NATIVE AMERICAN
ARCHITECTURE

Interior of Zuni Pueblo, New Mexico.
Photographed ca. 1900.

NATIVE AMERICAN ARCHITECTURE

PETER NABOKOV   ROBERT EASTON

OXFORD UNIVERSITY PRESS
NEW YORK   1989   OXFORD

Oxford University Press

Oxford   New York   Toronto
Delhi   Bombay   Calcutta   Madras   Karachi
Petaling Jaya   Singapore   Hong Kong   Tokyo
Nairobi   Dar es Salaam   Cape Town
Melbourne   Auckland

and associated companies in
Berlin   Ibadan

Published by Oxford University Press, Inc.,
200 Madison Avenue, New York, New York 10016
Oxford is a registered trademark of Oxford University Press

Library of Congress Cataloging-in-Publication Data
Nabokov, Peter.
Native American architecture / Peter Nabokov, Robert Easton.
p.   cm.
Bibliography: p. Includes index.
ISBN 0-19-503781-2
1. Indians of North America—Dwellings.
2. Indians of North America—Architecture.
I. Easton, Robert, 1940– .   II. Title.
E98.D9N33   1989   722'.91—dc19   88-9944
CIP

Printing (last digit): 9 8 7 6 5
Printed in the United States of America

CONTENTS

Sketch of Zuni Pueblo, New Mexico by Lewis Henry Morgan, after 1853.

TRIBES and LANGUAGE GROUPS

This chart lists Native American tribes
by language family and culture area.

Culture Area	Language Groups	Tribes
1 Northeast (including Great Lakes)	Algonquian	Abenaki, Chippewa (Ojibwa), Delaware (Lenape), Kickapoo, Menomini, Micmac, Naskapi, Passamaquoddy, Penobscot, Potawatomi, Sauk, Wampanoag
	Iroquoian	Cayuga, Huron (Wyandot), Iroquois, Mohawk, Oneida, Onondaga, Seneca, Tuscarora
	Siouan	Quapaw, Winnebago
2 Southeast	Muskogean	Chickasaw, Choctaw, Creek, Miccosukee, Natchez, Seminole, Timucua
	Siouan	Yuchi
	Iroquoian	Cherokee
3 Plains	Siouan	Assiniboin, Crow, Dakota (Sioux), Hidatsa, Mandan, Omaha, Osage, Oto, Ponca
	Algonquian	Arapaho, Blackfeet, Cheyenne, Prairie Cree
	Athapaskan	Kiowa-Apache, Sarsi
	Caddoan	Arikara, Caddo, Hasinai, Kichai, Pawnee, Wichita
	Uto-Aztecan	Comanche, Shoshone, Ute
	Tanoah	Kiowa
4 Plateau	Sahaptin	Nez Perce
	Salish	Chilcotin, Flathead, Klamath, Kutenai, Lillooet, Okanagan, Sanpoil, Shuswap, Thompson, Umatilla, Wanapum, Wenatchi, Yakima
	Penutian	Upper Chinook, Wishram
5 Arctic (including Subarctic)	Eskimo-Aleut	Eastern, Central, & Western Aleut Trans-Arctic Eskimo
	Athapaskan	Beaver, Carrier, Dogrib, Kutchin, Sekani, Slave
	Algonquian	Cree, Montagnais, Naskapi

Culture Area	Language Groups	Tribes
6 Northwest Coast	Athapaskan	Chilkat, Haida, Tlingit
	Penutian	Chinook, Tsimshian
	Wakashan	Kwakiutl, Makah, Nootka, Pacheenah
	Salishan	Bella Coola, Chemakum, Comox, Cowichan, Dwamish, Klallam, Lummi, Musqueam, Nanaimo, Pentlatch, Puyallup, Quinault, Sanetch, Squamish, Tillamook
7 California (including Great Basin)	Algonquian	Wiyot, Yurok
	Athapaskan (Na-Déné)	Hupa Tolowa
	Hokan	Achumawi, Chumash, Diegueño, Ipai, Karok, Pomo, Shasta, Tipai, Yuman
	Uto-Aztecan	Cahuilla, Gabrielino, Luiseño, Serrano
	Penutian	Costanoan, Klamath, Maidu, Miwok, Modoc, Nomlaki, Patwin, Wintu, Yokut
	Yukian	Yuki
	Yuman	Cocopa, Havasupái, Maricopa, Mohave, Quechan
	Uto-Aztecan	Bannock, Gosiute, Mohave, Mono, Paiute, Shoshone, Ute, Washo
8 Southwest I	Athapaskan	Apache, Navajo (Eastern and Western tribes)
	Uto-Aztecan	Papago, Pima
9 Southwest II	Tanoan	Isleta
	Tiwa	Picuris, Sandia, Taos
	Tewa	Hano, Nambe, San Ildefonso, San Juan, Santa Clara, Tesuque
	Towa	Jemez
	Keresan	Acoma, Cochiti, Laguna, San Felipe, Santa Ana, Santo Domingo, Zia
	Uto-Aztecan	Hopi, Huichol, Papago, Pima, Yaqui
	Zunian	Zuni

CULTURE AREA MAP

Following this book's organization, the map below indicates the commonly accepted culture areas of North American Indians. The Subarctic is covered in chapters 1 and 5; the Great Basin in chapter 7. Each culture area indication lists the following information: climate zone, ecology, raw materials, and major building types. A regional map at the beginning of each chapter generally locates the major tribes, selected sites, and important geographic features discussed.

1 Northeast/Great Lakes
Temperate
Woodlands
Saplings, birch and elm bark, sinew, reed
Wigwam, longhouse, Subarctic tipi

2 Southeast
Subtropical
Woodlands, tropical
Saplings, wattle-and-daub, palmetto thatch
Town house, chickee

3 Plains
Temperate, Continental Steppe
Prairie
Timber, saplings, sod, grass, hide, canvas
Earthlodge, grass house, tipi

4 Plateau
Continental Steppe, Highlands
Forest, prairie
Timber, saplings, sod, reed, canvas
Pit house, tipi, elongated tipi

5 Arctic
Arctic, Subarctic
Tundra
Snow, sod, timber, seal skin, stone
Winter house, iglu, tent, barabara, kasim

Subarctic
Mountains, tundra, forests, waterways
Timber, saplings, bark, snow, hide, canvas
Wigwam, tipi

6 Northwest Coast
Temperate
Forest, islands, waterways
Cedar timber, split planks, and bark
Plank house

7 California
Temperate, subtropical
Forest, mountains, valley, desert
Redwood timber and split planks, earth, timber, saplings, reed
Plank house, earthlodge, wikiup, bark tipi

Great Basin
Continental steppe, desert
Saplings, brush
Wikiup, tipi

8 Southwest I
Hot arid
Desert, valley, rivers
Adobe, timber, brush
Hogan, wikiup, ki, ramada

9 Southwest II
Hot arid
Desert, valley, rivers
Adobe, stone, timber, brush
Pueblo, kiva

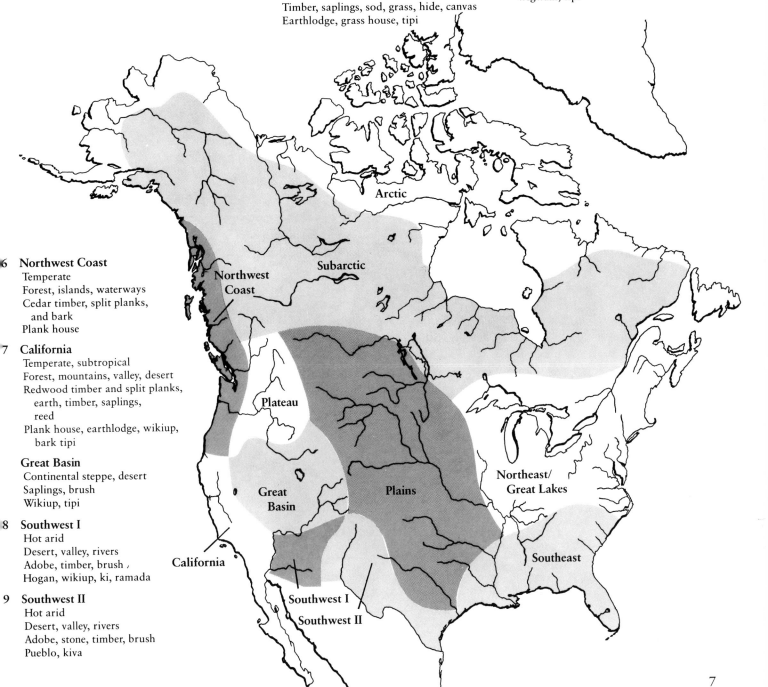

ACKNOWLEDGMENTS

For general assistance, guidance, and encouragement throughout this project we offer special thanks to Dr. Raymond D. Fogelson, Dr. George F. MacDonald, and Dr. William C. Sturtevant. For further assistance, we thank Mr. and Mrs. Armand Bartos and the Pinewood Foundation, which aided us with two grants, and John Watson, Mary S. Easton, James L. Easton, and Patricia Halloran.

We are especially grateful for the overall support and assistance of Dr. Joseph Epes Brown, Dr. Edmund Carpenter, Dr. Vine Deloria, Dr. James Deetz, Dr. Alan Dundes, Dr. Joseph Esherick, Paula Fleming, Dr. David Gebhard, James Glenn, Dr. Nelson Graburn, Dr. Frederick Hoxie, Lloyd Kahn, Dr. George F. MacDonald, Dr. Alice Marriott, Wayne Olts, Diana Parker, Dr. Carol Rachlin, Dr. Amos Rapoport, Dr. William S. Simmons, Dr. Dell Upton, Mrs. Abbie Lou Williams, Dr. Terry Wilson, and Don Congdon.

For print or pictorial research material, special advice, or editorial critiques regarding specific chapters we wish to thank the following individuals:

For information on the Northeast we are grateful to Mr. and Mrs. Lewis Cuppawhe, Dr. William N. Fenton, Benson L. Lanford, Dr. Nancy M. Lurie, Dr. Jay Miller, Gary Montour, Ernie St. Germaine, Dr. William S. Simmons, Dr. William C. Sturtevant, Dr. Thomas Vennum Jr., John White, and Dr. James V. Wright. Our chapter on the Southeast benefited greatly from the assistance of James and Trudy Baldwin, Roy Cypress Sr., Dr. Raymond D. Fogelson, Dr. Charlotte Heth, Houston Hicks, Dr. James H. Howard, Sunshine King, William Morgan, Archie Sam, Crosslin Smith, Lena and John Tigertail, and Dr. Amelia Bell Walker.

For material on the Plains we are indebted to Dr. Stanley J. Ahler, Gerard Baker, Dr. Ted J. Brasser, Dr. Joseph Epes Brown, Dr. Raymond J. Demallie, Jack Haley, Phyllis Howard, John Lovett, Adolf Hungry Wolf, George and Molly Kicking Woman, Dr. Lawrence Loendorf, Phillip Matthews, Lamar Newton, Dr. Douglas Parks, Dr. Joseph D. Porter, June Sampson, and Frank Vyzralek. We are grateful to Dr. Helen Schuster, Louis Thomas, Mary Thomas, and Dr. Roscoe Welmuth for information in the Plateau chapter.

Our chapter on the Arctic benefited greatly from the contributions of Tom Carnegie, Dr. Edmund Carpenter, Dr. Nelson Graburn, Molly Lee, and Dr. Gregory A. Reinhardt. For material on the Northwest Coast we are thankful to Fritz A. Fauchiger, Bill Holm, Tony Hunt, Richard Inglis, Dr. George F. MacDonald, Dr. Polly Sargeant, Bill Reid, and Dr. John Smyly.

To compile our California chapter we relied on gracious help from Dr. Leo Barker, Dr. Thomas Buckley, Dr. Lee Davis, Larry Dawson, Dr. Robert F. Heizer, Dorothy Hill, Dr. Travis Hudson, Weldon Johnson, Dr. Charles Lamb, Frank Le Pena, Malcolm Margolin, Dr. Polly Quick, Gene Prince, and members of the U.C. Berkeley, Dept. of Architecture museum presentation (1981) on Central California Indian architecture: Gerrit Fenenga, James Jackson, Julie Krieger, Nancy Weintraub, Kevin Matson, and Gretchen McGregor.

For our two chapters on the Southwest, the first owes a great deal to the contributions of Dr. David M. Brugge, Dr. Peter Iverson, Dr. Stephen C. Jett, Dr. Jeffrey King, and Jerome Pete; for the second we are thankful to Dr. E. Charles Adams, Dr. Bainbridge Bunting, William Lumpkins, Michael McCormick, Arthur Olivas, Dr. Alfonso Ortiz, Mary Powell and Marta Weigle, Dr. William E. Reynolds, Richard Rudisill, Dr. David G. Saile, Dr. Rina Swentzel, and William Webb.

For editorial assistance we are grateful to James Raimes, Susan Rabiner, William A. Darkey, Betsy Duncombe, Anne Edge, Anna-Ray Jones, Marcia Meier, Susan Meigs, and to the very special assistance of our editor, Joyce Berry.

We designed and produced the book in Santa Barbara. For help during production, we would like to thank John and Ginny Murray, Cindy Anderson, Tom Franotovich, Paul Kruip, Tom Buhl, Julie Honbo Taira, Greg Rech, Mary Schlesinger, and Tony Seiniger.

During the last year of this project, we have been grateful for the important editorial and production assistance of David Bricker, whose knowledge of architecture was invaluable.

Kickapoo wikiup interior, photographed in 1978 near Shawnee, Oklahoma.

INTRODUCTION

We were in a pasture outside of Shawnee, Oklahoma, when the elderly Kickapoo Indian couple we were searching for saw us first. They were heading home through the high grass, their arms cradling broken branches for firewood. We could follow them, they said. Soon we entered a clearing with three buildings: a white wood frame house with a porch, flanked by an old-time Kickapoo summer house, the *odanikani,* its lashed sapling frame and arbor naked without their roofing mats, and on the other side a traditional Kickapoo winter dwelling, the *wikiup.*

It was early October, and they had just moved the ochre-colored cattail mats from the summer house to the winter structure. They waved us inside. As the door hanging was held aside, a breeze fanned the embers in the central fire pit into flame, and smoke rose through a slit in the mats over our heads. Bent saplings framed the spacious interior. The Western style frame house was only their cookhouse, the woman said. It was here in the wikiup that they slept, under quilts spread over ground mats. This was how their people had sheltered themselves long ago, they told us. The Four Thunders, messengers of the Great Spirit, commanded the Kickapoo to build these homes, the old man added.

By the time of this first field trip in 1978, our collection of historical photographs of Indian dwellings was growing. We had begun to amass files of anthropological descriptions of dwelling types and village plans for every North American region. We were corresponding with scholars in pursuit of original data about Indian house-life. Stepping inside that wikiup, however, opened our appreciation of the role of Indian architecture in American Indian life.

We sensed the affection of this man and woman for their home, almost as if it were an older, revered member of the family. It was an attitude we would come upon again and again. We also realized that many of these architectural traditions might be alive today. From then on we tried to visit most of the tribal areas of North America, and to elicit from builders as well as scholars the deeper meanings of these buildings.

"By our houses you will know us," seemed to be the Kickapoo message. As our work progressed, we began to understand how different forces—economic, ecological, social, technological, historical, and religious—contributed to the outward appearance and unseen significance of Indian architecture. We began to discover in the grandest and the humblest of these structures a chronicle of American Indian cultural history.

In our view, the term "architecture" refers to more than just the design and decoration of buildings. It embraces what happens whenever human thought or action makes order and meaning of random space: naming places, designating sacred parts of "wilderness," clearing village areas and garden plots, claiming food-gathering areas, planning and constructing buildings, and arranging the spaces that surround and connect them. Finally, it includes the often unseen social and religious meanings which are encoded into buildings and spatial domains.

The wigwam, tipi, iglu, and pueblo—structures that have gained iconic status—are the only examples of Native American architecture most people can call to mind. Until this century the full range of Indian dwellings was not inventoried, nor were their diverse functions in Indian life comparatively studied. Native building traditions designated specific structures for sleeping, working, worshipping, meditating, playing, dancing, lounging, giving birth, decision-making, cleansing, storing or preparing food, caring for animals and honoring the dead. Furthermore, the ways in which buildings were grouped into larger aggregates such as camps, homesteads, villages, and towns had received scanty attention.

We became as interested in the building process as in the finished dwelling. We also were intrigued by settings and structures associated with actual dwellings which often may appear flimsy or impromptu: the arbors, windbreaks, outdoor kitchens, open-air council grounds, recreation yards, rooftops, and pathways that are rarely discussed. As spaces in which much of Indian life took place, they too fall under our definition of architecture as "a tangible expression of a way of life," in the words of architectural historian Bernard Rudovsky.

What appears random or haphazard in old photographs of Indian camps and villages often actually represents a pattern: the seasonal use of settings for special activities, possibly by certain members of the community. Indians were deeply attached to their architectural patterns, found them practical and enjoyable, and resisted the white man's attempts to change them. When the French advised the Abnaki to exchange their portable dwellings for European-style homes, their chief replied, "Why now do men of 5 to 6 feet need houses which are 60 to 80 ... do we not find in our dwellings all the conveniences and advantages that you have in yours, such as reposing, drinking and sleeping, eating and amusing ourselves with our friends. . . ."

Our intention is to do more than celebrate the skills of Indian builders who adapted to various climates and exploited local raw materials. As we describe Indian buildings and settlements from the Atlantic Coast to the Pacific, and from the Arctic Circle south to the Mexican border, we hope to show how this tribal architecture, as anthropologist Walter Goldschmidt puts it, "is responsive as much to the inner environment of cultural presupposition and social interaction as it is to the external environment of wind and weather." This responsiveness makes architecture one of the richest of all human expressions. Most aspects of our existence are played out—and leave behind some sort of trace—in buildings and spaces. By analyzing the ordered environment which American Indians created and inhabited, we hope to address Claude Lévi-Strauss's complaint that "there have been practically no attempts to correlate the spatial configurations with the formal properties of other aspects of social life." We want to explore how architecture embodied and reinforced the tribe's central notions about their society and its place in the cosmos. Finally, we wish to restore some historical dynamism to these diverse architectural traditions, and to illuminate changes in built forms that occurred before and after the arrival of European settlers.

The three hundred or so tribal groups who lived in North America when Christopher Columbus arrived built their homes and arranged their settlements according to singular patterns and principles passed on from generation to generation. Never intended as individual statements, these buildings were shaped by what folklorist Alan Dundes calls "inherited traditional forms." The Indians had no writing system before European contact—their

A woman of the Blackfeet tribe raises a tipi pole, northern Plains. Photographed ca. 1900.

Kwakiutl house frame, photographed at Mamalilikulla village, British Columbia, ca. 1927.

14

customs were transmitted through oral tradition and learned through repetition. Their traditions were their blueprints; social rules, their building code. They could and did build permanent structures. Division of labor in house construction was often determined by social custom and sexual roles, and in some tribes there was a degree of specialization in building skills. However, in Native America, it was largely tradition itself that designed these houses.

To help distinguish the native architectural traditions of North America we borrow from anthropology the inexact but useful concept of "culture areas." These are broad continental regions with a certain geographical and ecological distinctiveness and encompassing more or less similar ways of life. Subtle changes in landscape and differing tribal histories have made most of the American Indian culture areas home to more than a single architectural tradition, while tribal architecture straddling the boundaries of these areas often reflects a mixture of cultural influences. Within each of the following nine continental regions, however, built forms exhibit a certain aesthetic and cultural integrity.

First we examine the Northeast, where woodland people built domed barrel-roofed and gable-roofed houses of bent sapling frames covered with bark or mats. Then we look at the Southeast, from the prehistoric period of immense earthworks to today's enclaves of Southeastern Indians in Oklahoma and Florida, where vestiges of native building ideas survive. Next, in the Plains section we describe earthlodges, grass houses, and tipis. Between the Plains and the coast is the Plateau, an intermontane region where both pit houses and tipis covered with mats were prevalent. Moving northward we look at the Arctic with its sod winter houses, snow block structures, and summer tents. Along the Northwest Coast we study the monumental cedar plank houses that were built from Washington state to the Alaskan Peninsula. In California, we survey a profusion of house types which used earth, wood, and fiber for their coverings. We divide the Southwest region into two chapters, first describing the western tribes that occupied single-family dwellings arranged in seasonal camps, and then the Pueblo Indian world from the time of ancient pit houses to the communal stone-and-adobe villages found in the Southwest today.

The difficulty of tying an Indian society to a particular geographical location, however, is that one must then arbitrarily select a time period during which a tribe lived there. In pre-Columbian times, some architectural features were dropped, others retained and new ideas were adopted—a process that accelerated across North America once materials and ideas from Europe became available or were forced upon the tribes. It is also misleading to assign a time when any of these societies were most "traditional," or had arrived at their zenith. Maps that try to pinpoint the location of American Indian tribes usually tie them into an "ethnographic present" of around 1650. That date is earlier than the bulk of our documentation, and we have had to rely mostly on nineteenth- and twentieth-century ethnographic information. Only through circumstantial archeological evidence, suggestive narrative tradition, fragmentary observations by early travelers, and common sense can we surmise that an Indian roofing technique recorded in the 1890s was used in that same region by the builders' ancestors four centuries earlier. We have tried to bring the historical dimension into our chapters whenever our research has hinted at innovation, diffusion, or abandonment of architectural ideas.

15

DETERMINANTS OF FORM

It is impossible to single out why any Indian dwelling looked and worked the way it did. To be sure, Indians were responding to the climate around them and making the most of natural building materials at hand. But the evolution of a particular habitation also was affected by social organization, patterns of gathering food, religious life, and history. To understand the factors that form Indian architecture, one must look for what environment and culture made possible, not inevitable. Before proposing a major determinant for the design of a tribal building, one must undertake the "long and painstaking accumulation of recalcitrant detail," in the words of architectural scholar P.G. Anson, to clarify how the structure functioned in every aspect of life.

Amos Rapoport, the leading proponent of a multidisciplinary analysis of vernacular architecture, writes in *House Form and Culture*: "Materials, construction and technology are best treated as modifying factors, rather than form determinants, because they decide neither what is to be built nor its form." Our chapters interweave these "modifying factors" into a full-bodied narrative, but we consider six of them paramount: technology, climate, economics, social organization, religion, and history. Moreover, we are interested as much in how these factors help to interpret an Indian dwelling as in what the dwelling can tell us about Indian life. For one tribe, social factors may play a major role in determining building size; for another, the demands of gathering food might have a greater impact. For a third, the importance of a structure to religious beliefs might have the strongest consequences, and a fourth might manifest a struggle for dominance between Indian and non-Indian building traditions.

TECHNOLOGY

Indians had no choice but to build with raw materials from the land around them. They fashioned their dwellings from wood, bark, leaves, grass, reeds, earth, snow, stone, skin, and bones. Their principal types of construction were (1) tensile or bent frame with covering, (2) compression shell, and (3) post and beam (joined) wood frame with various walling materials.

The wigwam style of framing exemplified tensile construction. The dome-shaped frame gained enough springy strength from its bent saplings to support bark, mat, or thatch covers. In the compression shell, illustrated by the snow block iglu of the Arctic or the stone-and-adobe walls of the Southwestern Pueblo, the building material served both as structural support and wall covering. The joined-frame type was used for a variety of conical, rectilinear, or gabled structures found across North America. Their superstructure was made of straight poles or timbers which were tied together or otherwise joined and covered with planks, skins, or earth. Few, however, of the Indian house types conformed exactly to these methods. Both the pueblo (compression shell) and the Plains earthlodge (joined frame) were roofed with wooden beams covered by smaller poles and completed with a padding of fine twigs and grass and a layer of earth. Where joining required cordage, the means of preparing lengths of inner bark, slender withe, or root fibers was a basic craft that often escaped the scrutiny of early ethnographers. To a considerable extent, Indian architecture was tied, wrapped, and knotted together.

Raw materials

Earth	Organic	Hybrid
adobe	timber	adobe/timber
mud	saplings	sod (earth/fiber)
stone	bark	wattle and daub
	reed	
	fiber (grass)	
	brush	
	hide	
	sinew, bone	

Structural types

Bent frame	Post and beam	Compression
wigwam	lean-to	iglu
wikiup	shed	tipi
grass house*	pit house	hogan
ki*	earthlodge	pueblo**
	longhouse	town house*
	chickee	
	plank house	
	summer house	
	winter house	
	King Island house	

* combined with post and beam
** combined with beams

Building forms

Domical	Conical	Rectilinear
iglu	tipi	chickee
wigwam	forked-pole	longhouse
wikiup	hogan	plank house
grass house	earthlodge	pueblo
ki	pit house	summer house
cribbed-log hogan		winter house
barabara		King Island house

Tying a frame

The hands of Angel Quilpe, a Tipai man from Southern California, photographed by John Peabody Harrington as Quilpe lashed a grass house frame, 1925.

Although important to Indians in profound ways, houses were not usually conceived as articles of permanent craftsmanship. Much of their building technology had an improvisational and practical flavor. This is not to say that building methods were arbitrary. Construction techniques followed time-honored rules, but little attempt was made to preserve materials. On the Northwest Coast the woodwork in large family houses was painted or sculpted only where it was meant to impress onlookers. Even at the Pueblo Bonito ruins in western New Mexico, walls of elaborately patterned stone-work were plastered over, and, by historic times, pueblo walls were hastily manufactured and rarely bonded.

Constructing each house type called for special skills and tools. To bend a sapling into a smooth arch might call for debarking, trimming, aging, prebending, or steaming so that weak points would not splinter and crack. Felling trees, peeling bark, splitting boards, cutting and rainproofing hides, and making fiber ties were skills that were transmitted from the old to the young, often through prescribed interpersonal relationships and at appropriate moments in the tribal calendar.

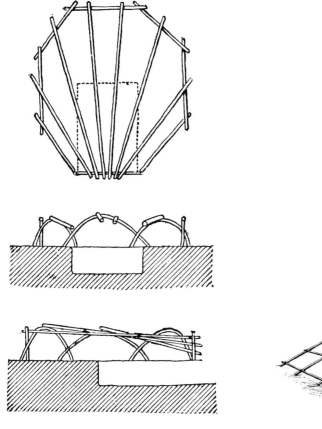

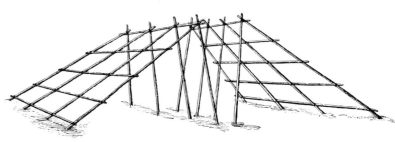

Arctic house　　　　　　　　　　　　　　　*Double lean-to*

Materials and construction techniques contributed to the appearance of Indian buildings, but did not restrict the ideas of their builders, who often pushed materials to their limits as they made structures in all shapes and sizes. We must stress again that the question of Indian architecture is less what they could build than what they wanted to build. Expanding a building to accommodate new family members, for example, could most easily be accomplished by rectilinear structures. In nearly every geographical area Indians built houses of extended length to meet social requirements. Early Eskimo structures of the late Dorset Period could be more than 150 feet long with stone sidewalls and, probably, a series of connected tent roofs. In the eastern woodlands, the Iroquois lashed together pole and bark longhouses exceeding 300 feet in length. The Coast Salish people of the Northwest put up shed-roofed plank buildings that were more than 600 feet in length, sheltering an entire tribe under one roof. The modular plan of both the Iroquois and Coast Salish structures allowed sections to be added or removed as new individuals married into the family.

It was difficult to enlarge circular structures, but they could be joined. When Eskimo families wanted more space, they clustered their winter snow houses, or joined two tents with an inner passageway in summertime. The Mandan of North Dakota, preferring smaller earthlodges during the winter, sometimes added sleeping chambers connected to the main lodge by a short tunnel.

Structural types

A basic camp structure was the double lean-to *(above)* built of lashed saplings by the Thompson Indians of the Plateau. Curved whale ribs and poles framed an Arctic house *(left)*. It was covered with two fitted and sewn seal skins filled with a thick padding of grass for insulation.

Indian structures were built with the three basic systems illustrated on the opposite page. The Kwakiutl of the Northwest Coast elaborated a post and beam system with carving. Photographed in 1900 *(near right)*. A compression roof *(far right)* of corbeled logs framed a Navajo hogan in the Southwest. A bent frame of small lashed saplings *(below right)* was used for wigwams and sweathouses throughout the Northeast and the Plains. This sweathouse was photographed by Edward S. Curtis in 1927.

Materials and techniques

The snow block iglu *(top left)* was an ingenious compression structure built by the Eskimo for winter shelter in the Arctic. At Old Oraibi Pueblo of the Hopi *(bottom left),* stone and adobe walls are shown being plastered with adobe mud. Photographed in 1908 in Arizona.

A bent frame wigwam *(top right)* is being covered with reed roofing mats by Mexican Kickapoo women. Mats could be easily moved from winter to summer houses. The frame of the Mandan-style earthlodge *(bottom right)* was a post and beam system. The builders of this reconstruction wove a grass matting over rafters which rested on the post and beam supports. The grass was then covered with tightly packed sod. Photographed ca. 1935 at On-A-Slant Village, Mandan, North Dakota.

Adaptable materials

A wide range of roofing and walling materials was used in basic construction. Seminole builders in Florida *(top left)* thatched their post and beam chickees with palmetto leaves. Conical pole tipi frames traditionally had a one-piece cover sewn together from tanned buffalo hides, as seen on this Apache tipi from the southern Plains *(middle left)*. Conical frames, a type of compression system, could be lengthened with a ridgepole and covered with many single-tipi canvas covers, as was this Flathead extended tipi *(bottom left)* built in Montana to honor a chief's dead son. Photographed in 1905.

The sapling frame and bark-covered buildings of the Northeast were ingeniously adapted to three different structural forms: the conical tipi and the domical wigwam, as seen in a western Cree camp in 1884 *(top right)*, and the rectilinear gable-roofed house, as in this summer house *(bottom right)* of the Sauk and Fox, photographed ca. 1885.

CLIMATE

Indian builders developed ways to keep the cold, rain, wind, and heat at bay. Techniques for warming or cooling were sometimes part of the hidden engineering of a dwelling and might have little effect on its outward appearance. The smaller and more subterranean the building, the easier it was to heat, but in chilly climates, dwellings often were built at ground level and were large and drafty.

Indians had other means of adapting to the weather besides designing their houses for protection. Partitions of hanging mats broke up drafts in large structures, and split-plank, adobe, or snow-block windbreaks frequently were built against doorways. Some Subarctic tribes relayered their floors with fresh, fragrant pine boughs every week. During the worst of a winter season some tribes migrated to warmer or more sheltered environs. They might wear heavy clothing indoors, and they were trained from childhood to tolerate variations in temperature. They also built a variety of structures and spaces in which to spend time during the different "seasons" of a single day.

Indian dwellings were generally heated from centrally located hearths, or separate family fires in large structures. A wide range of insulating methods was devised. The earth surrounding pit houses retained heat and was an effective barrier against wind chill. Southwestern Pueblos built above ground level used the same heat-retention principle. Their thick adobe walls soaked up heat from the sun during the day, and at night, radiated warmth into the rooms.

The versatile tipi

The seminomadic Plains Indians adapted their tipis to various climatic conditions. When the Cheyenne and other groups were forced onto reservations in the windy, dusty Oklahoma country, they devised windbreaks of bloodweed cane around their lodges *(above)*. Photographed ca. 1890. In freezing temperatures a double liner was hung around the interior of the tipi, the space between was stuffed with grass, and snow was banked outside around the base. This Blackfeet tipi *(above right)* was photographed during a northern Plains snowstorm, ca. 1900.

On warm summer days the tipi cover could be propped up on sticks to catch the breeze, or unfastened on one side, as was this Crow tipi *(bottom right)*, photographed along the Yellowstone River, 1871.

24

Rock Valley College - ERC

Arid and humid

Whenever it was hot, Indians lived outdoors beneath arbors or ramadas, as they were called in the Southwest. This Pima ramada *(left)* provided shade in the village of Sacaton, Arizona. The largest arbors were found in the southern Plains. A Kiowa woman named Good Eye is completing her arbor roof outside Anadarko, Oklahoma *(bottom left)*. Photographed ca. 1899.

Arbors were occasionally splashed with water for evaporative cooling. Heat was also diminished by inducing air flow. Seminole builders *(below)* raised their sleeping and working platforms to allow air to flow freely. Photographed near Ft. Lauderdale, 1917.

Indian builders employed a range of double-shelled walls. On the Plains, tipis had an inner liner that created an insulating air pocket. When temperatures dropped, this space could be filled with dry grass, and snow could be piled around the outside. In the Aleutian Islands, the natives built double walls of planks, stuffing moss or grass in between for insulation, and stacking sod against the outside walls and roof.

Relief from the heat was also important. Nearly everywhere Indian encampments included arbors. In the Southwest they were simple post and beam structures, shaded with leafy boughs, split cactus trunks, or cornstalks. In the southern Plains, the Kiowa and Wichita devised large bowed frames that they thatched with willow boughs to within a few feet of the ground. In scorching weather they frequently splashed the cover with water; evaporation lowered the shaded area's temperature by ten degrees or more. A long, running arbor shading an entire village was built by the Yokuts of the Central Valley in California.

In the Southeast, where humidity as well as heat was a problem, houses needed as much air flow as possible. The Seminole of the Florida swamps achieved this by constructing thatch-roofed, open-sided buildings with deep eaves and raised floors so that air circulated above and below. The raised floor also protected the occupants from the fluctuating ground water, insects, and snakes.

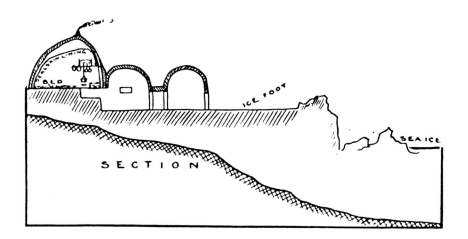

SECTION

ICE FOOT

SEA ICE

Response to Climate

In cold climates, dwellings were typically compact and smaller than those in temperate zones, where winter houses could enclose large open spaces or be long extended structures divided into family compartments.

When the Central Eskimos spent their winters on the sea ice, they built snow houses *(middle left)* directly on the sea ice, as sketched by Robert E. Peary *(top left)* in 1895. In summer they lived in skin tents, like this one in Labrador, photographed *(bottom left)* in 1864. Tlingit winter houses on the Northwest Coast had an excavated central hearth *(right)*. Photographed in 1888.

SOCIETY

Social organization significantly influenced the size of Indian dwellings and living arrangements. Local resources and methods of food gathering might restrict the size of a community, but social rules usually governed who lived with whom and who slept beside whom, where one moved after marrying, the size of dwellings, and their spatial relationships. The way in which tribal people arranged their spaces and used their dwellings reflected the way they organized their society as a whole. Architecture, then, was a principal tool for socialization—a means by which members of a tribe learned rules of behavior and a particular worldview.

Social customs also dictated who worked on the erection of the building, who owned it, and where it should be positioned in a village complex. Tribes such as the Siouan speakers of the Plains, and some Pueblo villages along the Rio Grande, split their societies into halves, social divisions known to anthropologists as "moieties." In some villages the residences of the two groups were placed on opposite sides of a stream or valley. During their summer gatherings, the Siouans pitched their tipis in a circle with an invisible line running north–south—dividing "Sky" clans from "Earth" clans. Many different housing patterns were found across Native America, from single dwellings for extended families, to grouped dwellings for single patrilineal families, to areas within large villages where clan members clustered together.

Men and women's roles in the construction and ownership of dwellings were sharply defined. Over most of central North America, women held sway over home and hearth, either building or supervising construction of their houses. Along the West Coast from Alaska to Southern California and on the eastern seaboard, however, men were largely responsible for building. In parts of the Southwest, and in pockets of the Great Basin, men and women shared the labor equally. Among the Mandan Hidatsa of the upper Missouri River, women held the right to erect earthlodges, but men cut and erected the frame.

30

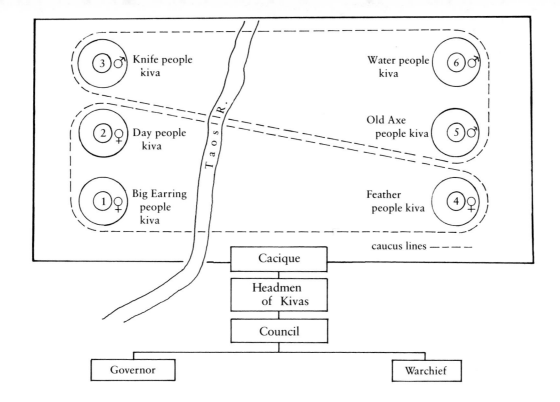

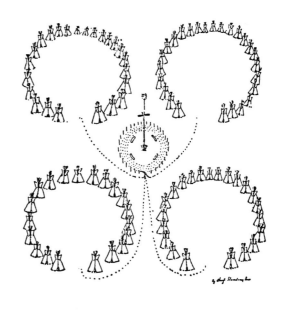

Community organization

Tribal social organization contributed to the outward form of communities. At Taos Pueblo in northern New Mexico *(top left, diagram top right)* the community speaks of itself as occupying "one nest," and the adobe wall surrounding the community imparts a sense of solidarity and separateness. Within that nest, however, is a complex social structure. One social division of the community is reflected in the division between the North and South Pueblo by the Taos River (Red Willow Creek). Another social division is based on the arrangement of the six active kivas in the community; they are assigned sexual identities, and three are associated with each "side" of the village. At birth every child is allied with one of these kivas. Kiva headmen advise the "cacique," or lifelong headman of the traditional theocracy which governs the community. The annually elected "governor," or bureaucratic head, handles day-to-day administration and official relations with the outside world.

When the Sioux of the Dakota Plains *(middle right)* gathered for games, ceremonies, and festivities, some arranged their groups into four circles of tipis surrounding a central sacred place, according to Sioux author Luther Standing Bear. The Winnebago of the Great Lakes arranged their wigwams according to social custom *(bottom right)*.

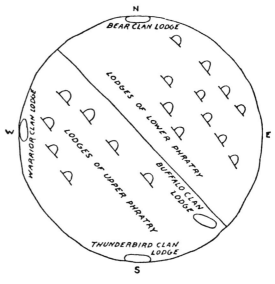

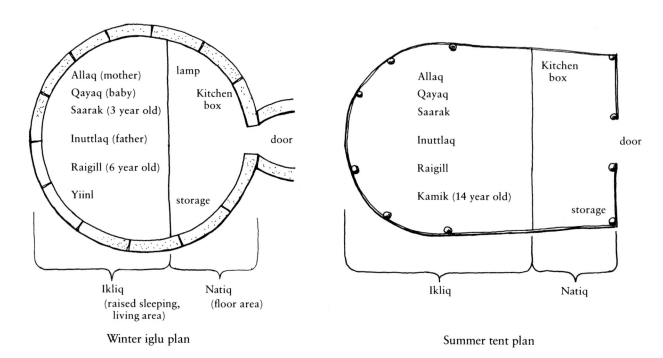

Winter iglu plan

Summer tent plan

Central Eskimo interiors

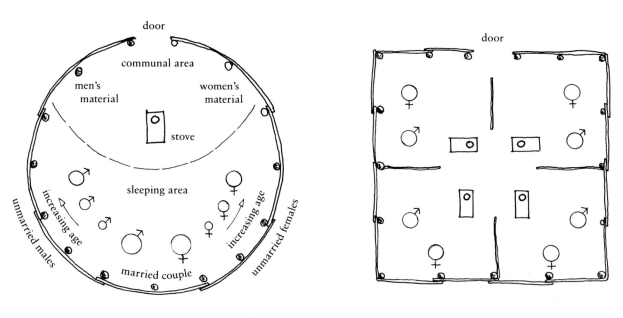

Individual camp lodge plan

Multifamily winter house plan

Mistassini Cree interiors

Cheyenne women had a "guild" which convened with feasting and prayer whenever they gathered to cut and sew covers and make porcupine quill ornaments for their tipis. Where kinship was traced through the female line and children automatically became members of the mother's clan, the house and its property were generally considered hers. Thus, among the Navajo, a divorce usually forced the husband to leave his wife's dwelling and return to his parents' home.

Sometimes house-building was a ritualized means of cementing relations among tribes, or between clans, moieties, and important families. Among the Hisanai of the southern Plains and the Kwakiutl of the Northwest Coast, kin or clan groups, each supplying specific materials and each with a different construction assignment, worked together, as in a barn raising. Such collaborative efforts often tightened kinship bonds and raised the status of the new occupants.

Within the confines of the house, rules concerning the use of space could be quite strict. Even for hunting people frequently on the move, such as the Cree of central Canada, temporary quarters and sleeping assignments were in traditional places determined by sex, family, marital status, and age. The Cree told of a supernatural woman who traveled ahead of the hunters to set up their tents and prepare camp—so that no matter where they moved, it was as if they were staying in the same place. Cree youngsters were warned not to count the tent poles in their lodges or her magic would fail. The Cree, Eskimo, Pawnee and many other groups also recreated that "same place" by carefully observing rules of domestic etiquette. In that way role relationships among tribal members were preserved and people found a measure of privacy and peace within spaces that most Europeans and Americans today would find too exposed and too cramped.

Household organization

Within the dwelling, social rules usually regulated where people slept, ate, and stored their possessions. Among the Central Eskimo, sleeping assignments were the same in both their winter iglu and summer tent *(top left)*. Among the Mistassini Cree in the Subarctic, age, sex separation, and marital status determined underlying sleeping assignments *(bottom left)*. When a Cree camp contained a number of individual lodges, they were lined up—facing a stream if it was summertime, the sunrise if it was winter. If the families lived together in a winter house, the higher status families slept nearest the door, and no wives slept beside men who were not their husbands.

A portion of a map *(below right)* dated 1691 shows Caddo Indian fenced homesteads with grass houses and arbors, near Texarkana, Texas.

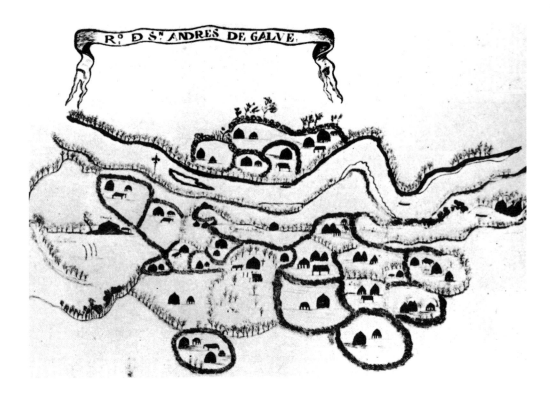

RＯ DＳＴ ANDRES DE GALVE

Seasonal residency

The abundance or scarcity of supplies influenced both the daily life and architecture of each tribe. All Indians had a "seasonal round," a pattern of relocating throughout the year for food-gathering. Many Northwest Coast Indians dismantled and reused the same cedar plank siding for both their permanent coastal winter houses and their inland summer dwellings. The frame of a Kwakiutl winter house *(above)* stands exposed in a village on the Salmon River. Other Northwest groups had more modest fishing shelters *(left)*, as they enjoyed the summer months of gathering berries and roots and catching fish. Photographed ca. 1867. As Plains Indians hunted the wandering buffalo herds, the tipi went along, the poles dragging behind a horse. This Crow woman was *(right)* photographed in 1880.

ECONOMICS

No Indian group had a single dwelling suited to all seasons; even Pueblo people were seminomadic, moving into summer quarters near their cornfields. Most tribes relied on different food sources at least for summer and winter, and occupied different camps in fall and spring. Each location commonly had its characteristic house type. Modern archeology refers to a hunting and gathering society's base camp as their "central place." Even if a band traveled widely, they often had one such location which was to them "home." Indians on the Northwest Coast considered themselves more "at home" in winter, when they occupied the family plank houses built on coastal sites that families had owned for years. Their summer fishing and berry-gathering camps were inland, up the rivers. When some tribes departed for the summer spots, they untied the wallboards of their winter houses, lashed them between canoes, and used them as siding for the more makeshift summer quarters. In the fall they returned to the bare frames of their winter homes and walled them up again with the same boards.

The opposite seasonal pattern was customary for the earthlodge dwellers of the northern Plains. They were more "at home" during the summer in large, cool, earth-roofed buildings, which were framed with heavy cottonwood timbers and situated on high river terraces. They left these structures to occupy portable tipis during their autumn hunts, moving into smaller earthlodges in protected, wooded areas along the Missouri River floodplain when winter came.

For more sedentary people such as the woodland dwellers of upper New York state, intense occupation of a single village site often exhausted both local building supplies and garden soil. Every ten or fifteen years, when the saplings they used as their primary building material became sparse, the Iroquois would resettle the entire community, often downhill from the original site. Insect infestation, overcrowding, and a pile-up of garbage could also cause a village to move on.

Fluctuations in supplies of food or water quickly affected population size, which in turn had an impact upon architecture. In Chaco Canyon in New Mexico, North America's most advanced expression of public architecture was achieved because Indians were able to divert rainwater that fell on surrounding mesas for agricultural use. But an apparent decrease in the amount of summer rain in the thirteenth century probably upset this fragile dependence, and the tribes could no longer support themselves nor their high-density apartment-house complexes.

Highly mobile native bands such as the Eskimo of the Arctic or the Paiute of the Great Basin stayed "at home" only when the weather forced them to. For the Eskimo in their turf or snow houses, winter was a time of seclusion; for the Paiute in their brush- or tule-covered shelters, the only time spent indoors was in January and February when the Nevada desert was frozen. For both groups winter was a period of family gatherings and storytelling, but afterwards they were anxious to be on the move again. The literature on Indian settlement patterns usually ignores the fact that a seminomadic existence not only made good sense, but that Indians deeply enjoyed it. Apparently some tribes followed a food-seeking, nomadic way of life because they had little other choice, but they also relished the sense of freedom, the reunions with distant kin, and the activity and change of scenery.

Food gathering and storage

After food was foraged, harvested, or hunted, it was frequently dried, as were these segments of squash *(left)* on a Hidatsa Indian rack in North Dakota. In anticipation of leaner times or the winter season, dried berries, roots, meat, fish, beans, and corn were carefully packaged and placed underground, hung on racks, deposited in special rooms, or placed in raised containers to deter rot and pests. This large woven Papago granary *(bottom left)* in the Southwest stood on stilts. Among the Pueblos, rooms were set aside for corn storage and grinding. A Hopi food storage chamber included an alcove for toasting the traditional piki bread *(right)*. Photographed ca. 1915.

RELIGION

The buildings of Native Americans encoded not only their social order but often their tribal view of the cosmos. Many Indian narratives tell of a "Distant Time" or a "Myth Age" when a "First House" was bestowed upon a tribe as a container for their emerging culture. Some tribes likened the creation of the world itself to the creation of a house, strengthening the metaphoric correspondence between dwelling and cosmos. Thereafter Indian peoples held the ritual power to renew their cosmos through rebuilding, remodeling, or reconsecrating their architecture.

The idea that houses served as models of the universe is suggested by the folklore and architectural terms of native groups as distant from one another as the Eskimo, the Mohave, the Navajo, the Hopi, the Delaware, and the Blackfeet. To the Navajo, mountains were models for the first house, its four principal posts symbolically equated with the four cardinal directions, and its floor space divided into day and night domains. The Hidatsa of North Dakota believed the universe was a mammoth earthlodge, its sky dome held up by four enormous pillars just like those of their own four-post lodges.

The mythological house and the buildings consecrated as their replicas could represent the four quarters of the sky, zenith and nadir, and the "sky-dome," which shamans could enter through a "sky door" or "sun hole," in order to obtain special powers. The "earth-navel" and cosmic tree, or center-of-the-world pole, were two other important cosmological concepts (which the historian of religions Mircea Eliade has named the "umbilicus mundi" and "axis mundi") that were often represented architecturally.

The tribal cosmos might also be multilayered. Usually there were three tiers, with the present world situated on the middle plane. The Delaware, though, envisioned their universe as twelve houses, one on top of another, which they symbolically entered during their annual Big House ceremony.

Origin myths also helped to teach tribal members the proper way to collect building materials, good construction techniques, and how to bless the finished building. Sometimes a myth was recited before construction began. The tale of the first Wichita grass house prescribed which materials should be harvested by women and which by men. It also regulated each phase of construction, described the prayers to be uttered, and dictated how the building, its doors and four cedar ribs jutting from the top, was to be aligned with the cardinal directions.

Symbolic correspondence between building and body was also common. Among the Tolowa of Northern California, a special sweathouse was dedicated to the spirit of an ancient supernatural salmon just before the annual spawn. As the hopeful fishermen entered to pray for a healthy catch, they believed they were entering the salmon's body; the ridgepole had become its backbone and the roof boards its ribs. On the Plains, the "Hugging Bear" design, found on both Blackfeet and Kiowa tipis, produced the effect of a giant furry creature embracing its occupants. For tribes as distant from one another as the Sanpoil of the Plateau and the Winnebago of the Great Lakes, the sweat bath was envisaged as the body of a sacred being which people entered to be purified or cured.

Houses and the materials that went into them were often considered alive. "Your house is a person," said an Achumawi Indian from Northern California during a visit to the linguist Jaime de Angulo. "It knows very well that I am

The cosmic house

Some Indian buildings symbolized world view, and embodied mythological ideas. For example, the large plank houses of Northwest Coast Indians were ritually transformed from secular to sacred structures for winter ceremonies. As suggested by the diagram of a Haida house (*top right*), the dwelling was symbolically at the center of the universe, which the Haida divided into three zones: the sky world, the earth, and the underworld. The souls of those to be born emerged from the sea (underworld), whose chief being was the Whale. People spent their transitory lives as social beings within the house which stood on the earth—family houses which were the architectural equivalent of their social group, or lineage. After death they were buried in a grave box near the forest, which was associated with the sky world, and its chief being, the Thunderbird.

During winter ceremonies a pole that extended through the smoke hole was planted in the house. This "cosmic tree" was climbed by a shaman to symbolize his access to the sky world, with its spirits and powers. In the photograph (*bottom right*), a facade painting on a Kwakiutl family house at Alert Bay, British Columbia contains some of these symbolic references. The shaman's pole is in place; the painting depicts a cosmic conflict between Whale and Thunderbird.

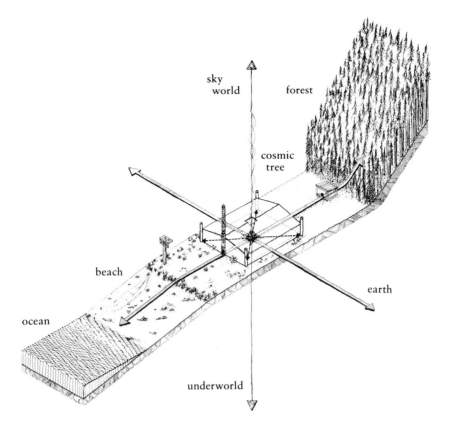

a stranger here. That's why I sent it tobacco smoke, to make friends with it. I said 'House, you are the house of my friend. You shouldn't do me harm. House, I want you to protect me.'" During the years of European domination such attention to the inner, sacred life of architecture focused upon ceremonial structures such as the Delaware Big House, the Apache puberty tipi, the Papago Rain House, and the Plains Sun Dance lodge. Among the Kickapoo of Oklahoma and Mexico, and certain tribes of the Southwest, however, the ritual renovation of domestic space is still observed.

Village plans also reflected tribal mythology. The Creek of the Southeast constructed their ceremonial "square grounds" to reflect the directional order in the universe and to signify the progression of a man's life through it. Four arbors, which were aligned with the cardinal directions, surrounded a four-log fire around which boys, middle-aged warriors, and aged men were assigned seating according to age. In the center of the circular plazas of the Mandan villages on the Missouri River, a shrine protected an effigy of their culture hero, Lone Man. He had instructed the Mandan in how to marry, hunt, and build houses, and had saved them from the Great Flood by placing them inside an enclosure symbolized by the shrine. The temple lodge on the innermost circle of buildings around the plaza always faced the direction where Lone Man disappeared after saying good-bye to his people. Everyday Mandan life revolved around these affirmations of their divine origins.

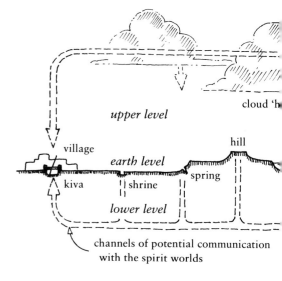

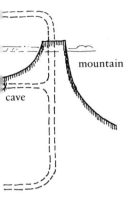

Symbolic houses and spaces

At the Kwakiutl village of Gwayasdums, on Vancouver Island, this house facade *(left)* emphasized the symbolic perils of the threshold. It brought to life the Northwest Coast belief that houses swallowed their guests, for during great occasions the lower beak of this monster raven would actually drop for visitors to climb through its throat.

Vision tipis of the Great Plains were painted with symbols seen during vision quests; the meanings of the designs and colors were usually personal and kept secret. This is the special vision tipi *(above)* of an Assiniboin medicine man from Montana named Nosey, who was said to have dreamed the designs for 32 different painted tipis during his lifetime. Photographed in 1906.

As suggested by the diagram of an idealized pueblo and environs *(above)*, the universe of a pueblo was bounded by four sacred mountains at its cardinal points. These were associated with particular colors, animals, and plants. Between them and the community were special shrines, sacred springs, and lakes—places of pilgrimage and prayer. Above were the "houses" of clouds, from whence came life-giving rains, and "houses" of the sun and other cosmic powers. Below were the various tiers of former worlds, where spirits still dwelled who might be contacted at sacred spots. Within the pueblo walls lay the ceremonial plaza, and at the heart of the pueblo was an altar within the kiva.

41

NORTHWEST · ELEVATION

Datum line

Roof line

Former grade

Present grade

Floor line

7'-10"

SECTION · LOOKING · SOUTHEAST.

Dirt roof

Datum line

Savine

Viga

Wood

See detail of Altar & Ladder

Adobe plaster wall

New post

New adobe base See note

Banco

Adobe floor

Banco

Wood

See Detail

New Wall

9'-5"

Ceremonial structures

All Pueblo groups constructed kivas, semisubterranean sacred chambers, which suggested symbolic communication between this world and the ancestral underworld. This elevation and section *(left)* of the desanctified adobe kiva at Nambe Pueblo north of Santa Fe was drawn by the Historic American Buildings Survey in 1934, and photographed *(below)* in 1969.

The Sun Dance lodge was constructed by over twenty Plains Indian tribes. Participants in the four-day ceremony fasted and performed acts to induce visions. This Cheyenne lodge *(right)* was photographed ca. 1910. The Yurok Indian sweathouse *(bottom right)* stood in the village of Pekwan in northwestern California. In Yurok thought, a sacred sweathouse stood at the center of their universe.

Graves

Indians paid respect to their dead in many ways, sometimes funerary rituals called for shelters or enclosures for the deceased. On the Northwest Coast, crest symbols associated with the lineage of a major figure were erected around the grave, as among the Kwakiutl *(left)* of Alert Bay. Photographed in 1899. Miniature grave houses of the Tsimshian *(bottom left)* show the influence of European architecture.

Less elaborate were those of the Chippewa *(bottom right)*, which often had a little aperture, or "spirit hole" to release the soul of the dead. Plains Indians elevated their dead on scaffolds or in trees *(right)*, which were often considered temporary resting places until the spirit could join what Crow Indians called "the other side camp."

45

HISTORY

Modifications in Indian architecture did not begin with the arrival of Europeans. Change had been under way for at least nine and a half thousand years—roughly the date of the oldest North American Indian house thus far identified, a 12-foot-long oval-shaped dwelling which stood near the Stanislaus River in eastern California. In pre-Columbian times numerous Native American societies flourished, and a succession of architectural ideas evolved. Some building forms developed rapidly, some gradually, and their rates of change can only be plotted in areas where archeological remains reveal considerable depth of time.

Scholarly interest in the pedigree of Indian buildings has been limited largely to one house type: the pit house. Indians burrowed into the ground to sink the floors for many different forms of dwellings, and tracing the distribution of semisubterranean houses has produced a kind of architectural family tree. The superstructure of the Kamchadal pit house in Siberia is similar to that of an early Pueblo kiva, which in turn was a survivor of an older domestic pit house form in the Southwest. Across the Arctic the semisubterranean winter house—commonly rectangular—is found everywhere. To the south are the pit houses of British Columbia's interior with their unique, slanting inside supports. In California, valley bands lived in dug-out dwellings that bore a remarkable resemblance to the Plateau pit houses. It has been argued that upper Missouri River earthlodges extended this tradition into the Great Plains, and that it continued into the partly excavated town houses of the Southeast.

Change

European contact changed forever the materials, forms, and meanings of traditional Indian buildings. Indian concepts of home and settlement were altered by trade, disease, depopulation, warfare, and the relocation of tribes to reservations. A Creek log cabin *(left)* from the late eighteenth century shows European influence.

Indian architecture in captivity is the theme of this photograph *(above)* of Fort Snelling on the Minnesota River, 1862. The tipis of 1700 Sioux stood behind an imprisoning fence after the Santee Sioux uprising against white settlers.

The problem with such hypotheses of direct architectural influence is that there is usually a dearth of minute data, a wide range of time periods, and too variable a range of terrains and climates to make them convincing. It might be more profitable to develop small-scale architectural sequences in limited geographical regions and time periods. What is probable, however, is that tribes retained outdated house types for other uses, either as ritual structures or for storage. Because of the gradual nature of architectural change in pre-Columbian Native America, tribal areas often became a sort of architectural memory bank.

With the arrival of Europeans, architectural change in Indian settlements accelerated. Disease, resettlement, and warfare forced the coalescence of some villages and building traditions, and the virtual abandonment of others. As metal tools and nails, then paints and cloth, and finally milled lumber and molded bricks became available, traditional materials such as buffalo hide, elm bark, and other natural supplies became harder to get. Reservation life also restricted the Indians' freedom of movement to obtain building materials. Indian agents and missionaries frowned on all "primitive" and "pagan" expressions of traditional Indian cultures, often singling out for disapproval old forms of house-life. Social reformers and East Coast "friends of the

Continuity

As the fur trade brought wealth to many Northwest Coast groups, villages consolidated in new trading settlements. Chiefs preferred to live in "Boston houses," and window glass, wooden doors, and non-Indian carpentry became the new status symbols. Tradition continued, however, as evidenced by the family crest painting in the gable end of this Tlingit chief's Boston house *(left)* in Sitka, Alaska.

The roof of the Comanche leader Quanah Parker's house *(top right)*, near Cache, Oklahoma, was decorated with star symbols.

Most Indian communities today display the results of generations of government housing programs. "Hud houses," produced by the Department of Housing and Urban Development, as shown at Acomita, New Mexico *(middle right)*, often acquire older architectural appendages, such as the adobe structure or bread ovens *(hornos)*.

Contemporary Indian designers have entered the mainstream architectural profession. A building designed by a part-Blackfoot architect from Canada, Douglas Cardinal, is nearing completion in Ottawa, Canada. The Canadian Museum of Civilization *(below)* encloses a million square feet, its undulating masonry walls wrap around a six-story Great Hall which houses a full-size replica of a traditional Northwest Coast Indian village.

49

Indian" reproduced in their publications photographs of tipis and bark houses with captions decrying the "old, unhealthy, disease-breeding mode of existence" that they represented.

Despite strong pressure to forsake their architectural heritage, some Indian groups were reluctant to give up the buildings and the way of life they represented. They had already retained outmoded house types out of nostalgia for a golden age; the Hopi *Kisi,* a brush shelter used during the Snake ceremony, or the Mandan *Okipa* (temple lodge) both were probably descendants of domestic structures. Instructed to behave like Europeans, a number of Indian groups clung to their traditional architecture even more tenaciously. Others viewed the structures blending European and Indian elements as the foundation of a new "traditional" identity. Many of the stories in this book describe a historical struggle between cultures waged on an architectural front.

It is tempting to make comparisons between Indian architecture and that of contemporary America, to forget that these traditional dwellings arose out of specific historical, demographic, ecological, and cultural circumstances. These buildings seem to offer what we miss so much. Their architectural imprint, often ephemeral, blends harmoniously with the land, and the ebb and flow between residents and surroundings is smooth. They are places where people can live together in comfort and tranquillity.

These buildings often resist description because there is so little to them in material terms; in large measure, they must be experienced to be fully understood. Yet many of their secrets will remain forever with the builders. A number of house types were never recorded, and most of those included in this book have been eclipsed. Like the oral tradition which passed them along, the intimate knowledge of their construction materials and building skills was always a few generations away from disappearance. The aesthetics and proportions which determined the right "look and feel" for many of these buildings, and their criteria for selecting the best natural materials for them are often irretrievable.

We have developed our chapters from four bodies of documentation: historical observations, archeological summaries, ethnographic descriptions, and our field experience. Archeology plays a great part in the chapters on the Southwest and Southeast because the architectural evidence is less conjectural and more dramatic. Elsewhere we describe only those pre-Columbian sites that contribute to our understanding of built forms of the later historic period.

As we study the cultural areas and their architecture, we follow in the wake of European exploration. From native memories and early ethnographic work we try to recreate the buildings and spaces that existed in the centuries between that first contact and this century. Our descriptive reconstructions would be impossible without the notes, photographs, and ideas of the pioneer ethnologists, and the equally important work of their Indian colleagues who answered endless questions, made models of traditional houses, and sheltered questioning scholars under their roofs. Our chapters close with our personal encounters in Indian communities today, where we have learned much from the buildings that still spring from tribal sources.

Kiva ladder, Picuris Pueblo, New Mexico, 1970.

50

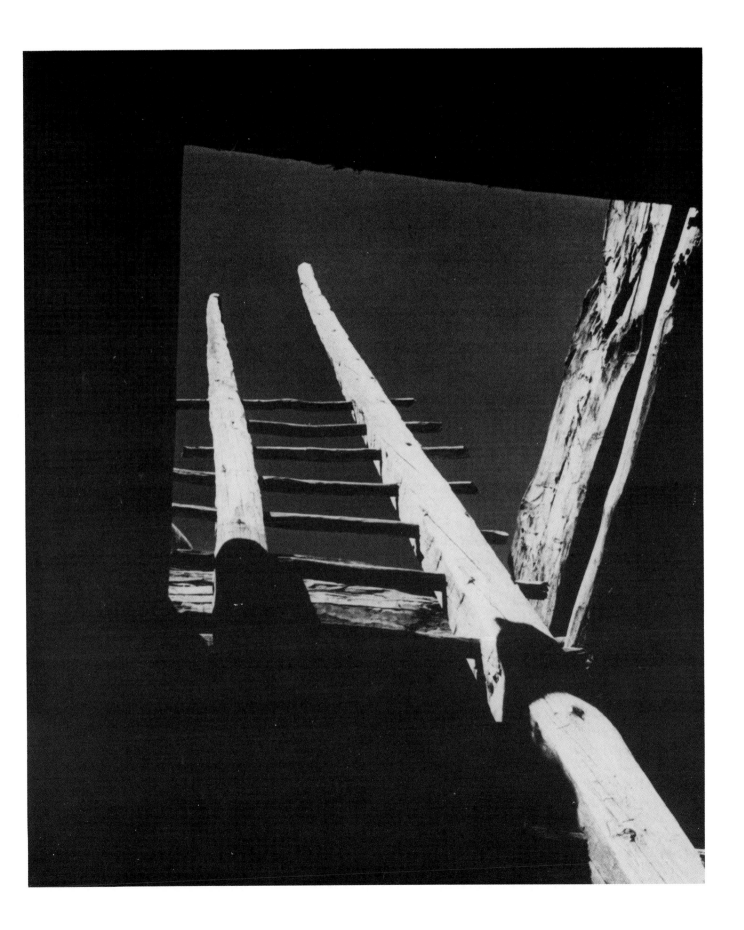

1 WIGWAM and LONGHOUSE

NORTHEAST and GREAT LAKES

In 1524, on the shores of Narragansett Bay, the Italian seafarer Giovanni da Verrazano became the first European on record to visit an Atlantic coast Indian camp. He wrote to his patron, Francis I of France, that he had discerned "no regularity of architecture." Of the houses, he noted that they were "of circular form about 10 to 12 paces in circumference" and were "covered with mats of straw ingeniously worked, which protect them from rain and wind." Inside one structure, which was slightly larger than the rest, he counted "nearly 25 to 30 persons." Since it was late winter when Verrazano landed, what he encountered was probably a temporary camp for Algonquian-speaking Indians who visited the coast each spring to fish and dig for clams.

The Eastern woodlands region was thick with pine and hardwood forests, stretching from the Maritime Provinces of eastern Canada to the western shores of the Great Lakes. To the north, it was bounded by sprawling Subarctic taiga—moist flatlands of spruce and fir—and to the south by the rise of the Appalachian highlands. This landscape of woodlands, mountains, seacoast, and lakeshore, with prairie on its western rim, was the homeland of tribes belonging to three major language families: the Iroquoian, the Algonquian, and the Siouan.

The basic building system that prevailed throughout the woodlands was a structural frame of saplings to which was lashed a covering of bark sheets or sewn reed mats. Woodlands architecture was extremely versatile; houses varied in shape and size in response to local climate and the particular tribe's economic, social, or religious practices. Along the St. Lawrence River, in upper New York state and west to the shores of Lake Ontario, the communal dwelling of the Iroquois and Huron tribes was the "longhouse." It was a large building—often 100 feet long or more—which was framed of bent saplings and covered with bark sheeting. It was occupied year-round by families related through the female line. To the east, south, and west of Iroquois country, the Algonquians constructed a wide array of bark- and mat-covered structures. Their most common house type has become known as the "wigwam." The term usually referred to a round or oblong dome-shaped hut perhaps 12 to 15 feet in diameter. Across northern New England and southern Canada, however, "wigwam" meant a conical, bark-covered structure framed with straight poles. The Siouan-speaking people, whose country was high-grass prairie interspersed with forests, built both woodland and Plains-style tipis or earthlodges depending on the location and season.

Verrazano wrote that the Algonquian Indians he met near Long Island "change their habitations from place to place as circumstances of situation and season may require." Portable roofing was an architectural asset to the coastal Indians' pattern of seasonal migration. In the winter they sought refuge in the deep woods, where they hunted and enjoyed easy access to fishing streams; in the spring they moved near ponds and clearings, where they gathered wild plants and cleared and cultivated the ground. From these spring settlements they would make short trips to the coastal spots where they hunted wild fowl and dug for shellfish. Summer dwellings were one- or two-family wigwams and larger, multifamily houses which chroniclers have loosely classified as longhouses, but apparently these communal structures were not imbued with the full cultural significance of the year-round Iroquoian longhouse.

The woodlands

The wigwams Verrazano described in 1524 possibly resembled this sketch *(above)* from Champlain's map of New France (1612). In 1605-6, Champlain observed such structures between the mouth of the Kennebec River in Maine and present-day Chatham, Massachusetts. Roofing mats appear to be separated from wall mats by a ring, which might be a bent sapling clamping them to the frame.

A Kickapoo Indian camp of winter wigwams *(bottom)* was photographed in Oklahoma, ca. 1890. Staunchly traditional, the Kickapoo have preserved their architecture as an essential part of their identity. Their present-day wigwams in Oklahoma and northern Mexico look much like those erected by their eastern Algonquian linguistic cousins centuries earlier.

Naskapi

Micmac

Subarctic

Canada
U.S.

Chippewa (Ojibwa)

Great Lakes

St. Lawrence R.

Montreal

Penobscot

Woodlands

Menomini

Huron

Chippewa

Draper site

Howlett Hill site

Sauk
Fox

Nodwell site

Iroquois tribes

Narragansett

Potawatomi

Niantic

Winnebago

Steamburg

Narragansett Bay

Grant Oneota

Coldspring

Kickapoo

Kickapoo

New York

Delaware

Woodlands

Appalachian Mtns

Atlantic Ocean

Mississippi R.

Ohio R.

Pamunkey

Powhatan

Roanoke Island

Pomeiooc
Secota

POWHATAN

Appamatuck

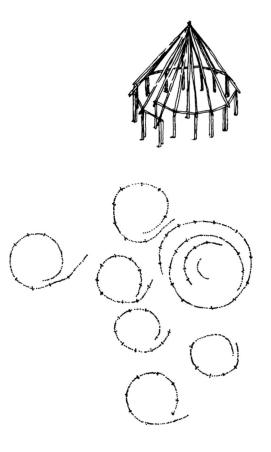

Algonquian archeology and towns

A plan view *(above)* of post molds from the habitations at the Assawompset Pond archeological site in southeastern Massachusetts. The hypothetical reconstruction drawing suggests how the roof might have been framed.

When artist John White visited the Carolinas in 1585, he produced watercolors of two Algonquian Indian towns. The community of Pomeiooc *(upper left)* was surrounded by a circular palisade. White's rendition of the village of Secota was embellished *(lower left)* by the Frankfurt engraver and printer Theodore de Bry. De Bry's 1607 idealized version of an Algonquian bark house interior in Virginia *(near left)* shows the legendary chief Powhatan at home. Powhatan is said to have reigned over thirty different tribes living in nearly two hundred loosely knit villages.

In the moist climate of the region, with its frequent freezes and thaws, building materials rot quickly, so little direct evidence of early architectural forms remains. Construction details of traditional Algonquian dwellings must be pieced together from historical accounts and scanty archeological data. One site that does bring us closer to the prehistory of perishable woodland architecture was uncovered at Assawompset Pond in southeastern Massachusetts in the 1950s. Its encampment of six circular structures averaging 36 feet in diameter was built by hunting and fishing people sometime between 2500 and 1800 B.C. The lodges appear to have been clustered around a larger, possibly ceremonial or council structure measuring more than 60 feet in diameter. Of particular interest are the "post molds," discolored remains of earth and wood fibers in the ground that indicate where saplings were once positioned for framing. At Assawompset Pond these holes are doubled, as if to support pairs of uprights that clamped the wall material together. The post holes also formed spiral patterns, indicating that the entryways into the lodges were curved, possibly to shield occupants from bad weather.

Sixty-one years after Verrazano saw the fishing camp at Narragansett Bay, Sir Walter Raleigh's first expedition to North America inspected an Algonquian settlement near the present-day North Carolina coast. He found a "village of nine houses, built of Cedar, and fortified round about with sharpe trees, to keepe out their enemies, and the entrance into it made like a turne pike very artificially [artfully]." From other early reports we know that while some Algonquian villages along the Atlantic Coast were similarly modest in size, others held upward of fifty structures and were spread over 100 acres. Village locations were selected for good visibility—which meant high ground—and access to running streams, stands of trees, and promising garden spots. Often they were protected by timber palisades.

A young English painter named John White joined Raleigh on his second voyage to Virginia and lived among the Indians for a year. At two Algonquian towns along the Carolina coast, White produced the first depictions of Native American village planning. One watercolor recreated "The Towne of Pomeiooc," between present-day Wyesocking Bay and Lake Landing. Fortifying it were tree trunks as "thick as a man's thigh" and about 15 feet high, set into 3-foot trenches. Shaped in a circle, the pointed stockade overlapped at the entrance, forming a fenced passageway into the village. Inside, eighteen mat-roofed structures were arrayed around a central plaza, with a fire blazing in its midst.

The frames for six of the town's buildings appeared to be built from saplings that were bent directly from the ground to resemble tunnels with flattened ends. White also depicted a few larger barrel-roofed structures elevated on vertical wall posts. Mats completely covered the smaller buildings, but on the large longhouses the wall coverings probably were rolled up or even removed to let in light and air. Inside, two rows of corridor posts supported sleeping porches a few feet above the dirt floor. It can be assumed that they were decked with puncheons—wood slabs split from logs—and furnished with grass mats and animal hides.

The horizontal trusses securing the house frames also held up storage racks. Two to four fires burned along the central aisle. Although White does not show them, matting or thatch partitions divided the corridor into bays. He notes one unusual building, a squat "temple, built without window," with a pointed roof. Opposite stood a large structure with seven posts on each side which White labeled a "king's house." It was probably a council chamber or receiving hall.

A three days' walk down the Pamlico River from Pomeiooc brought White to the village of Secota. Instead of a round plaza, a straight thoroughfare was used for community gatherings. Nor was Secota protected by a palisade, which to White made it a "fayre" place to live. The houses were barrel-roofed with vertical walls, draped in wall mats that could be removed for ventilation. White's drawing shows open spaces used for rituals: the central street with a feast in progress, a small dance area with dancers shaking rattles, and another ritual space surrounded by posts carved with effigies facing a blazing fire. He also depicted cornfields in three phases of cultivation: "newly sprung," "greene," and "ripe." A villager was perched in a special hut on stilts overlooking the ripened stalks to chase birds away.

In these more permanent villages, buildings ranged from 20 to 100 feet long and probably resembled the World War II Quonset hut. In the late seventeenth century, the Long Island Algonquians who had received Verrazano again hosted Europeans. Two Dutch travelers, Jasper Dankers and Peter Sluyter, described an extended wigwam that was some 60 feet long and about 15 feet wide. Its siding was reed mat, its roof, strips of chestnut bark. They counted eight families living there, and the Dutchmen observed that "all who live in one house are generally of one stock or descent, as father and mother with their offspring."

WIGWAM

Verrazano's descriptions of the hemispherical, mat-roofed dwellings that he visited at Narragansett Bay were Europe's introduction to the wigwam, a widespread American Indian house form. By the 1630s the Algonquian word was used by Massachusetts colonists for any Indian dwelling, and soon it preempted more specific architectural terms across North America; houses made of wood, bark, or even mud were labeled wigwams simply because Indians occupied them. However, in the mid-eighteenth century, chronicler Samuel Hopkins defined this Algonquian building type more precisely: "A Wigwam is an Indian House, in building of which they take small flexible Poles and stick them into the Ground, round such a space as they intend for the Bigness of their House, whether greater or less: those Poles they bend from each Side, and fasten them together, making an Arch over Head ... After which they cover the whole with Bark of Trees, leaving a Hole in the Top for Smoak to go out."

Strictly used, the word refers to a one- or two-family house of round or oblong floor plan built by woodland Indians. After its sapling frame of bent uprights was lashed together, horizontal pieces, or stringers, were tied in tiers to strengthen the frame and support the outer covering—reed or grass mats or sheets of birch, elm, or chestnut bark. Great Lakes tribes often left the naked wigwam frames standing at familiar campsites and transported only their rolled-up coverings.

Wigwam architecture

This early engraving of a Chippewa (Ojibwa) frame *(left)* is reproduced in Lewis Henry Morgan's *Houses and House-Life of the American Aborigines,* originally published in 1881.

The wigwam has remained a popular building type over the centuries. The bent sapling frame of a Winnebago house *(above)* is covered with reed mats. Wigwams varied from 7 to 20 feet in diameter and were covered traditionally with reed mats and bark.

Their separate frames and coverings made it relatively easy to transport wigwams. In 1691, an Algonquian told a Frenchman who was trying to persuade him to adopt a European house, ". . . we can always say, more truly than thou, that we are at home everywhere because we set up our wigwams with ease wherever we go and without asking permission of anybody."

The early Algonquian houses were likened by European observers to the garden arbors or bowers back home, or, as the Virginia colonist and historian William Strachey wrote in 1620, "at best like our sheppards cottages." Half a century later, the missionary and linguist Roger Williams admired this form of construction among the Algonquian-speaking Narragansett Indians with whom he lived: "They gather poles in the woods, and put the great end of them in the ground . . . and bendinge the topps of them in the forme of an arche, they bind them together with the bark of Walnut trees, which is wondrous tough."

In his report to Francis I, Verrazano noted that the Long Island house poles were "logs split in halves," which may have meant long saplings split lengthwise to make them bend more easily. In the 1960s, inventive archeologists seeking to replicate Algonquian building techniques in Virginia tried preforming the poles into arcs before planting them in 2- to 3-foot holes, but there is no field data to suggest the local Pamunkey Indians did the same. Some post molds at the Assawompset site appear to have been angled out, possibly so that the poles' tensile strength would be increased once they were bent inward, or so that the walls would lean outward and overhanging eaves would keep rain from dripping down them.

In this century, anthropologists have studied woodland Indians in the Great Lakes, whose dwelling forms were similar to those of their Eastern linguistic cousins. From detailed accounts of their technology we can make educated guesses about East Coast Algonquian architectural practice. Among the Chippewa, for example, we know that it was usually the men's role to chop the framing saplings, for which they sought young hickory, basswood, or elm trees. Some Chippewa groups preferred ironwood because it bent easily when green and toughened without cracking when it dried.

To secure the poles, the supple tips were wound around each other or overlapped, then lashed together with pliable strips of fresh white oak, tough roots, or inner basswood bark that had been made into cordage. The openwork arches, from 5 to 8 feet high, were secured with lighter saplings that reached to the central smoke hole.

Women took over at that point, sheathing the frame and installing the furnishings. They knew which bullrushes made the best wall mats and floor mats, and what size cattails should go into the outer roofing mats. The pulpy stalks were cut during September and October and stacked carefully to avoid mildew. Using 10-inch needles made from animal bones, the women sewed the slightly flattened cattails together with split spruce root, swamp milkwood, or nettle fiber, fashioning mats about 4 feet wide and 8 to 10 feet long.

They were fine house coverings for a mobile people living in an extreme environment. They were pliable, lightweight, and provided effective insulation. According to anthropologist Karen Peterson, this was because they utilized "the principle of insulation by means of walls enclosing a dead air space in which convection currents are retarded by filaments. The walls are the outer layers made up of the hard lower half of the leaves, while the filaments are the inner layers of thin leaf tips." Moreover, they were sewn together so that the stalks and leaves of the plants overlapped slightly to keep out rain and wind.

When they reached a new campsite, women unfurled the mats and unpacked the household items wrapped in them. European visitors often were amazed at the speed with which camps were set up. Once the wigwam frame had been erected, the cattail mats were tied in courses up to the smoke hole so that the grain of the reeds ran vertically for efficient runoff. The hearth area was cleared and sometimes slightly excavated, the earthen floor around it was spread with mats and hides, and the utensils and stores placed in customary spots. The seventeenth-century chronicler Thomas Morton wrote that the interior wall mats were "finely sewed together with needles made from the splinter bones of a Cranne's leg with thread made of their indian hempe." Additional mats were often fastened to the interior walls for decoration as well as warmth; among the Chippewa, Menomini, and Winnebago, wall or sleeping mats were plaited of cedar bark or bullrush in geometric patterns of brown and gray.

Bark sheets were heavier and more awkward to transport than reed roofing mats, so whenever feasible they were reserved for winter wigwams. Bark was harvested in spring when the sap was running and flats from elm, yellow birch, chestnut, oak, pine, black ash, or hemlock could easily be peeled off the living trees. When birch was used, sections of the bark about a yard square were sewn together with spruce root into 10- to 15-foot rolls, called *apakwas* by the Chippewa, which were stiffened at each end with cedar battens. After they had been stored for awhile, the brittle rolls usually were warmed over a fire until they were limber enough to be wrapped around the house frame. Great Lakes people often mixed the outer coverings, combining sidewalls of cattail mats with birch bark rolls draped over the round roof, or substituting black ash bark for mats on the sidewalls. A hide or a blanket served as the door; in freezing weather a double door-hanging was used.

The Chippewa wigwam

The house under construction was photographed in the early 1920s. The framing poles *(top left)* were set in the ground slightly angled out to increase tensile strength when bent.

Women and children tied the vertical poles together *(middle)*. Once the horizontal saplings were added *(right)*, the bark covering was unrolled and tied to the frame.

By nightfall the interior of the wigwam became a cozy shell, with intermingling odors of wood smoke, earth, bark, sweat, and food. Splinters of pitch pine sometimes were burned for illumination, but most of the light came from the central fire. Smoke escaped through a parting in the mats; sometimes the edges of this smoke hole were fireproofed with a mud lining that baked hard and black. Large wigwams had several hearths. Drying fish, strips of venison, and, later, metal kettles hung over them from crossbars or stakes. Within arm's reach around the hearth were earthenware pots, polished maple bowls, a hardwood mortar and pestle, and bark buckets made watertight with spruce gum caulking. Beds softened with mats ringed the hearths. As William Strachey observed shortly after he arrived in Virginia in 1606, "Round about the house on both sides are their bedstedes, which are thick short posts stalkt into the ground, a foot high." Far to the west, however, where the woodlands began to give way to prairie and the climate was not so damp, wigwam dwellers often unrolled sleeping mats or heaped skins on the ground.

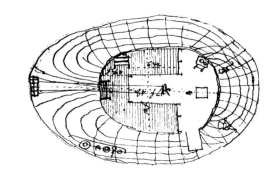

Early observers reacted differently to the comfort afforded by these native houses. Strachey praised the Virginia Indians for carefully siting their dwellings among protective trees so that "snowe or raine cannot assalt them, not the sun in summer annoye them, and the roof being covered, as I say, the wynd is easily kept out." The Jesuit missionary Father Paul le Jeune, who visited Indian wigwams along the St. Lawrence River in 1633, held another opinion, however. "This prison," he complained, "in addition to the uncomfortable position that one must occupy upon a bed of earth, has four other great discomforts—cold, heat, smoke and dogs," to which other chroniclers added fleas, cooking and garbage smells, and the absence of privacy. Yet Daniel Gookin of Massachusetts, writing forty years later, paid their dwellings this compliment: "I have often lodged in their wigwams, and found them as warm as the best English houses."

Wigwam coverings and interiors

A Chippewa house *(top left)* at Leech Lake in central Minnesota. Birch bark scrolls cover the roof and cattail mats form the walls. The leaning poles help hold the bark on the frame.

A top view sketch *(middle left)* was made in October 1761 by Ezra Stiles, president of Yale College. While visiting Niantic, Connecticut, Stiles called on Phoebe and Elizabeth Moheege and George Wawkeets, who lived in two of the six wigwams still standing in the Indian community of eighty-five people. A cutaway reconstruction sketch of the Moheege dwelling *(bottom left)* was made from Stiles' notes. The traditional raised sleeping platforms with mats were surrounded with furnishings of European manufacture.

The door flap has been thrown back to show the interior *(top right)* of a reconstructed Chippewa wigwam. Patterned woven mats are the floor; basswood fibers ready to make into string and tools hang over the skin-covered bed. A Chippewa house *(bottom right)* is covered with birch bark scrolls, sewn together with spruce root.

Elm bark

Elm bark being stripped from the living tree *(left)*. First a serrated ring is cut around the tree, then strips are peeled off with the aid of a wedge or ax. A Potawatomi house *(below)* in Kansas is covered with elm bark; an external sapling frame secures the stiff covering.

Algonquian conical wigwam

A Chippewa family, ca. 1866, inside a conical wigwam covered with birch bark scrolls, east of present-day St. Paul, Minnesota.

Conical Wigwam

The cone-shaped wigwam covered with yellow birch bark was the principal shelter for hunting tribes of the northern Atlantic coast and across much of the eastern Subarctic. Built by such Algonquian tribes as the Penobscot, Micmac, and Naskapi, who lived above the corn-growing belt, the conical wigwam provided sanctuary from the fierce winters. A simple, sturdy structure, it was framed of straight yellow spruce, cedar, or fir poles and encased in bark rolls sewn together from smaller birch bark flats.

The Micmac Indians of Nova Scotia began construction by lashing four 14-foot poles together and placing them upright with the bark intact. Secondary poles were laid into the crotches at the juncture, and a horizontal ring of small sticks near the midsection stabilized the cone. When the weather was especially bitter, insulating grass was layered over the frame, then the birch bark sheets were tied on by fastening fibercords to small flaps left on the bark.

More poles were leaned against the structure and then bound together at the top to clamp down the bark sheets. Inside the lodge, women laid the flooring with interlaced, sweet-scented fir boughs, curved side up, to make a fresh, springy mattress. Cooking gear hung from a rack of spruce twigs tied below the smoke hole. Space and furnishings in these houses had to be used with extreme efficiency. The Nova Scotia historian Duncan Campbell wrote of the Micmac wigwams he visited in 1873: "there is a place for everything and everything in its place. Every post, every bar, every fastening, every tier of bark, and every appendage, whether for ornament or use, in this curious structure, has a name, and every section of the limited space has its appropriate designation and use. Perhaps it would be impossible to plan a hut of equal dimensions in which the comfort and convenience of inmates could be so effectively secured."

GREAT LAKES DWELLINGS

The Indians of the Great Lakes survived on a mixed economy of hunting, fishing, growing corn, harvesting wild rice, and collecting maple sugar. The language groups concentrated in this region were central Algonquian-speakers, such as the Chippewa, and Siouan-speakers, such as the Winnebago. Each season they used a different pattern of structures and spaces, constructing lengthy bowers for grand annual ceremonies, small enclosures for shamanic performances, funerary shelters for the dead, sweat lodges, menstrual huts, and special sheds for processing maple sugar and other foods.

The Chippewa, who inhabited the forests and streams around Lakes Superior and Huron, built four different house types. Their domed winter wigwam was called *wagino gan,* which combines their word for "bent"—referring to its frame—with the root word for dwelling. This oval-shaped house could be easily enlarged to make a multifamily structure resembling a longhouse. The Chippewa also constructed a conical winter wigwam covered with yellow birch bark that was called a *na sawao gan.* Extending this building with a ridge pole, they created the *gino dawa,* or "long tent," to shelter several families in the winter. In summer they moved into the *gaka gaogan,* or gabled bark house, which usually was sided with slabs of elm bark.

In lodges occupied by more than one family, invisible boundaries divided the interior, and rules governed everyone's movements to ensure order and relative privacy. If four Chippewa families shared a long tent, there would be four door flaps, two at each end. Each family "owned" a door and slept beside it, but the two groups at each end, perhaps related through marriage, probably shared a cooking fire. Space also was divided according to sex. Men stored their tools in customary places; women had separate storage and work spaces. Men gathered around the central hearth to gamble or tell stories: when they left for the hunt, the hearth became the women's domain.

Protocol also governed the noise and activity within these cramped quarters. In the 1850s a German scientist named Johann Kohl spent a number of winters in Chippewa wigwams around Lake Superior and was struck by their peacefulness. "It was so quiet around, as if the huts were uninhabited, that we were quite astounded, on entering, to see a number of persons collected in groups in the room. This stillness is usual in all Indian wigwams.... As with every step you invade the territory of another family, and might see all sorts of things that a stranger ought not to see, respect demands that the guest should sit down directly, and fix his eyes on the ground. Indians, as a general rule, are not fond of restless people...."

For the summer, tribes of the woodland-prairie borderlands also built bark houses with gabled roofs, vertical walls, and high ceilings. When the Sauk Indians built these large square houses, they oriented the door to the east, naming that side "where daylight appears"; the west they called "where the sun goes down," while a wall post on the north was known as "noon." These summer buildings, constructed along the lines of the smaller, gabled Chippewa house, represented a house type that had probably been in use for centuries. That was the conclusion of archeologist Marshall McKussick, who in 1970 excavated an eleventh-century village in northeast Iowa. Called Grant Oneota, the site has ground remains of sizable buildings.

In re-examining the journals of early explorers, McKussick learned that in 1687, Henri Joutel, aide to Sieur de La Salle, had visited four Quapaw villages

Algonquian extended lodges

Domed wigwams could be easily extended, as was this birch-bark-covered Chippewa structure *(right).*

A Chippewa "long lodge" *(below)* on the St. Croix River in Wisconsin. The single-family bark and mat conical wigwam was lengthened by adding a ridgepole.

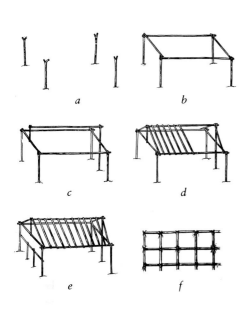

Summer house

Summer houses of the Great Lakes were gable-roofed and covered with bark. In front usually stood an arbor, or "ramada," used for shade and drying meat or corn. The house near Zoar, Wisconsin *(upper left)* of So'man Jim, a Menomini, is flanked by a ramada and a garden of native beans and squashes, ca. 1916.

The Sioux village of Kaposia in central Minnesota *(bottom left)* was painted by Seth Eastman ca. 1850. The scaffolds in front of the bark houses provided shade during the day and sleeping space above on hot nights. Bundles of corn were hung from the posts.

Artist Frank Sindelar recreated the interior of a Quapaw house *(top right)* built by a southern Siouan-speaking people whom the Marquette-Joliet expedition visited in the summer of 1673. These houses could hold two hundred people. The low platform lining the room was draped with furs.

Construction sequence for a Menomini summer house. Four upright crotched saplings: *(a)* are connected by poles *(b)* fastened in the crotches; crotched uprights support the ridgepole *(c)*, and rafters are lashed from ridgepole to connecting poles *(d)*. A horizontal pole is added to form the lintel *(e)*, and a framework *(f)* is constructed for the walls.

near the mouth of the Arkansas River. Joutel had come upon huge bark houses, each accommodating as many as two hundred inhabitants. Later, in 1806, the American soldier and explorer Zebulon Pike, while searching for the source of the Red River, visited an Osage Indian village in the Ozarks whose structures ran to 100 feet or more in length. In northeastern Kansas in 1811, the American Indian agent and explorer Major George Sibley encountered a summer village of Kansas Indians of more than a hundred "commodious" houses, averaging 60 feet long and 25 feet wide. In 1915, the Winnebago of Wisconsin told anthropologist Paul Radin that long ago they had lived in gable-roofed "ten-fire" buildings.

From such documentation McKussick hypothesized that during the summer, these big structures housed families related by clan. Some of their village plans probably reflected and reinforced their social organization as well. A Winnebago elder told Radin that in the past, villages had been divided by an imaginary line running northeast by southeast. On the northeastern side were placed the wigwams of members of the Winnebago clans, which were grouped within the Sky moiety, or division, of the tribe. Members of these moieties were exogamous; that is, they chose marriage partners from the opposite moiety. Thus a Sky person would be the spouse of an Earth person. The Sky clans took their names from such birds as the eagle and pigeon, and were led by the Thunderbird clan, which was responsible for handling civil matters. Their special wigwam served as a sort of courthouse, where internal disputes were resolved.

In the southeastern half of the community stood lodges of the Earth division, whose clans were named for land or water creatures, such as the wolf, fish, or snake. The leading clan of this moiety, the Bear group, issued declarations of war, prepared war medicine, and served as the tribal police. Community offenders were punished in a special Bear lodge. A sacred Bear sweathouse used in certain rituals symbolized the body of the clan's mythic ancestor. Its structure and furnishings corresponded to parts of the sacred Bear's anatomy, so that upon entering the lodge worshipers felt drawn into the protection of the animal's heat and power.

Sacred Enclosures

Certain religious ceremonies were accorded their own structures and spaces. A bower of sapling arches enclosed the rites of *Midewiwin* or Great Medicine Society which, some scholars argue, became widespread among Great Lakes tribes shortly after the arrival of Europeans—a period dubbed by some anthropologists as "contact traditional." The Midewiwin lodges were the largest structures built by Great Lakes people in historic times and quite likely evoked the form of outmoded domestic dwellings. Their barrel-roofed frames, known as *mite.wika.n,* extended 100 feet or more in length, and skins or cloth lined the perimeter of their earthen floors. Originally, they were walled waist-high with boughs, mats, or bark, but by the turn of the century, loosely draped canvas had largely replaced the natural materials. Sacred poles of cedar representing the "trees of life" rose from the lodge floor, which in turn the Chippewa associated either with the earth or Lake Superior. One rite, in which a solemn procession wove around the poles, possibly celebrated origin migrations. Members of the society were ranked by their progression through four "degrees" of initiation into the ritual's mysteries. The tiniest sacred building used by many native groups across the Great Lakes and much of the Subarctic was known to Europeans as the "shaking tent" or "conjuring lodge." It was a bent sapling frame no larger than a telephone booth, made

The Midewiwin lodge

The *mite.wika.n* or ceremonial lodge of the Midewiwin religious societies, was a major ritual setting for Indians throughout the Great Lakes. Ceremonies were held in long building frames made of bowed saplings, which were often partly covered by brush or cloth, and could extend for 100 feet or more.

Sacred birch bark scrolls of symbols, kept by special leaders of the society, recorded the procedures for the ceremonies and seem to depict the tribe's historical movements as a series of movements through the sacred lodges. The structure itself was sometimes known as the "blue house" and, in some accounts, was said to stand for Lake Superior itself. The drawing *(top)* is from a Midewiwin leader's scroll, ca. 1891.

The photograph *(below)* shows a long uncovered Midewiwin frame of the Seine River band of Chippewa in Rainy River, Ontario. A ritual procession *(opposite)* in a Grand Medicine lodge on the Lac Courte Oreilles Reservation, Wisconsin, 1899.

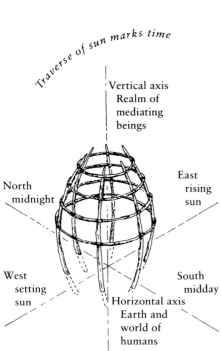

Vertical axis
Realm of
mediating
beings

North
midnight

East
rising
sun

West
setting
sun

South
midday

Horizontal axis
Earth and
world of
humans

When the shaman enters, he is at the center of the world, the place where he can make contact between two worlds: the horizontal world of humans, and the vertical world of mythological beings.

The shaking tent

The shaking tent, or "conjuring lodge," as early chroniclers also called it, was the setting for a divinatory rite performed by specially trained shamans across much of the Great Lakes and the Subarctic. It was a small booth built of saplings. The Chippewa customarily used three birch and three spruce uprights, and two birch and two spruce horizontal hoops to bind it together; other tribes used four or seven uprights. Three of the saplings were planted deeply in the ground and angled slightly outward so that when they were drawn together at the top the building was held in a state of tension. Rattles of caribou and deer hooves, or cups of lead shot, were tied to the frame. The floor was usually softened with freshly cut spruce boughs. After the shaman entered the frame, it was completely covered with bark or cloth. Onlookers could hear strange sounds issuing from inside as the tent swayed wildly from side to side. During his transcendent state, the shaman could dispatch a super-natural helper, usually a mystical turtle, to distant regions to answer questions from his audience about the most auspicious places to hunt, the well-being of distant relatives, and what would happen in the future.

A native observer, who reported seeing small lights like stars around the top, told anthropologist A. Irving Hallowell, "We cannot see them, but we understand that turtle rests at the bottom of the lodge, feet up, keeping it from sinking into the ground; that thunder is at the top, covering it like a bird; and that the other spirits are perched around the hoop that encircles the frame. They look like human beings about 4 inches tall, but have long ears and squeaking voices like bats."

The Chippewa lodge *(lower left)*, built near Little Grand Rapids, Manitoba, in 1934, is covered with a canvas top and birch bark walls. A Chippewa shaman *(below)* stands near a frame with its ribs tied at the top.

Drum Dance lodge

Chippewa Drum Dance lodge at Mille Lac, Wisconsin, ca. 1910 *(above)*. Examples of such many-sided dance lodges are also found across the Great Plains. These structures, which could hold gatherings of entire communities in private, represent the struggle of Indians during the early reservation period to preserve their religions and social traditions.

from special woods that had been harvested according to ritualistic instructions. After a shaman stepped inside, the booth was swathed in bark or canvas. From there he dispatched a supernatural helper to bring him answers to the questions of his rapt audience: Where was game? Were someone's relatives in good health? Were enemies nearby? Eerie voices and chattering birdcalls emanated from the enclosure as the lodge shook in convulsive movements, its top covering sometimes lifting into the air.

In the late nineteenth century, the Drum Dance ceremony began replacing the Midewiwin rituals. The Drum Dance was performed in a broad, open, circular arena ringed with logs and signifying the universe. In the center, a large, decorated drum was hung from four feathered staffs representing the cardinal directions. Over the years, the open arenas were replaced with roofed halls, whose form probably derived from the Plains Indian log-or-lumber dance enclosures that had become popular during the reservation period for housing the Grass Dance. The buildings were generally four- or six-sided, with turrets in the middle of their pitched, wood-shingled roofs. Inside they might have support posts colored according to sacred associations, such as red for south and blue for north. Wooden benches lined the wall, and the preferred floor was earth, beaten hard from dancing feet.

WIGWAM TODAY

The domed wigwam form survives in modern Indian communities largely due to the sweatlodge ritual. Sweat bathing, using different structures and wet and dry heating techniques, was practiced throughout Indian America, but the Plains Indian cleansing and prayer rite has become the most widespread. It takes place within a small bent sapling frame, usually of supple willows, tightly enclosed with quilts or tarps (originally, buffalo hides were used) to prevent the escape of steam. A pit in the center or to the side of the floor holds rocks that have been heated to a glowing red in a large fire near the lodge. With the frame completely shrouded and the participants huddling inside, a leader' ladles water over the hot rocks, and hissing steam fills the interior. As the heat grows in intensity, so do prayers, testimonials, and songs. In the past few decades, the rite has become a bonding experience in rural and urban Indian enclaves across America; even in some prisons, Indian inmates have been permitted to build sweatlodges in the outdoor exercise yard.

In its purest expression, woodland Indian architecture endures today far from its regional homeland. Segments of the Kickapoo tribe in Kansas, Oklahoma, Texas, and northern Mexico still use wigwams and follow seasonal residence patterns. Four hundred years ago the Kickapoo were a typical Algonquian-speaking woodland people living in separate winter and summer buildings of sapling frame and cattail mat in southern Wisconsin. But from the early 1700s until the late nineteenth century they resettled several times, splintering into different bands as they migrated southward to escape Euro-American encroachment. Their journeys eventually led some Kickapoo to Mexico, where, in the mid-nineteenth century, the Mexican government allowed them to stay in the northern state of Coahuila. Today, in hamlets outside McCloud, Oklahoma; Nacimiento, Mexico; and Eagle Pass, Texas, the Kickapoo still build wigwams using local materials.

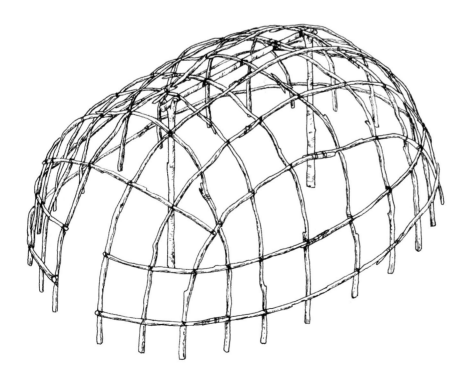

Wigwam frames

The typical sweatlodge frame *(above)*, found throughout Indian society today, of fifteen poles set in a round plan, roughly 7 feet in diameter and 5 feet high.

A Kickapoo wigwam frame *(left)*, 20 feet long by 14 feet wide and 9 feet high, is supported and stabilized by two interior posts and a horizontal ridgepole. The frame consists of 25 to 30 saplings set in an ovoid plan. Placed about 1½ to 2 feet apart, the thick ends are set firmly in the ground, then bent, overlapped about 1½ feet, and tied.

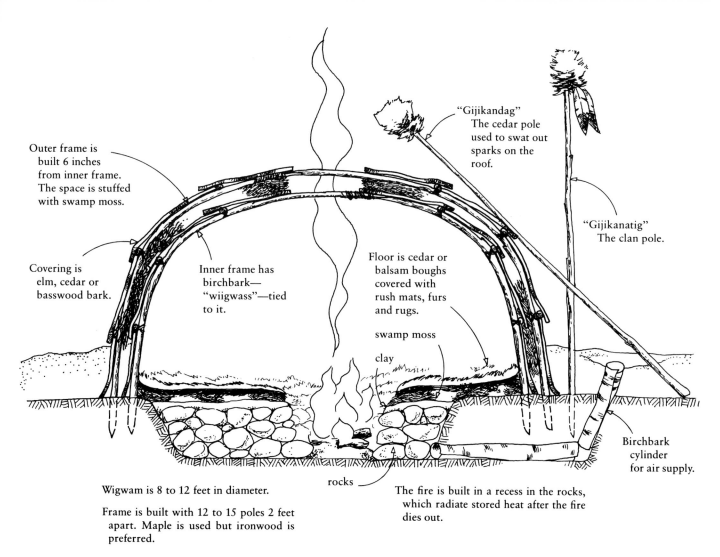

Outer frame is built 6 inches from inner frame. The space is stuffed with swamp moss.

Covering is elm, cedar or basswood bark.

Inner frame has birchbark—"wiigwass"—tied to it.

"Gijikandag"
The cedar pole used to swat out sparks on the roof.

"Gijikanatig"
The clan pole.

Floor is cedar or balsam boughs covered with rush mats, furs and rugs.

swamp moss

clay

Birchbark cylinder for air supply.

rocks

Wigwam is 8 to 12 feet in diameter.

Frame is built with 12 to 15 poles 2 feet apart. Maple is used but ironwood is preferred.

The fire is built in a recess in the rocks, which radiate stored heat after the fire dies out.

Modern wigwams

This inventive wigwam with radiant floor heat (*above*) was built by a Chippewa craftsman and farmer, Albert Isham, with his nephew Ernie St. Germaine. St. Germaine noted that the lodge originated among the Lac Courte Oreilles band of Chippewa, and that, according to his great-grandfather, it allowed his people to endure the cold winter. Neither the use of double-walling nor of radiant floor heating has been corroborated in the literature on Great Lakes Indians. St. Germaine said his great-grandfather was "a very ingenious man ... perhaps he may be the source of such a style of wigwam."

A twentieth-century tarpaper wigwam in Wisconsin (*right*). The Winnebago Indians of Wisconsin, who for a time were ineligible for government housing projects, used modern building materials for their traditional wigwams. In 1978, anthropologist Nancy O. Lurie documented these hybrid structures. Dr. Lurie believes that the modern wigwams appeared no earlier than 1910. "Forerunners," she noted, "developed from the dome or ovoid patterns in terms of substitution of both canvas and tarpaper for cattail mats and slippery elm bark coverings. An early variation, and some still exist, had a shedlike projection to hold a door."

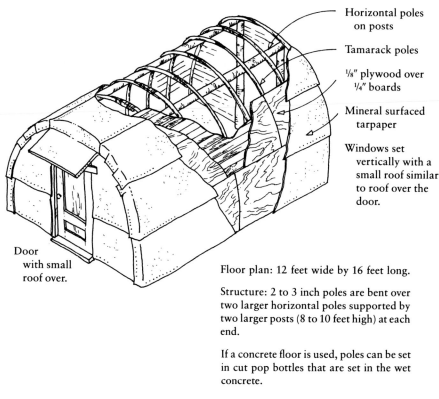

Horizontal poles on posts

Tamarack poles

1/8" plywood over 1/4" boards

Mineral surfaced tarpaper

Windows set vertically with a small roof similar to roof over the door.

Door with small roof over.

Floor plan: 12 feet wide by 16 feet long.

Structure: 2 to 3 inch poles are bent over two larger horizontal poles supported by two larger posts (8 to 10 feet high) at each end.

If a concrete floor is used, poles can be set in cut pop bottles that are set in the wet concrete.

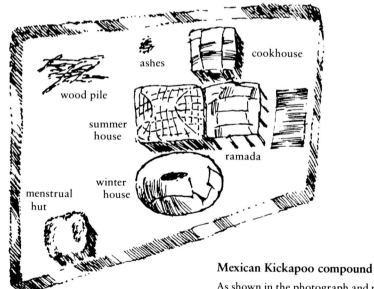

Mexican Kickapoo compound

As shown in the photograph and plan *(above)*, five structures (winter house, summer house with attached arbor, cookhouse, and menstrual hut) are the basic elements of a typical Mexican Kickapoo compound. The rectilinear enclosure, formed by a barbed-wire fence, also includes a woodpile and a spot for ritual ashes. The well-maintained open space of the compound is considered the property of the entire village. The structures, however, are the responsibility of private owners. The plan is of the compound that appears in the middle left of the photograph.

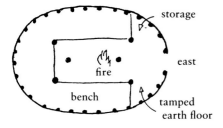

Wikiup plan

Plan of winter house (wikiup)
October to March occupancy.
20 feet long x 14 feet wide x 9 feet high
Woven frame.

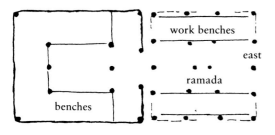

Summer house, ramada

Plan of summer house (odanikani) with ramada
March to October occupancy.
16-18 feet long x 15 feet wide x 11 feet high.

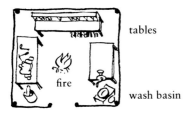

Cookhouse

Plan of cookhouse
12 feet square.

Kickapoo today

Mr. and Mrs. Lewis Cuppawhe stand next to their traditional wikiup *(right)*, near Shawnee, Oklahoma, late 1978. Each autumn the newer mats are tied on first, then the smoke-darkened, worn mats. Finally, the covering is battened down around the exterior with supple stringers.

The Mexican Kickapoo believed their creator, Kitzihiat, occupied the original *wikiup*, their traditional winter wigwam, and the first *odanikani*, their summer house. Kitzihiat showed his son, Wisaka, the proper materials and rituals for building and blessing these houses, and Wisaka, in turn, taught the first Kickapoo people. A Mexican Kickapoo woman's reputation remains bound up in her role as builder and proprietor of the house. Ownership of each house falls to the eldest female occupant, who must host other women helpers during fall and spring rites when roof mats are transferred from one structure to another and new fires are lit in their hearths.

By the 1960s, cattails for roofing mats were so scarce near Nacimiento that Kickapoo women had to ride commercial buses to a marshland more than 50 miles away to find them. Before the rushes were cut, tobacco offerings were made to the snakes, who were considered the owners of the marsh. At home the women soaked the 9-foot stalks in water to soften them, then laid them out on the ground to be sewn into roofing mats. Mats for sleeping and sitting benches were woven from the softened leaves of local sotol cactus. The buildings were framed with Montezuma bald cypress or one-seed juniper.

Kickapoo architecture also survives in the squatter camp in Eagle Pass, Texas. Over years of shifting residence between their Mexican and Oklahoma settlements by way of this border town, the Kickapoo became accustomed to stopping at Eagle Pass for seasonal work picking fruit and vegetables. Gradually they established this permanent camp and their nearby burial grounds.

On a neglected stretch of the Rio Grande floodplain stand their makeshift dwellings. Their summer houses are walled with cane cut from the riverbank and roofed over with cattail mats. But their winter wikiups are roofed with scavenged pieces of cardboard packing crates. They also manage to find saplings to frame arbors and cookhouses. Following a publicity campaign on their behalf, the city reluctantly piped in drinking water and provided portable privies, but the site has been earmarked for a community park. In this time capsule of Algonquian culture, the Indians dry corn, tan hides, and tend to their traditional houses underneath the International Bridge that connects Mexico and the United States.

LONGHOUSE

The longhouse has always been the dominant symbol of social solidarity for the Iroquois of upper New York state. The central role this building has played in their culture originates with the Iroquois genesis myth. Before mankind there existed only a sky world, illuminated by blossoms from an all-nurturing Great Tree. This domain was populated by "elder brothers," prototypes of the people and animals yet to appear on Earth. They occupied long, bark-covered houses aligned on an east-west axis. In each dwelling these mythological residents were related as clan kinfolk through the female line of descent. Single families occupied sleeping compartments along both sides of the central aisle, and cooking fires were shared by families opposite one another.

This mythic system gave the prehistoric Iroquois a model for organizing their living spaces and surroundings. Men were in charge of forests and lakes, and women were responsible for villages and gardens. The men offered prayers and choice tobacco to the forest spirits, who in turn let them clear the woods for houses and fields. The best town sites were level hilltops with clear views for spotting enemy war parties. They also had to have access to fresh water and timber for their dwellings and firewood. Trees were marked and girdled in the spring so they could be toppled by late August. Once the gardens were cleared with controlled burning, the women took over, praying to the spirits of the "three sisters"—corn, beans, and squash—before planting in the family plots.

Iroquois towns remained in one place as long as tillable soil, roofing bark, firewood, and stands of saplings for longhouse additions and stockades held out. After a decade or two, however, these resources often were exhausted, and heaps of refuse and invasions of fleas made the town unlivable. New longhouses were customarily built just downhill from the old site, where the bark structures were left to decay.

Iroquoian architecture

The centerpiece of Iroquois and Huron Indian life was the longhouse. This example *(below)* is a detail from an early French map of Fort Frontenac, ca. 1720. Longhouses were grouped together in large communities, the Mohawk town of Caughnawaga *(bottom right)*, located on the banks of the St. Lawrence River, ca. 1750. An idealized drawing of the fortified town of Hochelaga *(middle right)*, near present-day Montreal, was made shortly after Cartier's visit in October 1535. The longhouses shown in this drawing of an Iroquois village of the late seventeenth century *(top right)*, are far more accurate. They are aligned in two rows and are surrounded by a rectangular palisade.

Elevation des Cabannes Sauvages

LA TERRA DE HOCHELAGA
NELLA NOVA FRANCIA

MONTE REAL

A Eglise
B maison du missionaire
C Cabanes ou village des sauvages

veue de la mission
du Sault s.t Louis

PREHISTORIC LONGHOUSES

Archeologists believe this settlement pattern was flourishing by the mid-fourteenth century. One early longhouse site is the community known as Howlett Hill, south of Syracuse, New York, about four miles from Onondaga Lake. The village was in the heart of Iroquois country, midpoint on the Iroquois Trail, which ran from present-day Albany to Buffalo. In 1964 it was excavated by archeologist James Tuck, who found the floor remains of four longhouses. Based on radiocarbon dating of ceramic fragments, he estimated that Howlett had been occupied from 1380 to 1400. Residue of fish and deer bones, Indian corn, and hickory nuts revealed that the Howlett Iroquois had subsisted on a mixed economy of fishing, hunting, foraging, and farming.

The largest longhouse, a building 334 feet long and 23 feet wide, was particularly interesting. The outer wall appeared to have been framed with 3-inch poles set into the ground about a foot deep. Two rows of vertical poles 8 to 10 inches in diameter defined the inside central corridor and supported both sleeping bunks and roof. Tuck discovered that the main doorway had been placed precisely in the center of the west wall, unlike in the other houses, which were entered at either end. He speculated that the building was erected in one construction phase for a finite number of families totaling between 150 and 200 people. The more common Iroquoian practice was periodically to enlarge the longhouses to accommodate newly married couples.

Another early longhouse community, known as the Nodwell site, was established near Lake Huron. It was inhabited by members of the Huron tribe, who were neighbors (and often enemies) of the Iroquois yet spoke a closely related tongue and were culturally similar. Nodwell, in present-day Ontario, was, like most Huron villages, no more than a five-hour walk from a lake.

Archeological remains suggest that the Nodwell community flourished around the mid-fourteenth century. Its twelve buildings, built on well-drained loam, housed about five hundred people for at least twenty years. All the Nodwell houses apparently were extended at each end to accommodate newcomers who married into the house clan.

Between 1969 and 1973, Nodwell was excavated by Canadian archeologist James V. Wright. After uncovering the house floors, Wright and his students actually reconstructed on the site two of the huge longhouse frames, using the original post molds as sockets for freshly cut saplings. He based the building's proportions on a crude sketch of a longhouse built by the Oneida, a tribe belonging to the Iroquois Confederacy, which he discovered on a map of Fort Frontenac dating from 1720. This episode of "experimental archeology" gave Wright and his crew a hands-on appreciation of the construction problems Huron builders faced. From the experience they hypothesized that the interior corridor posts must have been slightly staggered to grip the horizontal poles

Iroquois archeology

The floor dimensions of this 334-foot-long building *(above)* were discovered at Howlett Hill, just south of Syracuse, New York, where archeologist James Tuck uncovered the remains of four large houses in 1964, dating from the fourteenth century.

At the Howlett Hill site *(right)* stakes indicate post mold alignment. The post mold floor plan shows the excavated areas of the site *(bottom right)*.

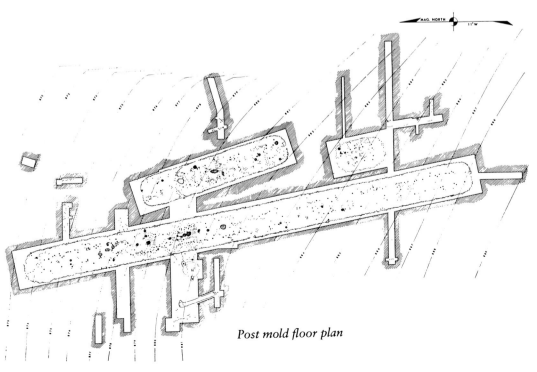

Post mold floor plan

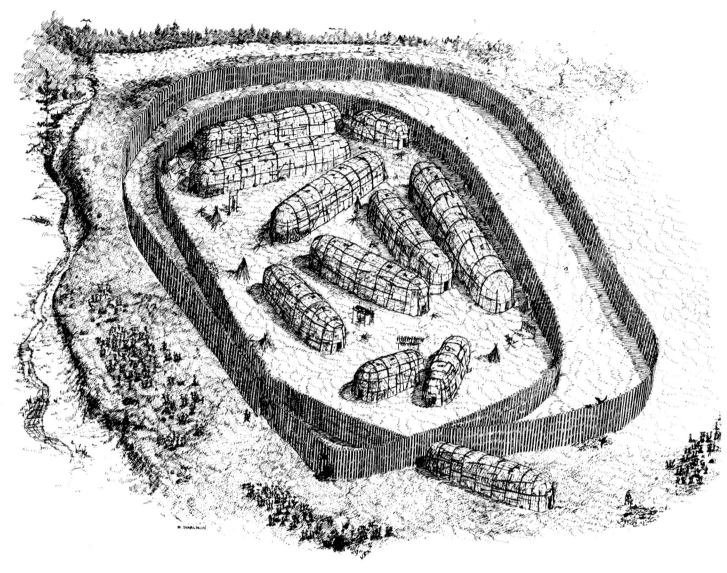

Nodwell site

Nodwell longhouse expansion
arrows indicate post mold locations of pre-expansion building ends

Core village

expansion 1

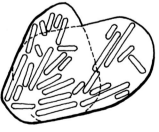

expansion 2

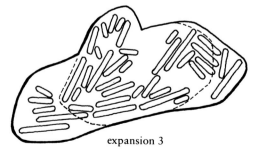

expansion 3

Draper site
showing possible expansion sequence

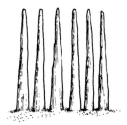

Palisade types

Huron archeology

Shown in reconstruction, the Huron longhouses of the Nodwell village site *(drawing, top left)* near Lake Huron seem less regularly arrayed than those of the Iroquois. At the Draper Site *(bottom left)*, archeologists have plotted the growth of a community of Huron longhouses. Both Iroquois and Huron villages were protected by palisades *(above)*, which ranged from fences of pointed posts to elaborate ramparts.

supporting the bunks and overhead storage racks. The reconstructed frames were left bare because cedar bark—which the Hurons had preferred for roofing—was scarce, and Dutch elm disease had practically eliminated the supply of elm bark, the traditional Iroquois wall covering.

Just north of Toronto, Ontario, Canadian excavators studied another Huron village, known as the Draper site, whose longhouses were similar to those at Nodwell. At Draper, however, the archeologists were able to plot sequential phases of village growth. The community developed rather rapidly around 1500 into a town of forty-five to fifty structures and within a few decades covered fifteen acres and supported at least two thousand residents within its triple palisade walls.

This expansion of the Draper site was a sign of the population growth that apparently took place throughout the Iroquoian world as it entered the historic period. For most of the fifteenth century, Iroquois villages were small—from five to fifteen longhouses on the average—but after 1500 the number of buildings increased dramatically and stronger fortifications were built to surround the villages.

In 1535, when explorer Jacques Cartier visited the major Iroquoian center Hochelaga, near present-day Montreal, he found its longhouses protected by a massive stockade. One of his chroniclers estimated that the community held 3,600 people living in fifty bark houses. The log walls stood about 18 feet high, but were raised even higher at points vulnerable to enemy attack, prompting some European observers to classify such Iroquoian towns as "castles." Sharpened vertical timbers in the middle row were interspersed with leaning posts that supported balconies from which the villagers could hurl rocks and shoot arrows at invaders.

By the late seventeenth century, the Iroquois settlement of Gannagaro in Ontario County, New York, contained 150 longhouses with thousands of residents. Most of the twenty-five major Iroquois towns of this period, however, averaged about six hundred residents. While longhouses in the early Huron settlements appear to have been randomly placed, these Iroquois buildings were sited quite formally. In 1634, a Dutch visitor to an Oneida and Mohawk town was impressed by "36 houses, in rows like streets, so that we could pass nicely." At the peak of its growth around 1615, the two-village settlement of Cahiague, between Lake Simcoe and Georgian Bay in Central Ontario, was said to contain two hundred bark structures, which sheltered nearly four thousand Indians.

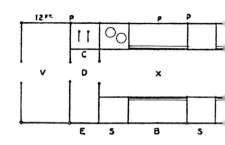

THE LONGHOUSE

The most authoritative account of Iroquois architecture comes from Joseph-François Lafitau, a Jesuit missionary who lived near present-day Montreal from 1712 to 1717. Lafitau was a studious observer of Iroquois life and had high praise for their architecture: "It is not without reason," he wrote, "that the name 'Hotinnosioni,' or builders of cabins, has been given to the Iroquois, they are indeed the most comfortably lodged of all America."

According to Lafitau, the Iroquois *hodensote,* or longhouse, of the early 1700s was from 40 to 400 feet long and from 20 to 30 feet wide. On the front and back entrances were representations of the house clan's totemic animal. The smaller, two-family dwelling called a *ganosote,* or bark house, was probably the core structure for many extended longhouses and may have been more commonly built than popular accounts of Iroquois society suggest. As the building was enlarged to accommodate new couples, its size became a rough indicator of how many in-laws it had acquired and of how long it had stood in the village. In each structure, the eldest woman held sway as the reigning longhouse "mother."

In his account, Lafitau gave details of the longhouses' appearance and construction and included a floor plan. He described them as "five or six fathoms wide, high in proportion, and [varying] in length according to the number of fires. Each fire adds twenty to twenty-five feet to the length of a cabin of a single fire, which does not exceed thirty or forty feet. Each of these cabins rests on four posts for each fire which are the base and support of the entire structure."

Lafitau compared the roof to "a vault or garden arbour," its framing "made with poles bent to the form of a bow." Early sketches show longhouses with barrel roofs, but a model commissioned by the renowned nineteenth-century anthropologist of the Iroquois, Lewis Henry Morgan, depicts a merging of barrel and gable profiles so that the rafters arch abruptly just before the ridgepole. By the late eighteenth century, however, almost all Iroquois bark houses had sharp gables, and the barrel-roofed longhouse had become a thing of the past.

While the Algonquians were partial to birch bark for their wigwams, the Iroquoians preferred the elm, celebrated in their folklore, to chestnut, hemlock, basswood or ash for sheathing their longhouses. The bark was peeled from the trees between late May and mid-July, when the sap was rising, then the thick sheets were flattened under rocks and kept moist to prevent warping or cracking as they dried. Punctured with bone awls, the bark was tied to the frame with strips of green basswood or slippery elm innerbark. Other accounts suggest that the bark slabs were considerably wider, but Lafitau described them as being about 6 feet long and a little over a foot wide. He wrote: "These pieces of bark lap one over the other like slate. They are secured outside with fresh poles similar to those which form the frame roof underneath, and are still further strengthened by long pieces of saplings split in two, and are fastened to the extremities of the roof, on the sides, or on the wings, by pieces of wood cut with hooked ends, which are regularly spaced for this purpose."

Smoke holes in longhouse roofs were the sole source of light, "in the same manner as the celebrated Rotunda built by Agrippe, which may still be seen

Longhouse plan

The plan of a five-fire longhouse *(above),* from a drawing in Lafitau's 1724 account. The single interior line marks the upper shelf, which runs the entire length of the house proper. The second line shows the lower shelf, which is used as a bed. The unit of measurement is the length of a man lying down, about 6 feet. V, exterior vestibule; E, entrance lobby; S, store room; B, bed; C, child's bunk; O, bark barrels; P, posts; X, fire; D, doors.

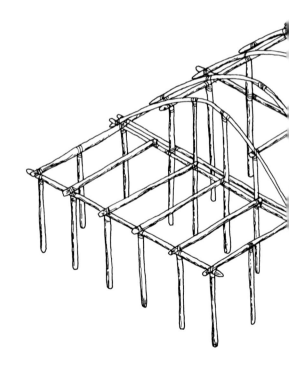

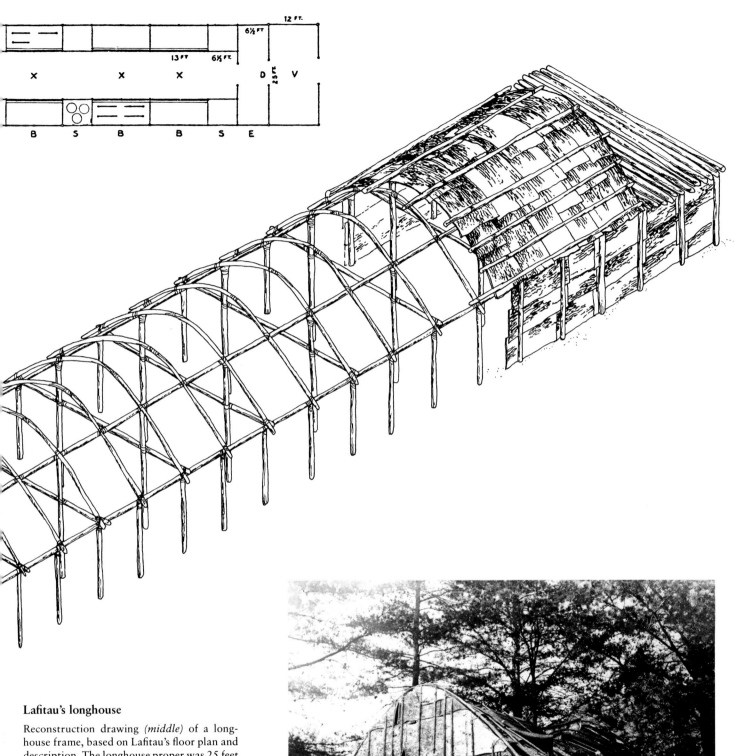

Lafitau's longhouse

Reconstruction drawing *(middle)* of a longhouse frame, based on Lafitau's floor plan and description. The longhouse proper was 25 feet wide by 110 feet long. The flat-roofed vestibules extended 12 feet from each end. The roof was not framed with a ridgepole; instead, slender poles were bent at the top and tied to form the rafters. The longhouse had no windows; doors were at each end.

A bark house *(right)*, built by Passamaquoddy Indians from Maine, Newell S. Thomas and Joseph Thomas, in Washington, D.C., 1896. Although of birch bark and originating from northern Algonquian country, the structure suggests how the two-fire Iroquois elm-bark *ganosote* house probably looked.

entire in Rome," commented Lafitau. In the late 1700s, however, some basswood bark houses built by the Iroquois had sliding wall shutters for illumination. By that time, too, longhouse doors were of hewn wood and swung from iron hinges obtained in trade.

Beneath the sooty ceiling, a central corridor divided the floor area. Every 20 feet or so a hearth with its own smoke hole was shared by two families whose compartments were across the aisle from one another. On either side, tiers of low bunks about 6 feet wide were lashed to the wall posts and the uprights, which extended from floor to roof. To Arthur C. Parker, an Iroquois writer of the early twentieth century, these interiors resembled "upper and lower beds in a sleeping car."

Each family's "room" was considered its private, domestic space. Beneath the sleeping platform, which was decked with stiff bark sheets and spread with mats and furs, was storage space for personal effects. Shelving above the beds might hold cornhusk mats, weapons, baskets, herbs, and dried tobacco. The uppermost loft, for bulkier items, could be transformed in summer into a spectator platform by removing a few bark shingles.

Day and night someone in the longhouse tended a simmering kettle of corn or meat from which all residents could partake. Hanging from the side posts and roof were drying fish and braided husks of drying Iroquois corn "so nicely done that it seems like a tapestry hung the whole length of the cabins," Jacques Cartier observed in 1535. Tall poles leaning against the storage racks were used to close the smoke hole covers when it rained, while smoke and draft were regulated by opening or closing the bark doors that hung from the lintel. At each end of the longhouse, flat-roofed vestibules held firewood in winter; in summer they were sleeping berths for the young.

Longhouse interior

Near an old Huron village site in Midland, Ontario, a Canadian archeologist has reconstructed a typical longhouse interior. Sleeping bunks run the length of the building. Braided corn, dried roots, and herbs hang from the rafters and support poles line the main corridor. Cooking fires are spaced along the central aisle.

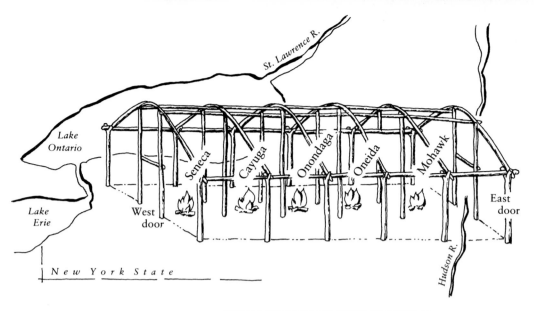

THE LEAGUE OF FIVE NATIONS

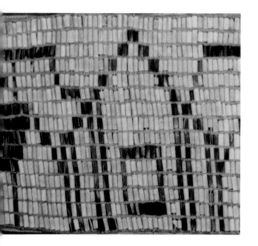

Longhouse of the League

Connected by the Iroquois Trail in upper New York State, the five nations of the League of the Iroquois symbolized their political and military unity by a longhouse of five fires. *(top)*

A ceremonial belt *(above)* depicting a longhouse. Strung of white and purple clamshell beads, wampum belts commemorated historical and religious events. Shown here is the central portion of the "Washington belt," which honors a peacemaking council between the Iroquois League—represented by the longhouse—and the "thirteen fires," or the American colonies.

Between 1400 and 1600, the longhouse—which sheltered the basic social unit, the matrilineal clan—became the unifying political symbol for a new federation of five Iroquois tribes. Sometime during that period two legendary heroes, Deganawidah and Hiawatha, formed a union of the Seneca, Mohawk, Onondaga, Cayuga, and Oneida tribes which came to dominate the fertile valleys and forested hills from the St. Lawrence River to Lake Champlain. They called themselves the "people of the longhouse"; to outsiders they were the League of Five Nations, or the Iroquois Confederacy.

At the famous council that is said to have formed their new league, the tribal delegates concluded in unison, "Have built longhouse." Ever afterwards, the Iroquois spoke metaphorically of their domain as a gigantic longhouse, which stretched 240 miles from near Albany to the shores of Lake Erie at Buffalo. Its symbolic central aisle was the Iroquois Trail, which hastened communication and provided mutual defense for the league. "To an Iroquois," the scholar Lewis H. Morgan wrote, "the League was not like a Longhouse. It *was* a Longhouse, extending from the Hudson to the Genesee, in which around five fires the five tribes gathered."

The eastern end of this stronghold was guarded by the Mohawks, who from then on were known as "keepers of the eastern door." The Seneca were "keepers of the western door." Such architectural figures of speech became part of Iroquois oratory and were used both in councils among themselves and in warnings to dangerous outsiders. "Secure the doors" meant for the Mohawks and the Senecas to keep a close watch on their territories. The west end of the house was said to be protected by slick sheets of green bark, which enemy invaders would slip on. Just inside the southern and northern "walls," respectively, lived the Cayugas and the Oneidas. In the center was the territory of the Onondagas, the "keepers of the fire." The Onondaga council house was said to stand directly beneath the longhouse's central smoke hole, and it was there that the entire league met for grand councils. The French were once warned to beware of threatening the Onondaga lest they fall through this smoke hole and burn themselves. Iroquois clan leaders, or *sachems*, were said to be the "braces" of the longhouse, while its "posts" were the tribal chiefs.

The Iroquois League represented the greatest military and economic alliance of Indians in seventeenth-century North America, but it began to lose power as the European struggle to retain the American colonies came to a climax. Following the Revolutionary War, American soldiers swept through upper New York state to take revenge upon the League for supporting the

85

British. Forty longhouse towns were burned and an estimated sixty thousand bushels of corn were destroyed. At about the same time smaller houses of log walls and bark roofs were beginning to replace the traditional longhouses, and furnishings of European influence—chairs, tables, trunks, and rugs—were proliferating.

The last enclave of Seneca traditionalists was a community known as Burnt House near Allegheny, New York. In 1798, visiting Quakers reported that in this settlement of four hundred Indians they found thirty bark-roofed houses, a building set aside for guests, and one council longhouse. Elsewhere, most Iroquois families lived in white-pine log cabins. By the mid-nineteenth century, when Morgan conducted his fieldwork among the Seneca, the traditional longhouse was but a memory. In his classic study of Iroquois society, *League of the Iroquois* (1851), Morgan included an engraving of an idealized longhouse with five fires and a trim gable roof. He noted, however, that "very little is now remembered by the Indians themselves of their form and mechanism, or of the plan of life within them ... A complete understanding of the mode of life in these longhouses will not, probably, ever be recovered."

The Handsome Lake Revival

The potency of the Iroquois longhouse as a collective symbol was revived around the close of the eighteenth century. In the Burnt House settlement lived a reformed alcoholic and charismatic mystic named Handsome Lake. His new religious doctrine, which attempted to revitalize Iroquois society through a blend of traditional seasonal rituals and Quaker moral teachings, was profamily and antiliquor. His followers met in a grange-type, rectangular meeting hall built of logs with a gable roof, but it was known as a longhouse and its members considered it their temple.

Scenes About a Seneca Bark Lodge
1905

From Handsome Lake's headquarters, messengers were sent east each autumn to recite his *Gaiwiiyo,* or "the good word," throughout a network of ten autonomous longhouses. Handsome Lake died in 1815, but his doctrine lives on. Today its adherents consider themselves the guardians of true Iroquois culture. Anthropologist Harold Blau has summarized the new, amplified significance of their buildings: "the Longhouse is utilized not only for religious purposes but also serves as a meeting place for tribal discussion and as a kind of hospital for the post-curative rites. The Longhouse is an informal schoolhouse for the young and carries on the process of traditional socialization; it is a dance center and a feast hall … The Longhouse as an institution is functionally integrated into almost every aspect of Iroquois life … [it is] the center of communication and the mainstay of ideological security."

LONGHOUSES TODAY

An unusual descendant of Algonquian extended-family dwellings was still in use by Delaware Indians in northeastern Oklahoma at the turn of the century. This was the "Big House," a barn-sized log house constructed according to tradition and used for the tribe's annual harvest ritual. Originally from the eastern seaboard, the Delaware had once lived in multifamily bark houses which, quite early in their history, were gable-roofed. It has been suggested that their skills at building log structures were picked up from Swedish immigrants.

As European settlers pushed them westward, the Delaware eventually were dispersed as far away as Oklahoma and Ontario, Canada. For years the more traditional groups held the Big House ceremony in old-fashioned, gable-roofed buildings that by then were built exclusively for this major ritual. Carved and painted faces, standing for the *manitou,* or spirits of the twelve layers of the Delaware cosmos, stared from the interior wall posts and from the sacred center pole, which was said to be the staff of the Great Spirit himself. The only remaining Big House—near Copan, Oklahoma—was robbed of its carved posts, and fell into ruin after the last complete ceremony was held there in 1924.

As for the Iroquois, a form of their longhouse is still being rebuilt and maintained on Iroquois reservations in New York state and southern Ontario. Today they are constructed with stud frames, clapboard siding, and shake roofs. The Seneca longhouse at Six Nations Reserve in Canada suggests their common plan. It commands an open field and measures 26 by 46 feet, with a cookhouse and eating house standing at right angles to its west wall.

Some Seneca examples in this region have been remodeled or entirely moved to new sites. Around 1913, for instance, the Senecas of the Allegheny reservation in southwestern New York tore down their Windfall community longhouse and, seven years later, demolished the Horseshoe community building because of shifts in population. When the "fire went out," as the Iroquois say, in another nearby longhouse, the structure was torn down, and surviving members recycled its timbers for a new cookhouse at their old Coldspring longhouse on the Allegheny reservation.

In 1964, the U.S. Army Corp of Engineers announced plans to flood the

Gable-roofed bark houses

In his publication on the social organization of the Iroquois, scholar Lewis Henry Morgan included an engraving *(above)* of an idealized late-period longhouse with a trim gable roof and five smoke holes. Actual bark houses of the eighteenth-century Iroquois, however, probably looked more like this two-fire bark house *(left),* sketched by Seneca artist Jesse Cornplanter, showing the gabled roof that succeeded the barrel shape. The roofing slabs are slightly scooped, overlapping each other over the underlying rafters like clay roofing tiles. Stringers fasten the bark tight to the frame. Cornplanter also shows braided corn drying on racks and corn being ground in oaken mortars with maple pestles.

Drawing by Spybuck 2720
Dec 23 Year 1912

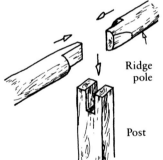

Center post and ridge

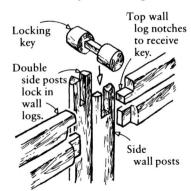

Wall post and beam

Delaware Big House

In the mid-seventeenth century, Delaware Indians were building bark-shingled dwellings that extended a hundred feet or more with steeply pitched roofs. Their "king's house," described by chroniclers as covered with split wood instead of bark, may be the forerunner of the Big House, the ceremonial log structure that housed their most sacred harvest rituals.

To the eastern Delaware, who were dislodged eventually to settle in the West, the Big House stood for the universe. Their New Year ceremony was staged in the fall after the harvest and lasted twelve days—one for every level in the Delaware cosmos, each of which was also represented by masks carved on an interior post. The building had a well-tamped earth floor. No iron could be used in its construction. Within its east (birth)-west (death) oriented interior, two fires and a central post were ringed by an oval "White Path."

The White Path, according to anthropologist Frank Speck, symbolized the passage of life: "As the dancers in the Big House ceremony wend their stately passage following the course of the White Path they 'push something along,' meaning existence, with their rhythmic tread. Not only the passage of life, but the journey of the soul after death is symbolically figured in the ceremony." The interior view *(above left)* by native artist Ernest Spybuck shows dancers on the White Path around the two sacred fires.

The drawing *(above right)* is based on the Big House near Copan, Oklahoma, 1909. The cutaway and detail drawings *(below left)* show intricate log work. The floor plan was 25 feet wide by 40 feet long by 18 feet high; the side wall plate was 6 feet high.

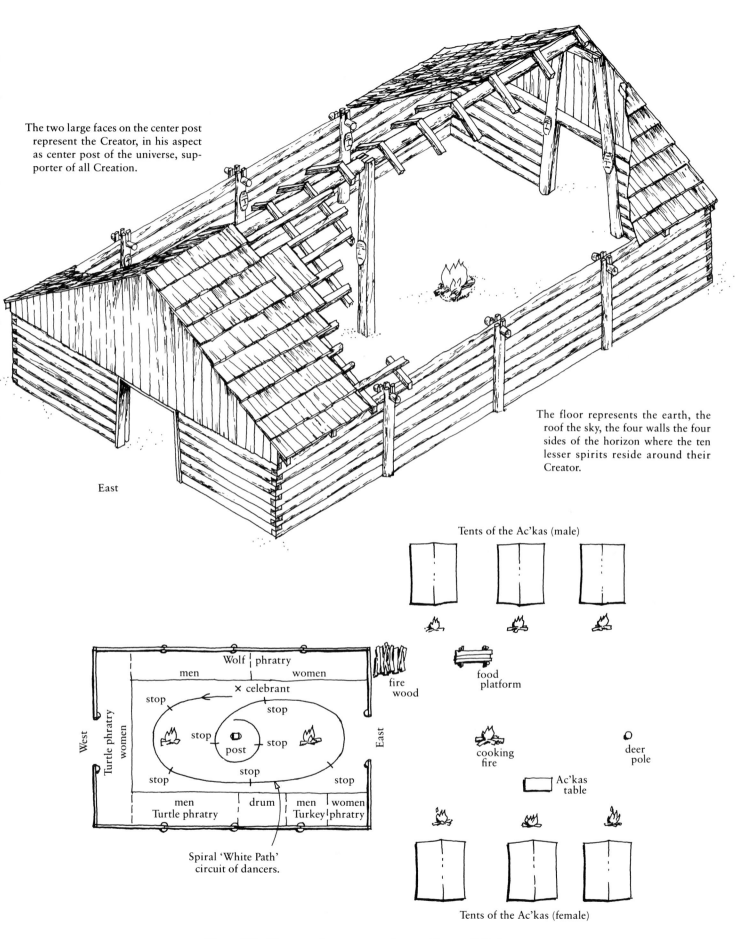

The two large faces on the center post represent the Creator, in his aspect as center post of the universe, supporter of all Creation.

The floor represents the earth, the roof the sky, the four walls the four sides of the horizon where the ten lesser spirits reside around their Creator.

East

Tents of the Ac'kas (male)

food
platform

cooking
fire

deer
pole

Ac'kas
table

Tents of the Ac'kas (female)

Wolf phratry

men   women

× celebrant

stop   stop

West   Turtle phratry women   East

stop   post   stop

stop

stop   stop   stop

men   drum   men   women
Turtle phratry   Turkey   phratry

fire
wood

Spiral 'White Path'
circuit of dancers.

Plan of Big House and camp grounds near Copan, Oklahoma

89

Allegheny River Valley, which would inundate the Coldspring community. After Seneca opposition to the Kinzua Dam proved futile, representatives of all the Iroquois longhouses convened at Tonawanda to compose an altogether new rite for desanctifying the old longhouse and consecrating its replacement in a new location. They also decided that the next building should have a few alterations. "It will be wider and not so high," said a tribal spokesman at the time. "Since the boys look in the tall windows, it would be better to raise them up; they can always come inside if they want to see the 'doings.'" In June 1965, tribal leaders delivered their final oratory in the cherished Coldspring structure, then sealed its doors with prayer and took its sacred shell-beaded belts to the new longhouse in Steamburg, New York.

In the autumn of 1976, we traveled along the old Iroquois Trail, now Interstate 90, to visit the Upper Cayuga reservation's longhouse. Every now and then we glimpsed a nineteenth-century cabin still in use, its hand-hewn logs occasionally visible beneath overlays of tarpaper or plywood. We slowed down as we passed longhouses at the new Tonawanda and Allegheny communities—austere, undecorated buildings standing alone on well-kept lawns, almost indistinguishable from country schools or Shaker churches. We were hesitant to approach, however, without invitation. Finally we crossed into Canada and arrived at the Six Nations Reserve, where roughly one-fifth of the community members consider themselves "followers of the longhouse."

At the lovely site once known as "medicine spring where the fire is," now called Sour Springs, we visited the oldest longhouse in the vicinity. When the original structure built in nearby Brantford in 1784 burned down in the mid-nineteenth century, a replacement structure was erected close by. Its adze-squared logs were later moved to this third site. The log walls were laid up once more with doorways at either end, their joints were chinked, and a new gable roof was added.

We strolled around the framed dining hall and the cookhouse, which exuded the fragrance of wood smoke from the last strawberry and maple-sap harvest feasts. Through the windows of the longhouse the spare interior seemed to be patiently awaiting the next ritual gathering. The hearths that had once lined the central aisle were represented by a pair of wood stoves. Simple wooden benches pressed against the walls. Hanging above them were ceremonial rattles made from the dried bodies of large snapping turtles. Two doors opened on opposite ends of the long walls—the west for women, the east for men. In the rites of the Handsome Lake religion, the *Okiwen,* or Feast of the Dead, is held in the spring and during the Six Nations councils; the etiquette for entering, sitting, and leaving the buildings still echoes the old social divisions and spatial domains of seventeenth-century Iroquois longhouses.

We paid a call on the Upper Cayuga longhouse, hoping to photograph the interior. As we drove up, a native work crew was dismantling the cookhouse in preparation for a new one. But when we asked permission to enter, we were eyed suspiciously. "You don't understand, you can't do that," said one man in denim coveralls. "You didn't get permission from the council." Another worker added, "It might look like just a building to you, but this is like our church, not a place for your camera. You have to respect what this building means to us."

Longhouse today

The longhouse photographed at Sour Springs, Six Nations Reserve, Canada *(right).* The logs in this sacred meeting structure of the Upper Cayuga people were hewn in the 1870s. When Frank Speck photographed the building in 1943, the old-style cook house, with a smoke hole in the roof instead of a chimney, still was standing.

Standing at the men's doorway to the Sour Springs longhouse *(above)* are singer Willie John and Bill Johnson, who wears an Iroquois false face mask, 1962.

90

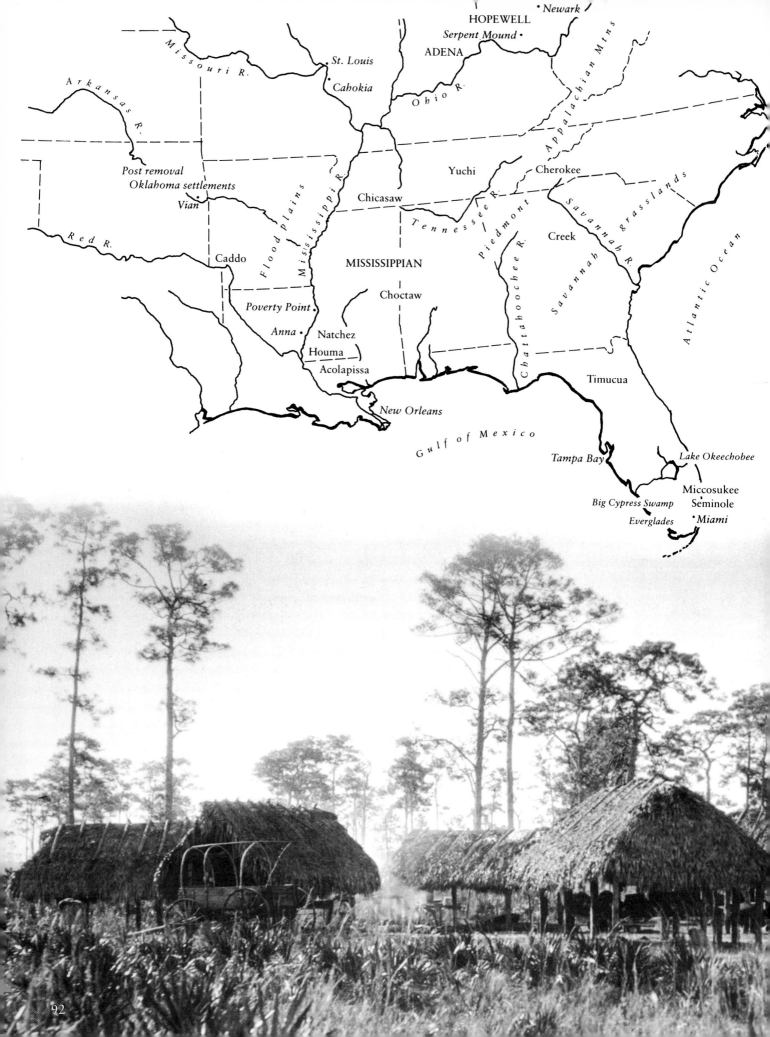

Missouri R.

Arkansas R.

St. Louis

Cahokia

HOPEWELL

Newark

Serpent Mound •

ADENA

Ohio R.

Appalachian Mtns

Post removal
Oklahoma settlements

Vian

Yuchi

Cherokee

Chicasaw

Tennessee R.

Piedmont

Creek

Savannah grasslands

Red R.

Flood plains

Mississippi R.

Caddo

MISSISSIPPIAN

Choctaw

Chattahoochee R.

Savannah R.

Atlantic Ocean

Poverty Point •

Anna •

Natchez

Houma

Acolapissa

Timucua

New Orleans

Gulf of Mexico

Tampa Bay

Lake Okeechobee

Miccosukee
Seminole

Big Cypress Swamp

Everglades

Miami

Southeastern temples and camps

This temple *(above)* was drawn by French engineer A. de Batz in 1732 from a structure in an Acolapissa Indian village north of New Orleans. Cane mats covered its domed roof and sacred bird effigies were mounted on reed steeples. The Seminole Indian camp *(below)* was headed by John Jumper, photographed by M.R. Harrington in 1908.

In late May of 1539, only days after landing on Florida's west coast, the Spanish explorer Hernando De Soto and his party came upon an Indian town named Ucita—the first of many examples of Southeastern Indian architecture the Spanish soldiers would record as they trekked across the steaming lowlands of the deep South. Located near present-day Tampa Bay, Ucita was a fairly representative settlement of the local Timucua Indians, containing, according to one expedition chronicler, "seven or eight houses, built of timber, and covered with palm-leaves."

Ucita also exhibited the native Southeast's most ancient, widespread, and characteristic architectural form: the shaped earth mound. Overlooking its palm-roofed dwellings from either end of town stood two of these man-made earthworks. Throughout the history of Southeastern Indian cultures, such monuments were used to entomb the bodies of dignitaries, often playing a central role in funeral rites, or to support civic buildings or temples on their flattened summits. Carefully positioned in geometric clusters, the mounds also demarcated formal, open-air plazas.

At Ucita, the Spanish learned of another of the mounds' functions. According to the De Soto scribe, the earthwork nearest the beach was "very high ... made by hand for defense" and supported a "Chief's House," a large cabin built of plastered wattle-and-daub, which was the common walling technique used throughout the Southeast. Ucita's other mound, located on the inland boundary of town, was of special interest to the gold-hungry Spanish, for its rooftree featured an effigy, "a wooden fowl with gilded eyes."

After staying in Ucita for five weeks, De Soto left a military detachment behind and continued north, soon encountering another Indian town, Ossachile, on Florida's northern peninsula. The chief's house in this settlement was built on a mound with steep sides; it was reached by climbing an 8-foot wide ramp of earthen steps secured by squared retaining timbers. At Ossachile, the Spanish also learned how the Indians laid out their communities. "They choose a place where they bring a quantity of earth which they elevate into a kind of platform, two or three pikes high ... They then trace, at the bottom of this elevation, a square place conformable to the extent of the village which they would make; and around this place the most important persons build their dwellings."

De Soto and his men had begun a journey through the heart of the Southeastern culture area, which stretched westward from the Atlantic to the Mississippi and from the Ohio River to the Gulf of Mexico. To the east, its broad coastal plain supported savannah grasslands, scrub forests, and marshy lowlands. Beyond the coastal plain, rising to the Appalachian Mountains, were rolling hills and fertile river valleys forested with hickory and oak. As the expedition party left Florida for Georgia and the Carolinas, they continued to encounter earthworks, public buildings, and town squares. The soldiers learned to distinguish burial temples from chiefs' houses, and they noticed a shift in construction materials from palmetto to cane as they moved north. Of the Creek town of Toalli in southern Georgia they observed: "The houses of this town are different from those behind [in Florida]. [These] are roofed with cane after the fashion of tiles. They are kept clean; some have their sides so made of clay as to look like tapia [puddled adobe] ... Throughout the cold country every Indian has a winter house, plastered inside and out, with a very small opening which is closed at dark and a fire being made within, it remains heated like an oven, so that clothing is not needed at night. He has likewise a house for summer and near it a kitchen, where fire is made and bread baked."

Toalli's architecture also seemed to express a class structure and a form of taxation: "The difference between the houses of the masters of principal men and those of the common people is besides being larger than the others, they have deep balconies on the front side, with cane seats like benches, and about are many barbacoas [granaries] in which they bring together the tribute their people give them of maize, skins of deer, and blankets of the country."

De Soto's men headed west into Tennessee, followed the Alabama River south, and finally turned westward, soon crossing the Mississippi to enter the Southern Plains. In many of the Creek and Chickasaw communities they noticed a pattern of separate residences for summer and winter. In other Creek towns they found all-season gabled structures, framed with upright southern pine, locust, or sassafras posts. These buildings were walled with cypress planks or wattle-and-daub—cane lath which was plastered with a mixture of clay and grass—and finally coated with a whitewash made from ground oyster shells or white chalk. Their floors were puddled and plastered, with sunken central hearths. Within the domestic compound, corncribs held the harvest. Inside the house were raised cane beds softened by mattresses and thick animal furs. Baby boys slept on panther skins and baby girls slept on soft, tanned fawn skins, which the Indians believed would impart the appropriate masculine and feminine traits to their children.

The De Soto chronicles confirm the range across the entire Southeast of an

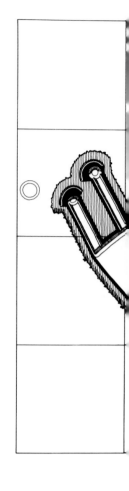

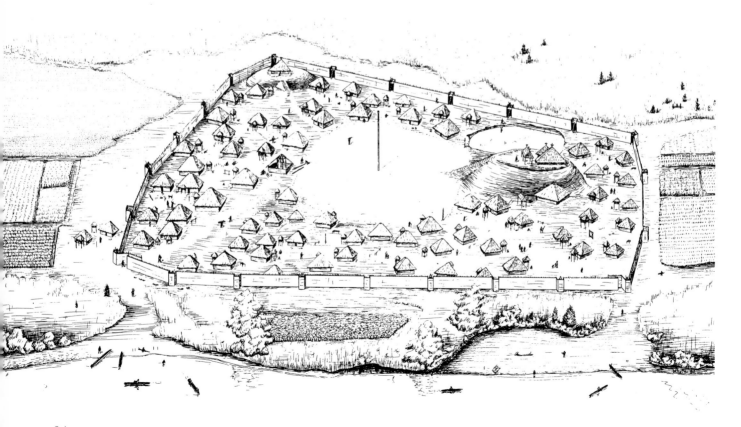

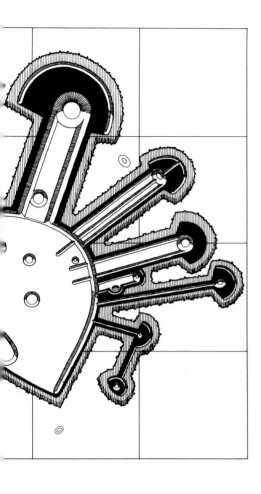

orderly pattern of towns with municipal and religious structures raised on mounds and organized around ceremonial town centers. The Southeast then had a thriving native population, with an estimated 120,000 Indians living in long-established towns. But early Spanish contact brought warfare, slavery, and disease, virtually eliminating the native societies along the eastern Gulf of Mexico and in Florida.

By the eighteenth century the native American South consisted of such major tribes as the Muskogean-speaking Creek, Choctaw, Chickasaw, and Natchez; one group of Siouan-speaking Yuchi; the Iroquoian-speaking Cherokee; and some Caddoan speakers who dwelt along the region's western boundary. Most of these nations comprised many towns, whose members lived in family compounds of thatch-roofed houses dispersed along streams near civic centers. As in prehistoric times, the town proper contained playing courts for ritualized ball games, a winter council house—sometimes still raised on a low mound—and, in the Creek and Yuchi villages, a "square ground," or ceremonial plaza.

These communities were directly descended from the pre-Columbian mound-building cultures that left thousands of earthworks throughout the eastern and central United States. The archeological record indicates that with the Woodland Period, which began around 2000 B.C., earthworks started to appear inside village confines. Initially, the mounds interred dead chiefs or were arranged to enclose formal plazas. Later, influenced by native traders who brought architectural ideas from their homeland in northeastern Mexico, the mound builders began to shape their earthen heaps into platforms for temples.

After European culture penetrated their territories, increasing numbers of Cherokee, Chickasaw, and other tribespeople began to move into log cabins and plantation-style structures. As missionary Samuel Worcester observed in 1825: "The houses of the Cherokee are of all sorts, from an elegant painted or brick mansion, down to a very mean cabin. If we speak, however, of the mass of the people, they live in comfortable log houses generally one story high, but frequently two; sometimes of hewn logs, and sometimes unhewn; commonly with a wooden chimney, and a floor of puncheons, or what a New England man would call slabs." Added to this medley of architectural styles were square-ground arbors and ancient council or winter houses, with sacred fires that were tended by Indian "full-bloods," the staunch traditionalists.

In the 1830s, however, Andrew Jackson's administration responded to the clamor of the new settlers and gold miners demanding access to the fertile Southeastern Indian lands. In the largest forced resettlement in American history, the Cherokee, Chickasaw, Choctaw, Creek, and Seminole nations—known collectively as the Five Civilized Tribes—were rounded up and moved to the newly created Indian Territory in present-day Oklahoma. Some Cherokee families evaded capture, however, and their descendants may still be found in the Great Smoky Mountains of North Carolina. Earlier, in the marshes of southern Florida, renegade groups of Creek tribespeople had also avoided resettlement and later emerged as the Miccosukee and Seminole nations. In their swampy hideaways they revised old architectural forms to produce the deep-eaved, open-sided dwelling of cypress poles and palmetto thatch known as the *chickee*.

Mounds and towns

The ancient Indian earthwork known as Big Mound City *(above)* was located near Lake Okeechobee, Florida. The site was occupied from 500 B.C. to A.D. 1600. This plan by architect William Morgan shows a crescent-shaped embankment enclosing a central area with eight radiating causeways. The embankments may have provided a raised foundation for buildings in a flood-prone region. The scale of the grid is 200 by 200 meters.

Hernando De Soto probably visited communities much like the late Mississippian town of Toqua *(left)*, shown here in an artist's recreation based upon archeological information. Located in southeastern Tennessee, the proto-Cherokee community was active around A.D. 1500. The large mound, facing an open plaza and ball pole for public games, contained the remains of a burned structure on its summit. The town was surrounded by a wooden palisade.

MOUND

When travelers in the nineteenth century first encountered the remains of the monumental earthworks in the Mississippi and Ohio River valleys, they attributed them to a highly civilized vanished race they called "mound-builders." But this hypothesis of a mysterious Indian Golden Age ignored De Soto's accounts of mounds in everyday use, early eighteenth-century French accounts of the mound-building Natchez people along the Lower Mississippi, and the late eighteenth-century reports of English-speaking travelers that the Cherokee and Creek worshiped in temples raised on man-made hills of earth.

By the time the French visited them, the Natchez were the only remaining mound-building Indians. In 1718, a French architect-engineer named Antoine le Page du Pratz was befriended by a Natchez nobleman known as "Tattooed Serpent," who presided over the "Grand Village" of the Natchez. This site, located on bluffs along St. Catherine Creek in the vicinity of the present-day city of Natchez, Mississippi, is known today as the Fatherland site. Du Pratz lived among the Natchez for four years and described the architectural settings of their complex social and ceremonial life. The average Natchez settlement contained about four hundred people living in thirty to forty rectangular, plastered dwellings. The domestic compounds were clustered around nine ceremonial town centers, generally overlooking the creek just east of the Mississippi and protected by a combination of natural cliffs and log palisades. The tillable floodplains supported individual family gardens of corn, beans, and pumpkins, and a communal garden in which everyone in the community worked.

Du Pratz, perhaps the first trained architect to document a Native American culture, paid close attention to how the Natchez built their homes. "The cabins of the natives are all perfectly square," he observed. "There is not one which measures less than 15 feet each way, but there are some more than 30 . . . The natives go into the young woods in search of poles of young walnut [hickory] trees 4 inches in diameter by 18 to 20 feet long. They plant the largest at the four corners to fix the dimensions and the size of the dome."

After constructing the wall frame, the Natchez bent the extended corner poles together into a high, bowed roof frame, "giving the whole the appearance of a bower in a greenhouse such as we have in France," du Pratz added. Canes were lashed onto the frame, and adobe stiffened with Spanish moss was plastered over them to create 4-inch-thick walls. Carefully fitted soft cane mats formed the outer layer. The roof was thatched with grass "clipped uniformly, and in this way, however high the wind may be, it can do nothing against the cabin. These coverings last twenty years without repairing."

The Natchez preoccupation with social hierarchy and sun worship was apparent in their formal architecture. Temples and residences for the elite were built on flat-topped earth mounds that were reached by stairway ramps with log-reinforced steps. At the Grand Village of the Natchez the sun temple stood south of the ceremonial plaza. A temple guardian resided there, tending a perpetual fire of hickory logs—revered as a fragment of the divine sun itself. Painted wooden bird effigies were displayed on the roof.

Tattooed Serpent, the Great War Chief, commanded a full view of the settlement from his centrally located 10-foot house mound. He occupied a building 30 feet long and 20 feet high from tamped earth floor to thatched roof. Its wattle-and-daub construction was without windows, but beautifully

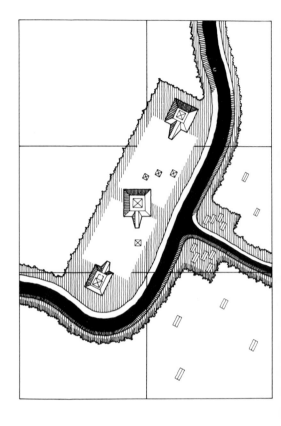

Natchez capital

The ceremonial center of the "Grand Village" of the Natchez Indians *(above)* was located along St. Catherine's Creek, a few miles southeast of Natchez, Mississippi. Known to archeologists as the Fatherland site, the town was settled some time after A.D. 1200, and remained occupied until the 1720s. The middle mound is believed to have been the residence of Tattooed Serpent, a Natchez chief, while the southern mound supported a temple which was 40 by 65 feet. The scale of the grid is 200 by 200 meters.

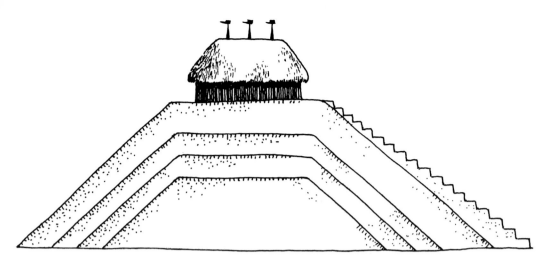

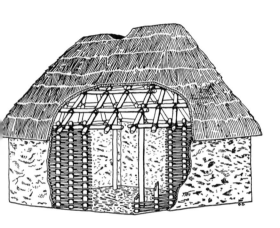

Mound and house construction

A typical platform mound *(top)* was composed of superimposed layers of earth added in stages, generally upon the burial of a dignitary. The form resembles Mesoamerican stone pyramids. The chief's house or temple at the summit was rebuilt with each construction phase.

Domestic structures and temples of the prehistoric Southeast were probably similarly constructed *(above)*. Floor plans were generally rectangular, and the houses ranged in size from 15 to 30 feet long. The floors were earth, and the interior walls were formed of rows of poles set vertically into narrow trenches (sometimes a horizontal pole braced the verticals). The exterior walls were wattle-and-daub; roofs were covered with cane mats or thatch.

The Caddo were probably descendants of prehistoric Southeastern people who once built mounds. A Caddo Indian house *(above right)* was photographed in 1870 in Oklahoma.

woven mats covered the interior walls. Before his mound lay the ceremonial plaza, 250 paces wide and 300 paces long, which du Pratz described as a "parade ground."

Natchez builders seem to have taken greater pains building their mounds and positioning them around formal plazas than they did in constructing their domestic quarters. This contrast between ceremonial and utilitarian architecture in the Southeast was apparently even more pronounced in prehistoric times. Of the early period earthworks in the Southeast, Poverty Point, in northern Louisiana, is the grandest in scale and design. Its construction, believed to have been begun around 1200 B.C., required considerable manpower to shape an estimated half-million yards of dirt into six concentric ridges separated by four outward-radiating aisles.

The function and use of Poverty Point remain a mystery; however, the archeologist James A. Ford contends that the site flourished during a pivotal era, when hunting and dispersed small camps were giving way to farming and settled towns. Ford also suggests that Poverty Point was settled by Mexican Indian traders who crossed over by way of the Gulf of Mexico. Materials excavated there came from as far as the Great Lakes, the Appalachians, and the Florida Peninsula, indicating that the settlement was a center of extensive trade. Presumably its residents occupied simple thatched shelters framed with saplings—possibly built along the narrow ridges—and cooked on outdoor hearths.

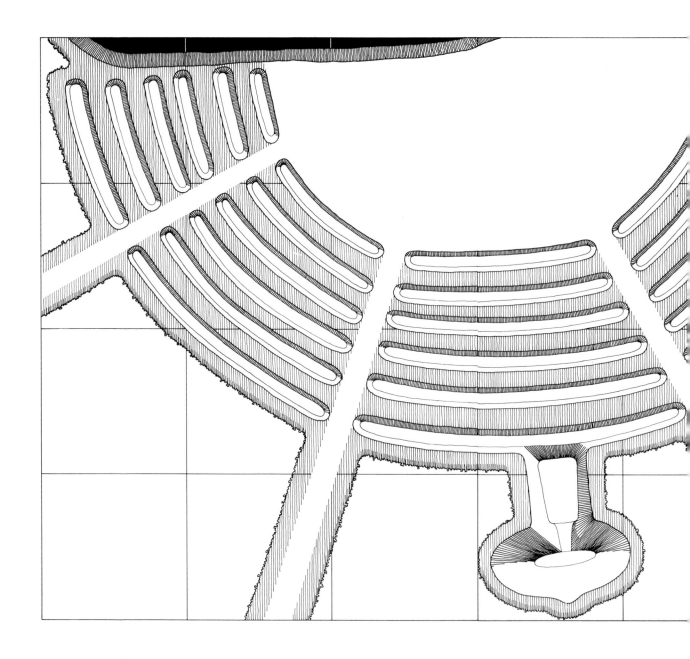

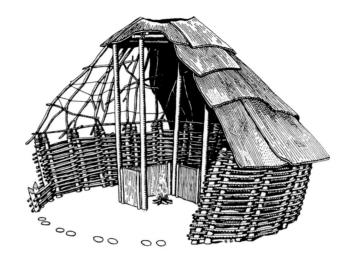

Poverty Point

Poverty Point, located in northern Louisiana *(below)*, is an early and extremely large mound complex. Its construction began around 1200 B.C. and its concentric ridges enclosed a plaza over 1800 feet across. (In this plan, north is to left, and the scale of the grid is 200 by 200 meters.) The drawing of the Adena period house *(right)* is based upon post-mold remains from the Cowan Creek Mound in Ohio. Excavations indicate structures with outward-leaning posts which were paired, possibly to hold horizontal laths. The roof form is highly speculative; it more likely was framed like a wigwam with wall uprights arching across the top.

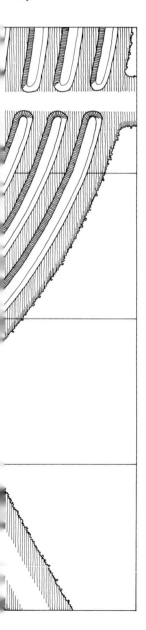

A few centuries after the flowering of Poverty Point, the Adena culture appeared in the Ohio River Valley; it lasted until about A.D. 200. Common Adena dwellings were circular, from 20 to 70 feet in diameter, and were clustered in compounds of two to five houses. One structure might house a single family or up to forty people. It contained a central cooking fire with food storage pits dug into the floor. Probably simpler prototypes of the later Natchez dwelling, the structures were walled with wattle-and-daub and roofed with grass thatch. Beginning with Adena times and continuing well into the historic period, monumental Southeastern architecture emphasized funerary ceremonialism and burial mounds. However, embankments demarcating ritual spaces, as well as effigy earthworks, would also develop in complexity from the Poverty Point period until the reign of the Natchez.

While late nineteenth-century mound explorers like Ephraim G. Squier and Edwin H. Davis of the Smithsonian Institution believed that the Ohio mounds were possibly refuges from flooding rivers, their student Cyrus Thomas—who debunked the myth of a separate race of mound-builders—showed that most Ohio earthworks actually were built on terraces safely above the floodplain. Thomas acknowledged, however, that mounds in the lower Mississippi Valley were constructed on vulnerable bottomland and could have played a role in flood control and agriculture. More recently, the architect William Morgan has suggested that the complexes of linear mounds and causeways in Florida, such as Fort Center, Big Mound City, and Big Tonys, used excavated fill to elevate agricultural plots, control water levels, circulate irrigation water, and provide escape from periodic inundation.

In the fully elaborated Adena burial mound, the adorned corpse was laid in a crib-work log tomb together with the bodies of retainers who had been sacrificed after his death. The tomb was set afire, and earth molded into a cone shape covered the ashes. The circular embankments sometimes associated with these mounds—over 300 feet in diameter—did not necessarily support buildings, as they might have at Poverty Point, but defined communal areas where people from dispersed hamlets gathered for worship and celebration. The Adena people also refined the Poverty Point tradition of building effigy mounds, manipulating tons of dirt to depict bears, panthers, reptiles, and birds—an earthwork form that eventually spread from Wisconsin to Louisiana. The function of these "geoforms" is not known, but they may have represented supernatural beings or ancestors of clans in the Adena social system.

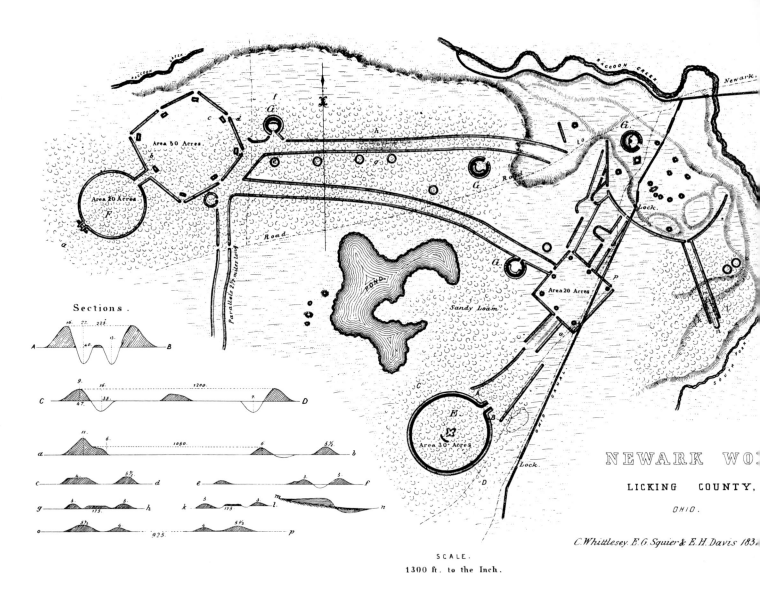

Sections.

NEWARK WO[

LICKING COUNTY,

OHIO.

C.Whittlesey. E.G.Squier & E.H.Davis 183

SCALE.
1300 ft. to the Inch.

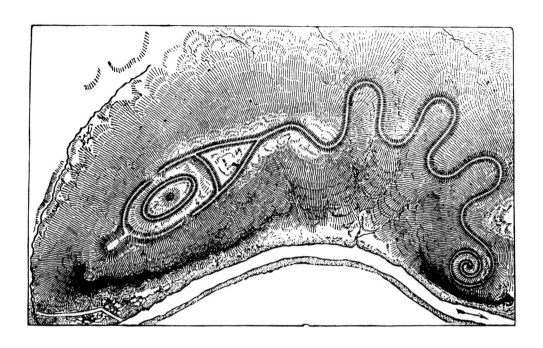

Monumental earthworks

The Hopewell site of Newark in Ohio is shown in plan *(top left)* and aerial photograph *(bottom left)*. Little is known of the function or construction procedures for such mound complexes. Newark was in use by A.D. 200. The site was surveyed by E.G. Squier and E.H. Davis for publication in 1847 by the Smithsonian Institution. The photograph was taken in 1934, and emphasizes the precise geometric forms; the circle is 1200 feet in diameter. The Serpent Mound *(above)* in southern Ohio is one of the most dramatic examples of an effigy mound, a long-lasting construction practice in the prehistoric Southeast. More than 600 feet long as shown in this Squier and Davis plan, it was possibly built by Adena people, between 800 B.C. and A.D. 400.

Just before the beginning of the Christian era, an extensive network of communities, known collectively as the Hopewell culture, replaced Adena society in the Ohio Valley. The Hopewell builders' elegant earthwork architecture used the monumental circle, square, and pentagon constructions found at such sites as Marietta, High Bank, and Newark in Illinois and Ohio. Hopewell people also elaborated upon funerary architecture for the priestly or high-born, with 70-foot earth mounds built over the incinerated remains of elaborate log tombs. Despite intriguing efforts to discern astronomical alignment or mathematical consistency in the orientation and proportions of these larger Hopewell sites, the function of their elegant, geometrically precise arenas is still uncertain.

Between A.D. 700 and 1000 there was a surge of mound-building in northern Georgia, which eventually swept across the southern states into Illinois and southern Missouri. Known as the Mississippian tradition, it appears to have synthesized previous architectural styles and produced a network of ritual centers that spread from the upper Great Lakes to the lower Mississippi Valley.

Mississippian constructions and rich pictorial artwork have invited tentative interpretations of the culture and its underlying beliefs. The religious life of these people revolved around what archeologists call the Southern Cult, a constellation of beliefs and practices including sun worship, the "Black Drink" (a ritual emetic brewed from yucaipa holly leaves), sacred fires that were ceremonially rekindled upon the first harvest of the year, ceremonial games, and the periodic enlargement of their architectural forms.

Mississippian settlements honored traditional burial mounds, ridge mounds, effigy mounds, and earthen causeways, but they also set aside grounds for the ritual *chunkee* game and built ceremonial earthlodge forms with tunnel entrances. Their trapezoidal, flat-topped mounds supporting thatch-roofed temples or earth-roofed chief's houses are reminiscent of pre-Columbian pyramidal forms in Mexico and seem to be further evidence of a long-standing trade route from the northeastern Mexican coast through east Texas and into the southeastern river valleys.

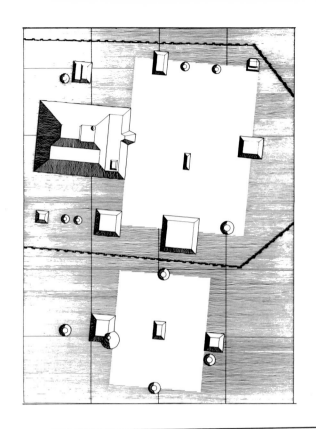

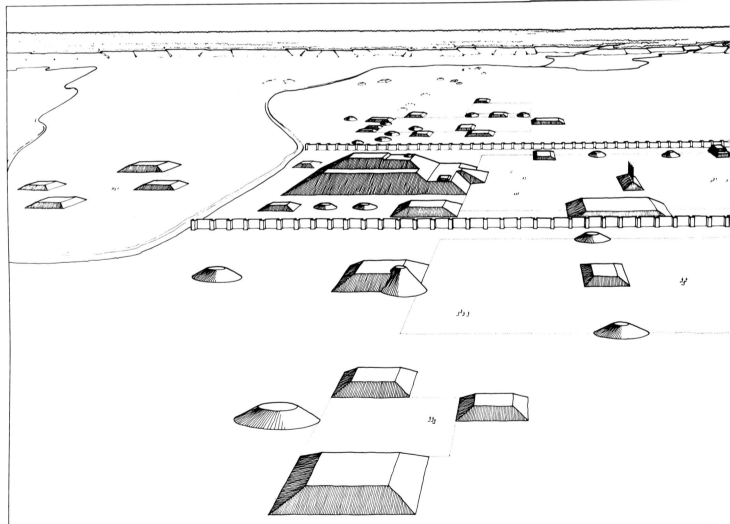

Cahokia

Cahokia was the center of Mississippian culture and represented the peak of earthwork building in the prehistoric Southeast. Located near St. Louis and the confluence of the Mississippi, Missouri, and Illinois Rivers, Cahokia was the political, religious, and trading center for many towns and hamlets along these rivers. The central pyramid, as shown in William Morgan's plan *(left)* and perspective *(below)*, was the largest mound north of Mexico. A timber palisade is believed to have enclosed the central plaza.

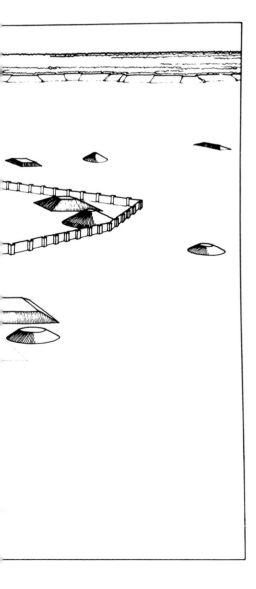

Cahokia, ten miles from present-day St. Louis, was the major metropolis. Construction on its mounds began around A.D. 800, also making it one of the oldest Mississippian sites. The city was occupied until A.D. 1500, but the population reached its peak around 1100, when an estimated forty thousand people lived, traded, and worshiped within the city limits. About a hundred mounds were positioned around six major plazas, comprising a city center that covered six square miles. Cahokia probably controlled the most complex and extensive sociopolitical network in North America.

Overlooking the Cahokia complex stood a mammoth earthwork that rose out of the town's inner precinct, an area that some archeologists believe was surrounded by a log stockade. Known as "Monk's Mound" after French Trappists took over the site around 1800, this terraced edifice had grown in size over three centuries and through fourteen different building phases. As each new layer of fresh earth was placed on its sides and top, the temple or royal residence on its summit was also rebuilt. After the last resurfacing, the mound extended about 1,080 feet in length, 710 feet in width, and stood 100 feet high, covering fourteen acres at the base. The final wattle-and-daub structure on its crest is estimated to have extended more than 100 feet in length and to have measured 50 feet from floor to roof.

When Tattooed Serpent died in 1725, his entombment was the finale to a millennium of architectural ritual. Du Pratz was among the onlookers as the chief's wife and aides were strangled and interred with him in a trench in the Grand Village's temple mound. Following tradition, the building atop the earthwork was burned to ashes, and the entire mound was covered with basketfuls of earth, raising it one last layer. Within a few years, bloody wars between the Natchez and French colonists virtually annihilated the culture. Neighboring tribes gave the Natchez survivors sanctuary; the group harbored by the Cherokee took on mystical stature as the last representatives of the Southeast's Mississippian heritage.

Mound ritual

In 1725, the French architect Antoine du Pratz witnessed and sketched *(right)* the funeral ceremony for his Natchez friend, Tattooed Serpent. The bier containing the Great War Chief's body appears to be spiraling up the south mound for its burial within the earthwork.

103

TOWN

Late in the eighteenth century, the botanist and artist William Bartram visited Indian villages across the Carolinas, northern Florida, and Georgia. He was among the earliest white travelers to the Creek Confederacy in the South's heartland, whose territory included Upper Creek towns along the drainage of the Coosa, Tallaposa, and Alabama Rivers, and Lower Creek communities along the Chattahoochee and Flint river system. There were some eighty towns in all, each with its own ceremonial courtyard or "square ground," winter council house, ball field, and civic identity. Bartram also ventured into the country of the Yuchi, a tribe who shared with the Creek the architectural tradition of open-air plazas, wattle-and-daub arbors for summer ceremonies, and large "town houses."

Cherokee town

This depiction of the Cherokee settlement of Toqua was based upon the observations of Louis Philippe, Duke of Orleans and later King of France. In 1799 he visited the community and noted its domestic log cabins and the conical town house behind them. The cabins were chinked with mud and the town house was 50 feet in diameter.

Bartram was particularly taken with one Yuchi settlement along the Chattahoochee River in Georgia, "the largest, most compact and best situated Indian town I ever saw: the habitations are large and neatly built; the walls of the house are constructed of a wooden frame, then lathed and plastered inside and out with a reddish well-tempered clay or mortar, which gives them the appearance of red brick walls, and these houses are neatly covered or roofed with cypress bark or shingles of that tree. The town appeared to be populous and thriving, full of youth and young children...." Just north of Creek territory lay the homeland of the Cherokee. Their towns lacked formal plazas, but, even in Bartram's day, the Cherokee built large winter houses on low mounds. To the northwest of the Creek lived the Chickasaw, and to the southwest the Choctaw. Both societies built enclosed winter structures, although the Choctaw shifted to open-sided dwellings to endure the Gulf Coast summers. The decline in mound building between De Soto's and Bartram's journeys is difficult to explain. By the end of the 1600s, the barter economy that had developed, based increasingly on European trade goods, may have weakened the older economic, religious, and architectural customs.

More tenacious than monumental earthwork construction, however, were the architectural concepts and symbols of the Mississippian Southern Cult, whose traces in the Creek and Yuchi towns Bartram recorded. He learned that their citizenry still believed that the "heart" of each community was its sacred fire. During the great late-summer religious festival known as the "Busk," or Green Corn ceremony, the town rekindled the fires, thereby renewing their strength and spirit for another year. Bartram also visited the open-air square grounds where such rituals were conducted. He noted the "four-log" fires in the center and the shed-roofed shelters known as "clan beds" that bordered this sacred arena in the cardinal directions. The square ground was the male domain. The arbors were furnished with tiered benches, and seating was strictly assigned by clan membership and age status: youths, warriors, and old men.

The numerous towns of the Creek Confederacy were functionally divided into red towns and white towns, which were readily identified by colored doors, flags, or wooden posts. The red towns handled executive and judicial decisions. Their prime responsibility was to declare war and organize military action. White towns, on the other hand, were peacemaking towns, which presided over the internal and religious affairs of the Creek world. During the ritualized ball games, however, when disputes between towns were resolved, this strict division might shift, white towns assuming red duties and vice versa.

Homestead

Creek families' homesteads were either in the immediate vicinity of the ceremonial town centers, or dispersed along nearby streams and connected by footpaths. But they all were required to remain within a drumbeat's call of the square ground. Bartram describes the typical Creek domestic compound as covering perhaps a quarter-acre; it included up to four buildings, which were positioned around a common work yard in a rough approximation of the formal town square arrangement.

The family's winter house, often resembling a smaller version of the communal winter house, also served as a sweatlodge. The summer house generally was built of wattle-and-daub walls on a rectangular floor plan and was roofed with thatch. An affluent Creek household might have a warehouse for storing deer hides on a third side of the courtyard. On the fourth side they might put up a two-story structure, its bottom floor used to store food and equipment and its upper level reserved for guests and formal meetings.

While the guest quarters were the male domain, Creek women controlled domestic space. Clan membership was inherited through the female line, so a new husband commonly moved in with his wife's family. Although a man might spend most of his adult life in this household, he would regard his true "home" that of his own clan's womenfolk.

The domestic architecture also included granaries, corncribs, and animal pens. The Creeks tilled their family gardens, but all adults were required to put time into the common gardens, which were used to restock communal granaries supervised by town officials.

Town House

Prehistoric prototypes of the southeastern communal town house—known to Europeans variously as "hot house," "rotunda," and "assembly room"—probably were erected on mounds and had dome-shaped, earthen roofs much like the earthlodges of the Great Plains village people. By the 1770s, however, when Bartram visited Creek villages, most of these multifunctional winter structures—which the Creeks called *chakofas,* meaning "house-inside"—were built at ground level. Their walls were plastered and painted, and their high conical roofs were thatched or shingled with bark. Inside, Creeks held

A HOTT HOUSE

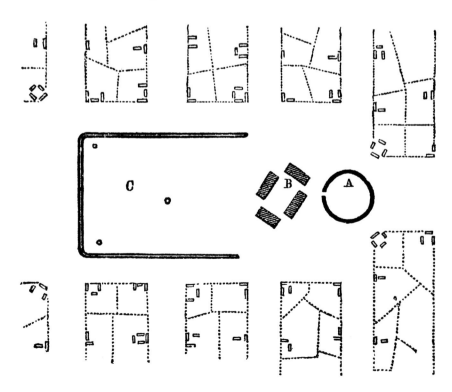

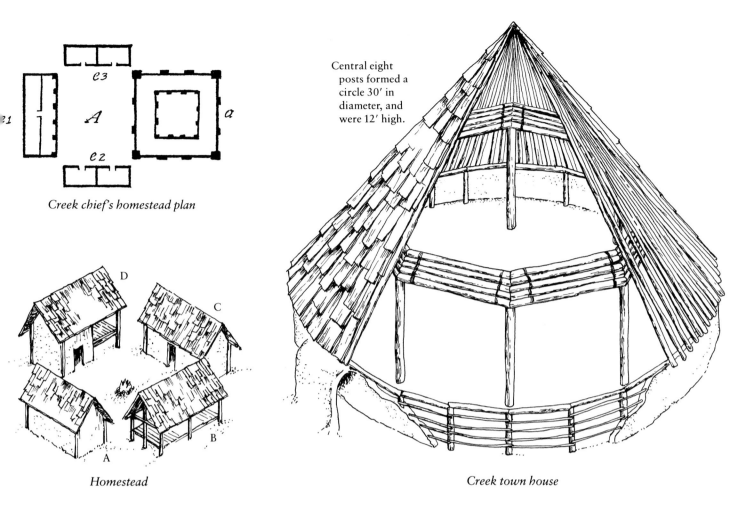

Creek chief's homestead plan

Central eight posts formed a circle 30' in diameter, and were 12' high.

Homestead

Creek town house

Creek architecture

In the late eighteenth century, William Bartram traveled through the Southeast and published drawings and descriptions of Creek towns and homesteads. These communities were primarily composed of a winter house, clan arbors or "beds" positioned on four sides of a sacred square ground, and surrounding domestic compounds. Bartram's plan of a generalized Creek town *(bottom left)* includes (A) hot house *(chakofa)*; (B) square ground; (C) ball court. Homesteads and gardens surrounded the public area and Bartram noted that they were "placed with considerable regularity in streets or ranges...." The ball court was roughly 600 to 900 feet long, with an earth ridge around it for spectator seating.

Bartram also prepared a plan *(top)* of a Creek chief's homestead situated near a river in Alabama. He noted that the "villa" was beautifully sited and well-built. (A) courtyard; (e1) common hall, lodging house; (e2) cook house; (e3) warehouse for skins; (a) open pavilion, with an interior two-level raised platform.

The drawing *(above)* is based on Bartram's account of a Creek homestead. The buildings enclosed a courtyard. (A) cook house and winter lodging house; (B) summer lodging house and guest reception house; (C) warehouse for skins; (D) a two-story granary or provision house with a closed storage room and an open-

sided storage area on the ground. On its upper floor was a council room and an open loft "where the chief of the family reposes in the hot season."

The Southeastern winter town house was often called a "hot house" by European visitors because of its well-heated interior. The frame was of oak, pine, black locust, cypress poles, or in the Gulf region, palmetto. Walls were wattle-and-daub (usually cane plastered with a mixture of clay and grass). They were often covered with a whitewash made from ground oyster shells and then painted with religious symbols. Woven cane mats also were used as roof coverings (sometimes sandwiching a thatch layer). Other roofing materials were mud plaster, thatch, and cypress, pine, or chestnut bark.

This drawing of a Creek town house *(above right)* construction is based on a description by the Indian agent Benjamin Hawkins (1848). The houses could vary from 30 to 60 feet in diameter, their conical thatched or shingled roof sometimes reaching 30 feet in height. Large structures seated up to 500 people on tiers of raised platforms encircling the interior. The drawing shows a layered plate beam linking the interior post tops that supported the long sloping rafters.

council meetings and special rites, but the structures also served as shelters for the old and indigent during the damp and cold southeastern winter.

When the artist John Mix Stanley visited the re-established Creek town of Tukabatchee near the Canadian River in 1843, he recorded "a building of rather a singular and peculiar construction, used during their annual busk or green-corn dances as a dancing house. It is of circular form, about sixty feet in diameter and thirty feet high, built of logs." What makes Stanley's report especially interesting is its glimpse of cooperative architectural practice. First, the medicine man cut little sticks "in miniature of the building, and distributed them proportionately among the residents of the town, whose duty it was to cut logs corresponding with their sticks, and deliver them upon the ground appropriated for the building, at a given time." During the six days it took to organize construction, the medicine man fasted. On the appointed day, the building was quickly assembled on the site, "as intended by the designer," Stanley added.

The typical Creek town house was octagonal in shape, with a mud-plastered entry portico spiraling out from the building for 5 or 6 feet and sealed with a door. Inside, reed or oak mats were hung along the rear wall; dividers between the rear and central posts partitioned the seats, forming bleacher-like sections. As in the summer square grounds, one's designated place was assigned by age and status, with town officials, warriors, and other important officers seated closest to the central sacred fire. The floor might be paved with a tempered clay which, when dampened and dried, formed a durable surface. The spiritual focus of these buildings was the sacred fire, which was tended with utmost respect. The fuel was carefully selected; the Creek preferred well-seasoned Black-Jack oak branches because they burned almost smokelessly—chakofas usually did not have smoke holes—and were hot enough to keep the inside warm and dry both night and day.

Bartram was allowed to watch a ritual firekeeper bring dry cane stalks into a winter "rotunda" prior to a council meeting: "... these are previously split and broken in pieces to about one length of two feet and then placed obliquely crossways upon one another on the floor, forming a spiral circle round about the great centre pillar." Eventually the spiral grew to about 24 feet in diameter "according to the length of time the assembly or meeting is to continue. By the time these preparations are accomplished, it is night, and the assembly have taken their seats in order." Before Bartram's eyes the end of the kindling mysteriously burst into flame, burning inward all night long "with the course of the sun" until its fuel was spent just as the council broke up at dawn.

Each Southeastern tribe put its stamp on the town house form. The Chickasaw built somewhat smaller houses than the Creeks, using four central support posts instead of eight and covering the outer wall with grass. Like the Creek, the Cherokee also built theirs without windows or smoke holes but often constructed them with seven sides (standing for the tribe's seven clans) and covered the cone-shaped roofs with earth.

In the early 1760s, an American military officer named Henry Timberlake spent three months with the Cherokee on the Little Tennessee River and visited their immense town house at Echota, considered the tribal capital. By this time the Cherokee no longer made domestic use of the smaller winter house, but in each of their towns an expanded version of it served as the hub of religious and social life. "It is built in the form of a sugar loaf," Timberlake wrote, "and is large enough to contain 500 persons … Within it has the appearance of an ancient amphitheatre, the seats being raised one above another, leaving an area in the middle, in the center of which stands the fire."

Unlike the Creek town houses, some Cherokee versions still were being built on mounds into the historic period. In 1887, a shaman named Swimmer told anthropologist James Mooney that old-time Cherokees began the construction of a town house by lighting a sacred fire at ground level. A hollow log was propped above the hearth and dirt was mounded around it to shape the base. The structure was built upon this foundation, its fire fed by a caretaker who dropped tinder down the wooden shaft.

During the Reconciliation Festival held by the Cherokee in late autumn, when uncleanliness was purged and personal animosities forgiven, a new fire was kindled in the town house to be distributed throughout the community. Another new-fire festival was held during the first moon of spring, when home fires again were extinguished and hearths swept bare. A fire was lit in the town house by twirling a wooden drill in the pit to ignite goldenrod tinder, which then was used to light the inner bark from seven different trees. Women from every household carried away embers to light their family fires, which they believed revitalized the entire Cherokee world.

Ball Court

Another ceremonial zone in most Creek town centers was a field known as the "swept area." Kept free of litter and periodically strewn with fresh sand, this open space stretched for about 250 yards. Here the ancient game of *chunkee* was played, using disc-shaped stones. A second ritual sport, somewhat like field hockey, pitted men against women. The goal post was a stripped pine trunk standing about 30 feet high. The rules and political functions of these games—some of which were played between the towns as a means of deciding political alliances and settling disputes—are difficult to reconstruct, but they appear to have been an essential feature of Southeastern ceremonial centers.

Square Ground

The Creek word for town, *Italwa*, signified more than a physical location. It implied spiritual membership in and social responsibility for a civic ceremonial center with a square ground and, most important, its sacred fire. The American Indian agent Benjamin Hawkins once likened these summer courtyards to Italian piazzas. In 1820, the British missionary Adam Hodgson visited the largest of the Lower Creek settlements, Cussetah, near present-day Columbus, Georgia, and described its formal arena: "In the center of town, we passed a large building, with a conical roof, supported by a circular wall about three feet high: close to it was a quadrangular space, enclosed by four open buildings, with rows of benches rising above one another: the whole appropriated, we were informed, to the Great Council of the town, who meet, under shelter, or in the open air, according to the weather. Near the spot was a high pole, like our May-poles, with a bird at the top, round which the Indians celebrate their Green-Corn Dance."

Creek square ground today

Abihka was one of the early nineteenth-century Creek townships whose members were forcibly removed in the 1830s to Indian Territory in Oklahoma. Shown here is the square ground and ball pole of this township today, the Abihka "stomp grounds," located five miles southeast of Henryetta, Oklahoma, where its members still celebrate the Green Corn Ceremony.

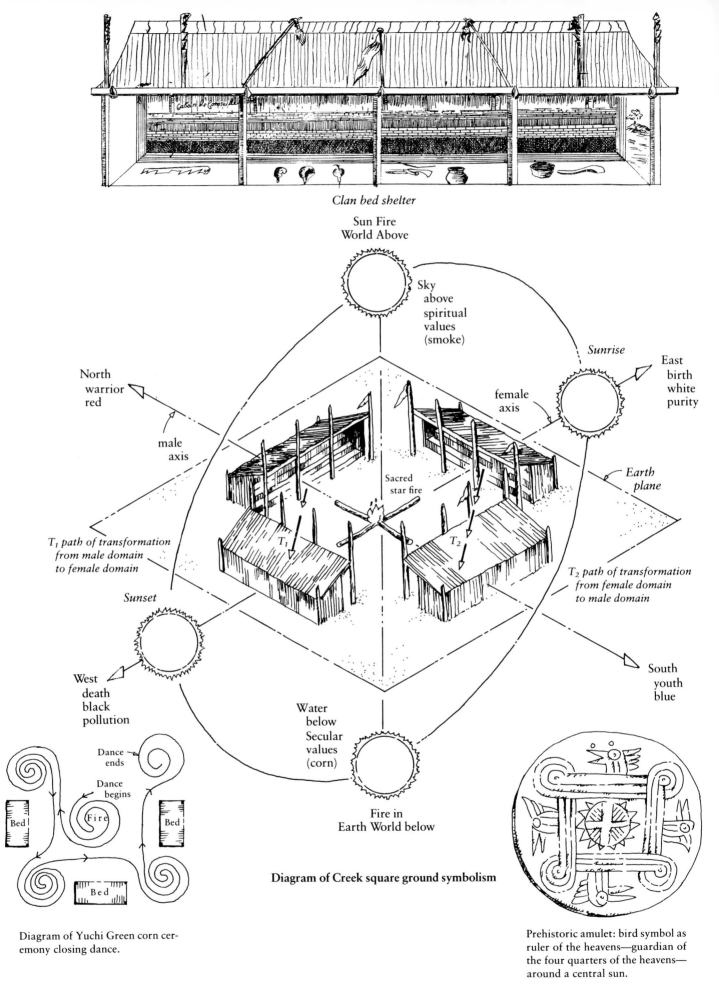

Clan bed shelter

Sun Fire
World Above

Sky
above
spiritual
values
(smoke)

Sunrise

East
birth
white
purity

North
warrior
red

*female
axis*

male
axis

*Earth
plane*

Sacred
star fire

T_1 path of transformation
from male domain
to female domain

T_1

T_2

T_2 path of transformation
from female domain
to male domain

Sunset

South
youth
blue

West
death
black
pollution

Water
below
Secular
values
(corn)

Fire in
Earth World below

Diagram of Creek square ground symbolism

Dance
ends

Dance
begins

Bed

Fire

Bed

Bed

Diagram of Yuchi Green corn ceremony closing dance.

Prehistoric amulet: bird symbol as
ruler of the heavens—guardian of
the four quarters of the heavens—
around a central sun.

It is debatable whether these square grounds evolved from the prehistoric Mississippian plazas or were open-air expansions of the ancient temple room arrangement that guarded the sacred fire. In the Creek vocabulary the precinct enclosing both square ground and council house was known as *d'jogo t'akko,* or "big house." When Bartram visited the Creek towns, he paid special attention to the westernmost building, where the leaders held court, and its secret rear apartment which held "all the most valuable public things, as the eagle's tail or national standard, the sacred calumet, the drums and all apparatus of the priests."

The square ground, its shelters, and the ritualized movement of males through them expressed Creek ideas about the structure of the tribal universe—of which the square ground was a symbolic microcosm—and the proper place of human beings in it. The passage of a man's life from birth to warriorhood to old age was indicated by his shifting seating assignment in the clan arbor. This symbolism was most explicit during key ritual periods, especially during the intense four to eight days of the annual Busk.

Among the rites of the Busk—the animal dances, the use of the emetic Black Drink, the ritual bloodletting—was the Creek version of a new-fire ritual. Like the Cherokee, the villagers in preparation for the festival would douse their home fires, clean up the ashes, sweep their floors, and throw out refuse. Then, using a drilling technique until a tendril of smoke appeared, the signal to add dry tinder, spiritual leaders would ignite a fire in the middle of the square ground. The flame, which represented the sun itself, was believed to renew the vitality of their homesteads, town, and cosmos.

Trail of Tears

At the beginning of the nineteenth century, American settlers began pushing into the fertile river valley lands of Georgia, Tennessee, and Alabama. Feeling the pressure, some groups of Lower Creeks sought freedom farther south. Other Creek, Cherokee, Choctaw, and Chickasaw communities tried to graft the white man's institutions to their own, developing their own school systems, building their own Southern-style plantation houses, learning English, publishing their own newspapers, drafting their own constitutions, and holding trials in their own courthouses. All the while more traditional members maintained the older sense of tribal identity in the square grounds.

But this Indian initiative was disregarded under the removal policies of Andrew Jackson and his Congress. Through a series of edicts in the 1830s, Jackson ordered the eviction of practically all Indians from the Southeast. Over the next decade, hundreds of Indian families were forcibly removed—often under armed military escort and in the dead of winter—from townships and territories they had considered their divine birthright. Some religious leaders salvaged ritual utensils and sacred embers from the town square grounds, guarding them on forced marches to Indian territory west of the Mississippi. During these tragic journeys—over a route known to the Cherokee as the Trail of Tears—fires from the precious coals were kindled at overnight stops. When they arrived in the hill country of eastern Oklahoma, their chiefs cleared new square grounds from the scrub and red clay and laid the treasured coals in new hearths.

Square ground symbolism

The interpretative diagram of a Southeastern square ground is based upon Yuchi and Creek sources and work by anthropologist Amelia Bell Walker. The square ground was the summer location of the sacred fire and the traditional center of a town's political and religious activities. Four shelters, called "clan beds," were situated around a square plaza.

The drawing shows the square ground at the time of the Green Corn Ceremony. Held in late summer, the festival was intended to renew tribal and cosmic vitality and affirm social structure. On the fourth day of the festival the sacred fire was rekindled and camp fires were relit from it.

Color was symbolic in the square ground. Red clan beds (war) were built astride the male axis, the white beds (peace) on the female axis. A man's seating assignment reflected his change in age and role from boy, to warrior, to old man. It suggested the male passage from the world of his mother to the world of men and finally, as an elder, a return to the female domain.

A clan bed (*top left*) at an Alabama square ground, sketched in the early 1700s. Two cane benches in the shelter are covered by a shed roof. Such clan beds could measure 40 by 16 feet.

Architectural survivals

Some traditional Southeastern house types lasted into the nineteenth century.

Thatched house *(top)*. Palmetto leaves covered the pole frame of this old-style Choctaw house photographed around 1881 in Louisiana on the shores of Lake Ponchartrain.

Wattle-and-daub house *(middle)*. This Houma house was photographed in 1900. Like the Seminole and some Cherokees, the Houma evaded removal and remained in the lower Mississippi region.

Log cabin *(bottom)*. This Cherokee cabin was photographed on the Qualla Reservation in North Carolina in 1888. Influenced by early pioneer buildings, Creeks and Cherokees built notched-log cabins from the mid-eighteenth century on.

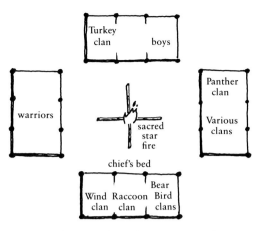

Close-up plan of square grounds.

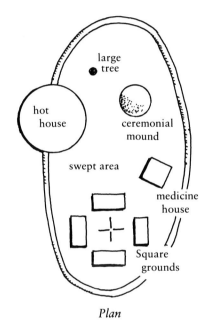

Plan

Stomp ground

After their forced removal and relocation to Oklahoma in the 1830s, the Indians of the Southeast recreated their old square grounds. They became known as "stomp grounds" and were usually found in the backwoods.

Plan of the Tukabahchee stomp grounds *(above)*..The most traditional of Creek towns, Tukabahchee had a large hot house, 60 feet in diameter, even after its sacred grounds were reestablished in Oklahoma. The clan beds are shown in the close-up plan as they were arranged in 1912.

TOWNS TODAY

In the years following the federal resettlement of the 1830s, most Creeks built log or frame houses after the fashion of their white neighbors, but back in the hills they established more than fifty separate "stomp grounds," recreating their old Southeast township names and their square grounds. Here the Creek and Yuchi medicine men observed traditional summer ceremonies and revived rites that harked back to the ancient mound festivals of Mississippian times.

Early in spring 1978, we were guided into the Cookson Hills of eastern Oklahoma for a look at a few of the twenty or more remaining stomp grounds where Creek and Yuchi Indians still hold the Green Corn rites. Our escort was Archie Sam, the grandnephew of Watt Sam, the last speaker of the Natchez tongue. Archie Sam led us into the humid woodlands between the Canadian and Arkansas rivers, where Creek who were moved from the Southeast initially re-established their town centers. Outside the town of Gore we drove to the site of his family's old grounds, once known as Medicine Spring. It had become a weedy pasture where farmers dumped their garbage; less than a century ago it was the setting for games, dances, and curing rituals.

Recently some Creeks near Gore had petitioned Sam to "bring back the fire" of the Medicine Spring ground. First he established a "rehearsal ground" for them to practice the old dances. Its four clan benches—Wind clan at the north, Alligator to the east, Bear to the south and Bird to the west—surrounded the hearth of a four-log fire. Nearby stood a goal post, topped by a revolving fish effigy, for the men-vs.-women ball game. But Sam was not convinced that the petitioners would demonstrate the stamina and dedication necessary to "keep alive its fire," and if not, he said, the power generated by the ancient rituals might turn against them and cause them to suffer. He led us to two Yuchi square grounds, one belonging to the Duck Creek community and the other to the Kellyville community. Over the previous winter the leafy boughs of the clan arbor roofs had turned brown and moldy. Soon they would be replaced with fresh willow branches for the sequence of preliminary gatherings leading up to the major mid-July rituals.

At Duck Creek, Sam showed us another goal post, topped by a cow skull, and warned us not to violate the invisible axis between the central hearth in the square ground and the westernmost "chief's" arbor, which sheltered three plank benches. At the Kellyville grounds he demonstrated how the dancers leaped over a hump of ochre-colored earth just to the east of the fire, leaving us to wonder if this might not be a token of a prehistoric town house mound.

Off a country road twelve miles from Vian, we visited a Cherokee stomp grounds with seven arbors grouped around a raised earth hearth. In pre-European times Cherokee towns never had such ceremonial courtyards, but around the turn of this century a charismatic Cherokee named Redbird Smith apparently blended Creek and Cherokee concepts. At the time, Smith was rallying Cherokee resistance to the U.S. government's attempts to subdivide native land into individual family parcels and to obliterate Cherokee tribalism. Smith had a vision of renewing the ancient sacred fire, which was surrounded now by seven arbors, one for each of the seven clans.

Our second visit to the Cherokee hill country coincided with a birthday celebration for Redbird Smith. At midday we entered the Stokes Smith stomp grounds, which was named for the son who assumed Redbird's mantle. A

113

feisty ball game between men and women was under way near the seven arbors. The men, not permitted to touch the small, hide-covered ball, gripped it between pouches at the end of two short-handled sticks. Women, however, could use their hands to hurl it at the goal. Points were scored by striking the fish and were tallied by scratching marks on the ground.

Following the game, a potluck feast with dozens of native dishes was laid out on a hundred-foot table beneath the kitchen arbor. During the afternoon, eloquent speeches were given in the center of the ceremonial ground by officials of the Keetowah Society, the conservative brotherhood whose importance was revived by Redbird Smith. These men were the custodians of sacred Cherokee shell and bead "wampum belts" that had been brought over the Trail of Tears.

As they proclaimed in their native tongue, punctuating their stories with stylized gestures, they paced around the sacred hearth, a carefully shaped mound built up of a year's accumulation of earth and old ashes. Kindled at sunrise with flint and steel, its fire smoldered in the center of four large logs which pointed in the four cardinal directions. That night more wood was heaped onto the coals and stomp dancers spiraled around the bonfire until sunrise.

Cherokee sacred ground

The Stokes Smith ceremonial ground *(bottom)*. This stomp ground with seven arbors was conceived by the early twentieth-century Cherokee visionary Redbird Smith. Standing in front of its raised mud hearth, which held the four-log fire, Archie Sam—of Cherokee and Natchez ancestry—points to the shake-roofed arbors that shelter members of the seven Cherokee clans during ceremonies: *(clockwise from left)* the Warpaint, Deer, Bear, Wolf, Savannah, Longhair, and Bird arbors.

CHICKEE

Seminole and Miccosukee home

Pole and thatch shelters called *chickees* are the traditional housing for Seminole and Miccosukee Indians in the southern Florida swamps and forests. They are arranged in camps occupied by single or extended families related through the female line.

The sleeping and working chickee *(above)* has a raised platform. Photographed in 1910 at Cow Creek, Florida.

The Lower Creek groups who had escaped the brunt of Jackson's removal policy by fleeing south emerged in the mid-nineteenth century as the Seminole and Miccosukee tribes of Florida. Isolated in the subtropical swamps of the southern peninsula, they survived bloody but unsuccessful efforts by U.S. troops to flush them out. Slowly their numbers increased, and by 1900 nearly a thousand people were estimated to be living in houses called *chickees*, small buildings framed of cypress pine or palmetto log and thatched with palmetto fronds. The first ethnographer to penetrate the secluded Seminole camps, Clay MacCauley, observed in 1880 that the average chickee, about 16 by 9 feet, was "actually but a platform elevated about three feet from the ground and covered with a palmetto thatched roof, the roof being not more than 12 feet above the ground at the ridge pole ... This platform is peculiar, in that it fills the interior of the building like a floor and serves to furnish the family with a dry sitting or lying down place when, as often happens, the whole region is under water."

Like the dome-shaped snow iglu of the Eskimo, the chickee was an ingenious adaptation to an extreme climate, using local materials and basic design principles. Its raised floor, originally decked with split palmetto or cypress logs, was replaced later with sawn boards. Whether lashed or nailed directly to the building's main heart-of-cypress posts, or freestanding on legs,

115

these elevated pallets were cooled by ventilation both below and above the living area. They also protected the inhabitants from the swamp's insects, snakes, alligators, and flood tides. At the roof ridge, the thatching was weighted down by a row of inverted, crossed logs. Deep, low eaves offered shade and shelter during torrential rains. At night the families slept together on these raised platforms; in the daytime they rolled their bedding into a corner or tucked it into the open roofing frame and used the platforms as working space.

The chickee form may have derived from the old Creek two-story storage and guest house structure, while the technique for thatching it with palm leaves could have come from the Gulf Coast Choctaw or Timucua Indians who occupied Florida until the Spanish arrived. Whatever its origin, the form soon diversified into different sizes and styles of buildings for cooking, eating, sheltering guests, working, and sleeping.

By the 1950s, the Creek Indian descendants had divided into several groups: an East Coast Seminole band that occupied secluded camps on the outskirts of Miami, the northerly Okeechobee, and encampments of the Miccosukee tribe dispersed throughout the marshes west of the great Everglades.

A Seminole or Miccosukee camp was customarily hidden in the sand-pine woods or on swampy islands known as "hammocks," which could only be

Chickee variations

Florida Indian camps might include different types of chickees. Among the raised-floor structures for sleeping and working there would always be a cook house *(left)*. It lacked a platform and contained a "star fire," which was fed by moving the logs inward as they burned. A guest house *(above)* had separate sleeping platforms, an extended hip roof, and diagonal corner braces. These photographs were taken at the Seminole camp of Little Tiger at Big Cypress, Florida, 1910.

reached by dugout canoe. The encampments themselves generally were set up on the northern end where the land was highest. Usually undetectable from afar, a camp was approached by an inconspicuous path hacked through the surrounding underbrush. Silt and weeds that had accumulated around tree roots formed the spongy camp grounds.

A chickee compound consisted of four or five buildings. It sheltered four to twelve people related through the female line. As in the old Creek homesteads, the other, special-use buildings were modified along the basic chickee lines. An open-gabled shelter without a deck served as the cookhouse; in its center was the "star fire," consuming four or more extremely long logs that met at the cooking hearth and extended like rays beyond the building. As they burned, the logs were nudged toward the center to feed the flame.

A large camp might also contain a chickee for communal eating, thatch-roofed sheds, and an extremely long chickee for guests, with a single-hipped eave and angled logs at the corner posts serving as buttresses. Nearby was a garden, possibly bordered by banana trees. Members of these dispersed family hamlets convened at isolated ceremonial grounds for such religious festivals as the fall Hunting Dance and the midsummer Green Corn ceremony.

117

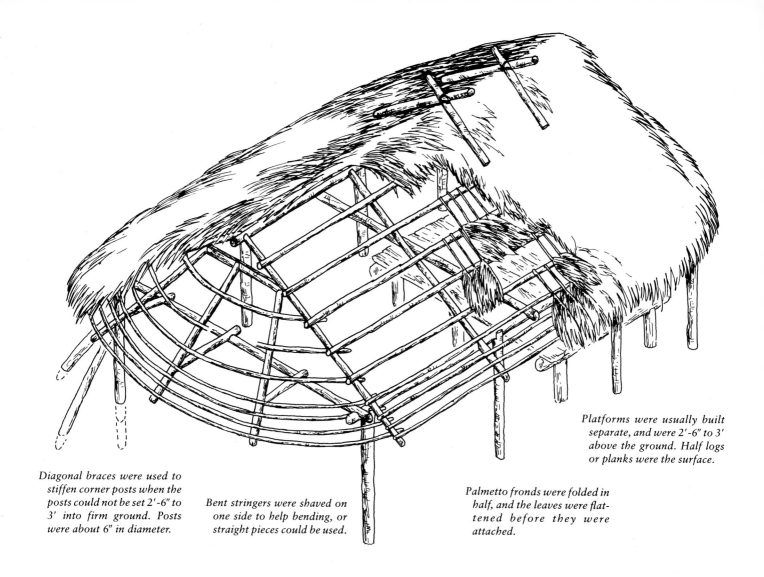

Diagonal braces were used to stiffen corner posts when the posts could not be set 2'-6" to 3' into firm ground. Posts were about 6" in diameter.

Bent stringers were shaved on one side to help bending, or straight pieces could be used.

Palmetto fronds were folded in half, and the leaves were flattened before they were attached.

Platforms were usually built separate, and were 2'-6" to 3' above the ground. Half logs or planks were the surface.

Chickee architecture

Chickee construction in southern Florida was first recorded by Clay MacCauley in 1880. The drawing *(above)* is based on anthropologist William Sturtevant's notes taken at Big Cypress Seminole camp in 1952.

Chickee floor plans vary in size from 7 by 12 feet to 16 by 21 feet. The typical size is apparently about 9 by 16, with either three or four posts per side. Raised floor platforms provide the protected work or sleeping surface.

Posts are set 2 to 3 feet deep; where they cannot be dug in that deeply, diagonal corner post braces are sometimes used to support them. Palmetto, pine, or heart of aged cypress logs are used as framing materials because of their resistance to rot. Today frames are nailed; in the past, bark ties fastened the frame and the thatch. Sometimes the rafters and ridgepole were framed separately on the ground, then placed on the plate beams. Closed gable-end eaves were preferred for all but the cook house. They were framed with either two or three projecting rafters supported by horizontal members. From horizontal cross-tie rafters hung clothes, tools, and other gear.

Palmetto thatch is carefully nailed to cross members and shingled so that the stems on the underside form a straight pattern. Crossed logs weigh down the extra layers at the ridge. Today, roof ridges are often further protected by sheets of corrugated iron or tar paper.

The plan *(right)* of Big Charley's camp at Cow Creek, Florida (1939), indicates placement of special-use chickees. An aerial view *(far right)* shows another Seminole chickee camp, in Big Cypress, Florida, about 1920.

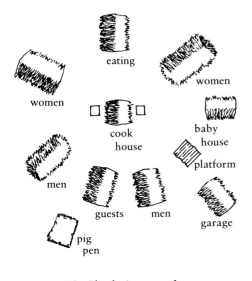

eating

women

women

cook
house

baby
house

platform

men

guests   men

garage

pig
pen

Big Charley's camp plan

CHICKEES TODAY

One can inspect chickee construction at the Miccosukee tribe's museum and visitor center on Highway 41, which follows the old Tamiami Trail that bisects southern Florida. The roadside chickees, many with TV antennas, are wired for electric lights, fans, and the sewing machines used by the Indian seamstresses who demonstrate crafts.

In the 1960s, the U.S. Bureau of Indian Affairs built new homes for the Miccosukees who live by the highway—cement-walled houses with high thatched roofs, raised floors, and screened windows. The Indians found them uncongenial, and objected to the inflexibility of the planned community concept: they were discouraged from building additions for coming-and-going clan folk, and clan uncles were not assigned adjoining residences. Some of the Miccosukees soon abandoned the rent-free dwellings in favor of the breezy, traditional chickees, which could be put up or taken down in an afternoon.

The only chickee compound in the Everglades that we were allowed to visit stood on a hammock four miles north across the shallow marshes from the Tamiami Trail. In 1979 it was occupied by the family of John and Lena Tigertail and was reached by a noisy airboat for five dollars. The craft skimmed over the shallow grassy water, veering around overgrown islands, on many of which were abandoned chickee camps. Unlike the brush on most occupied hammocks, the protective screen of reeds and sawgrass at the Tigertails' compound was chopped back, presenting the visitor on the rickety boat dock an idyllic tableau of the traditional Indian family at home.

The clearing was blanketed with close-cropped grass to the shoreline, where a garbage-eating alligator glided among the reeds. A girl in a cloth appliqué skirt greeted us. When we approached the cluster of chickees, Mrs. Tigertail was sitting cross-legged in the ample shade of her chickee, working at an antique Singer sewing machine. She was piecing together the multicolored garments that her people sell to tourists along the Tamiami Trail. We studied the ceiling, noticing the cross-braces nailed diagonally to strengthen the roof frame, and we sketched the intricate framing of peeled cypress poles that supported the projecting eaves. We wondered if they cantilevered that far in the days when fiber cordage was used.

We walked into the centrally located cookhouse and noticed its metal grate over a convergence of long, smoking firewood poles—the traditional "star fire." We photographed it and the sheds protecting tools and building materials, then followed a footpath that led to a vegetable garden fringed with banana palms. Back at the clearing, the family ignored us as we waited for the airboat's return and listened to the rattle of the sewing machine's pedal and the soft conversation from the chickees.

Later we learned from a government Indian Service employee that the Miccosukee Green Corn ceremonial grounds were hidden in the Everglades, but that only trusted outsiders were invited there. Florida Indians were reluctant to say much about their buildings and ritual spaces, but we did catch up with a Seminole construction crew roofing a modified chickee in a Miami suburb for a white businessman. Two thatchers climbed around the frame while helpers passed poles and palm leaves up to them. Once again we were steadfastly ignored as they peeled and nailed the last cypress pole braces and began to place the first layer of thatch.

First they folded the fan-shaped leaves back upon themselves, bunching them to fix the thatching at a proper outward angle as it advanced, course by course, up to the ridgepole. On the ceiling the palm leaves produced a herringbone pattern, the stalk lines pointing straight to the ridge, the leaf spines fanning outward. Finally, the five or six log weights, which today often rest on a protective ridge cap of tarpaper or tin, were placed on the roof.

All that the workers would disclose about their building customs was that it generally takes two days to build a chickee, that a single thatching normally lasts about seven years, and that when a new husband joins his wife's family, it is customary for him to build a new star fire in the cooking chickee. With a note of pride they added that when Hurricane Cleo struck Miami in 1965, apartment buildings were leveled while the Indian chickees remained standing.

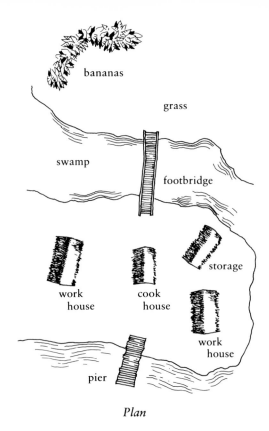

Plan

Tiger Tail camp

The Miccosukee camp of Lena and John Tigertail *(above)* is located on a "hammock" island just north of the Tamiami Trail in southern Florida. The central cook house is surrounded by larger chickees for sleeping and working. Near the boat dock is a path to the water and a bathing area. Behind the camp a footbridge leads to a small garden and banana trees.

Palmetto roofs

When a Miccosukee roofer *(left)* begins thatching a chickee with palmetto leaves, he folds back the spines on the first layer. Outrigger members *(right)* extend from the main roof frame to support the extended eave. Photograph of an abandoned chickee near Everglades City, Florida, 1944.

The circle motif

For the Plains Indians, most notably the Sioux, the circle was a central, abiding symbol. It appears often in their architecture. During the Pawnee's Hako ceremony, a communal blessing for the well-being of children, a priest drew a circle with his toe and placed eagle down inside it. "The circle represents a nest, and is drawn by the toe," a Pawnee explained to anthropologist Alice Fletcher in the late nineteenth century, "because we are imitating the bird making its nest . . . If you go on a high hill and look around, you will see the sky touching the earth on every side, and within this circular enclosure the people live. So the circles we have made are not only nests, but they also represent the circle Tirawaatius [the Pawnee Great Spirit] has made for the dwelling place of all people."

The drawing *(above)* of an historic Arikara earthlodge at the Leavenworth site in South Dakota show a circular ground plan. The tipi ground plan was also circular.

A tipi petroglyph *(right)* carved into rock at Castle Butte, Montana, suggests that tipi building is an enduring tradition on the Great Plains.

ment in villages expressed beliefs about how the universe was organized and the proper role of human beings in it. The Mandan earthlodges on the upper Missouri River encircled a plaza, and key religious officials occupied the innermost dwellings. On important religious, decision-making, trading, or hunting occasions, tribes who spent more time on the move commonly pitched their tipis at traditionally fixed positions within expansive circular encampments.

Sometimes these formal assemblies were conceived of as the base of a gigantic tipi, as if the entire tribe were under one symbolic roof. The architectural metaphor might even extend to the broader landscape. As a Crow chief named "Sits in the Middle of the Land" told a U.S. government emissary in 1873: "When we set up our lodgepoles, one reaches to the Yellowstone, the other is on the White River; another goes to Wind River; the other lodges in the Bridger Mountain. This is our land."

For the Oglala Sioux of the Dakota Plains, the more cosmic symbol of the circle was the model for their encampments. "The sun and the sky, the earth and the moon are round like a shield," an Oglala told the ethnographer James Walker. "It is also the symbol of the circle that makes the edge of the world and therefore of the four winds that travel there. Consequently it is also the symbol of the year. The day, the night, and the moon go in a circle above the sky. Therefore the circle is a symbol of these divisions of time and hence of all time. For these reasons the Oglala make their tipis circular, their camp-circle circular, and sit in a circle at all ceremonies."

EARTHLODGE

Earthlodges had first appeared around A.D. 700, housing the earliest farming cultures on the Plains. They were constructed by seminomadic villagers in three areas of the Plains. In the Dakotas, the Mandan, Hidatsa, and eventually the Arikara erected their earthlodge villages near streams that emptied into the Missouri River. In the central Plains of Kansas and Nebraska the Pawnee built their earthlodge towns. To the northeast lay the territory of a third group of linguistically related tribes—the Omaha, Ponca, Oto, and others—who also built earthlodges.

All of these people put up their lodges in more or less the same fashion. Four or more central posts—generally cottonwood—were planted in the ground and joined at the top by cross beams. A wider ring of shorter posts and beams encircled this square frame. Radiating from the central smoke hole was a wheel of roof rafters that rested on the outer ring. To complete the frame, a slanting, or vertical, sidewall of covering posts or split planks—known as puncheons—was placed around the basic structure to hold the earth walls. Smaller sticks overlaid with brush or grass provided a thick padding for the heavy layer of sod or loose earth. Some tribes finished off the outer layer with a final coat of wet earth, which dried like a plaster shell.

What gave the upper Missouri tribes the collective name of "village Indians" was their emphasis upon relatively fixed settlements, places where the more nomadic people could count on a market for their buffalo hides in exchange for vegetables and, later, horses. The villages were established on natural bluffs for security, with the sides that might be exposed to attack often protected by dry moats and log stockades. Between spring and fall the people sowed, harvested, and processed eight varieties of corn, nine kinds of squash, and beans, watermelons, and tobacco in family-owned plots along the floodplain that were enclosed with living fences of four different kinds of sunflowers. They usually used their tipis on brief trips during the summer, or during the longer buffalo hunts of fall and late winter. For most of the winter, however, the summer villages that they considered their true homes were left for smaller earthlodges nearer the floodplain, where dense tree cover provided firewood and a buffer from windstorms.

Archeological work in the Dakota Plains suggests that the earliest earthlodges were rectangular. In the Middle Missouri earthlodge, two central pillars appear to have borne the weight of a ridgepole, while the "Republican" house type of the central Plains used four posts and was squarer, with rounded corners. Only in historic times, apparently, did the dwellings become circular.

The earthlodge played a central role in the myths and rituals of the Mandan, Hidatsa, Pawnee, and Arikara. In Mandan cosmology the four pillars on which the dome of the sky rests are equated with the four main earthlodge posts. To the Hidatsa, the earthlodge was a living entity whose spirit lived in the central beams. The Pawnee, who worshiped a host of celestial deities, incorporated astronomical symbolism in their earthlodges and the layout of their villages.

While these conservative cultures clung to older building customs, the architectural patterns of other earthlodge dwellers such as the Omaha and Ponca were more responsive to the new horse culture. During the agricultural season in early summer, new husbands, according to custom, moved into earthlodges with their wives and her relatives, who owned the houses and

Arikara earthlodge

Medicine man Four Bears poses in front of an Arikara sacred lodge for a photograph by F.B. Fiske ca. 1900, near Beaver Creek, North Dakota. Its floor plan *(right)* shows the location of the center posts, firepit, and western altar mound.

126

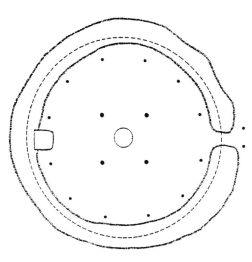

gardens. But hunting season prompted a move into tipis and a change from this female-centered pattern. Because the horse allowed greater penetration into distant buffalo country at the same time that intertribal feuding was on the rise, defense became a major concern. Tipi encampments were more vulnerable than palisaded earthlodge villages, so the layout of the summer camps began to reflect the man's role as provider and protector. In the northern sector of a camp circle were tipis of clan-mates associated with the sky division of the tribe, while the southern side was made up of fellow clansmen belonging to the earth division.

MANDAN

In early December 1738, the French explorer Pierre de la Verendrye and his sons were the first Europeans to visit an earthlodge village. As he entered one of six Mandan villages not far from present-day Bismarck, North Dakota, de la Verendrye was struck by its orderliness: "... the street and squares [are] very clean, the ramparts very level and broad; the palisade supported on cross-pieces mortised into posts of fifteen feet." He counted 130 earthlodges, which were "large and spacious, separated into several apartments by thick planks; nothing is left lying about; all their baggage is in large bags hung on posts, their beds made like tombs surrounded by skins."

The Mandan are believed to have settled on the Plains around A.D. 1100, introducing agricultural techniques and absorbing the older hunting traditions that had been the way of life for Plains Indians for perhaps ten thousand

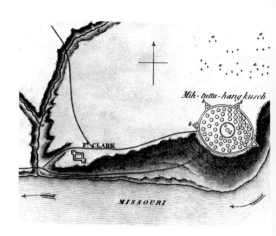

years. Their first earthlodge villages generally contained twenty to thirty rectangular structures built on terraces overlooking rivers. After 1400, wars between villages over scarce resources forced them to add the defensive moats and log stockades. These fortified towns expanded in size and population until the 1500s, when droughts significantly reduced the amount of arable land, and the number of earthlodges shrank accordingly. In the late sixteenth century, the rounder style of earthlodge identified with the central Plains was brought north, possibly by the Arikara, an offshoot of the Pawnee tribe.

By the early seventeenth century the Mandan were reduced to three subtribes inhabiting a cluster of earthlodge towns where Heart River meets the Missouri. By then their villages consisted of an inner circle of lodges facing an open plaza about 150 feet in diameter. In its center stood a barrel-like shrine of split cottonwood planks that enclosed a red-painted cedar pole. It symbolized Lone Man, their mythic culture hero, and the structure he had built to save his Mandan children during the primordial flood.

De la Verendrye encountered the Mandan on Heart River, but by the time other Europeans began arriving the villages had moved north, to the mouth of Knife River. The stories that drifted back to Europe praised the tidy roominess of the Indian earthlodges and the hospitable sophistication of their cultures. By then the villages were renowned as a well-established center of trade in which dried vegetables were exchanged for buffalo hides, and where by 1780 one might find goods from the Plains, the Great Lakes, and even Europe. Paintings of the villages were made in the early 1830s by visiting artists, notably the chronicler George Catlin and the Swiss watercolorist Karl Bodmer. Their work captured the expansive Mandan plazas and the dramatic vistas of the blufftop sites.

The innermost circle of Mandan lodges that faced the central, circular plaza was reserved for important religious officials. Behind lay a maze of earthlodges, underground storage pits with their ladders, rickety platforms made of poles for processing corn and drying wood and thinly sliced meat for making pemmican, and alleyways that were well-policed by the warrior societies. The earthlodges were typically 40 to 60 feet in diameter but could extend 90 feet from wall to wall. In 1805, the fur trader Alexander Henry was invited into one of these larger Mandan earthlodges and found a family resting on comfortable couches sewn together from willow wands and spread with buffalo robes. "Upon this, a Mandan sits all day, receives his friends, smokes, and chats the time away with greatest dignity. On the left side of the host, begins their range of beds; the master and his favorite wife always occupy the first bed." Henry noticed an altar in the rear holding a pair of buffalo skulls, shields and weapons hanging from the posts, a pestle and its hardwood mortar "fixed firmly in the ground," and the hearth area, which was swept every day.

Both outside and inside were 6- to 8-foot-deep storage pits where the summer's produce could be stored until the lean months of late winter. Within the earthlodge a windbreak of split cottonwood planks set apart an intimate space for craftwork and storytelling around the fire. In one corner might stand a bent sapling dome, which would be covered with hides when sweat baths were in progress. In another corner might be a corral for favorite horses. Homemade black pots and horn spoons were hung around the cooking

Fort Clark village

Fort Clark village *(above)* became a major Mandan Indian trading community after Europeans began to visit the Plains in the early nineteenth century. Located where the Knife River joins the Missouri River in present-day North Dakota, it contained a plaza surrounded by large earthlodges. Called Mittahantush by the Indians, Mandan, Hidatsa, and Arikara tribespeople occupied it at different times. After Lewis Henry Morgan visited the settlement in the 1860s he included this plan in his publication on Indian architecture.

When the Swiss watercolorist Karl Bodmer visited the village during the winter of 1833-1834, he portrayed its site on the bluff above the river *(below)* and painted an interior view of a lodge *(above right)* occupied by a warrior named Diapauch and his extended family, including favored horses.

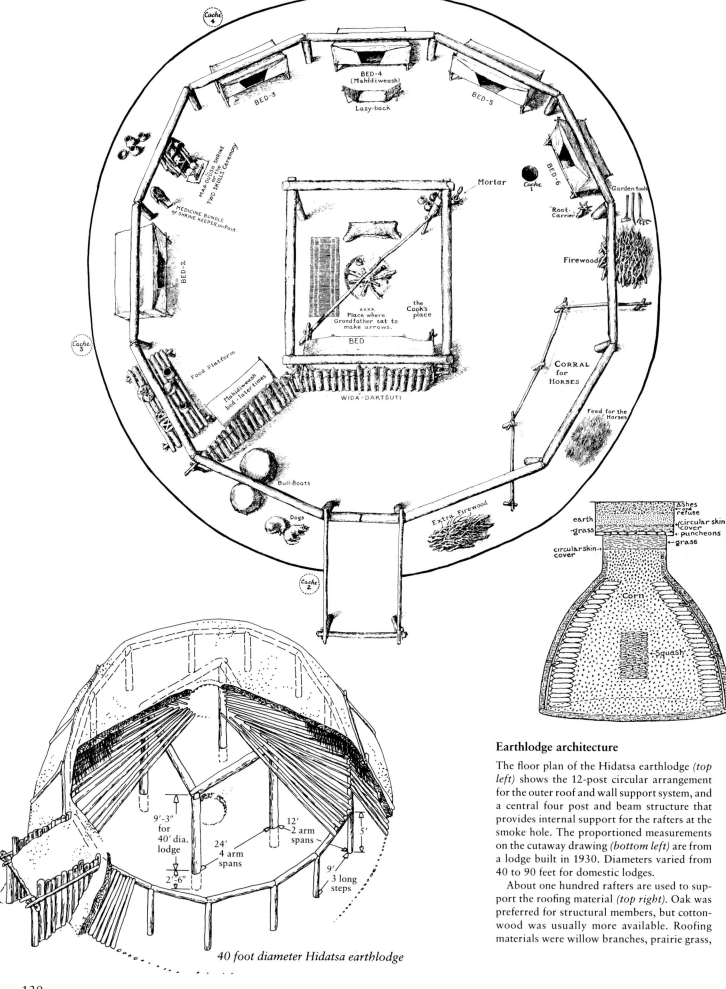

Cache 4

BED-4
(Mahidiweash)

Lazy-back

BED-3

BED-5

MAA DUUSH SHRINE
or the
TWO SKULLS Ceremony

MEDICINE BUNDLE
of SHRINE KEEPER, on Post.

Mortar

Cache 1

BED-6

Garden tools

Root-
Carrier

Firewood

BED-2

xxxx
Place where
Grandfather sat to
make arrows.

the
Cook's
place

BED

Cache 3

Food Platform

Mahidiweash
bed - later times

WIDA-DAKTSUTI

Corral
for
Horses

Feed for the
Horses

Bull-Boats

Dogs

Extra Firewood

Cache 2

ashes
and
refuse

earth
grass

circular skin
cover

circular skin
cover
puncheons
grass

Corn

Squash

9'-3"
for
40' dia.
lodge

12'
2 arm
spans

5'

24'
4 arm
spans

9'
3 long
steps

2'-6"

40 foot diameter Hidatsa earthlodge

Earthlodge architecture

The floor plan of the Hidatsa earthlodge *(top left)* shows the 12-post circular arrangement for the outer roof and wall support system, and a central four post and beam structure that provides internal support for the rafters at the smoke hole. The proportioned measurements on the cutaway drawing *(bottom left)* are from a lodge built in 1930. Diameters varied from 40 to 90 feet for domestic lodges.

About one hundred rafters are used to support the roofing material *(top right)*. Oak was preferred for structural members, but cottonwood was usually more available. Roofing materials were willow branches, prairie grass,

130

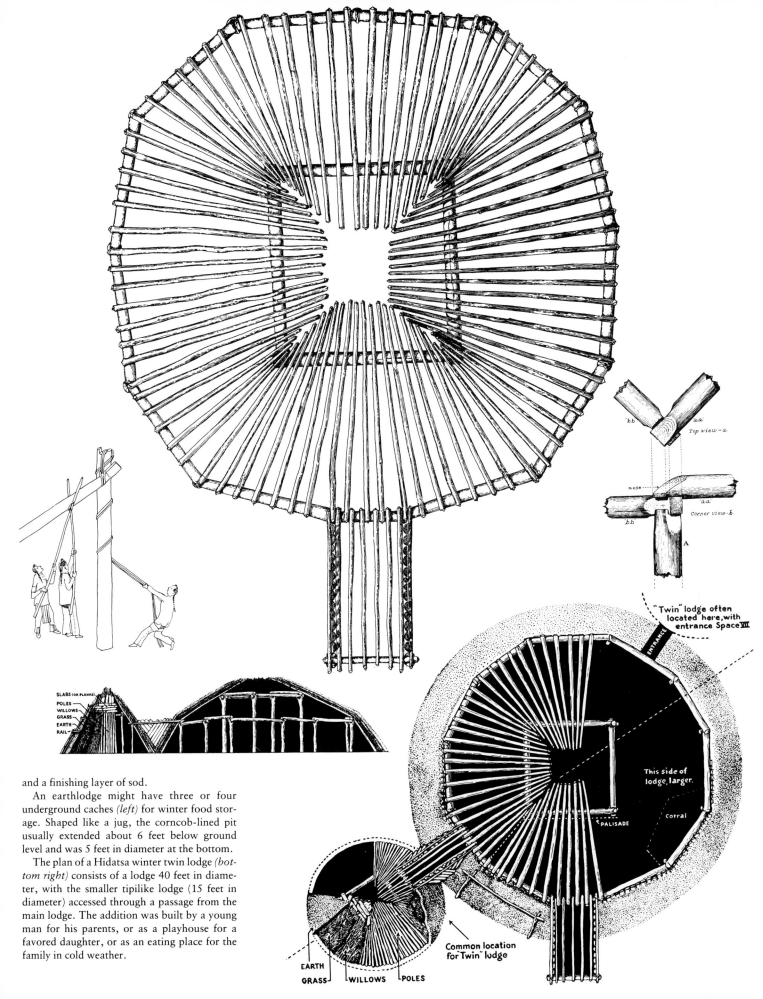

_bb_ _aa_
Top view – a

nose _aa_
Corner view – b
_bb_
A

"Twin" lodge often located here, with entrance Space VII

ENTRANCE

This side of lodge, larger.

PALISADE Corral

SLABS (OR PLANKS)
POLES
WILLOWS
GRASS
EARTH
RAIL

and a finishing layer of sod.

An earthlodge might have three or four underground caches _(left)_ for winter food storage. Shaped like a jug, the corncob-lined pit usually extended about 6 feet below ground level and was 5 feet in diameter at the bottom.

The plan of a Hidatsa winter twin lodge _(bottom right)_ consists of a lodge 40 feet in diameter, with the smaller tipilike lodge (15 feet in diameter) accessed through a passage from the main lodge. The addition was built by a young man for his parents, or as a playhouse for a favored daughter, or as an eating place for the family in cold weather.

Common location for "Twin" lodge

EARTH
GRASS WILLOWS POLES

131

Missouri River earthlodges

Indians at North Dakota's Fort Berthold Reservation continued to build earthlodges into the twentieth century. Scattered Corn *(top left)*, daughter of the last Mandan corn priest, and, to her right, her companion Mrs. Sitting Crow are shown as they begin to construct an exhibition earthlodge in Bismarck, North Dakota, in 1930.

One of the last Hidatsa earthlodges *(bottom left)* was occupied by Hairy Coat. The sleeping alcove, smoke hole, and rack for suspending pots over the cooking fire can be seen in the interior. Scattered Corn and her husband, Holding Eagle, lived in this earthlodge *(below)* in 1902.

A Hidatsa Indian named Edward Goodbird sketched the earthlodge *(near right)* which his grandfather, Small Ankle, inhabited at Like-A-Fishhook village in 1878. Goodbird also showed the ethnographer Gilbert L. Wilson an Hidatsa winter earthlodge *(far right)*, which was smaller, more steeply pitched, and built within tree cover along the river bottom.

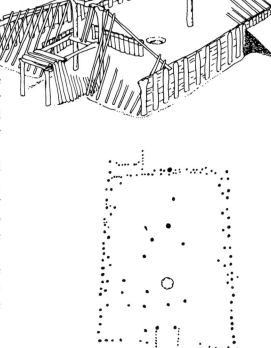

hearth. During the daytime children might spend as much time playing on the earthlodge roofs as they did inside them. The roof was also a vantage point for Mandan men to greet the sunrise and sunset with special songs, to sit and gossip, and to keep an eye out for enemy tribes who might try to steal their horses or vegetables, or set fire to their homes.

Mandan ceremonialism perpetuated a complex social organization and also reconciled the contrasting subsistence activities of farming and hunting. Their sacred Okipa lodge was consecrated by burying blessed buffalo hair beneath two of its central posts and planting sacred seed corn under the two other posts. Every year the Mandan revitalized their culture through the Okipa ceremony, staging some of the rites within the large, flat-fronted lodge. The structure was built in the form of the old rectangular domestic earthlodge and, as such, was considered a reminder of Mandan origins. In the plaza in front of the lodge a throng of costumed performers would dance around the Lone Man shrine, bringing Mandan mythology to life.

HIDATSA

The Hidatsa are believed to have started building their earthlodges in Mandan territory around the mid-1500s. According to Mandan folklore, when the newcomers appeared on the Missouri's eastern shore and asked to cross over, the Mandan told them to build their lodges upstream, so as to be "close enough to be friends, and not so far as to be enemies." Thereafter the Hidatsa held to their upriver position, practicing agricultural arts they probably acquired from the Mandan. But the Hidatsa probably influenced the Mandan by introducing the outer ring of angled wall-posts in the earthlodge, which created the distinctive triangular storage alcove the Hidatsa called the *atutish*.

By the seventeenth century the Hidatsa villages were found just north of the Mandan near the mouth of Heart River. The largest held over 150 dwellings and was protected by a palisade that changed form over time from rectangular to circular. While the Hidatsa apparently had few plazas or set patterns of lodges, particular lodges sheltering powerful religious shrines were identified by feathered standards outside their entryways. The area toward the rear or western wall was often designated as sacred space in Hidatsa lodges.

For all earthlodge people, lodge ownership and the rights to initiate construction were inherited through the female line. Women staked out the dimensions on the ground, marking where the holes for the four central posts should be dug, and supervised the men erecting the heavy frame. In both Mandan and Hidatsa folklore, women and fecundity often are associated with earthlodges. One belief held that babies actually were born from tiny earthlodges beyond the village, and tribesmen claimed to have seen little footprints at dawn in the sandhills. In the mythic earthlodge of Old Woman Who Never Dies, the supernatural regulator of seasons for the Hidatsa, a steaming pot of corn mush remained magically full, while from another earthlodge in the north, a supernatural figure known as Buffalo Woman controlled the plentitude of buffalo. To memorialize her great gift to them, the Hidatsa lodge-builders tied buffalo hides around the four central posts. Hidatsa priests piled offerings of corn and sunflower seeds on rooftops as they prayed for a blessing on the season's crops.

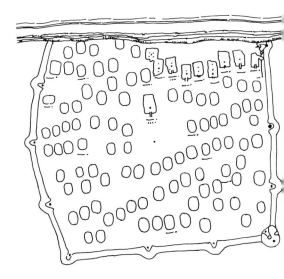

Middle Missouri archeology

Excavations in both South and North Dakota have revealed evidence of rectangular Missouri River houses, precursors to the circular earthlodge of the historic period. The village plan, floor plan enlargement, and speculative reconstructed house sketch *(above)* are from a sixteenth-century Mandan village at Huff State Park in North Dakota. More than 100 houses were protected by a palisade on three sides and by the river bluff on the fourth side.

Religious theatre

Five years before the disastrous 1837 smallpox epidemic, artist-explorer George Catlin spent two weeks among the Mandan. The summer sojourn coincided with the spectacular Mandan celebration called the Okipa. Catlin, who would be the only white man ever to witness the ceremony in its total glory, was overwhelmed by what he saw: a huge earthlodge, with flattened front, vibrating with pounding drums. Inside, young men dangling from rafters by thongs fastened to skewers piercing their chests. Outside, full-painted dancers in shaggy buffalo head masks, shaking spears; women chased by a clownlike character wielding a three-foot wooden penis; symbolic intercourse between the buffalo figures and women. The liturgy was uttered in an ancient dialect, decipherable only by initiates.

To the Mandan, the annual four day-and-night Okipa was the ultimate in communal piety, a collective prayer for tribal welfare and the success of the hunt. When Catlin's 1841 account of the ritual gained notoriety, he was publicly accused of dreaming up the Okipa. To whites, its self-mutilation, sexual imagery, and exhausting duration fulfilled their fantasies of rampant paganism. Although he was known to have doctored up his painted scenes of Indian life, the Okipa was no figment of Catlin's imagination. The ceremony was possibly ancestral to the Sun Dance, which is known to have been performed by over twenty Plains tribes in the nineteenth century.

The "Walking the Buffalo" interlude between dancers and women symbolized sexual intercourse which bestowed supernatural power; it was believed to pass from the buffalo demigod to the woman to her husband. The self-torture and fasting intensified young men's yearnings and prayers as they sought life-guiding visions. A special ceremonial lodge signified the Dog Den Buttes where, according to Mandan mythology, all living things had once been imprisoned, before their release by the Mandan culture-hero, Lone Man. The entire ceremony dramatized the Mandan creation story; its dances, chants, prayers, and mythic scenes re-established the Mandan's sense of tribal history and assured their survival. The Mandan celebrated the Okipa for perhaps five centuries. It was last performed in its entirety in 1881.

Pawnee earthlodge at Loup Fork village.   William H. Jackson 1871.

PAWNEE

Five hundred miles south of the Mandan-Hidatsa homeland, in what is now Kansas and Nebraska, lay the Pawnee villages. The date of the Pawnees' arrival on the central Plains is especially intriguing, because their customs and language hint of affinities with both Mississippi Valley and Southwestern prehistoric cultures. By the 1600s their fortified villages were strung out along the Upper Republican River.

Between 1500 and 1700, Pawnee lodges underwent a subtle change in shape from square with rounded corners to circular, and the villages became more compact. Unlike the Upper Missouri earthlodges, Pawnee floors were dropped to a depth of up to 3 feet. One entered by descending a long, tunneled ramp. Inside, the sloping sidewall met ground level slightly outside the excavation, forming a storage shelf just beyond the outer ring of short posts. Another characteristic of Pawnee lodges was their number of central posts— as many as eight or even ten in special religious structures constructed into the late nineteenth century.

According to Pawnee belief, each of their villages was founded by a particular star; every community treasured its sacred star bundle and revered the hereditary chief who was bundle-keeper and celestial representative. Village priests mediated between these star dieties and the community. The Pawnee also believed in earthly spiritual beings, who usually took the form of animals. These supernatural beings occupied their own "animal lodges" out in the countryside, and aspiring shamans visited them to fast and be blessed

Building a Pawnee earthlodge

These three photographs *(right)* are stages in a construction sequence recorded at the St. Louis World's Fair in 1904. The entire sequence is listed here: (1) A circle 60 feet in diameter was drawn with a rawhide lariat by the two leading medicine men. (2) The floor was excavated to about 2 feet. (3) The outer circle of twenty 6-foot forked top posts was put up and a circle of poles laid across (cottonwood was used for the structural members). (4) The long entrance passage was built *(top)*. (5) Wall poles, mat grass, and sod were packed around the outer circle. (6) Eight (or ten) center forked, 12-foot posts were set in an inner circle, and joining beams were laid in the forks *(middle)*. (7) Radial rafters were set from the outer circle over the inner circle, leaving a smoke hole in the center. The photograph *(bottom)* shows willow mats on the nearly completed structure. Grass was placed over the mats, then topped with sod to complete the lodge.

with special powers. Every fall and spring, special earthlodges were outfitted for shaman or "doctor" dances, colorful performances in which the shamans tried to outdo each other in feats of theatrical illusion—swallowing a deer's head and antlers whole, bringing mud duck decoys to life, shooting a boy full of arrows without harming him, and commanding the fire to rise and fall. Elaborately costumed shamans performed animal dances and enacted myths as the climax of the month of ceremonial dances in the earthlodge.

Pawnee earthlodges housed other rituals as well; the Hako, a ceremony for the welfare of children, was among the most important. In one phase of the Hako the earthlodge served as a "spiritual" sun dial. "As the Sun rises higher, the ray, which is its messenger, alights upon the edge of the central opening in the roof of the lodge, right over the fireplace," a Pawnee told anthropologist Alice Fletcher. "We see the spot, the sign of its touch, and we know that the ray is there ... The ray is now climbing down into the lodge. We watch the spot where it has alighted. It moves over the edge of the opening above the fireplace and descends into the lodge." Songs of thankfulness followed throughout the day as the sun shone through the smoke hole, its beam moving across the floor. The most potent moment of their recitation came as hearth, smoke hole, and sun aligned in a shaft of light.

Around 1905, a half-Pawnee named James Murie recorded the last house-building ritual among his people in northern Oklahoma. An officiating priest reminded everyone how the deity Tirawa chose the center of the earth for the Pawnee and marked the spot with an ash tree. Once the world's birds and animals swept the site clean, the gods of the four semicardinal directions brought forked posts for the central pillars of the cosmic earthlodge.

As Murie watched, the medicine men planted an ash pole on the altar and related each architectural element to the earth, the sky, the clouds, and key stars. After five days of hard work, the building was done and a medicine man proclaimed: "Let us stand in this lodge as Tirawa stood when he created the Earth." Everyone inside the building yelled in imitation of the birds and animals who they believed had similarly celebrated the world's first house.

ARIKARA

The origin of the Arikara tribe is attributed, in one native account, to the disappearance of a village of the Skidi branch of the Pawnee people sometime in the late sixteenth century. The community had gone north on a hunting trip and never returned. A migrating central Plains people speaking the Skidi dialect were soon named Arikara by Europeans and, by the 1800s, were alternately fighting and trading with the Mandan and their old Pawnee kinsmen. They occupied earthlodges that they built themselves or that had been abandoned by the Hidatsa.

Archeological work at the historic Leavenworth site in South Dakota has turned up house floors excavated in Pawnee fashion but constructed with only four central posts. Two sectors made up the Leavenworth village, which was encircled by a single log stockade and is considered an extremely large Arikara community. On one side of a little creek was a group of 64 houses, and on the other side stood 75, perhaps reflecting a division of the village into complementary social halves.

Village at Loup Fork, Nebraska, photographed by William H. Jackson in 1871.

The altar or place-where-things-are-performed represented the garden of Evening Star. The sacred area also represented the original camp circle in the sky.

The skararu, a foot deep square hole, represented the throne of Tirawa in heaven.

The wiharu, or sacred space, could not be walked across. Circulation was to the east, the head of the lodge sat to the east, no one passed in front of him ...

The path for gods in heavens to pass outside the lodge and create and later return to their stations.

The lodge was both universe and womb of woman, the household activities represented her reproductive powers—the women's beds were arranged by age to represent the main stages in a woman's life—the youngest women in the west near the garden of Evening Star. The mature women in the middle of each side. The beds of the old women near the passage, for they were "on their way out ..."

West
Evening Star
Beautiful woman, Goddess of night
Germination—in her garden the corn and buffalo were constantly being renewed so the people could eat.

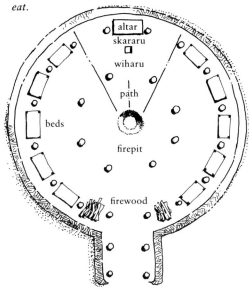

East
Morning Star
God of Light, Fire, War
Every morning poured his beam into the lodge and lit fire in act of cosmic procreation, symbolizing his first union with Evening Star—from their mating came the girl who was the first human being to be placed on earth.

Dwellings typically had 4 center posts, lodges of chiefs had 8 posts, and lodges of medicine-men had 10 posts. The other posts represented stars also holding up world ...

A westernmost post became the Evening Star—an easternmost post was Morning Star, head chief of all stars was the North Star, whose mystery was symbolized in a North Post, the southern post represented the Milky Way ... actually the flickering campfires of dead Pawnees.

Space around firepit symbolized the horizon. The firepit is the open mouth of Tirawa, the earth removed was mounded outside the passage and symbolized his words.

The circular outside wall also represented the horizon—the 20 posts stood for minor gods.

The star gods poured down their strength from their appropriate directions in a constant stream through the roof.

Pawnee earthlodge symbolism

Tirawa, the Pawnee's supreme deity and creator, was not symbolically represented in the earthlodge. His domain was the vast expanse of sky above, which was visible through the smoke hole, and his presence was manifest in the shaft of light that came through the smoke hole to the fireplace—a symbolic link connecting the heavens above to the center of the earth below.

The paths of Tirawa's power were also toward the sky in the four semi-cardinal directions: northwest, northeast, southwest, and southeast. The circular plan of the earthlodge evoked the Earth's extension in all directions, and its wall and roof form served as a reminder of the sky above.

Among the Skidi Pawnee (a tribal subgroup), a group of five villages joined together to form a constellation on Earth. One village was to the west (evening star), and four villages were situated to form a square (semi-cardinal direction stars). These five villages (and their stars) are symbolized in each earthlodge by the altar at the west and the four central roof supports.

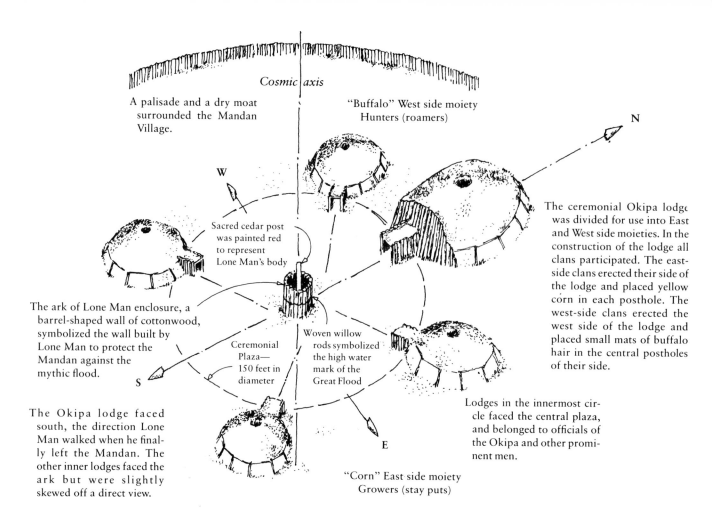

Cosmic axis

A palisade and a dry moat surrounded the Mandan Village.

"Buffalo" West side moiety
Hunters (roamers)

W

N

The ceremonial Okipa lodge was divided for use into East and West side moieties. In the construction of the lodge all clans participated. The east-side clans erected their side of the lodge and placed yellow corn in each posthole. The west-side clans erected the west side of the lodge and placed small mats of buffalo hair in the central postholes of their side.

Sacred cedar post was painted red to represent Lone Man's body

The ark of Lone Man enclosure, a barrel-shaped wall of cottonwood, symbolized the wall built by Lone Man to protect the Mandan against the mythic flood.

Ceremonial Plaza— 150 feet in diameter

Woven willow rods symbolized the high water mark of the Great Flood

S

The Okipa lodge faced south, the direction Lone Man walked when he finally left the Mandan. The other inner lodges faced the ark but were slightly skewed off a direct view.

Lodges in the innermost circle faced the central plaza, and belonged to officials of the Okipa and other prominent men.

E

"Corn" East side moiety
Growers (stay puts)

Like-A-Fishhook village

Photograph of Like-A-Fishhook village after it was abandoned, ca. 1887.

Mandan village iconography

Located along the bluffs of the Missouri River, Mandan sites were typically concentric groupings of lodges surrounded by a circular palisade and a dry moat *(top left)*.

A bird's-eye view of a Mandan village *(bottom left)* was sketched by George Catlin, ca. 1832 and then painted later.

LIKE-A-FISHHOOK VILLAGE

In the late eighteenth century, debilitating smallpox epidemics coupled with increased aggression by Sioux Indian horsemen forced the Mandan and Hidatsa to move closer together for mutual protection at the mouth of the Knife River near present-day Stanton, North Dakota. By 1840, more disastrous assaults of smallpox had decimated the tribes. In the worst epidemic in 1837, the Hidatsa lost fifty percent of their people, the Mandan ninety percent. Abandoning the Knife River communities, the survivors moved up the Missouri River to Like-A-Fishhook, a familiar site where the river makes a sharp bend. This new refugee village afforded the protection of high bluffs on three sides, good pasture, enough driftwood for earthlodge frames, and ample alluvial flats for their gardens.

In the early 1860s a wave of Arikara arrivals also built earthlodges at Like-A-Fishhook. Within this community of earthlodges, ceremonial centers, corn-drying racks, and pioneer-style sod-roofed cabins, the old village Indian lifestyle was kept alive for another twenty-five years. As these earthlodge traditions accommodated each other, the Hidatsa turned over the southeastern corner of Like-A-Fishhook to the Mandan so they could replicate their circular plaza and the Lone Man shrine. In turn, the Hidatsa were permitted to use the Mandan sacred lodge for their Bear rituals. Both Mandans and Hidatsas occupied the inner ring of earthlodges around the plaza. The Arikara kept to their own sector, and the other tribes watched with interest as they danced around their holy cedar tree.

For the Hidatsa women, a community bell signaled the beginning of the work day in their gardens. In the village proper, the Black Face warrior society policed the clean streets and made sure that the earthlodges were kept up. But

141

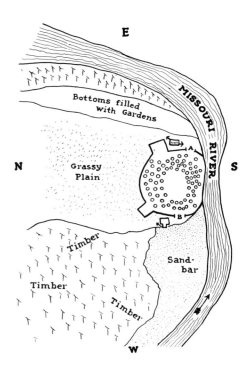

Like-A-Fishhook's florescence was brief. By 1870 the buffalo were almost gone, and the trading post that helped stabilize the community was closed down. In 1887, the federal policy of subdividing tribal lands forced Indian families to abandon the village. The government program called for each Indian family to live like an Anglo household, farming 160-acre allotments, attending schools and churches, and dwelling in single-family log cabins or wooden frame houses.

Soon, the building of an earthlodge became almost an act of cultural defiance. At Nishu, near Beaver Creek in North Dakota, an Arikara holy man named Four Rings oversaw the construction of one of their last earthlodges and—against the missionaries' wishes—his people danced around its cedar tree on sacred occasions until 1908. A Hidatsa named Old Dog built a hybrid earthlodge around the same time. It was half log cabin, half old-style earth-roofed dwelling and became a popular spot for community gatherings. One well-known holdout against the white man's way was Crow's Heart, a Mandan who lived in an earthlodge and safeguarded the Lone Man shrine through this period of cultural upheaval. "We no longer live in an earth-lodge," said a Hidatsa woman who had been forced to leave Like-A-Fishhook, "but in a house with chimneys.... Sometimes at evening I sit, looking out on the Big Missouri. In the shadows I seem to see our Indian village, with smoke curling upwards from the earthlodges...."

TODAY

In a windswept, open pasture in northern Oklahoma's Cimarron Valley, Pawnee elder Phil Matthews led us to a circular depression—all that remained of a Pawnee lodge built around 1905. The grassy basin was about 36 feet in diameter, with the lumpy ridge that had once been the outer wall broken only at the east where the door tunnel had been. Matthews said he remembered watching the last rituals held in this sod-covered lodge as a boy. He also guided us to a weedy pasture outside Pawnee, Oklahoma, where we discovered a hexagonal wooden hall, its doors nailed shut and windows boarded up. Built by Pawnees around 1910, it seemed to be an approximation in milled lumber and shingles of their traditional earthlodge. Through splintered shingles we glimpsed brass beds, steamer trunks, and clothes rotting on racks. Its gabled entry tunnel faced east. Stretching up to the smoke hole were eight central posts made from slender four-by-fours. Four were in the semicardinal directions, symbolizing the Evening Star, Morning Star, North Star, and Southern Star (which in Pawnee mythology is associated with the Pawnee land of the dead).

Our search for Plains earthlodges also took us to On-A-Slant, a pro-tohistoric Mandan village site outside of Bismarck, North Dakota, that was abandoned when Lewis and Clark passed in 1804-1805. The sunken remains of seventy-five earthlodges still can be counted. In the 1930s a Depression-era federal project employed Civilian Conservation Corps workers to reconstruct four lodges. They mistakenly constructed the Okipa ceremonial structure in the round, but otherwise the buildings were fashioned authentically, and local Indians supervised the weaving of prairie grass into the frame before roofing them with sod.

Like-A-Fishhook village plan and pictographic symbol.

Pawnee hall

This Pawnee building *(right)* for dances and community meetings was built ca. 1910 outside Pawnee, Oklahoma.

Though they no longer lived in earthlodge villages, the Mandan, Hidatsa, and Arikara descendants—known collectively as the Three Affiliated Tribes—still cherished their old townsites. In the 1940s they joined in opposition when the U.S. Army Corps of Engineers proposed a dam across the Missouri River. The Garrison Dam launched one of America's largest archeological salvage operations, in which old earthlodge villages up and down the Missouri were plotted and excavated. Yet this gave little satisfaction to the Indians, who watched as the rising waters broke their reservation into five sectors and flooded townsites along the river where they had lived for nearly a thousand years.

The Lone Man shrine was secretly transferred to a new home above the Garrison Reservoir. Today the shrine is maintained in a secluded field in the Twin Buttes sector of the reservation. Periodically its caretakers honor it with fresh red cloth and pay homage to the last emblem of the oldest civic architecture in the Great Plains.

144

GRASS HOUSE

In 1540 Coronado saw and described an example of a second major Plains Indian house type, the grass house, close to what is now Dodge City, Kansas. Its aesthetic trademark was a double-curve profile produced as its thatched roof bent in, then up, where the grass twisted into a spire. It was built extensively by Caddoan-speakers of the southern Plains, tribes such as the Hasinai, Kitchai, Wichita, and Caddo. Coronado admired how their thatch was sewn "in and out in such an ingenious manner that each bunch of grass overlaps the bunch below."

The grass house was framed of poles that were bent over an interior ring of posts and beams and bound together at the top. Horizontal sapling stringers strengthened the frame, which could be as wide as 60 feet across at the base. The thatch was tied on in tight bunches, and exterior rows of stringers held it fast.

In the early eighteenth century, a Spanish priest witnessed the protocol of grass house construction among the Hasinai of east Texas. After a tribesman had informed the chiefs of his need for a house, a building site was chosen and overseers were dispatched throughout the village. They left a stick at each house, a sign that its occupants were obliged to cut and clean one rib of the frame. The women of each house were expected to contribute a load of grass "coarser than the largest wheat." That night the overseers slept at the building site. At dawn the villagers were told to plant their prepared ribs in designated holes. In the middle of the house site a man climbed the branch stubs of an oak tree ladder. By means of ropes tied to the tips of the ribs he gathered them in "until they formed a figure like half an orange." Next the overseer had the ribs "covered with heavy timber," presumably meaning the encircling rows of

Grass house

Grass house *(left)* photographed by Edward S. Curtis, ca. 1927.

This somewhat stylized illustration *(bottom)* of a village of Wichita grass houses on Rush Creek was published in *Exploration of the Red River of Louisiana in the Year 1852*, by Captain Randolph Marcy and Captain George B. McClellan, 1854. The buildings would actually have had pointed-dome roofs, and the smoke, instead of pouring through gaping smoke holes, would have seeped out through the grass roofs.

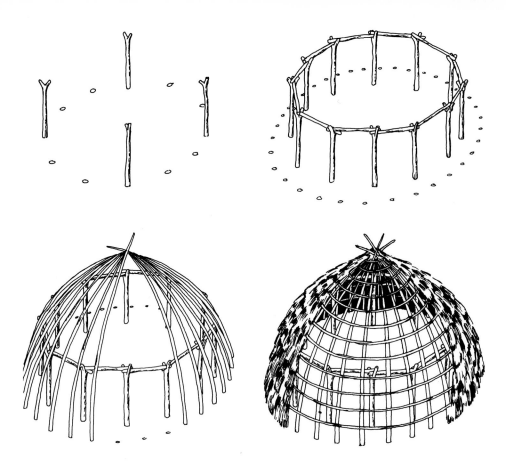

horizontal stringers. Starting at the base, the frame was thatched "with grass to a thickness of three hand breadths." By midday the job was completed, and a feast of venison and ground corn served in earthen pots celebrated the house-raising.

Each Hasinai settlement constructed sacred buildings to house a holy fire, which stood for their culture hero. In the capital of the Hasinai confederacy a priest kept vigil over a sacred flame inside a "fire temple." The Hasinai believed that beyond the safety of their immediate communities lay the domain of a horned serpent, and only fire kept his threatening presence at bay. Their mythology also reveals a suggestive symbolic link between wombs, acorns, and grass houses. Their culture hero is said to have first emerged from an acorn shell buried in another acorn shell. This shell was enclosed in an earthen pot, which in turn was safeguarded in a grass house.

Grass houses also figured in the folklore of the Wichita tribe. In one tale a mythic visionary dreamed of an eagle who told the wandering Wichita where to settle. Upon their arrival there the Indians offered smoke and prayer so the Four Directions would protect their new village. After building their domestic dwellings, everyone pitched in to erect a dance lodge. The hero directed the cutting of its main ribs, trimming the saplings himself so they would bend evenly. One after another, the east, south, west, and north poles were set into holes that had been bedded with water moss. Using soapweed ties softened in hot ashes, they bound these four first, then completed the circle. Supple willows were the horizontal stringers, and the grass was tied on with buffalo-hide thongs.

Another Wichita narrative, collected in the 1920s by the photographer Edward S. Curtis, focuses upon a culture hero named Red Bean Man, messenger of the great spirit Kinnikasus, who told a Wichita emissary how to divide the work of harvesting materials for the first grass house between male

Instructions from Red Bean Man on building a grass house

During his visit to the Wichita in the 1920s, Edward S. Curtis collected this text on the sacred origin of the grass house:

"... in the future the homes for all the people will be as this house which the spirit told me how to build; for they are good, and in them the tribe will have good health. First, the women will make the ground ready: they will cut away the sod on the chosen space and make smooth the surface with the pure earth. In shape it will be round like the sun. The men will go to the forest and cut many short cedar posts with crotches at the top. Of these, four of the best will be planted in the ground, in the shape of a square, beginning at the east. All of these posts must be made fine and smooth, or the spirits will say our work is not good. When the four posts of the house are secured in position, then you will set up others about them that the form of the house may be round. In the crotches you will lay other fine cedar timbers, against which will rest all outer timbers. Next you will divide the workers into four parties, the leader of each taking his men to one point of the land; the first to the south, the next to the west, then one to the north and one to the east. Each party will cut and prepare a fine long cedar. These four from the four winds are the strength of the house. They are like the chiefs who hold up the tribe. Before these men and their leaders go out to look for the fine cedars, they will pray to Kinnikasus that their work may be good; that the cedars which they find may give the house great strength, and that through the strength of the house the people may prosper ..." *(left).*

146

Grass house camps

Traditional grass houses and arbors *(above)* make up the Oklahoma homestead of Ska-Wa-Cer, a Wichita Indian, ca. 1890. In the summer arbors the ribs are exposed. The presence of log cabins and tents suggests that building traditions were in a state of rapid change.

and female villagers. Each stage of construction faithfully followed his instructions. Finally, with the frame ready for thatching, a crew leader climbed a notched log ladder to the peak where four of the bent ribs stretched out to honor the Four Directions. Then he uttered the prayer which Red Bean Man had taught them:

> Kinnikasus, this is your house.
> It is good; I am thanking you for it.
> Guide us and help us in all things done in it.
> This house is your work;
> Let me tie these poles well
> That the people may have health and happiness.
> Look upon us, that this work be blessed.

During the early 1800s, the Wichita occupied large villages of seventy or more grass houses. Usually they were situated on the lower slopes of fertile valleys so the Indians could plant gardens close by. By the turn of the century, however, the only surviving grass houses were found in family compounds on Oklahoma's Wichita reservation, which had been given to the tribe in 1867.

In 1915 an Oklahoma newspaper reported that only four grass houses still stood in the region just north of the Washita River. Pecan, elm, or hemlock trees, harvested in late winter and stripped of their bark, provided the ribbing. Swamp grass was collected by the women when the rivers had dried. Upward of seventy ribs might be used for an extremely large dwelling. Stringers were of willow, and the frame was overlaid with tied grass bundles. The women sewed them on from the base up using a yard-long cottonwood needle to pass the cord back and forth through the grass wall. Four poles extending beyond the peak still stood for the Four Directions, and only two doorways led into a building.

148

Building grass houses

This grass house *(above left)* was under construction at the Trans-Mississippi International Exposition in Omaha, Nebraska, when it was photographed by James Mooney in 1898. The interior of a Wichita grass house *(bottom left)* was photographed by Edward S. Curtis, ca. 1927. In traditional times, coarse prairie grass was used for the external roof thatching and softer grasses collected along the riverbanks for the interior walls along sleeping areas. Contemporary Wichita builders are shown *(above, left and right)* building grass houses near Anadarko, Oklahoma, 1978.

TODAY

In Anadarko, Oklahoma, we visited the Wichita Indian reservation in the hope that some tribespeople could tell us about the old grass houses. We knew that most old examples had been destroyed by careless fires, and local Indians suggested that the dilapidated examples at the nearby tourist center of "Indian City" were "done wrong." Our guide around the community was tribal chairman Lamar Newton. He led us to a fenced-in plot, where we discovered a two-family grass house in mint condition, indicative of recent community interest in old traditions.

Once inside we could make out toy birds with corncob bodies and wooden wings hanging from the ceiling. They were there to clear away cobwebs, we were told. A smoke hole had also been cut through the thatch just below the top. Thatching the peak had been tricky, Newton said, referring to the uppermost clumps of grass twisted into a rainproof peak. Except for a sunken area for a hearth and a crescent of dried mud to prevent rainwater from splashing through the door, the interior was bare.

Newton hinted we might be interested in continuing down the dirt road we had come on. Soon there loomed through the trees the skeletal frame for an immense grass house. Just under construction, its hemispherical webbing bulged up 40 feet and consisted of fifty-two split red cedar ribs tied with leather thongs to a grapevine hoop at the top. Because the building was so large, the ribs required short extensions for them to meet. Their experience on the smaller house had turned the Wichita builders into purists; instead of thatching this building with swamp grass, they had driven fifty miles to cut the more traditional buffalo grass, bringing it back in the trunks of their cars.

One worker told us they had begun rather ignorant of many techniques, such as splitting the cedar ribs from the tip rather than the butt end so they would divide neatly down the grain and not shear off. They had hoped to use an old-style notched log ladder but converted to pipe scaffolding when chopping steps into the tough oak became too time-consuming. We wanted to inspect the grapevine hoop, so we clambered up the wobbly frame. A ponytailed man clung to the top, securing the last tier of stringers. Down below we could see the men and women working on the first of twenty-three rows of thatch. Their division of labor followed the pattern authorized in the Red Bean Man myth, with men completing the frame and hauling bundles of grass to women who worked together, one inside, one out. They sewed the thatch on by pressing the bundles against the horizontal stringers with their knees as they passed a long cottonwood needle through the grass.

TIPI

The Spanish explorer Don Juan de Oñate followed Coronado into the southwestern Plains twenty years later, where he too encountered nomadic architecture. Near eastern New Mexico he saw "fifty tents of tanned hides, very bright red and white in color and bell-shaped, with flaps and openings and built as skillfully as any house in Italy." Closer inspection revealed that they were "so large that in the most ordinary house, four different mattresses and beds are easily accommodated." He praised their tanned hide covers: "although it should rain bucketfuls, it will not pass through nor stiffen the hide, but rather upon drying it remains as soft and pliable as before...." The coverings were sewn from five to seven buffalo hides. They could be folded and loaded onto "travois," V-shaped drags that were yoked onto dogs. Other dogs towed the short framing poles.

The evolution of these ancient tipis has been the subject of recent speculation by Canadian scholar Ted J. Brasser, who has analyzed both the "tipi ring" evidence and building practices of Subarctic people. He believes the full-fledged Plains tipi grew out of two traditions, the old shorter tents of uncertain framing that existed at least five thousand years ago and possibly developed into the four-pole framing system, and the northeastern woodland conical tent that used three poles and was brought into the Plains by the Cree around 1600.

The fully developed Plains tipi was not a true cone. Its steeper, rear side braced the tilted structure against the prevailing westerly winds, and its doorway faced the rising sun. Nor was its plan a true circle; the wider end of its egg-shaped base lay in the rear. Because horses could drag a far heavier travois, tipis soon doubled in height and their furnishings became more comfortable and decorative.

Portable dwellings

The equestrian tribes of the Plains transported their tipi covers folded and packed on a travois, such as this Northern Cheyenne example *(bottom)*, ca. 1900. Tipi poles were also bundled together and dragged by the horses.

Plains tipis were sometimes painted with scenes of warfare or sacred symbols. In this photograph *(right)* by F.B. Fiske, on the Standing Rock Sioux Reservation, two pictographic tipis underscore the importance of horses to Plains Indian warrior-hunters. The tipi in the foreground belonged to Old Bull, a Hunkpapa Sioux who was a nephew of Sitting Bull.

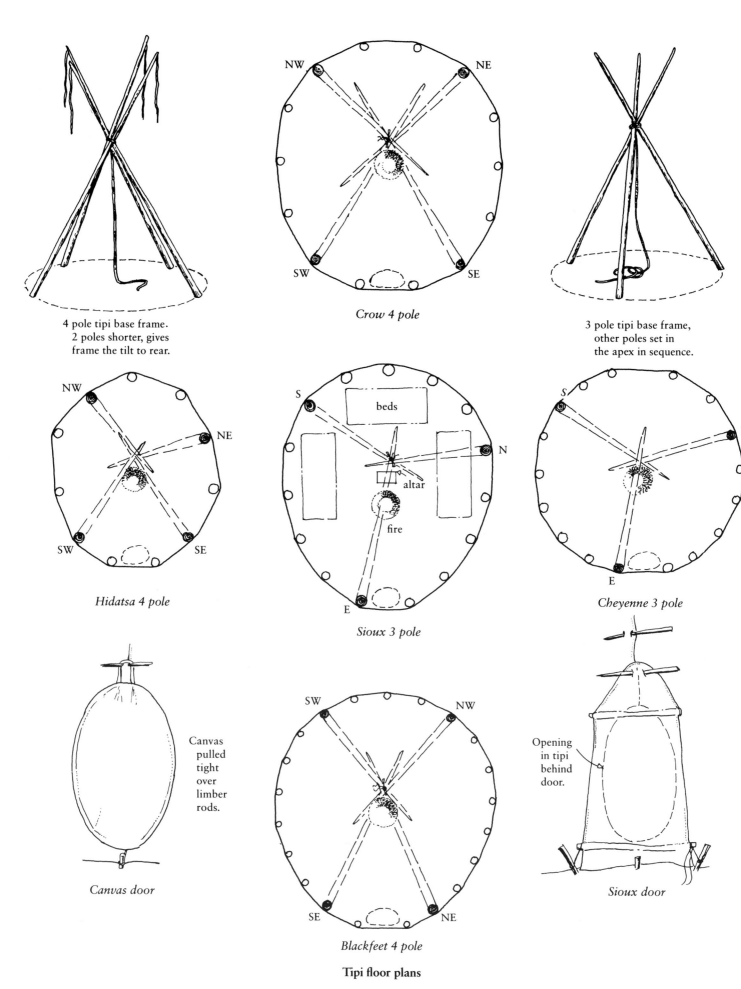

4 pole tipi base frame. 2 poles shorter, gives frame the tilt to rear.

Crow 4 pole

3 pole tipi base frame, other poles set in the apex in sequence.

Hidatsa 4 pole

beds

altar

fire

Sioux 3 pole

Cheyenne 3 pole

Canvas pulled tight over limber rods.

Canvas door

Blackfeet 4 pole

Opening in tipi behind door.

Sioux door

Tipi floor plans

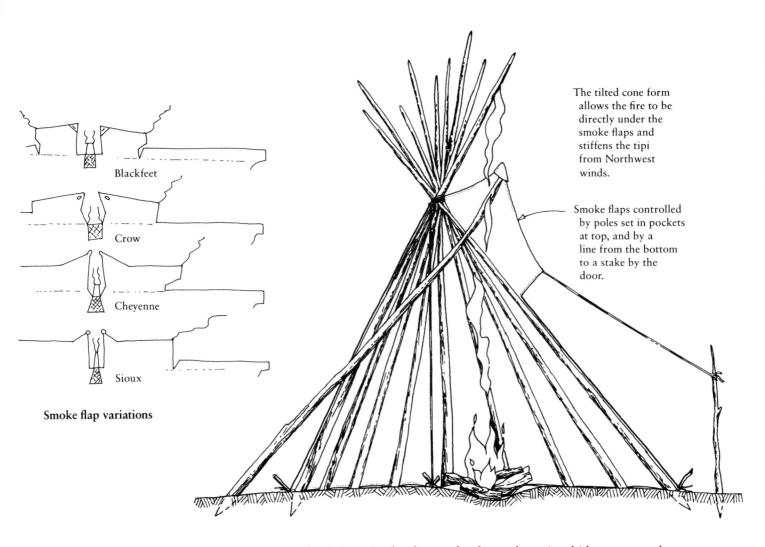

Smoke flap variations

The tilted cone form allows the fire to be directly under the smoke flaps and stiffens the tipi from Northwest winds.

Smoke flaps controlled by poles set in pockets at top, and by a line from the bottom to a stake by the door.

Blackfeet

Crow

Cheyenne

Sioux

Tipi architecture

Tipis were erected in two ways. A tripod foundation was common in the southern Plains, and a four-pole foundation was generally found further north. Additional poles were carefully placed into the apex of poles. The floor plan was roughly egg-shaped; four-pole tipis allowed for a more generous interior. The profile of the structure resembled a tilted cone with its steeper side facing westward, the direction of the prevailing winds. The cone of poles had to be positioned so the cover would fit snugly at the front, where it was laced together with willow pins, and at the base, where it was pegged to the earth. The smoke flaps (*above*) were adjusted from the inside with a pair of long poles.

The tipi required only wood poles, stakes, pins, hide covers, and ropes to provide a quickly assembled and easily dismantled shelter in both sweltering and freezing weather. To erect a tipi, a three- or four-pole frame was lifted into place. The preferred wood was young, straight, and extremely long lodgepole pine, but red cedar was an acceptable second choice. All but one of the remaining poles were lifted onto the crossed poles from proper places around the ovoid floorplan. Women sewed the semicircular cover together with sinew from twelve or more tanned buffalo hides, using split sinew for thread and making sure their stitching produced a waterproof cover. Smoking the finished tipi cover prevented it from cracking after a rain.

The finished cover was tied to a final pole at the western side of the frame. Then it was pulled around both sides to meet at the doorway, where it was laced from the bottom to the smoke hole with carved willow pins. Stakes or rocks held the cover on the ground. The smoke flaps, or "ears," were extended out using lengthy poles. Small adjustments in the position of poles and stakes helped to stretch the cover as smooth and taut as a drum.

After canvas became available in the late 1800s, regional variations in tipi construction and appearance evolved. Tipis with the tripod foundation predominated in the south, while the four-pole frame was prevalent in the north. In the southern Plains, tipi poles usually did not lift as far above the smoke hole as those in the north, where long poles often sported colorful streamers or trophy scalps. In the north, small cross pieces were attached to the guide poles, which were inserted through grommets in the smoke flaps; in the south the poles generally fit into corner pockets. Around the hem of the northern tipis, hardwood stakes were driven into the ground through cloth

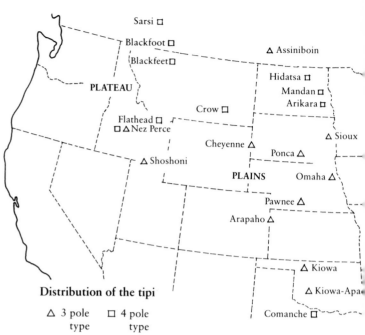

Distribution of the tipi

△ 3 pole type □ 4 pole type

Sarsi □
Blackfoot □
Blackfeet □
PLATEAU
△ Assiniboin
Hidatsa □
Mandan □
Arikara □
Crow □
Flathead □
□ △ Nez Perce
Cheyenne △
△ Sioux
Ponca △
△ Shoshoni
PLAINS
Omaha △
Pawnee △
Arapaho △
△ Kiowa
△ Kiowa-Apa[che]
Comanche □

Tipi construction

The tipi building sequence *(left)* shows Sarsi Indians on the Canadian Plains erecting the frame of a four-pole tipi, then covering it with a painted canvas cover. In the late nineteenth century, canvas began replacing tanned buffalo hides as covering material. This traditional hide tipi *(right)* was occupied by Little Big Mouth, an Arapaho, and used a three-pole foundation.

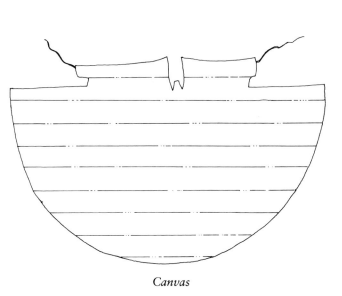

Canvas

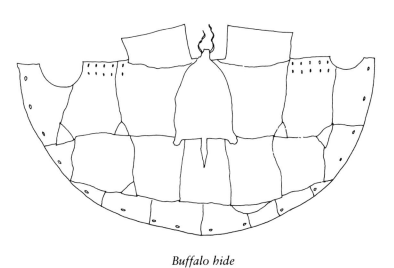

Buffalo hide

loops; in the south, one was more likely to find stones knotted into the cover cloth, with ties that formed loops for the ground stakes. The southern tipi doorway was usually an inverted V, created by pulling back the sides below the lacing pins; northern tipis often had an oval door tailored into the cloth.

During windstorms a rope was stretched from the crossing of the poles at the top to stakes in the floor to anchor the dwelling; during rainstorms guide poles outside the cover enabled occupants to fold the smoke flaps over each other. An inner liner known as a "dew cloth" was fastened to a line tied about 5 feet up the poles; it helped provide an upward draft for drawing out smoke and, more important, insulated the tipi. Often decorated with geometric border designs, this liner also kept the rain that inevitably ran down the poles from dripping on sleepers. To further prevent unwanted moisture in the sleeping area, the poles were scraped to remove bumps. During extremely cold weather the air pocket between liner and cover was stuffed with grass, and snow was banked outside for insulation. In summer the hem of the tipi was often propped up with sticks to catch the breeze and provide shade.

Seating, sleeping, storage, and the placement of holy objects within the home followed social custom. Doorways almost invariably faced the rising sun, and the oldest male occupant customarily slept at the rear, western side of the lodge. Among some tribes it was bad form to step between him and the fire. Men usually sat on the northern side of the tipi, women on the south. If the tipi housed multiple families or more than one wife, household goods defined each person's sleeping place. Sacred medicine bundles were hung on tripods inside the tipi or were tied high upon the outside cover. Firewood, food, and cooking implements were kept near the door.

Tipi elaboration

As horses instead of dogs began to pull their travois, and lightweight canvas replaced buffalo hide, Plains Indians began building larger and more elaborate tipis. The canvas tipis of the Crow of Montana (above) were distinguished by lofty sprays of poles above the smoke hole. Tipi furnishings included backrests of willow sticks, painted rawhide trunks and beaded robes, and beds softened by tanned furs. This interior view of a Flathead tipi (right) in western Montana shows dance garb hanging from tipi poles.

The Cheyenne, who in the seventeenth century had been seasonal nomadic earthlodge farmers in the eastern Dakotas, rapidly abandoned their old life to become buffalo-hunting warriors. By 1830 they had moved west and split into Northern and Southern Cheyenne groups who lived in tipis all year long. When they were on the move, the Cheyenne chose campsites with good drainage and avoided pitching their tipis under trees that might drop morning dew or dead branches.

Whenever the scattered hunting and warring bands of Cheyenne gathered as an entire nation or in formal camp circles for councils, Sun Dances, or other ceremonies, the position of each lodge depended on which clan or religious association it belonged to. The camp circle faced east; special painted tipis that housed significant tribal objects such as the sacred Buffalo Hat were pitched at time-honored spots within the hallowed inner ground of the circle itself.

Individuals who painted their own tipi covers either illustrated their battle exploits or, more commonly, depicted symbols related to their experiences during fast-induced visions. A man ventured into the hills to fast for up to four days. Sometimes a supernatural animal, a "guardian spirit," answered his prayers for power by bestowing upon the seeker his own "lodge," which included instructions on painting a tipi cover and sacred materials linked with the dwelling. Thereafter the tipi was part of a sacred kit which included the narrative of the original fasting, the sacred objects, and songs associated with the dwelling. The spiritual power and social status associated with such tipis often was ritually passed on for generations.

Tipi camps

The Cheyenne, like most Plains tribes, arranged their tipis into highly organized and well-policed camps. When the nomadic bands assembled for ceremonies or councils, each tribal division, band, and individual tipi had its assigned spot. An older form of Cheyenne tipi circle, for occasions when the tribe's original two groups, the Sutayo and the Cheyenne proper, camped together, is diagrammed here *(right)*. The C-shaped ring might extend up to a mile in diameter. Sometimes Indians likened these camp circles to the circle of stars in the night sky, or to the base of a gigantic tipi whose door faced east. Such a camp might contain up to a thousand tipis in a ring three or four dwellings deep.

Cheyenne painted tipis are shown during a warrior society's feast *(left)*, painted by a Cheyenne artist named Cohoe. A southern Cheyenne camp *(above)* includes a lone painted tipi decorated with the Maltese Cross design, which stood for the sacred Morning Star, ca. 1880.

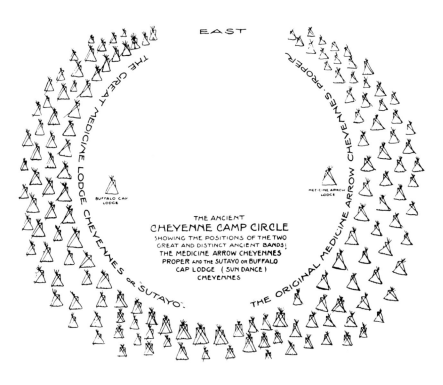

EAST

THE GREAT MEDICINE LODGE CHEYENNES OR "SUTAYO".

THE ORIGINAL MEDICINE ARROW CHEYENNES PROPER.

BUFFALO CAP LODGE

MEDICINE ARROW LODGE

THE ANCIENT
CHEYENNE CAMP CIRCLE
SHOWING THE POSITIONS OF THE TWO
GREAT AND DISTINCT ANCIENT BANDS:
THE MEDICINE ARROW CHEYENNES
PROPER AND THE SUTAYO OR BUFFALO
CAP LODGE (SUN DANCE)
CHEYENNES

159

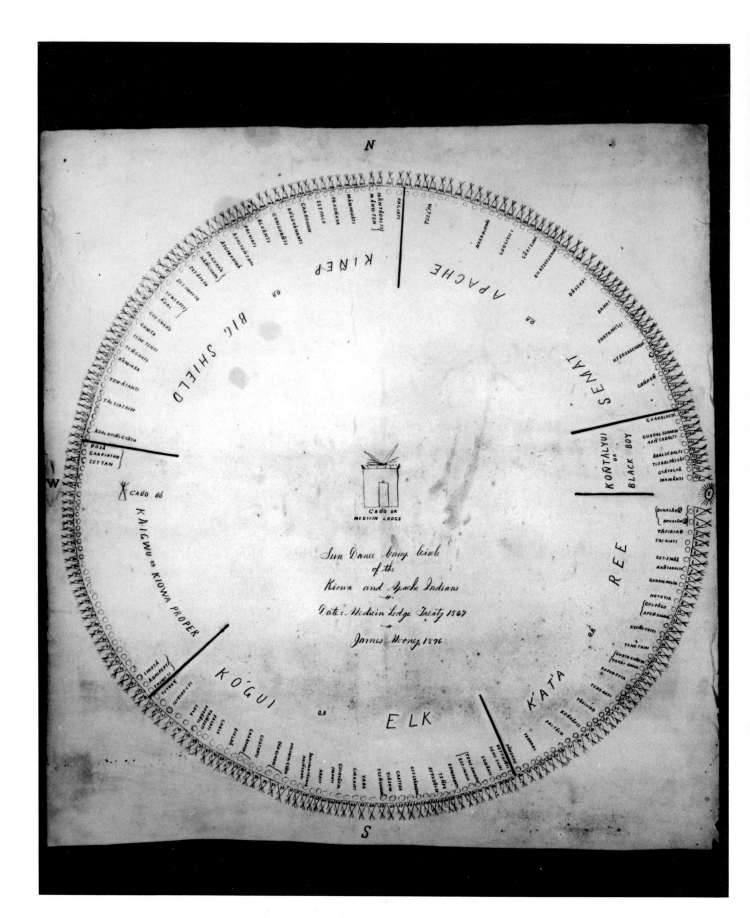

Sun Dance Camp Circle
of the
Kiowa and Apache Indians
—
Date: Medicin Lodge Treaty 1867
—
James Mooney, 1876

The Kiowa tribe was a neighbor to the Southern Cheyenne and roamed across southwest Kansas and western Oklahoma. They used three-pole tipis, about one in twenty of which was decorated with this form of sacred heraldry. When anthropologist James Mooney studied the Kiowa in their Oklahoma reservation in the 1890s, only one painted tipi remained in use, but the people told him about many of the old designs. Mooney documented their dream-origin stories and their owners' names. Kiowa warriors were remembered long after they had died for the magical power of tipi designs which they had received in visions. For example, Chief White Man's Hugging Bear tipi design had the power to heal the sick, while Black Cap's Porcupine tipi was known to keep children healthy.

Mooney wanted to recreate the Kiowa Sun Dance encampment of 1867 for the 1897 Tennessee Centennial Exposition. At that final gathering of the tribe before they were placed on a reservation, 238 tipis, about sixty of them painted, were erected in one great circle. Each of the six Kiowa bands had their designated section, and each dwelling, identified by its owner's shield hanging from a tripod by the door, was pitched in its assigned spot. In the center was the Sun Dance lodge. Using commercial paints and deerskin panels about 4 feet wide and 26 inches high, Mooney's Kiowa artists managed to produce thirty-one replicas, far short of the quantity Mooney wanted for the exhibit.

Another Indian group renowned for its painted tipis was the Blackfeet of Montana and Canada. Their three tribal divisions rode horses and used guns as early as 1730. About a century later, Prince Maximilian of Germany described their tipis: "they are, at first, neat and white, afterwards brownish;

Kiowa and Blackfeet camps

Anthropologist James Mooney compiled this diagram *(left)* of the last gathering of Kiowa and Kiowa-Apache tipis, in 1867, before the tribes were consolidated on their Oklahoma reservation. It locates the six major bands and the individual tipis of major warriors and their families.

The zigzag lines on the Thunder tipi of Cream Antelope *(below)* in a Blackfeet camp represent lightning.

and at the top, where the smoke issues, black, and, at last, transparent, like parchment, and very light inside." The Blackfeet erected hundreds of tipis in circles up to a mile in circumference during summer Sun Dance encampments. About one out of ten Blackfeet tipis were painted, each illustrating the guardian spirit its original owner had received in a vision, and each with a song repertoire, a sacred medicine bundle, and a lineage of owners.

At the height of their prosperity—achieved largely through their trade with early fur companies—the Blackfeet were building the largest tipis in the Plains. Each cover used at least eighteen buffalo hides. Very large tipis, however, could call for as many as thirty-eight hides and were sometimes so heavy that they had to be cut in half for transportation. Up to forty poles might support such a tipi, and the two parts were buttoned together up the back with old Hudson's Bay Co. brass buttons and fastened up the front with wooden pins. The floor area was large enough to accommodate three or four fire pits.

After a year or more of steady use, tipi covers acquired holes, tears, and burned spots. Usually they were patched, but if a cover was too tattered, the leather was recycled. The spongy, smoke-softened darkest section around the smoke flaps sometimes was cut into diapers for babies. The Blackfeet woman who needed a new tipi cover invited her friends or clan relatives to a feast and then passed out needles, awls, and sinew bundles. On the first day the women

Circles of tipis

Blackfeet tipis (above) were photographed in 1896 by Walter McClintock, when the tribe gathered for their Sun Dance. McClintock later wrote, "The camp had hundreds of smoke-colored tipis and was more than a mile in circumference."

The social organization of many Plains groups was encoded in the layout of their tipi encampments. The Omaha camp circle, called the *Huthuga (right)* exemplified the tendency of Siouan-speaking tribes to divide their tipi circles into halves, standing for the earth and sky respectively. Five of the clans positioned their tipis on one side, and five on the other, a division that was preserved even when it was inconvenient to build the camp circle with its opening precisely to the east. During the gathering of the Omaha for their last buffalo hunt in 1872, 133 tipis were on the northern half of the large camp and 147 on the southern side.

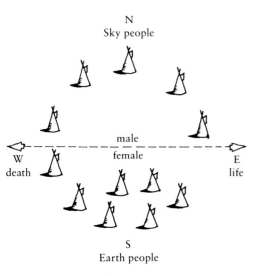

N
Sky people

male

W   female   E
death   life

S
Earth people

**Omaha camp circle
'Hu'thuga'**

prepared 2-foot lengths of sinew thread. On the second day they each unrolled two or three hides while an experienced elder woman directed the cutting and patching. When the cover was cut and sewn, it was stretched over its frame, the smoke flaps were closed, and the inside was cured with heavy smoke scented with sagebrush to keep it supple, waterproof, and fragrant.

If the cover was to be painted, its semicircle of sewn and smoked hides was spread on the grass. Skilled specialists outlined the animal figures and border designs in charcoal, using rules of red willow to keep the lines straight. The symbols and designs for the bottom and upper panels of the tipi originated from a combination of received tribal forms, while the designs for the middle area represented vision experiences and supernatural guardians significant to the warrior of the household. Originally paint was mixed from mineral or vegetable coloring with a glue base made from boiled buffalo hooves, but the white man's commercial pigments soon became coveted trade items. Friends and family helped the visionary apply the coloring with brushes made from sticks softened by chewing, bound buffalo hair, or porous bone joints.

It took little more than an hour for Blackfeet women, who actually owned the tipis, to erect them. One band of Canadian Blackfeet in Alberta hastily set up a painted tipi named the Thunderbird Lodge whenever their camp was threatened by a storm. No undue noise was permitted in its vicinity so that its depictions of sky, hail, and rain could deflect the angry skies around the camp.

163

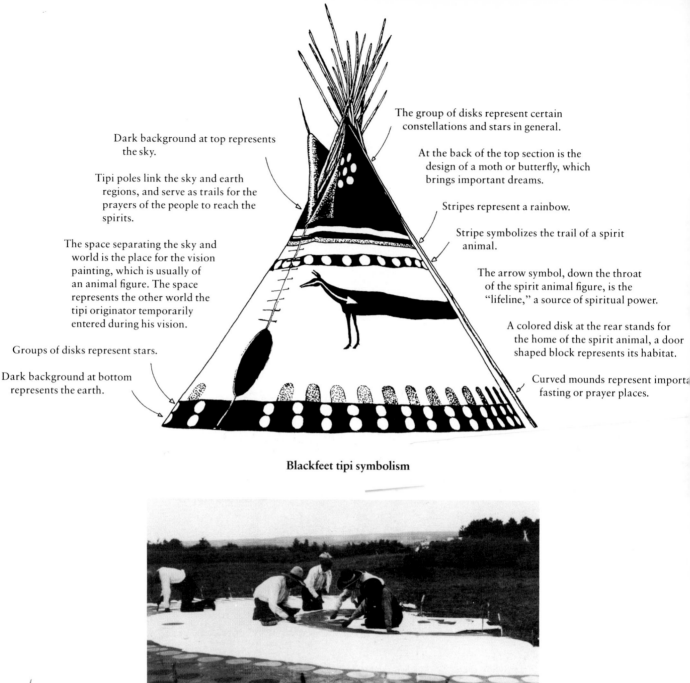

Dark background at top represents the sky.

Tipi poles link the sky and earth regions, and serve as trails for the prayers of the people to reach the spirits.

The space separating the sky and world is the place for the vision painting, which is usually of an animal figure. The space represents the other world the tipi originator temporarily entered during his vision.

Groups of disks represent stars.

Dark background at bottom represents the earth.

The group of disks represent certain constellations and stars in general.

At the back of the top section is the design of a moth or butterfly, which brings important dreams.

Stripes represent a rainbow.

Stripe symbolizes the trail of a spirit animal.

The arrow symbol, down the throat of the spirit animal figure, is the "lifeline," a source of spiritual power.

A colored disk at the rear stands for the home of the spirit animal, a door shaped block represents its habitat.

Curved mounds represent importa[nt] fasting or prayer places.

Blackfeet tipi symbolism

Painted tipis

Paintings on Plains Indian tipis depicted war exploits of the dwelling's head male occupant, or supernatural creatures associated with sacred powers he or his direct ancestors had received during vision quests.

The Kiowa of the southern Plains and the Blackfeet of the northern Plains were renowned for their decorated tipis. For the Blackfeet a standard arrangement of panels *(top left)* was customary. Paints were applied while the semicircular tipi cover was spread on the ground, as shown in this photograph *(middle left)* of Blackfeet decorating a canvas tipi cover. A Blackfeet camp *(bottom left)* photographed by Walter McClintock features the Horse, Snake, and Deer tipis. An Omaha tipi *(above left)* associated with the sacred white buffalo medicine, shows highly realistic cornstalks. The vision tipi *(above right)* of Mother of Bull Weasel, a Crow from Montana, has a gigantic eagle on its western wall. The eagle and mythic Thunderbird were the principal messengers of the Creator and represented the most powerful guardian spirits one could receive through a vision.

Around the turn of this century, the anthropologist James Mooney hired Kiowa artists to recreate original tribal designs on miniature tipis. Three of these covers are shown *(overleaf)*: the Bear tipi *(top left)* of the Kiowa Apache, Chief White Man. According to myth, Chief White Man's maternal grandfather, Lone Chief, had a vision of a great bear grasping a tipi in this way, and was told by the bear, "make this tipi and I shall always hold you up." The bear was believed to have the power to cure sickness.

Considered to be the last painted tipi of the tribe, the Battle tipi *(bottom left)* of the Kiowa warrior Little Bluff portrays actions against United States soldiers and enemy tribes in the late 1800s. The original design was given to an ancestor of Little Bluff by a Cheyenne as a token of friendship. The Star tipi *(top right)* of Black Magpie was last set up during the Oak Creek Sun Dance of 1887. The circles represent stars; the cross symbolizes the morning star. A buffalo tail hangs from the unpainted center stripe.

The original version of this Sioux tipi *(bottom right)* was probably associated with the ritual of the Sacred Pipe. The stylized pipe stem on the western wall has wings to emphasize its transcendent power, and is broken into seven sections, standing for the seven original Sioux tribes. Symbols relating to Sioux cosmology cover both sides; the large suns on the east and west walls are feathered, for the Sioux believe the sun is a bird which flies from east to west every day.

165

N

W ● ● E

S

unchi

earth
mound

sacred path

peta
Owihankeshni
'fire of no end'

plan

side view

Sweathouse

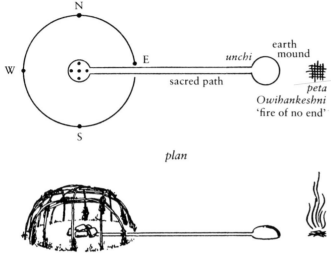

Painted tipis

Paintings on Plains Indian tipis depicted war exploits of the dwelling's head male occupant, or supernatural creatures associated with sacred powers he or his direct ancestors had received during vision quests.

The Kiowa of the southern Plains and the Blackfeet of the northern Plains were renowned for their decorated tipis. For the Blackfeet a standard arrangement of panels (top left) was customary. Paints were applied while the semicircular tipi cover was spread on the ground, as shown in this photograph (middle left) of Blackfeet decorating a canvas tipi cover. A Blackfeet camp (bottom left) photographed by Walter McClintock features the Horse, Snake, and Deer tipis. An Omaha tipi (above left) associated with the sacred white buffalo medicine, shows highly realistic cornstalks. The vision tipi (above right) of Mother of Bull Weasel, a Crow from Montana, has a gigantic eagle on its western wall. The eagle and mythic Thunderbird were the principal messengers of the Creator and represented the most powerful guardian spirits one could receive through a vision.

Around the turn of this century, the anthropologist James Mooney hired Kiowa artists to recreate original tribal designs on miniature tipis. Three of these covers are shown (overleaf): the Bear tipi (top left) of the Kiowa Apache, Chief White Man. According to myth, Chief White Man's maternal grandfather, Lone Chief, had a vision of a great bear grasping a tipi in this way, and was told by the bear, "make this tipi and I shall always hold you up." The bear was believed to have the power to cure sickness.

Considered to be the last painted tipi of the tribe, the Battle tipi (bottom left) of the Kiowa warrior Little Bluff portrays actions against United States soldiers and enemy tribes in the late 1800s. The original design was given to an ancestor of Little Bluff by a Cheyenne as a token of friendship. The Star tipi (top right) of Black Magpie was last set up during the Oak Creek Sun Dance of 1887. The circles represent stars; the cross symbolizes the morning star. A buffalo tail hangs from the unpainted center stripe.

The original version of this Sioux tipi (bottom right) was probably associated with the ritual of the Sacred Pipe. The stylized pipe stem on the western wall has wings to emphasize its transcendent power, and is broken into seven sections, standing for the seven original Sioux tribes. Symbols relating to Sioux cosmology cover both sides; the large suns on the east and west walls are feathered, for the Sioux believe the sun is a bird which flies from east to west every day.

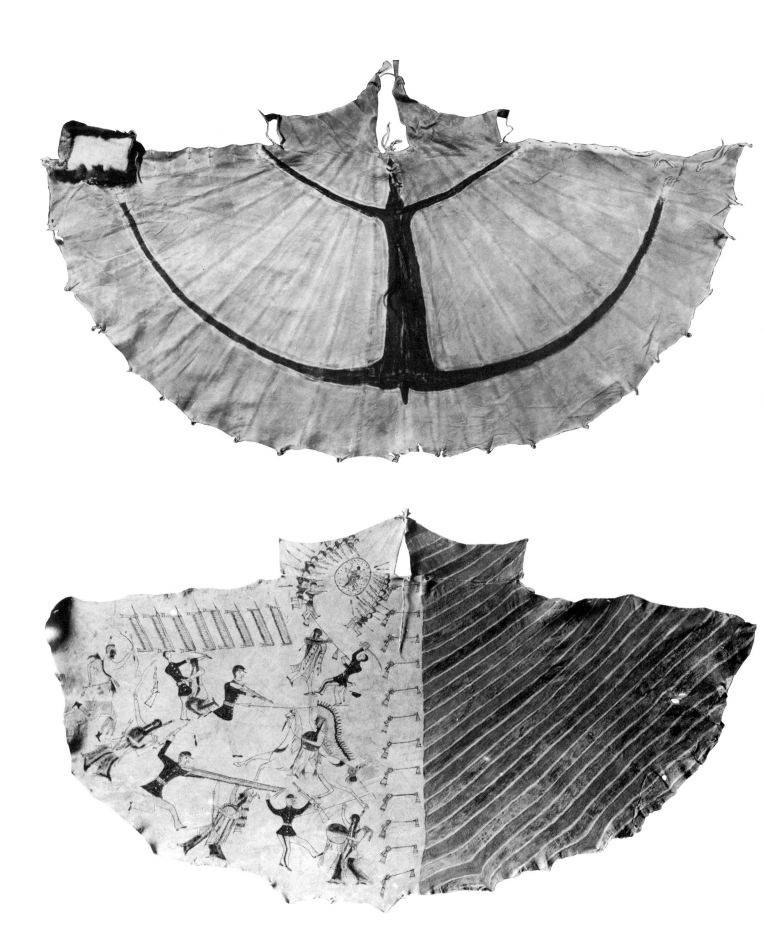

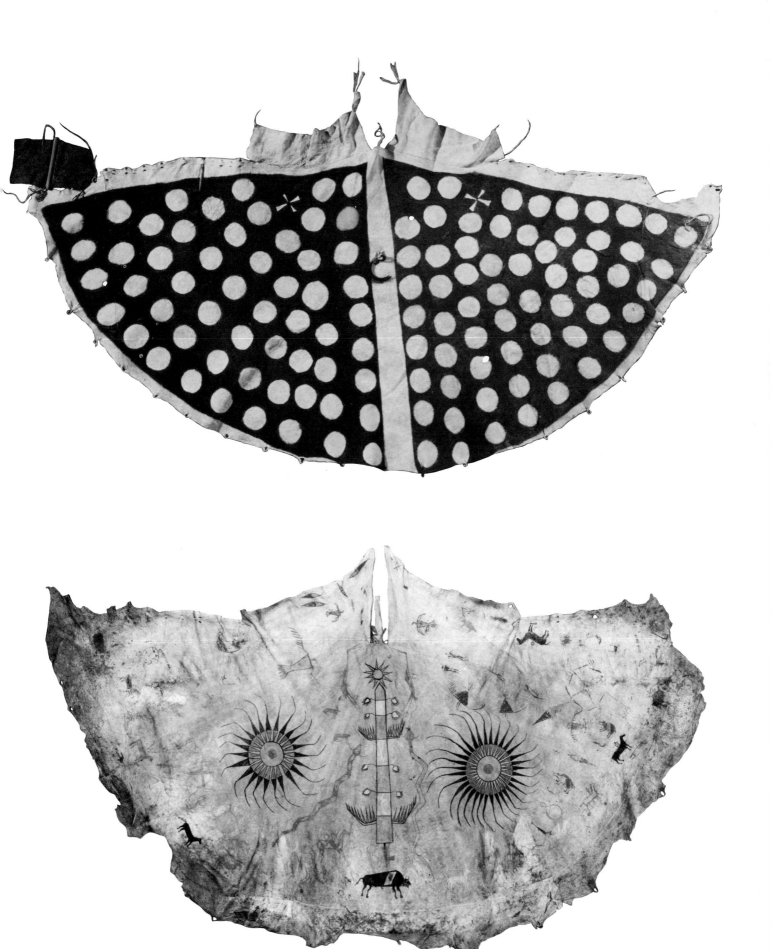

CEREMONIAL STRUCTURES

Special tipis, built and decorated to house ceremonies and sacred objects, occupied honored spots inside the camp circle. Within the Huthuga camp circle of the Omaha, three such lodges were set up adjacent to the clans responsible for them. In addition, the keepers of the seven sacred pipes of the Omaha erected their dwellings at designated locations.

The holiest religious structure built by most of the twenty or so major Plains Indian tribes was for the Sun Dance. According to the Cheyenne myth, the look and construction of their Sun Dance lodge originated in an ancient vision quest. The tribe, facing starvation, met in a large tipi circle and chose a man named Erect Horns to undertake a quest for their salvation. Accompanied by a chief's wife, Erect Horns traveled many days before discovering a hollow mountain. The couple entered the mountain and, during a lightning storm, saw that the interior resembled a Sun Dance lodge. There they learned how to construct the building and perform its ceremony. Upon their return, they conducted the first Cheyenne Sun Dance, and the buffalo herds returned.

Sun Dance lodges resembled circular fences about 40 to 50 feet in diameter, connected to the fork of a centrally placed cottonwood tree trunk by long radiating rafters. During the ceremony, this Sun Dance pole was the pivot of the cosmos, the conduit for collective prayers and individual sacrifices made inside the lodge. Always chopped down under a Sun Dance priest's instructions, it was borne to the construction site by appointed men who could not let it touch the ground. The crotch atop the pole was stuffed with willow branches or buffalo grass to represent the nest of the Thunderbird, the mediator for the dancers who pledged to fast and dance for four days in order to receive life-guiding visions.

Like all Sun Dance lodges, the structure built by the Arapaho, a tribe

Sun Dance lodges

Over twenty Plains tribes built temporary enclosures for their highly sacred Sun Dance. Its centerpiece was a forked cottonwood tree, freshly cut each year. Sapling rafters radiated out to a circular fence enclosing the central area for prayer, fasting, meditation, curing, self-mutilation and rituals for the renewal of the tribe's cosmos and welfare. This center pole and frame of an Arapaho Sun Dance lodge *(right)* was photographed in 1893. The side walls and sometimes the rafters were covered with brush or, later, old canvas tipi covers.

A Cheyenne drawing *(bottom right)* shows a typical Sun Dance lodge in profile, with a line of dancers who have pledged to go through the ordeal facing the central pole. As shown in a floor diagram of a contemporary Ute-Shoshone Sun Dance lodge *(bottom left)*, a buffalo head often hung from the central pole.

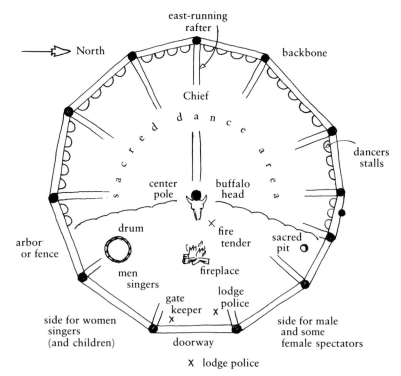

Modern Sun Dance lodge plan

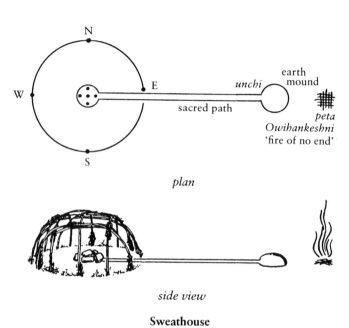

N

W

E

S

unchi

earth
mound

sacred path

*peta
Owihankeshni*
'fire of no end'

plan

side view

Sweathouse

Sacred structures

Sweathouses are still built by all Plains Indian tribes. The plan *(far left)* of the Sioux *Inipi,* or purification lodge, shows the sacred path between a fire, where rocks are heated, and the lodge pit where the rocks are watered to produce steam once the lodge frame is covered with hides or cloth. Plenty Bird, a Northern Cheyenne from Montana, sits within his sweathouse *(top left).* The frame of a special Crow sweathouse *(middle left)* contains 44 willows, as decreed in a vision.

Another sacred structure by contemporary Indians is the tipi that shelters Native American Church services, which use the peyote cactus as a sacramental food. Kickapoo artist, Ernest Spybuck shows a peyote meeting *(bottom left)* in progress. In the Cheyenne engraving *(bottom)* on a silver water cup of a peyote meeting's floor plan, the centerpiece is the crescent-shaped earthen altar with wood laid in its curve ready to light. Celebrants sing and pray around the perimeter; stars indicate seating for ritual officials. Firewood is piled outside the eastern doorway.

closely allied to the Cheyenne, faced east. Inside on an altar lay sod, rabbit bush, a buffalo skull, and a small wooden disc, all of which were said to symbolize the Earth and its waters and abundance of fruit and meat. At the center, the cottonwood tree stood for a cosmic tree that was climbed by a mythic woman in order to reach the upper world. It both symbolized the Indians' supreme deity and transmitted their prayers to him. An old-style garden digging stick laid in the crotch was said to represent the tool the woman used to uproot a bush and peer down on the world below.

In the 1880s, the Sun Dance was banned by the U.S. government. Christian missionaries frowned upon all aspects of native religion, but especially the self-torture, a form of personal sacrifice involved in the ritual. Later, however, a version of the ceremony omitting self-torture passed from the Shoshone to the Crow. Observers who happened upon the ritual now were told that the rafters of the Sun Dance lodge stood for the twelve apostles of Jesus Christ. After the ban was lifted in 1934, piercing the flesh as an offering to the Great Spirit was practiced again, first on the Rosebud reservation in South Dakota among Sioux traditionalists, who passed it on to other tribes.

Another ritual structure built by the Plains Indians was the sweat bath. It was made of bent saplings covered with buffalo hides. Often the wood was willow, and the pieces either were tied together or the leafy boughs were wound around each other to hold them fast. Offerings of tobacco tied in little bags often were fastened to the frame, and a buffalo skull was placed beside or on top of the hut. To create a sweat bath, carefully chosen sandstone rocks were heated in a large fire until they were cherry-red and then taken into the lodge and dropped into a central pit. After the participants entered, the door flap was dropped and water was ladled onto the rocks. Each tribe had its own symbolic interpretation of the structure and its own procedure for prayer and song. The participants used whips of sage or buffalo tail to draw the stinging steam into their skin. After the ritual, it was common to bathe in the river, even in winter.

Plains tribes built other structures and spaces for sacred occasions. The Crow constructed a ten-pole conical frame with a rolled-up cover that was fringed with leafy willows for the initiation rites of their Tobacco Society, a religious association that cultivated a rare species of tobacco believed to bestow prosperity on the entire tribe. Blackfeet women's societies met in special enclosures walled by upright travois frames. On their vision-seeking fasts deep in the wilderness, young men carefully built stone and grass platforms on prominent buttes, where they prayed and fasted for days as they sought visitations from supernatural beings.

In the late nineteenth century, the tipi was chosen as the temple for the Native American Church, a sect whose sacramental food is the hallucinogenic cactus known as peyote. These tipis still are erected with special care for the all-night ritual of prayer, song, and confession. Ground cloths are arranged around the grassy perimeter for worshipers to sit on. Firewood, cut to uniform length, is stacked outside the eastern doorway and fed to a blaze tended by a "fire chief" using a carved poker. The fire burns all night beside an altar hearth of earth, finely shaped like a crescent moon, with a line symbolizing the "peyote road" running along its crest.

TODAY

Tipis are widely used today by Native Americans and non-Indians alike. Cottage industries advertise mail-order canvas versions in all sizes, and manuals provide instructions for adding wooden floors, stoves, rain covers, water-catching basins, and truck racks for transporting tipi poles. In our pursuit of traditional tipis, we visited North Dakota's new state museum in Bismarck a few years ago to examine a patched-up buffalo hide tipi cover. Museum records revealed little about its origin, but to Sioux specialist Raymond J. DeMallie its designs suggested Sioux provenance. Stylized pipe stems lined the western wall above a buffalo head, feathered suns were on the north and south walls, and more pipe stems were positioned above the door.

What particularly drew our attention, however, were two drawings flanking the eastern entrance. To the right, a woman was leading a horse whose travois carried a hide bundle. A dog pulled a smaller travois beside them. The left panel showed the tipi in place—the woman was using the lacing pins as her ladder while she finished closing the cover near the smoke hole. On the south wall of her dwelling hung a bright yellow sun. A story seemed to unfold: A man had drawn on the doorway of his home the tipi-as-world in the stages of its creation and had proudly emphasized the role of his own wife as archetypal woman in that process. It was the only time we ever saw Indian architecture illustrated on a building itself.

During the 1979 Festival of American Folklife in Washington, D.C., we witnessed the continuity of tipi artistry. We had invited George and Molly Kicking Woman from the Blackfeet reservation near Browning, Montana, in the hope they would replicate a tipi painting known to be the ceremonial property of her family. Mrs. Kicking Woman was unwilling to reproduce that still-potent cover merely for display. It was the wrong time of year for the proper preliminary rites, and assistants were missing. However, she did reproduce another well-known tipi whose rights and responsibilities of

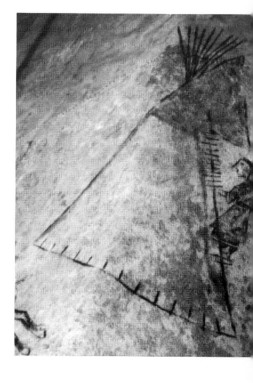

172

Architectural continuity

The woman's role in tipi construction is illustrated *(above left)* in a painting near the entryway of a buffalo hide tipi from North Dakota. The tipi maker laces the lodge together while standing on the pins already inserted below; a yellow sun blazes at her left. At the 1979 Festival of American Folklife in Washington, D.C. *(bottom left)*, Ernest Doybei, a Kiowa from Oklahoma, wove willows into a traditional arbor roof, while beside him fellow Southern Plains builders enclosed a three-pole tipi with a bloodweed windbreak. Crow Indians of central Montana *(above)* host the world's largest gathering of tipis every August along the Little Big Horn River, photographed in 1982.

ownership had expired. It was the Yellow Otter tipi, whose design had been dreamed by a warrior named Big Snake long ago. With help from festival staff and passers-by, the magical otters that had once guarded Big Snake and his family were depicted on a tall tipi beside Constitution Avenue.

The largest collection of tipis in the world can be found on the Crow reservation in south-central Montana on the third weekend in August. The Crows were renowned for their tanned white tipi covers and their love of tall poles, which extended almost as far above the smoke hole as they did below it. Today, tipis, tents, and trailers cover the traditional Sun Dance grounds along the Little Big Horn River during Crow Fair, a time for Crows to host Indian and other visitors from across the country. Some years ago we helped Bill Russell, then a tribal judge, cut new tipi poles for the event. In the Pryor Mountains we found thick stands of tall lodgepole pine. Cutting and trimming twenty-five poles, we loaded them on to a special pickup frame he used to transport his tipi to peyote meetings and summer powwows. Back at Russell's family camp near Lodge Grass we stripped off the bark and smoothed the knots with a draw knife.

On the eve of Crow Fair we helped erect the tipi on the spot where Bill's family camps each year. Among the hundred or more modern tipis were the last of the old canvas covers painted with dream symbols. Leaning against the nearby cottonwood trees were bunches of graying tipi poles from former encampments. Among the forest of tents from different tribes, the Crow lodges were easily identifiable by the evergreen tips of their freshly peeled poles.

4 PIT HOUSE and EXTENDED TIPI

PLATEAU

On a trek through the Nicola Valley of interior British Columbia in the 1890s, an amateur ethnographer from the Shetland Islands named James Teit inspected the caved-in remains of an old-style Plateau Indian "pit house." Teit's Thompson Indian guides described how these circular, dug-out dwellings were framed, roofed with dirt from their own floor excavation, and heated with central fires that kept their inhabitants alive through the long Canadian winters.

Teit settled among the various Salish-speaking tribes of the western Plateau, learning their languages and becoming a staunch advocate for their civil and cultural rights. As he won their trust, the Thompson tribe shared their beliefs with him. They described their concept of the world as a huge, circular lodge divided into four compartments, each associated with one of the four cardinal directions. This pattern is reflected in the spatial arrangement of their old pit houses, which were divided by four roof beams. They believed that after death one's soul left the world and crossed a river to the east where it resided in the land of ghosts. Teit learned that this afterworld also was imagined as a round dwelling made of granite enclosing a landscape of trees and hills. Once a soul arrived there, it enjoyed a good life, joking and dancing with old friends. To the Thompson, as to many Indian people, it seemed natural to envision their cosmology in architectural terms.

The Plateau region of northwestern America is an expanse of tablelands, high valleys, and lava beds locked between the Rocky Mountains to the east and the coastal and Cascade mountain ranges in Canada and the United States, respectively, to the west. In the northerly stretch where Teit traveled, pine forests alternate with grasslands along the great bend of the Fraser River. Here, Salish-speaking tribes such as the Thompson, Shuswap, and Lillooet fished and hunted and foraged for wild plants. To the southeast lay other Salish-speaking tribes such as the Okanagan, Flathead, and Sanpoil and their Sahaptin-speaking neighbors, the Kutenai, Yakima, and Nez Perce. Their diet of ground tubers, fish, and berries was supplemented by hunting buffalo. Along the upper Columbia river system lived tribes who spoke Upper Chinook and lived off wild carrots, sturgeon, and salmon.

Even before the coming of Europeans, the Plateau was a crossroads for cultural influences. Trade goods and ideas for building rectangular houses came by way of rivers that cut west to the Northwest coast. European culture made an impact here before Europeans actually arrived. Through mountain passes that opened eastward to the Great Plains came the trappings of an equestrian and buffalo-hunting life style, most notably the hide-covered tipi. While the architectural ancestry of the region remains unclear, most tribal traditions seem to agree that their oldest house form was the pit house.

In the "Chinook jargon," which western Plateau Indian traders used to haggle in a common tongue, the word for pit house was *kekuli* house. Each tribe dug out, framed, and sized the dwelling in its own way. Despite this structural variety, however, early anthropologists proposed an intercontinental pedigree for the western pit house based upon the common feature of being constructed over an excavated floor. The diffusion hypothesis offered in the early twentieth century by such scholars of Indian architecture as T.T. Waterman and Ralph Linton was that an earth-insulated, semisubterranean lodge had originated in northeastern Asia and then passed across the Bering

174

Plateau houses

The Plateau region was a crossroads for trade and architectural influences. Bounded by the Fraser and Columbia River drainages, it encompasses southern British Columbia, Washington state, and parts of Oregon and Idaho, as shown on map *(left)*.

North America's oldest house type, the pit house *(right)* was superseded on the Plateau by the mat lodge. With the availability of canvas, the mat lodge form expanded. The large cloth lodge *(below)* was photographed on the Umatilla reservation in northern Oregon on July 4, 1900.

"reservation" July 4, 1900.
Maj. Moorhouse

Strait, where it was expressed in the Arctic winter house. It was then borrowed by Plateau people, and next moved southeast to emerge as the Great Plains earthlodge. Finally, the idea was transmitted to the Southwest, where it produced the Mogollon and Basketmaker pit house forms. The problem with this grand scheme is that it treats a common-sense solution to extreme cold—semisubterranean flooring—as a specific trait suggesting single invention and group-to-group diffusion.

By the time of classic Plateau culture, which archeologists date from A.D. 1200 to 1300, most tribes were concentrated in the north and west and occupied pit houses in permanent winter encampments along major streams. Prehistoric sites reveal clusters of three or four of their saucer-shaped floors, most averaging 3 feet deep and from 25 to 40 feet in diameter. Shortly thereafter the wood-house forms of the Northwest Coast apparently proved attractive to tribes like the Wishram, who lived along the Plateau's western rim. The nearby Yakima apparently kept their traditional mat coverings, but placed them over pole frames modeled after the gabled Northwest Coast buildings.

By the mid-eighteenth century, some tribes in the southern Plateau had begun to abandon pit houses in favor of mat-covered, multifamily structures, while the more northerly groups followed suit less than a century later. It is unclear whether this housing shift signified changes brought about by European diseases, changes in social organization, or food-gathering strategies, or a combination of such factors.

In summer, many Plateau Indians set up lighter pole-framed shelters, including small conical lodges, lean-tos, and double lean-tos that faced each other. All were roofed with sewn reed or grass mats and usually were pitched at favorite fishing grounds or in open meadows. Once they had acquired horses, however, the southern and eastern Plateau groups carried their buffalo-hide tipis year-round. Then, as cloth became available through trade or government issue after the 1880s, canvas rapidly replaced skins as tipi coverings. Tribes like the Nez Perce and Yakima elongated the tipi frame, draping it with many covers, for festive gatherings at seasonal foraging camps and to accommodate guests during formal gift exchanges and relatives and friends at funeral rites.

PIT HOUSE

The Thompson Indians escorted Teit to their old campsites in the river valleys, where the climate was mildest and mountains to the east blocked the wind. Three or four pit houses made up each hamlet, with fifteen to thirty residents in each dwelling. When a new house was needed, the Thompson would begin to measure the floor excavation around mid-November. First they crossed two bark ropes the length of the proposed pit at right angles, pointing their ends in the semicardinal directions. Stakes marked the center and quarter midpoints; then quarter circles were scored in the ground to complete the circumference. Using sharpened sticks and flat-bladed wooden scrapers, the women broke up the earth and hauled it to the side in baskets until they had a hole 3 to 4 feet deep, with sloping sides.

Freshly cut logs were dragged to the site and stripped of bark. Four served

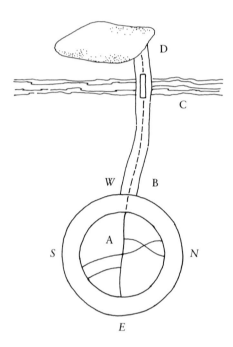

Pit house cosmology

Pit houses figured in the cosmology of the Thompson Indians of interior British Columbia. Drawn by a Thompson Indian, the diagram *(above)* shows his concept of the afterlife. (A) After death the soul leaves this world, depicted as a four "room" pit house. (B) Toward the sunset across a river (C) there lies the land of ghosts (D), a huge granite lodge where the soul jokes and dances with old friends.

Pit house architecture

The plan and cross-section drawings *(right)* by James Teit show the Thompson Indian pit house in stages of construction, ca. 1900. The plan drawing, viewed counterclockwise from noon, shows the basic framing, its layering with tightly nestled poles, and its final cover of pine needles, grass, and earth. The cross section reveals the angled support posts and the entry ladder tipped into the sunken floor. The floor is about 24 feet in diameter, and the smokehole is about 15 feet above the floor.

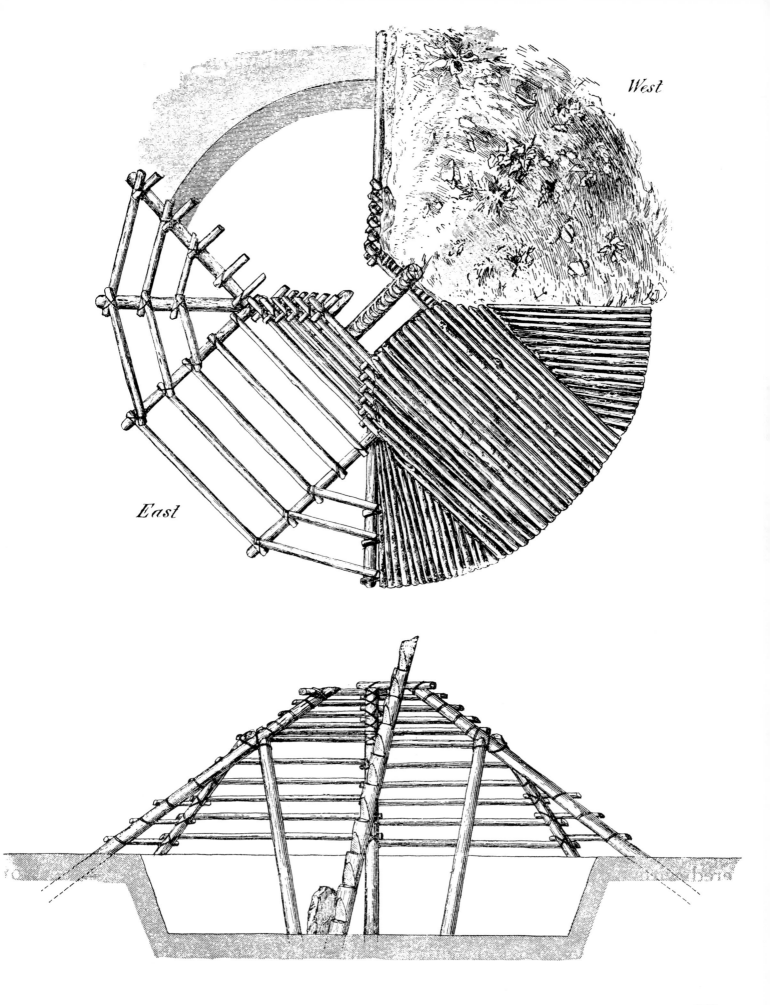

Plateau pit house construction

The shape and construction of pit houses varied throughout the Plateau region. Photographs of abandoned Nicola Valley dwellings *(above and left)* show the style of the Thompson Indians. Although this pyramidal form was typical of the north, the nearby Shuswap sometimes added two more central posts and main beams, producing a hexagonal smokehole.

Neighbors of both the Thompson and Shuswap, the Lillooet dug a rectangular pit and set the rafter butts in the corners at the pit's base, supporting the main beams with struts that sloped diagonally into the floor. Among the Klamath, the winter house combined a pit house foundation with a mat-covered tipi-style structure of crossed poles, but the pit was shallow and earth was banked against the exterior.

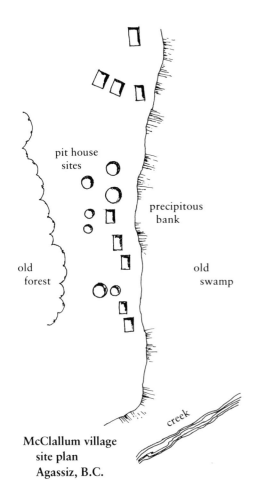

McClallum village site plan Agassiz, B.C.

pit house sites

precipitous bank

old forest

old swamp

creek

as main house-posts and were planted in holes in the floor at an angle roughly parallel to the excavation walls (in treeless regions driftwood was saved for this purpose). Their tops were notched to support the four main roof beams, whose butt ends were sunk 2 feet into the topsoil at steep angles. Supple willows fastened these beams, which almost converged at the smoke hole, and also secured pairs of struts that braced them.

A webbing of spaced rafters was lashed in concentric circles from pit to smoke hole. This supported a snug layer of poles that was thickly padded with pine needles or grass. In the upper Plateau, where rainfall was heavy, cedar bark with the curved side up was laid at this stage. Finally, earth from the original pit was spread over the roof and stamped down, and a notched-log ladder was lowered through the smoke hole. With twenty to thirty people cooperating on the building, a pit house could be finished in a day. The following spring, grass sprouted on the roof and, but for the ladder, the dwelling seemed a living part of the landscape.

Pit house shape and construction varied throughout the Plateau. The Shuswap in the north sometimes used six central posts and beams instead of four, producing a conelike profile once the dirt was added. The Lillooet, who lived between the Thompson and Shuswap, dug a more rectangular pit that gave the building a wedgelike look. The Sanpoil adopted a flat-roofed structure, placing their ladder entry at one side and the hearth on the other side. Their roofs were simpler to construct but also drained less effectively. The Shuswap occasionally added a secondary side tunnel that faced southeast, while in the squarer pit houses of the southerly tribes this side entrance was the sole access to the building.

Teit also learned that the Thompson had once paid special attention to the pit house ladder. Its top sometimes was carved into a bird or animal head and then painted to represent the man of the household's guardian spirit. Customarily, it was tilted against the eastern edge of the smoke hole. It was proper to descend the log ladder facing northeast, supporting oneself by gripping the grooves in the back of the ladder with the right hand. The northern Shuswap reversed that protocol, keeping the left hand on the ladder and turning their faces to the southeast. A fireplace usually was located on the north side of the ladder, which was protected from burning by a stone slab. In the main space, the areas marked by the four main posts and beams were known as "rooms," and each was named for a semicardinal direction.

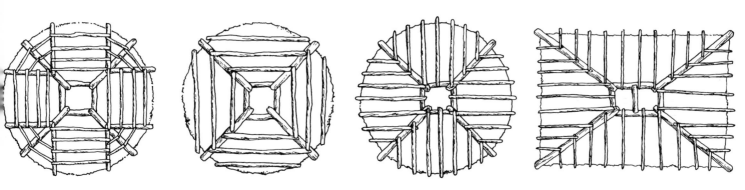

Pit house roof framing plans

MAT HOUSES

The winter mat houses of the southern Plateau were occupied from mid-October to mid-March and had floors dropped a foot or two below ground. They could be extremely long, as the American explorers Lewis and Clark discovered when they visited the Nez Perce along the Columbia River in the winter of 1805-1806: "This village of Tumachemootool is in fact only a single house one hundred and fifty feet long . . . It contains twenty-four fires, about double that number of families, and might perhaps muster a hundred fighting men."

The multifamily structures were a series of simple A-frames secured by horizontal poles lashed in parallel courses about 3 feet apart from base to top. When one or both ends were rounded, they were framed with a semicircle of poles that resembled a tipi frame sliced in half. Perhaps the tribes began to favor these buildings over the older pit house because they were already affected by European stereotypes, which compared Indians to animals; when the Flathead, for instance, were asked whether they had ever built pit houses they would only say that an earlier race of Foolish Folk had made them, who they derisively described as living "in holes in the ground like animals." At the start of the nineteenth century, however, mat houses were already a way for Plateau families who shared clan or kin affiliation to live together. The year before Lewis and Clark's journey, the fur trader Alexander Ross described the inside of a typical Plateau mat lodge: ". . . the fires are made in the center, directly under the ridge pole, and about six or eight feet apart and are in proportion to the number of families who live under the same roof."

The common winter mat house was 25 to 60 feet long, 12 to 15 feet wide, and stood from 10 to 14 feet from floor to ridgepole. The Sanpoil began roofing at ground level, tying on about 4 feet of grass banked with about a half-foot of earth. Then twine-tule roofing mats, about 5 feet wide and from 10 to 15 feet long, were lashed up to the slitlike smoke hole with 3 to 4 inch overlaps. Variations in design were determined by available materials and local climate. The Shuswap sometimes used only grass on the roof; their northern neighbors, the Carrier Indians, squared off one end of the house but partitioned the other into a dog shelter and storage room for food. Most of these winter homes had slightly sunken floors, whose sleeping areas were softened with slough grass mats. In colder regions they were banked with earth and used double doors.

In the nineteenth century, the multifamily winter mat lodge changed from habitation to temple. The Prophet Dance, one of many revitalization movements that provided psychological relief to Indians who were dispirited by disease and warfare, used this building to symbolize the pre-white values it tried to restore. In defiance of government and missionary pressures to abandon these native structures, messianic Indian leaders like Smoholla of the Wanapum tribe held their rituals in converted mat lodges. Smoholla's central Prophet Dance lodge at Priest Rapids on the Columbia River in eastern Washington was about 100 feet long and could hold 120 followers. Today, this religious and cultural movement survives among the Yakima as the *Washat* religion, and its meeting place is still called a "longhouse."

Plateau mat houses

The mat-covered winter structures which were converted into shelters for the late nineteenth century nativistic religions were built along the major watercourses of the southern Plateau. At Priest Rapids on the Columbia River, a group of Wanapum builders unroll tule mats over the frame of a mat house *(top left)*, ca. 1952. In the mat house frame *(bottom left)* one can see the slightly excavated floor. These buildings served tribespeople as sacred structures during ceremonies *(bottom right)* which gave thanks for the natural foods—fish, berries, and roots—of their region.

SUMMER HOUSES and TIPIS

Extended tipis and mat lodges

Plateau people had always enlarged their mat houses to accommodate new occupants. When they obtained canvas, this practice continued. The Yakima holiday lodge *(above left)* was photographed by Edward S. Curtis ca. 1910. After the Nez Perce Chief Joseph died in 1904, a feast in his honor was held in an extended canvas tipi *(lower left)* photographed by Curtis. The gable-roofed, mat-covered house *(above)*, built by the Umatilla, was probably a version of an older type of extendable rectangular house.

For temporary use during fishing and berrying seasons, Plateau people put up new pole-and-mat structures or simply repaired those from the previous summer. The fishing shelters usually were built on the first terrace above the rapids for easy access to the river banks. Their dimensions often depended on how much volume was needed for hanging fish-drying racks, but they averaged 60 feet in length. However, in 1811 at Cabinet Rapids along the Columbia River, the surveyor David Thompson visited a Wentchi fishery where the two rectangular houses loosely covered with rush mats were large enough to contain 800 people.

As early as pit-house times, most Plateau people also used during the summer one- or two-family conical dwellings covered with mats. To craft their mats, the Lower Kutenai gathered Indian hemp or dogbane after the leaves had dropped in autumn. Then they split, scraped, and seasoned the stalks for a year before braiding them into long ropes that were sewn together. Three or four of these large coverings could roof a single dwelling.

The Upper Kutenai, however, used buffalo-hide tipi covers after the practice of the Plains Indians. Once they acquired canvas, the Nez Perce, Umatilla, and Yakima expanded the cloth tipi much as they did the mat tipi. For influential leaders like the well-known Nez Perce Chief Joseph, such homes signified resistance to government pressure to adopt the white man's ways; when he died in 1904, his funeral feast was held in such an elongated tipi.

Building with mats

Mat-making was an important skill for Plateau peoples. Coarse tules or cattails were sewn together from materials gathered *(right)* along lake shores and marshes. Instead of tule, the Lower Kootenai used dogbane or Indian hemp and twined the mats that softened their floors. Mats were overlapped on a tipi frame *(left)*, or they were tied and held down with additional poles *(above)*, as among the Umatilla.

185

TODAY

The floorplan of the winter mat lodge of the Nez Perce and Yakima Indians of eastern Washington was preserved by the Washat religion. Most of its meeting houses are aligned on an east-west axis and retain the rounded western end and squared eastern end. Instead of poles and mats, however, they are built of concrete blocks and, with the exception of the earthen-floored buildings at the Yakima's White Swan and Priest Rapids communities, have floors of bricks or planks.

The Priest Rapids structure near Vantage on the Columbia River was reputedly the most conservative. Until 1956, when high winds blew it over, it retained its tule-mat roof and was surrounded by smaller, mat-covered family houses. Despite the storm, enough framing still stood to support a new corrugated metal roof. Longhouses for the Washat faith were erected by the Nespelem, Umatilla, and Nez Perce as recently as the 1960s.

As for pit houses, by the 1900s most Plateau people were reluctant to discuss how they had been made, fearing the ridicule of outsiders who might still compare them to the dens of hibernating animals. Among a few traditional Chilcotin and Shuswap families, however, such lore was not lost. The Mary Thomas family of Salmon Arm, British Columbia, for example, smoked salmon in the old way, tanned hides, and occasionally built a kekuli house. Mrs. Thomas and her sons had built a full-size pit house for display in 1974 for exhibition at the Kelowna Museum south of Salmon Arm. Five years later we invited them to construct a second exhibition pit house for the 13th Festival of American Folklife in Washington, D.C.

When we interviewed Mrs. Thomas at the festival in 1979, she explained that the older Shuswap style reserved the separate, side doorway for women. Narrow troughs extending from the western sides of abandoned house depressions along the South Thompson and Little rivers tend to confirm her claim. During the demonstration, Louis Thomas and his brothers notched and lashed the main beam braces and horizontal purloins so that the frame resembled, as they described it, "a spider web made of wood." They stomped on pine bark to flatten it and laid it on the roof frame, topping it with grassy sod. A wedge-shaped section of roof was left open, however, so visitors could stand in the shadow of the Washington Monument and peer down into the oldest house type in the Western hemisphere.

Pit houses today

The knowledge of how to construct the ancient Plateau pit house has not been lost. At Anahim Lake in the central plateau of British Columbia, Museum of Man archeologist Roscoe Wilmeth excavated pit house remains, then engaged local Chilcotin Indians to reconstruct one on the site *(above)*. At the 1979 Festival of American Folklife in Washington, D.C., Mary Thomas and her sons built a Shuswap version *(right)* of the old semisubterranean house form.

North Pole

Bering Strait

King Island

Bering Strait
Eskimo

Point Barrow

North Alaskan
Eskimo

Arctic Ocean

THULE

Greenland

Aleutian Islands

Aleut

Kobuk R.

Mackenzie
Eskimo

Davis Strait

Alaska
Canada

Kutchin

*Gulf of
Alaska*

Mackenzie R.

*Pelly
Bay*

Iglulik

Netsilik
Eskimo

Central
Eskimo

Baffin Island

Greenland
Eskimo

Copper
Eskimo

Arctic Circle

Pacific Ocean

Subarctic

Hudson Bay

Frobisher Ba

Mistassani Cree

Labrado
Eskimo

Montagnais-Naskapi

5 WINTER HOUSE, IGLU, and TENT

ARCTIC

Seasonal houses

To survive harsh winters and brief summers in the Arctic required effective patterns of camp movement and house building. In each season, the Eskimos traveled to familiar locations for fishing and hunting and used appropriate building types.

The stone cut (above), by native artist Joe Talirunili, illustrates summer and winter architecture—a skin tent (summer) and a snow house (winter)—and hunting by kayak in summer and dog team in winter, ca. 1965.

Copper Eskimo build a snow house settlement (below) at Bernard Harbor, ca. 1915.

On the Norsemen's second voyage across the Atlantic a thousand years ago, a Viking scouting party found in Labrador what was probably the first sign to Europeans that any people existed in the Americas. Their *Graenlandinga Saga* relates that in searching for a settlement site near the shores of what is today Lake Melville, they noticed "three humps on the sandy beach just in front of the headland. When they went close they found that these were three skin-boats, with three men under each of them." These overnight shelters used by the Labrador Eskimos sound remarkably similar to the temporary camps improvised from overturned walrus-skin boats called *umiak*, which still are used by some Eskimo hunting groups. Consistency of architectural pattern over considerable time and geographical range is one hallmark of Eskimo culture. Another is the ingenuity that went into Eskimo building design, which allowed survival in one of the harshest climates on Earth.

From northeastern Siberia along the countless bays and inlets of the Arctic to eastern Greenland, the coastal homeland of the Eskimo who lived north of the timberline covered more than 4,000 miles. Their separate cultural worlds were distinguished by subtle variations in language and life style. Each was a small, seminomadic dialect group whose patterns of summer and winter hunting were dictated by variations in animal resources, building materials, and environmental conditions. For purposes of study, however, scholars have distinguished six provinces of Arctic Eskimo culture: (1) Greenland Eskimo; (2) Labrador Eskimo; (3) Central Eskimo—including the well-known Baffin Islanders, the Southhampton Eskimo, the Iglulik, Netsilik, Caribou, Copper, and other groups; (4) Mackenzie Eskimo; (5) North Alaskan Eskimo; and (6) Bering Strait Eskimo, including the Aleut people who occupy islands farther west.

Everywhere, however, Eskimo subsistence patterns, thought, and architecture were influenced by the natural division of their existence into summer and winter, seasons of constant light and incessant darkness, outdoor life and indoor life. In 1577, explorer Martin Frobisher, the first European after the Vikings to visit the Eskimo, observed this stark seasonal division in their dwellings. While around him the Eskimo were living in "tents made of Seale skinns," he did not have to look far to notice winter structures "raised of stones and Whale bones," which they moved into when autumn began.

Like every Arctic visitor, Frobisher was impressed by the way in which their architecture enabled Eskimos to endure such an extreme environment. At the time of his arrival, their "Great White Desert" was home to well over fifty thousand people. Each year, families dispersed to hunt and fish during the summer, then regathered along the sea ice in winter. Between the spring and fall equinoxes, they lived in a world of nearly constant light, which allowed the isolated families to roam the coastline, tundra, and coastal lakes for food. Their route was dictated by caribou migrations, fish spawns, and the brief availability of sparse plant life. During the winter, however, their movements were greatly restricted. They might not see the sun for weeks, and temperatures normally plunged to between 30 and 50 degrees below zero.

While the snow-block dwelling popularly known as *iglu* comes to mind as the characteristic Eskimo house, iglus were probably a recent development limited to the Central Arctic Eskimos. Far more common, across thousands of miles of lakes, rivers, glaciers, and tundra, were winter structures that

exploited the same heat-preserving principle of the snow house, but were framed with whale bone, stone, or driftwood—depending upon available materials—and insulated with layers of dirt, sod, skins, or packed snow. The third Eskimo house type was the summer tent—a pole frame covered with sewn walrus, caribou, or seal skins, and constructed in a myriad of styles— which actually better typified the Eskimo way of life than the iglu.

Eskimos also built a variety of special-use buildings, of which the *kashim*, the men's assembly house used for dancing, singing, and special events, was most prominent. In the Central Arctic these communal enclosures were large snow-block domes that opened into separate domestic sleeping chambers. Elsewhere they were expanded versions of the driftwood or sod winter house. Several Eskimo groups also built menstrual huts, special child-bearing shelters, and dwellings for a mother and child's first three months together. For the brief spell between winter and summer, there were hybrid shelters with ice, sod, or stone walls, and skin roofs. Farther west were found the stilt dwellings of Alaska's King Island or the sod-covered *barabaras* of the Aleutian Islands.

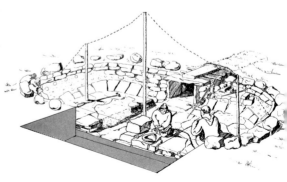

The history of Arctic architecture possibly goes back 25,000 years, according to archeological analysis of house floors along the Kobuk River in Alaska. But clear evidence of early house forms begins with the Old Bering Sea cultures, which archeologists call the ancient Western culture. The remains of their dug-out floors, extended entryways, and rear sleeping porches date back to at least 500 B.C. and resemble the ancient semisubterranean houses of northeastern Asia.

By that time, however, the eastern Arctic was occupied by a prehistoric people known as the Dorset culture. Their unique architectural contribution—which never found its way into the later Eskimo architectural inventory—were long enclosures constructed of waist-high boulder walls and, presumably, a series of tent roofs held up by inner poles. According to Canadian archeologist Peter Schlenderman, who discovered these structures in 1978 on the Knud Peninsula, Ellesmere Island, they were built by late Dorset folk around 800 B.C. From the rows of outdoor hearths apparently associated with these "longhouses," Schlenderman surmised that the structures housed hunting families who gathered along the coast each spring to hunt and fish.

Beginning about A.D. 1000, the Thule, direct ancestors of today's Eskimo, spread their remarkably uniform material culture from the Pacific Coast eastward, reaching Greenland about 1200. Along with such tools as soapstone lamps, dogsleds, and toggle harpoons, the different forms of Thule architecture seem but regional expressions of a common cultural kit. The people spent the summer in tents and the winter in semisubterranean houses. The tents were weighted down with rocks and their fire pits placed outside. The winter houses nearly always faced the shoreline and had lowered floors with raised sleeping platforms and cold-trap passageways to maximize interior temperatures.

WINTER HOUSE

Because building material was extremely scarce across the Arctic, Thule builders framed their winter houses with whatever they could find—rocks, driftwood, chunks of sod, and the ribs, jawbones, skull, and vertebrae of the bowhead whale. The jawbone sometimes served as an arch over the entrance, curved ribs were side posts, bone chunks became wall filling, and baleen was fashioned into drying racks to hold clothing above the soapstone lamps. The most critical Thule innovation was to angle a narrowing passageway steeply down into the ground, then tip it up so that one crawled through a trap door, emerging through the floor into a room 9 to 12 feet in diameter. The effect was that of an ingeniously designed elevated cave. By sealing the passage inside the narrowing tunnel during fierce storms, and carefully tiering the working and sleeping levels within the chamber, body heat and the lamp's flame maintained a livable environment.

This construction system had changed little by the time of Frobisher's visit. The gaping entrance of the Baffin Island winter house was "not much unlike an Oven's mouth," he observed. Its outer walls were built of sod or stone and rose to 4 or 5 feet around the pit. Whale rib or driftwood posts reached from the sides and back to meet rib and jawbone supports in front. One method of covering a roof was to layer seal or walrus skins with dried moss for

Winter houses

Beginning with the Thule Eskimo culture, about a thousand years ago, natives along the polar rim partially sank their houses into the earth or banked them heavily with earth. The sod-roofed winter houses *(above)* of Nunivak Eskimo were photographed at Hooper Bay, Alaska, ca. 1928.

Beside the Ruggles River in northern Ellesmere Island, archeologist Moreau S. Maxwell uncovered in 1958 a thirteenth-century winter house, reconstructed *(left)* in a speculative drawing. The oval floor was 3 feet below ground level; flat sandstone slabs lined floor and wall. Skins, which were probably insulated with snow and supported by center poles, presumably roofed the structure.

insulation. Stone slabs sometimes paved the entrance tunnel. On the front of the house, directly over where the tunnel merged with the floor, was a window made from the dried intestines of the bearded seal. This parchmentlike material, which did not rot and resisted frost, became a translucent window that acted as a beacon for hunters returning home in winter darkness.

One or two soapstone lamps stood on platforms on either side of the sleeping porches in the back half of the interior. Scholar Molly Lee calls such lamps the "cornerstone of life" in these houses. The stone was carved into crescent-shaped basins, with mossy wicks to burn melted blubber. The flames were constantly tended and were crucial "monitors" of the air quality in the heavily insulated structures. If heavy bad air was not forced back down the passageway, and the lighter bad air was not sufficiently vented through a central hole in the roof known as the house's "nose," the flame turned yellow. The turf plug in the nose would then be pulled until the flame burned white again. Ventilation also was regulated by adjusting the passageway doors. With such constant fine-tuning of the winter house's climate, the inhabitants could even feel layers of temperature. At one's feet the air could be quite cool, at waist level a temperate zone prevailed, while one's head, as Eskimo scholar Kaj Birket-Smith put it, projected "a good way into the tropics."

The winter house took various shapes and sizes. Eastern Greenland Eskimos constructed their walls of flat stones, whale ribs, and sod, and commonly backed them steeply into a hillside. An early visitor compared them to "hulls of ships with their keel uppermost." The Northern Greenland Polar Eskimo, whose houses were pear-shaped with high rear walls, constructed their roofs of corbeled sandstone slabs which were counterweighted with boulders and further supported by interior driftwood or bone uprights. Over this was laid sod, earth, more sod, and on occasion a final waterproofing layer of old skins rubbed with fat. Up to three translucent windows might be stitched into the front wall.

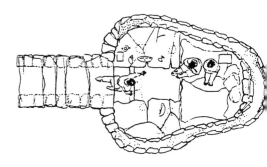

Thule engineering

Thule Eskimos developed an efficient method for warming a winter house. As shown in the elevation and plan *(above)*, they recessed the entrance to the living area, and raised the sleeping platform to take advantage of rising heat. The building also featured a gut-skin window, a ventilation hole, driftwood roof beams, and a sod cover. This was essentially the same technique still used many hundreds of years later in historic-period sod winter houses, such as this abandoned one of stone and turf *(below)* in northern Greenland, photographed ca. 1909. Note the two side door-ways which lead into storerooms, and the window opening for illumination, which would have been covered with gut.

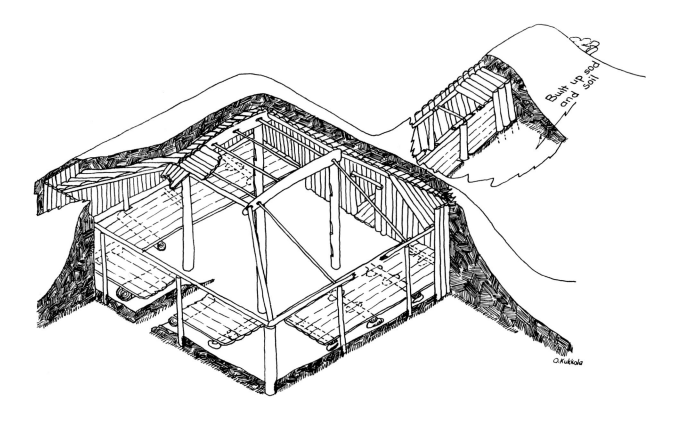

Built up sod and soil

O. Kukkola

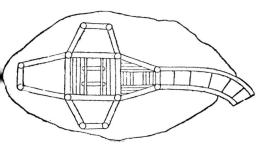

Western house variations

In the western Arctic, where timber was available, sod-covered houses were wood-framed. This reconstruction *(top)* of a western Eskimo house is based on remains at Kukulik on St. Lawrence Island, near the Bering Strait. The structure measured 16 by 17 feet. Two of its posts had notched steps; it was ventilated by a section of hollow whale vertebra attached to the center of the roof. The Mackenzie Delta Eskimo built an unusual cross-shaped house *(above)*, which was framed with logs. This diagram is based on documentation by Émile Petitot, who visited the western Arctic in 1876.

The extremely wide Eastern Greenland winter house was distinctive in that sleeping platforms lined both front and back walls. Softened with layers of dry heather and skins, these areas were used as work space and for children's daytime play, but became communal beds at night. Up to fifty people might share a sleeping platform, which might be 14 feet long and up to 50 feet wide. But sleeping spaces were strictly assigned by family or age: young, unmarried men and guests generally slept against the front walls, while families lay together beneath skins in 4-foot-wide spaces in the rear. The wife in each family owned her own soapstone lamp, cooking pot, and rack for drying damp garments.

Farther west, the type of house built by Eskimos living near the mouth of the Mackenzie River featured a distinctive cruciform floor plan. Since trees were available, the roof was framed of ax-dressed and cribbed logs, with four long posts holding up the major roof beams. The leaning-log walls were chinked with humus, then layered with dirt and snow, and sometimes finished with a ladling of water, which quickly froze into a heat-retaining ice shell. The living area inside was divided into three single-family alcoves, each with its own sleeping platform. During the winter, families departed from and returned to this central house, moving temporarily into snow houses to hunt seals on the sea ice.

The greatest variety of wood-framed winter houses was found along the North Alaskan coast. Local forms differed in their length and number of entry tunnels (some that were also used in summer had an above-ground doorway), the location of their sleeping platforms, and whether they were heated by central fireplaces or oil lamps. In the southernmost Alaskan territory, the Indian architecture of the Northwest Coast was highly influential. There, marginal Eskimo groups used sod-covered gabled structures built on a rectangular plan apparently modeled after the plank buildings of the Tlingit Indians.

IGLU

The Eskimo word iglu originally meant any permanent, roofed dwelling made of solid materials—in brief, any winter house. In the nineteenth century, however, when, some scholars suggest, the Polar Eskimos learned the technique for vaulting snow blocks from Canadian immigrants, the term among non-Eskimos became associated solely with the domed dwelling built of snow blocks.

For most Eskimos to the east and west, these snow houses were used only for protection against winter weather for short periods or as temporary bases while hunting. Only the Central Eskimo groups between Labrador and the Mackenzie Delta occupied them all winter, and they engineered iglu complexes with connecting passageways, cold traps, and communal dance chambers.

Although recorded Eskimo mythology has no tales of the origin of the snow house, some of their stories suggest that the iglu played a role in their culture. The Iglulingmuit people tell of snow-domed houses that rose from the ground and took their occupants on flights into the night. Their account of the birth of the sun and moon describes a mythic pair of siblings who chase each other out of a snow house and spiral up to the "dome of the heavens."

Whether iglu construction was of native origin—deriving possibly from the domed skin tents used in parts of the Arctic—or was a foreign import, it was a feat of engineering. The catenary shape of its roof prevented caving or bulging due to its optimum height-to-diameter ratio. Skilled iglu builders could complete the basic dome in a few hours, whereupon it could be adjusted to exploit all of the heating principles developed by the Thule builders.

Constructing an iglu usually took no more than two men, but often the whole family pitched in, with women and children helping to chink between the snow blocks and pack on the last coating of snow. The quality of snow selected for the iglu blocks was the builder's first concern. The Eskimo builder

The snow house

The basic iglu was a hemispheric shell of frozen water. It could be built by one man for an overnight shelter, or it could grow into a cluster of snow bubbles linked by inner passageways to house many families for much of the winter. An Eskimo piles up blocks *(above)* for his small iglu at Spence Bay, Northwest Territories, ca. 1951. The basic tool for snow-house building was the snow knife *(right)*, which was originally made of bone. Generally two men worked together on an iglu, as shown in this photograph *(below)* from the Canadian Arctic Expedition among the Copper Eskimo, 1913-1918.

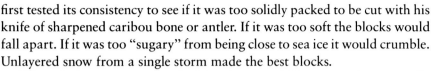

first tested its consistency to see if it was too solidly packed to be cut with his knife of sharpened caribou bone or antler. If it was too soft the blocks would fall apart. If it was too "sugary" from being close to sea ice it would crumble. Unlayered snow from a single storm made the best blocks.

Although the arrangement of Eskimo houses within a camp was generally random rather than socially patterned, the placement of houses was critical to shield inhabitants from the weather. After the sea ice had frozen, the Eskimos began to cluster their iglus out on the ice on east- or south-facing drift slopes to avoid prevailing winds. East or south orientation of the individual houses kept snow from covering the ice window or the ventilation "nose" of the iglu. The passageways also were turned away from incoming drafts. If built on land, the dwellings nestled into the protective lee of cliffs and faced the beach.

First the builders determined the iglu's diameter, which could be between 6 and 15 feet, depending on whether the house was to be a "traveling" structure or more permanent. With the site chosen and floor size established, the block-cutter worked inside the dwelling while the block-positioner remained outside. The cutter first excavated the snow blocks from the floor and passageways of the iglu. The blocks were set in a circle, then seesawing motions of the snow knife shaved them snug and curving slightly inward. Banging on the top and sides of the blocks caused the ice crystals to melt quickly and refreeze—in effect, welding them together.

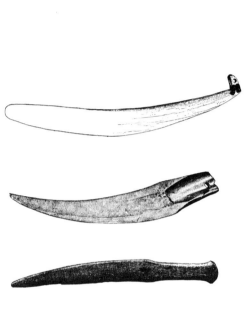

Next, the top of the first layer was angled so that a continuous row of canted blocks could rise to create the dome. The cutter inside passed the snow blocks to his partner outside. Each block, sized by eye and heaved in place, was deliberately cut large so that a few deft swipes of the snow knife could trim it to a tight fit. The blocks spiraled up to the top like a screw. Finally only a keystone snow block capped the shell; it was cut large, twisted out through the top opening, then beveled flush to complete the structure. As the men constructed the passageway tunnel, angling it down then up, the women and children stuck wedge-shaped pieces of snow into the large fissures on the outside of the blocks, then packed the exterior with loose snow, using wooden shovels. Inside, a natural seal was created as the snow aged and iced over. To let in light, a chunk of translucent ice—preferably freshwater ice, often transported by sled from another camp—was fitted into the roof just over the entry tunnel. Sometimes a reflecting snow block was set at right angles to this window to intensify the illumination. A smaller "porch" iglu was almost always added in front.

As work progressed, special taboos were often observed, some suggesting a symbolic tie between house and womb. The first blocks to be cut were for what were known as the "long sides"—where the vital soapstone lamps were to be placed. Blocks for the "broad side," or the rear of the iglu where people slept, were cut next to ensure good luck. If a man desired many children he used a serrated knife to cut the first block for the broad side, slicing outward so the household would not suffer bad fortune. Loose snow chips had to be cleared away from the interior so the house's children would enjoy good luck. Special attention was given to the final building step: The opening for the keystone block had to be as large as possible to ensure easy childbirth for the women. If a family hoped for a son, that block had to be bigger than the block preceding it, and its softest side had to face the rear of the house.

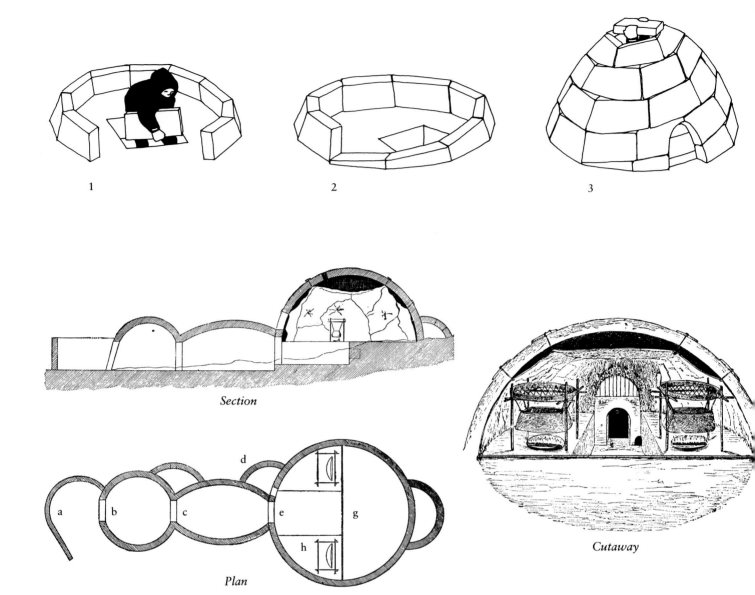

1   2   3

Section

Plan

Cutaway

Iglu architecture

The drawings *(top row)* illustrate iglu construction: (1) A circle is marked in the snow. Snow blocks are cut from within the circle, and the first course is set. The bottom of the trench will be the iglu floor. (2) The first course of blocks is trimmed to begin to form the spiral dome. (3) Blocks are added in a spiral to complete the dome. The edge of each block is angled to slope inward, creating the domical shape. A door hole is cut on the side facing away from the wind. From within the iglu the builder places the final block, shaping it with his knife to fit into the opening. Snow is packed over the blocks to seal all cracks. Tunnels and storage chambers are added.

The plan, section, and cutaway of a two-family snow house was documented by anthropologist Franz Boas at Repulse Bay: (a) Curved wall to prevent wind and snow from blowing directly into the house. (b) Small dome about 6 feet high; the door is about 2 ½ feet high. (c) Elliptical domed passage. The door to the main room is about 3 feet high, and

the floor of the room (e) is 9 inches higher than the floor of the passage. (d) Small domed compartments that may be entered from inside or out and are used for storing clothing, harnesses, meat, and blubber. In the main room is a snow platform 2 ½ feet high that contains a bed (g) and (h) places for lamps, meat, and other goods.

The dropped floor area is known as *Natiq*, and is associated with men, their tools, and the sea. The raised, sleeping platform is called *Ikliq* and is associated with women, their soapstone lamps and gear, and the land. The interior cutaway looks from the bed platform toward the entry tunnel below the clear ice window. It shows oil lamps, stone kettles, and liner skins, which are hung by ties drawn through the snow walls and secured to outside toggles. A small hole in the roof provides ventilation. With the heat generated by the inhabitants and the lamps, the snow surfaces of the interior walls tended to crust.

Communal iglus

Snow houses served a society that had to stay flexible in its comings and goings in order to survive. During the winter, Central Eskimo families often clustered their iglus for various lengths of time, depending on personal compatibility and food supply. The diagrams *(below)* show iglu combinations documented by Arctic scholars. Based on work by Asen Balikci, who studied the Netsilik Eskimo of Pelly Bay in the 1960s, four iglus (1) could be joined by means of a snow dome (2), with doors cut into this shared space. Franz Boas recorded a Central Eskimo house (3), with two iglus sharing an entrance and protected access to storage units.

Diamond Jenness of the Canadian Arctic Expedition of 1913 to 1918 documented iglu-cluster patterns among the Copper Eskimo of the Liston and Sutton Islands. In late 1914, Jenness drew a group of three iglus (4) that shared an entry tunnel, and a year later, a larger iglu complex (5) with four living chambers opening into a central dance house. The families who lived in this complex were very likely close friends or relatives who broke through their house walls in order to share games, song, and food.

Among the Iglulik of Hudson Bay, explorer Charles Hall noted in the 1860s a complex (6) of four domestic iglus leading into a domed hall, while in 1822 and 1823 Sir William Parry recorded three domestic iglus (7) around their common feasting room. When Therkel Mathiassen visited the Iglulik in 1922 during the 5th Thule Expedition, he saw a larger complex (8) with four domestic iglus on Aua's River, and one cluster (9) on the Melville Peninsula with two living units plus rooms for clothing, dog harnesses, a meat locker, and a dog kennel.

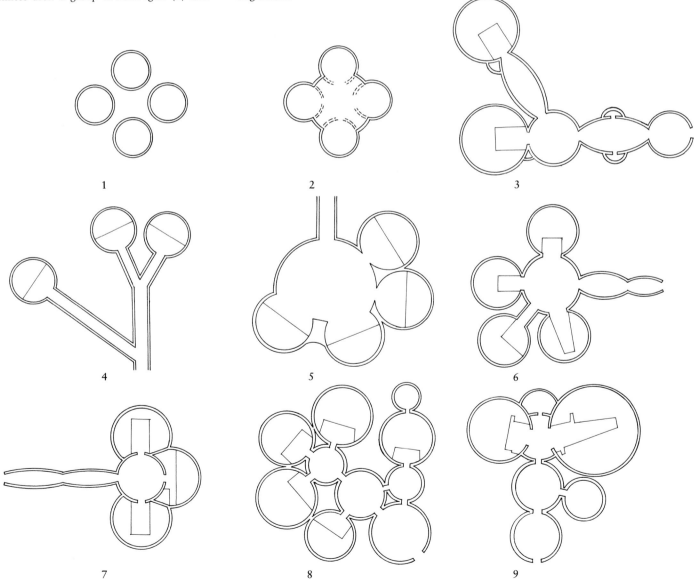

1

2

3

4

5

6

7

8

9

Iglu interior

The snow-block roof of this Iglulik dwelling, photographed in 1903 by Albert Low at Cape Fullerton, covered a 27 ½-foot diameter floor. It stood 12 ½-feet high. Women and children occupied skin-covered sleeping platforms, and kettles were suspended over oil lamps.

The average iglu housed five or six people. However, the severity of the weather, the number of dogs to shelter, and the amount of gear and food to store sometimes called for building smaller rooms off the central chamber or the tunnel. As kin and visitors congregated for sealing expeditions farther out on the ice or to join other camps, a snow-house cluster could be expanded or made smaller. A young man who had recently married might attach his iglu to that of his wife's family, then open up the adjoining wall. New domes might be linked with connecting passageways, or disconnected iglus might be constructed, while temporarily unused units might be sealed off to conserve warm air. When two or more iglus were attached, a larger alcove dome often was built for festive occasions such as feasting, game playing, song rituals, or sleight-of-hand feats by shamans.

When British explorer Captain George Lyon crawled into an Iglulik iglu cluster on Winter Island in 1822 he found himself within a glowing cavern, "a cluster of cone-shaped edifices, entirely constructed of snow, which, from their recent erection, had not been sullied by the smoke of numerous lamps that were burning, but admitted light in most delicate hues of verdigris green and blue. . . ." One hundred and thirty years later, the anthropologist Edmund Carpenter also was inspired by an Iglulik snow house: "Visually and acoustically the igloo is 'open,' a labyrinth alive with the movements of crowded people. No flat static walls arrest the ear or eye, but voices and laughter come from several directions and the eye can glance through here, past there, catching glimpses of the activities of nearly everyone."

The room inside the iglu was almost equally divided between sleeping porch and floor. To the side of the porch stood the soapstone lamp. The floor might be crowded with horn dippers, blubber pounders, urine buckets, tools, and frozen meat that could be sliced whenever someone was hungry. Suspended over the lamp were platforms for drying damp clothing. Toggled around the inner walls might be seal skins for additional insulation. The snow sleeping platform would be laid with willow, heather, or baleen mats and soft furry hides.

To Europeans these cramped quarters were often claustrophobic and disorderly. "Picture to yourself a room about twelve feet in diameter," the anthropologist Franz Boas wrote to his wife in 1884. "Vaulted ceiling lined with sealskin . . . in the back also a big pile of things, skins clothing, etc. . . . The kettles hang over the lamps—above this for drying a network of skins, which is full of clothes day and night . . . on one side the provisions, on the other the garbage—it is difficult to accustom oneself to the sight." But to the Eskimo the chambers were wonderful winter havens. Indeed, the arrangement of these interior spaces seemed to mirror the division of their wider world. The floor area held the remains of the world of men: the sea, marine animals, winter hunting. The sleeping platform with its lamps was associated with the world of women: summer, fur-bearing mammals, and light.

Iglus could be used all winter; if left empty they often were occupied by anyone traveling the same route. If there was a death in an iglu, however, the Eskimo believed that the structure attracted malevolent spirits who envied the life force. Some groups broke a hole in the wall to remove the corpse and abandoned or destroyed the structure; others merely observed the taboo against scraping frost from the ice window for a while. If a revered parent died inside, the family might seal the corpse in the iglu and move on.

TENT

Around May, as the sod winter houses grew soggy and dripped, or iglu domes got crusty and tumbled in, Eskimos devised short-term living quarters. These spring and autumn interseasonal buildings were called *qarmaq*. The Eskimo might continue to use an old iglu's walls and tunnel entry, but the roof would be spanned with skins with the support of an interior pole. An unexpected cold snap might call for a hasty layer of insulating snow. In autumn, if snow was late in coming, ice blocks were often shaped into octagonal walls, with summer tent covers serving as roofs, the furry side of the skins facing in.

When summer arrived, all Eskimos moved into some form of tent, or *tupik*. They divided the space inside between a sleeping area toward the rear with designated positions for family members, and storage space for clothing and tools. A row of rocks or logs marked the two interior zones, and, incidentally, served as headrests. This plan almost duplicated the layout of the winter house, with the important exception that food generally was cooked over an outdoor fire pit.

Eskimo tents varied in construction according to group and locale. Their covers were sewn from caribou or seal skins, depending upon which animal the group hunted most. The Central Arctic groups built tents using frames both with and without ridgepoles. The simplest, lacking the ridgepole, were made of ten or more caribou skins with the fur left on except where it was scraped off to admit a glow above the doorway. As in the winter houses, this was the "window." The cone of pole supports protruded from the smoke hole; the hems were weighted down with large stones. Another non-ridgepole form used a narwhal tusk for a central pole; the skin cover was draped over support thongs that radiated from it and were tied to rocks on the ground.

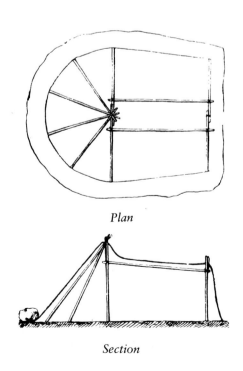

Plan

Section

200

Summer and interseasonal dwellings

In summer all Eskimos erected various forms of tents, or *tupik*. The Polar Eskimo lashed a seal skin cover to a wooden frame *(left)*, and scraped the hide over the doorway to admit light. Photographed at Neqi, northwestern Greenland. Rectilinear tents with a semicircular rear formed by crossed poles were more common *(bottom left)*.

During the fall and spring, Eskimos built various forms of *qarmaq*, an interseasonal shelter. In this spring dwelling of the Copper Eskimo of Cape Yackyer *(bottom right)*, a tent roof has been raised over the walls of a winter iglu whose roof has collapsed. Photographed ca. 1915. Drawings of another qarmaq *(top right)* show a structure with stone slab retaining walls set into a hill. Whale rib arches support poles over which a seal skin cover, insulated with dried moss, is placed; the window is of dried and sewn seal intestines. Large boulders held secure this spotted seal skin tent *(middle right)*, photographed on Baffin Island, 1924.

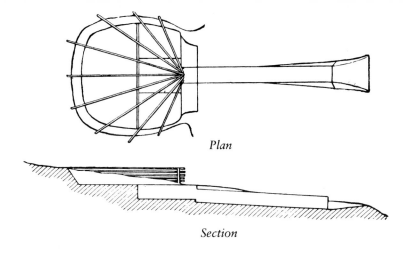

Plan

Section

Ridgepole tents, offering somewhat more floor space, used a portable H-shaped frame made of two pairs of slanting poles that were fitted into sockets in a carved cross piece. The poles toward the rear were set farther apart, and additional poles fanned around them, giving the tent an apsidal shape with poles sprouting from the top. The caribou or seal skin cover sloped toward the narrower front pair and additional poles. Where wood was scarce, whalebone or narwhal tusk would be used, and a taut thong might serve as the back-to-front ridgepole. The women who crafted and erected the tents often sewed pockets to secure the cross pieces so that the tent could be assembled on the ground and then raised by drawing all the guy thongs tight and lashing them to heavy rocks. Sometimes ridgepole tents belonging to congenial families were joined together. A curved whale rib supported a crawl space between them, much as two or more family iglus were linked by private passageways. When mosquitoes were bothersome, smudge fires were kindled close to the tent door.

Tents in Greenland were considerably larger, up to 15 feet in diameter. They sloped steeply toward the back over sawhorselike frames and sometimes featured a double cover. The outer skin was sewn of fifty to sixty seal skins turned inside out, using a needle made from seagull or rabbit bone and a waterproof "blind stitch" that didn't completely penetrate the skin. These covers were drawn like a coat over the tent and fastened in front. The perpetual Arctic summer daylight allowed most of the parboiling and roasting to be done outdoors, and the soapstone lamps were packed away. But the Greenland tents sometimes had an illumination curtain, sewn from alternating strips of light and dark dried seal intestine, that hung from the door frame.

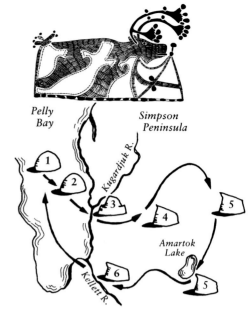

Pelly Bay *Simpson Peninsula*

Kugardjuk R.

Amartok Lake

Kellett R.

1	Midwinter (seal)	4	Midsummer (fish)
2	Late winter (seal)	5	Early fall (caribou)
3	Spring (seal)	6	Late fall (fish)

Nomads' shelters

During the winter the Netsilik Eskimo *(above)* lived in iglus on the sea ice; in summer they moved to tents on land. From their winter settlement on the ice of Pelly Bay, the Netsilik set out on a food gathering circuit of the Simpson Peninsula, from early spring through fall. The drawing of a "Caribou Tent" is by a Cape Dorset artist, Padloo, 1973. In the summer, Alaska Eskimos often made temporary shelters *(below)* from walrus-hide boats (umiaks) turned on their sides. Photographed ca. 1906.

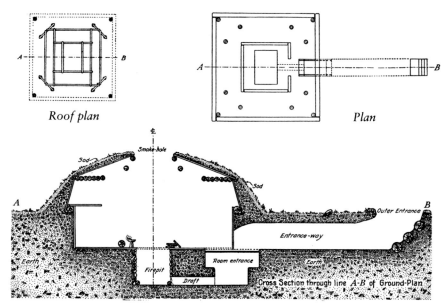

Roof plan

Plan

Section

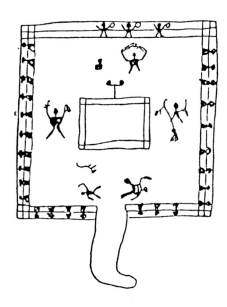

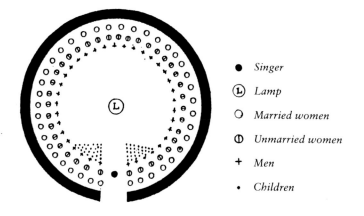

- ● Singer
- Ⓛ Lamp
- ○ Married women
- ⊕ Unmarried women
- + Men
- · Children

Dance houses

For feasting, socializing, and conducting sacred activities, most Eskimo winter settlements of any duration had their oversize gathering place. This Eskimo *kashim (top right)* from Alaska was framed with split wall timbers and pole rafters, and roofed with sod. Franz Boas published this diagram *(middle right)* of the floor plan of a Greenland Eskimo singing house, with the locations for the singer (s), lamp (L), married women (O), unmarried women (ϕ), men (x), and children (.). The building, a large snow dome, was 20 feet in diameter and 15 feet high. The lamp stood on a 5-foot snow pillar.

The pictographic representation of a square dance house *(above)* by an Alaskan Eskimo illustrates a shaman curing a patient. While the audience watches from side benches, the shaman proceeds through the three phases of the ritual cure. Above the T-shaped pole holding two lamps, he stands in front of three drummers and chants before his patient. To the right of the fire, he drives out a bad spirit. To the left, with his curing charm in hand, he chases the spirit toward the door, through which two helpers hurry it out of the dance house.

KASHIM

Throughout the Eskimo world special structures housed social and religious gatherings. These assembly chambers were known as *kashim* in south Alaska, *qaggi* in coastal Canada, and *qashe* in Greenland, and were generally more circular in plan in eastern areas and more rectangular in Alaska. Some were specially outfitted with trapezes and secret passageways for theatrical performances by shamans, known as *angakok*.

An over-sized iglu served this communal function for the Central Eskimo. The explorer Vilhjalmur Stefansson measured one such "feast house" of snow blocks that was 30 feet in diameter and could house at least a hundred people. Missionary accounts from Labrador describe them as 16 feet high and 70 feet across. In Alaska the kashim developed into a vital social institution for men, serving much the same function as the *kiva* of the Pueblo Indians of the Southwest. There the young underwent initiation rites, and it was also a men's club, sweathouse, gambling house, workshop, and temple for major religious and curing ceremonies.

During special feast days a sequence of animal dances was performed in the kashim in which guests and performers mingled freely. At the climax, according to folklorist Charles Hoffman, "the angakok donned his spirit mask, [and] ran about in circles until he collapsed in a trance. The people believed he was communing with the spirit guests in the fireplace below the kashim. After a time the angakok revived and told the people that the spirits had been pleased with the dances and promised a successful hunting season. When appropriate offerings of meat, drink and tobacco had been made to the spirits through the chinks in the floor, the celebrations ended."

In some communities, a man would only join his father's kashim, and kashim brotherhoods often united to form whaling crews. In some of these structures every man had his appointed seat. Women only entered as guests. One Eskimo tale describes a girl who arrives at a kashim feast uninvited; when the building's spirit tells her that it has eyes, nose, arms, legs, and male genitals, she dashes home in fear.

In the 1850s at Alaska's Point Barrow, a populous village might have had as many as three kashims, all constructed on ground slightly higher than that of the surrounding winter houses. All were framed of wood and measured about 18 by 14 feet. In each, benches lined the four sides and there was a tunnel entrance. Missionaries, in their effort to stamp out the pre-Christian Eskimo religion, often tried to prevent the kashim activities.

SUBARCTIC SHELTERS

South of the Arctic rim lay the vast Subarctic, the continent's largest culture area. Its native housing was modest yet varied, reflecting the harshness of the climate the seminomadic hunters faced and their need to improvise. To the east the Montagnais-Naskapi used conical, bark-covered wigwams. Among the Mistassani Cree, brush-covered conical lodges and tents served in summertime, while earth-covered conical structures framed with axe-hewn planks, or log cabins with moss-insulated roofs and spruce bough flooring, gave winter shelter. In the Northwest Territories were double lean-tos, enveloped with bark slabs, caribou skins, or brush. Where the far western Indians had contact with the Northwest Coast tribes, they built simple split-plank houses. A critical feature of most Subarctic camps was the food cache, which was either a simple sack of meat hung from a tree or a complete log building raised high on stilts to keep provisions away from scavenging animals.

In the northwest taiga, where caribou migrated and Indian groups traded or warred with the Eskimo, a variety of tents were used in both winter and summer. One unusual type, developed by the Kutchin, was a dome-shaped, portable structure carried on hunting trips. Its wooden poles were carved into curved supports; its cover of caribou skins was tailored and sewn into two sections.

When the hunting families moved from one camp to another, the poles and hide were lashed compactly to their dog-drawn toboggans. At the new site the Kutchin women positioned the poles and then tightened the covers over them so that the completed shelter resembled two half-bowls meeting at the smokehole. Snow was piled against the tent for added insulation. These dwellings were occupied by two families, one under each arching side.

Food storage

Subarctic Indians built permanent camps at favored fishing spots, even when they resided there for only limited periods. This view of the Tutchone fishing camp at Klukshu in southern Yukon Territory shows log cabins and raised food-storage caches, all of which are sod-roofed, 1948.

BARABARA

Among the largest native homes of the Arctic was the semisubterranean *barabara*, built by inhabitants of the Aleutian Islands. When Captain James Cook stopped there in 1778, he found oblong-floored barabaras measuring approximately 50 feet long by 20 feet wide. Cook's men were repelled by the smell from urine pots, which were used for washing hands and soaking raw hides. Russian seamen, who dominated the trade in sea otter furs, described considerably larger barabaras, up to 180 feet in length.

Among the unique features of these sod-roofed communal buildings was the roof doorway. One climbed down a notched log or plank ladder that protruded through the thatch underlying the sod roof. Framing for the roof was driftwood or whalebone, which rested on posts that stood some 6 or 7 feet inside the building's support walls. These posts also defined the sleeping stalls, which were swathed in woven grass mats, while the floor was padded with loose dried grass. The most honored occupant lived in the compartment at the far back of the house. Secret alcoves were dug along the sides to hide children in the event of enemy raids. From a ceiling beam hung a figurine that hunters would address before going after game.

The thatched roof, sealed over with grassy turf, blended into the terrain; after domestic cattle were introduced, it was not unusual for a grazing cow to tumble through the sod into a barabara. The last manifestation of the structure, regarded as "traditional" in the memory of Aleuts today, was a gable-roofed, double-walled plank house with moss insulation between the timbers, an external skin of sod bricks over walls and roof, and a sunken, moss-covered floor.

Aleut housing

John Webber based this engraving of an Aleut communal house on sketches he made in 1778 when he accompanied James Cook's third expedition to Unalaska, at the western end of the Aleutian Island chain. The *barabara* roof was first framed with driftwood, then thickly layered with dry grass, and finally topped with sod. In this example, there were actually two roof openings: one for the notched entry ladder, and the other for light. The inhabitants slept in mat-draped trenches along the walls. Early Russian accounts describe these buildings as from 50 to over 200 feet long, up to 40 feet wide, and holding as many as 150 residents.

The stilt-supported homes of Ukivok village on King Island were photographed by Edward S. Curtis, ca. 1928. Overlooking the Bering Sea, they were plank-framed boxes wrapped with walrus hide and tied with rope. The structures were supported by tree trunks which stood up to 20 feet tall, and hide boats were stored on racks under the floors.

POLE HOUSES

On King Island, a treeless granite mountain rising 700 feet at the entrance to the Bering Sea, was Ukivok, a coastal village with unique houses on stilts. The boxlike structures stood shoulder to shoulder in rows and were anchored to the cliff face by wooden pilings. No one is sure when these structures were invented as adaptations to the steep site. Their front pilings, tree trunks more than twenty feet long that had been towed in skin boats from the mainland, extended above the structures to support platforms for drying skins and food. Slung underneath the houses were the skin whaling boats, ready to launch whenever sea mammals were sighted. Steep wooden staircases and connecting plank ramps served as town streets.

The houses were framed of hewn or whipsawed boards. They were divided into two rooms, with 6-foot ceilings, the larger storage room in front measuring about 16 by 10 feet, the rear living space partitioned into sleeping rooms about 8 by 7 feet. Outside, the wooden walls and roof were lashed with a double layer of walrus hides, each sewn together from about thirteen green skins that formed tightly to the frame as they dried. Moss insulation was wadded between the wood and skin, and, until the turn of the century, when glass was introduced, light entered through small side windows glazed with sewn intestines. According to photographer Edward S. Curtis, the wood floors were highly polished, a seal-oil cooking lamp was placed just below the window, and the chamber was kept scrupulously clean.

In the 1920s, twenty-nine of the structures were still standing on the island's south side, arrayed in seven terraces with the lowest only 10 feet from the waterline. It was here the islanders returned after their annual summer visit to Nome, Alaska. By 1952, only about 150 Eskimos still made their home on this forbidding outpost. While the village still stands today, only a handful of families return each year, and pole structures are no longer built.

TODAY

Hired by the U.S. Army to write its World War II Arctic survival manual, Vilhjalmur Stefansson could not improve on what the Eskimos had taught him; he simply set down step-by-step instructions for building the snow block iglu. Few traditional Eskimo winter houses, or summer tents for that matter, have been used in the Arctic since the advent of prefab housing three decades ago. But the skills of jerry-rigging survival dwellings based on traditional building techniques have persisted. Arctic anthropologist Edmund Carpenter wrote us that in the winter of 1951-1952, "I came across a sailing spar protruding from the snow, and a stream of vapor beside it. These marked the entrance to the smallest conceivable home: a pocket in the snow like a cocoon, in which a man, woman and infant lived, cooking, keeping warm, laughing."

In 1960, at Lake Harbor, Baffin Island, anthropologist Nelson Graburn saw a winter house that had been modernized. Its wooden frame was covered with a double layer of duck cloth with moss stuffed in between and snow banked against the walls. Inside, the family had replaced its old soapstone lamp with a metal lamp that burned seal oil.

According to Graburn, some experimental Styrofoam iglus were introduced in the traditional community of Cape Dorset in the 1950s. The synthetic iglus proved to be poor insulators compared to the snow house, however, and required wood stoves as well as oil lamps to heat them. Among those who tried them out was a crippled elder named Kingwatsiak, an artist whose memories and skills represented a crucial link to the traditional Eskimo way of life. When the rest of the community was in church one Sunday, Kingwatsiak's synthetic iglu caught fire and he died inside it.

Since the 1960s, Graburn told us, the Canadian and American governments have introduced major housing programs to supply free or low-rent housing to Eskimo communities across the Arctic. He noticed, however, that even the assembly line uniformity of these prefab units often bowed before ingrained customs of usage, and residential grouping was still by extended family. Between 1965 and 1975, Graburn said, some Eskimo families culturally transformed their one- to three-bedroom government-issued homes. They nailed an entry alcove together in front of the door to help retain warm air throughout the house. As in the old winter houses, this vestibule's roof was used to dry frame-stretched furs and sleds and to keep them out of the dogs' reach. They also remodeled the back bedrooms. One became common sleeping quarters for parents and young children, with a raised platform extending across the room, storage area underneath. Unused bedrooms were converted to workshops for carving soapstone. In some of the houses the bathroom was turned into a meat locker, where the window was left open and game was stashed in the tub. Butchering and eating took place on the floor beside the kitchen table. Just as soapstone lamps had been allowed to flicker in the iglus through the entire night, a kerosene lantern was kept burning on the kitchen table until dawn.

Interior passage at Pueblo Bonito, Chaco Canyon, New Mexico. The dwelling complex was occupied by the Anasazi from A.D. *900 to 1300.*

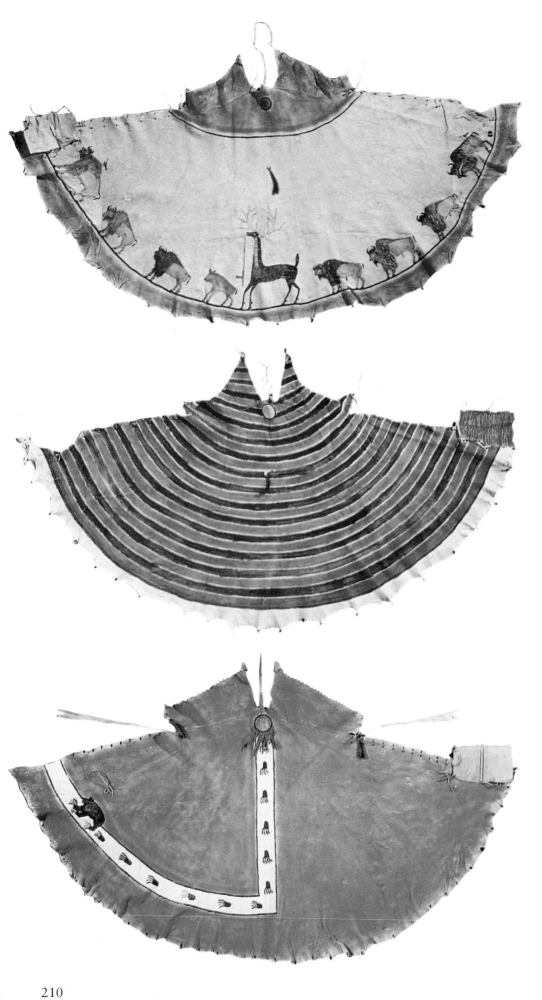

Indian encampment on Lake Huron,
painted by Paul Kane, ca. 1845 (below).
Painted Kiowa tipi covers, Great Plains,
1891 to 1904 (left).

Plains earthlodge interior, painted by Karl Bodmer, ca. 1833 (right). Earthlodge reconstruction at Like-A-Slant Village, Mandan, North Dakota (above).

Chippewa maple sugar camp, Great Lakes, painted by Seth Eastman, ca. 1840 (above). Reed mats cover a Kickapoo wigwam, Shawnee, Oklahoma (right).

Great Kiva at Pueblo Bonito (left). *A southwestern kiva interior, New Mexico* (above).

Acoma Pueblo, New Mexico (below). *Taos Pueblo, New Mexico* (right).

*Big House ceremony of the Delaware,
painted by Kickapoo artist Ernest Spybuck
in Oklahoma, ca. 1912 (left). Maidu
roundhouse, painted by Maidu artist
Frank Day, ca. 1970 (above left). Maidu
roundhouse, northern California (above).*

Papago ceremonial arbor and Rain House, Arizona (above). *Navajo hogan frames, northern Arizona* (top and bottom left).

Tlingit house reconstruction, Ketchikan, Alaska (above). *Tsimshian totem pole, Kitwancool, British Columbia* (right).

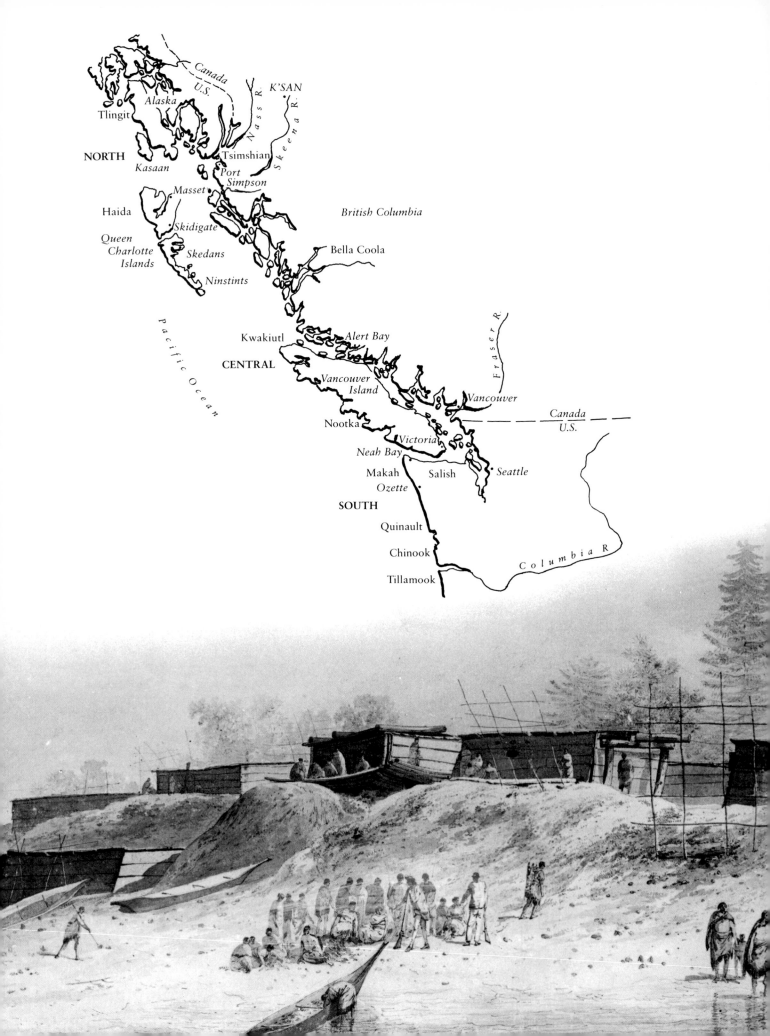

6 PLANK HOUSE
NORTHWEST COAST

In 1778, the world traveler and British Navy captain James Cook brought his ship *Resolution* into Nootka Sound, a protected inlet on Vancouver Island's wild western shore. As Cook dropped anchor in a natural harbor he named Friendly Cove, he met a typical Northwest Coast village scene: three rows of large cedar-plank houses lined imposingly above the tide line. Banked walkways served as "main streets" running in front of the buildings, which faced a beach strewn with fishing gear and dugout canoes.

Cook climbed a notched-log stairway from the beach to examine the most sophisticated wood architecture in North America. In his journal he recorded that "The height of the sides and ends of these habitations is seven and eight feet; the back part is higher than the front, by which means the planks that compose the roof slant forward; they are laid on loose, and are moved to let out smoke and admit air or light. Inside, Cook found that "the whole might be compared to a long stable, with a double row of stalls, and a broad passage in the middle."

Cook had mixed feelings about life inside these voluminous interiors. They seemed full of "filth and confusion," yet their Indian builders clearly had invested them with great symbolic importance. Cook was struck by the images that decorated many of the houses: "These are nothing more than the trunks of very large trees four or five feet high, set up singly or by pairs, at the upper end of the apartment, with the front carved into a human face, the arms and hand cut out upon the sides, and variously painted, so that the whole is a truly monstrous figure . . . When [the natives] did unveil them, they seemed to speak of them in a very mysterious manner."

In his observations of a major Nootka Indian village, Cook identified key elements of the architectural system that prevailed for an estimated 75,000 native people who occupied the 1,200-mile coastline from the lower Alaskan panhandle in the north to southern Oregon. For convenience, scholars have grouped the dozen or more major Northwest Coast tribes by three subregions: Southern, Central, and Northern. All of these tribes traditionally constructed wood houses, using massive logs for their post-and-beam frames and split and adzed planks for their walls and roofs. The house shape, construction details, and symbolic decoration in each region, however—and sometimes each tribe—displayed distinguishing characteristics.

Cook had entered the last American Indian world below the Arctic that was virtually unknown to the white man. The Northwest Coast was a dramatic environment of thundering surf, mist-shrouded islands, hidden bays, lofty mountains, and dense rain forests. In winter, temperatures rarely dropped below 35 degrees. Among the wettest regions on Earth, its annual rainfall averaged more than 80 inches. Its forests, coast, sounds, and rivers offered its Indians diverse food sources. Extended family groups owned traditional rights to shellfish beds, salmon-fishing riverbanks, berry patches, and hunting areas in the valleys. This freedom from want fostered the development of highly stylized art forms, which adorned their clothing, tools, ritual paraphernalia, sea craft, and architecture. With it also developed a complex social organization that placed a premium upon ancestry, status, prestige, and wealth—all of which were amply displayed in the architecture.

Each of the subregions produced a singular house type. The Salish-speaking tribes of the South lived in extremely long, undecorated shed-roofed houses.

Large gable-roofed structures framed around a central rectangular pit were built by such Central tribes as the Nootka, Bella Coola, and Kwakiutl. In the North, tribes such as the Tlingit and Tsimshian constructed similar gable-roofed, two-beam houses, but the Haida of the Queen Charlotte Islands devised the unique six-beam house.

Red cedar was the wood most commonly used, either in the round or split into wide planks. In the most northerly reaches of Northwest Coast culture, however, yellow cedar, spruce, and hemlock were more common. But cedar was generally preferred, for reasons which Haida carver William Reid explained in 1975: "The wood is soft, but of a wonderful firmness and, in a good tree, so straight-grained it will split true and clean into forty foot planks,

Kwakiutl house

A painted housefront on milled lumber, in Kwaustums village on Gilford Island. The design is of a loon encircled by a rainbow, on which is painted a two-headed *sistiutl,* a mythic being whose two mouths, hidden by bushes, are said to swallow visitors who enter the building for a feast. Photographed by Edward S. Curtis, ca. 1914.

four inches thick and three feet wide with scarcely a knot. Across the grain it cuts clean and precise. It is light in weight and beautiful in color, reddish brown when new, silvery grey when old. It is permeated with natural oils that make it one of the longest lasting of all woods, even in the damp of the Northwest Coast climate ... you can build from the cedar tree the exterior trappings of one of the world's great cultures."

Except that it could not be consumed, cedar was to Northwest Coast craftsmen almost what the buffalo was to Plains Indians. Its inner bark was woven into mats, cloth, rope, and ritual costumes, and its outer bark shingled the roofs of their houses. Its wood—composed of thin-walled cells with large spaces between cells—offered naturally insulating walls. Not surprisingly, most Northwest Coast tribes also believed the tree was endowed with spiritual power.

Villages varied in size from large autonomous towns to smaller communities of fewer than a dozen houses. These coastal settlements were permanent winter residences, considered home from about October to May. Usually sited along the curving beachfronts of sheltering coves, they were protected from winter winds, stormy surf, and surprise attack. Some tribes also erected palisades around their villages, or propped their houses on stilts in hard-to-reach coastal overlooks, to protect against the threat of unfriendly tribes hunting for slaves or booty. In summer, families canoed inland on river channels to resettle near favorite salmon-spawning stretches, berry plots, and groundhog-hunting areas. There they erected short-term shelters, often sheathed with large wall boards they had brought from their winter homes, lashed between canoes for the trip inland. Individual families enjoyed inherited rights to fish, hunt, and gather. They netted and speared up to five kinds of salmon during upstream spawning runs. The fish were then smoked in special houses or dried on huge outdoor racks.

Northwest Coast society was ranked into two classes, commoners and nobles, with the aristocratic families dominating the villages. Slaves stolen from other tribes were considered outside the social order. The extended-family lineages placed the utmost value upon inherited or accumulated prestige. Noble families usually owned the houses, whose large plank facades and sculpted posts boastfully announced their social standing. Mythic characters, considered part of the ancestral heritage of prominent families or clans, were symbolically depicted in "crests" of highly stylized faces and body forms on the large facade, the upright posts in and outside the building, and on interior painted screens. Arranged marriages between high-ranking families often were formalized by the ritualized construction of a new house, which was then decorated with the combined iconographic inheritance of the occupants.

Considered almost as living entities, most houses were given proper names; some acquired reputations for their wealth and prestige. Through the accumulation of crest carvings and other inherited treasures, the "noble house" continued to strengthen its history and totemic imagery even though the original building might fall into disrepair and be replaced or repaired on the site. In midwinter, the time of year when house interiors were converted into sacred spaces during religious festivals, the layering of symbols portrayed on them came to life as wooden panels were erected behind the large fire

hearth to separate public and secret zones, and the buildings became stages for ritual dramas.

These buildings also housed the ostentatious gift-giving rituals known as "potlatch," during which family lineages or even entire tribes competed in dispensing immense quantities of goods. Such formal events reaffirmed the networks of important social relations and were also mechanisms by which local chiefs enhanced their power and reputations. During formal speeches at these give-aways it seemed as if the houses themselves, rather than their temporary occupants, were vying for attention and status.

European traders who arrived after Cook soon discovered how readily Northwest Indians would offer sea otter pelts for coveted metal. Before Cook's appearance they had salvaged iron from shipwrecks washed ashore, but it was probably not essential to their carpentry. Experiments by archeologists at Canada's Museum of Man in the 1970s suggest that their distinctive art style could have been achieved using adzes and chisels edged with clam or mussel shell, along with stone mauls, hardwood or sheephorn wedges, and bone bores and awls. In Nootka Sound, Captain Cook examined a typical Indian carpenter's kit that contained "[a] maul, chisels, wedges, D-adze, straight adze, simple drills, grindstones of sandstone for finishing, sharkskin for fine polishing. . . ."

Other scholars argue that the blossoming of Northwest Coast architecture occurred with the proliferation of metal chisels, axes, nails, and saws. Archeological evidence of the antiquity of the plank house tradition is meager because the damp climate rots wood and fiber. Yet excavations in the Skeena River Canyon on the mainland in British Columbia have uncovered fishing villages of rectangular houses that date back nearly 5,000 years. Moreover, Canadian archeologists working in the present-day Kwakiutl region near Prince Rupert claim to have found traces of equally ancient plank house communities.

There is only circumstantial evidence for the origin of Northwest Coast house forms. Wood houses in Siberia's Amir region bear a resemblance to the rectangular plan of Northwest plank houses, as do traditional Ainu homes from northern Japan. Closer to home, Alaskan Eskimos just north of Tlingit country used planks, and their technique of sinking the floors to conserve warmth was shared by some Northwest Coast builders, who stepped their rectangular floors in tiers down to the fire pit.

There is no argument, however, that metal tools increased the quantity of Northwest Coast architectural art. Museums from New York to Moscow today abound with interior posts, free-standing crest poles, house screens and furnishings, and even entire building facades. It was the interpretive scholarship of Northwest Coast art launched by ethnographer Franz Boas in the 1880s that first correlated the tribes' material culture and social life, contributing to the fledgling discipline of anthropology.

These Northwest Coast Indian housing traditions have suffered from economic change, disease epidemics, the abandonment of many ancestral villages and suppression of native lifeways instigated by the Europeans. Yet today, at some native communities and art centers such as Alert Bay, Skidegate and K'SAN, architectural craftsmen still carve totems, adze wallboards, and paint house facades in traditional fashion.

Haida house

Named "House Where People Always Want to Go," this six-beam Haida house was photographed at Haina, Queen Charlotte Islands, ca. 1900.

Images of animals, mythic beasts, and humans are carved in the frontal pole, popularly known as the "totem pole." It is often difficult for an outsider to disentangle and interpret the images in Northwest Coast architectural art. For the Indians, however, they represented an age of mythic history. "It was an age," writes the anthropologist Edmund Carpenter, "of extraordinary events and noble deeds, when men lived as equals with animals and mythic beasts, and the plan of raven and eagle, frog and beaver, thunderbirds and whale established all that was to be. When depicting that reality, Northwest Coast artists often showed two beings simultaneously occupying a single space by sharing various parts. Such visual puns did more than express complexity; they depicted transformation. Before one's eyes, bear became wolf, then bear again. The image didn't change, of course. What changed was the observer's organization of its parts. But the effect was one of transformation."

Southern plank houses

Makah shed-roofed plank houses at Neah Bay,
Washington state, photographed by Edward S.
Curtis, ca. 1915.

SOUTH

In 1792, Captain George Vancouver explored Elliot Bay, near what is today Seattle Harbor, then landed in North Bay to examine an Indian building whose single-pitch shed roof sheltered over six hundred Dwamish tribespeople. Known to them as Tsu-Suc-Cub, or the "Old-Man-House," the structure extended in length more than 380 yards—almost a fifth of a mile.

Its interior was divided lengthwise into eight sections, each of which housed a clan chieftain and his followers. Each clan domain was identified by its prominently displayed carved totem. At the higher, front side of the house, the mighty support posts stood about 20 feet high. Over 5 feet thick and positioned about 25 feet apart, they were paired with other posts at the rear which stood between 5 and 6 feet high. The log beams spanning these uprights and setting the building's width were just over 60 feet long.

More than a dozen coastal Salish- and Chemakum-speaking people—tribes such as the Chinook, Tillamook, and Quinault—inhabited the bays and islands that extend from Puget Sound in the south to the Gulf of Georgia in the north. Their shed houses, commonly hundreds of feet long, were actually a sequence of post-and-beam modules that were added on whenever new households, related through the father's line, married into the family.

It was customary for the principal leader and his entourage to live in the central, largest unit—a chamber up to 90 feet in length—and the houses might grow in both directions. A family's social position thus could be inferred from their proximity to the middle room, with more important households usually closer to the main quarters. Compared with the coastal traditions further north, however, this southern architecture appeared less concerned with displaying rank and status. The hierarchical order and societal rules were more flexible, and families would even change houses on occasion, which would have been unthinkable further north.

Coastal villages contained some gable-roofed structures and an occasional large, flat, or mansard-roofed feast house. Most settlements held from three to five multiple-family houses, usually laid out in rows with the long side facing the shoreline. Diversity in the size and design of Salish communities was not unusual, however. An entire Squamish hamlet might live beneath a common roof, yet a Musqueam village described in 1876 contained 76 separate buildings arranged in a semicircle. In a Lummi settlement in Washington the structures were aligned in an L-shape, in accordance with mythic instructions their culture hero received to build his house at right angles to the main village.

Some of the best-documented shed houses were found along the banks of the lower Fraser River. A few tribes on Vancouver Island are reported to have excavated their floors, but generally the topsoil was simply scraped level. Front posts often stood 18 feet high, while rear posts, 40 to 50 feet back, were raised about 10 feet high. Long beams connected them, producing a succession of parallel post-and-beams that held the lattice of lighter rafters. Sheathing the building on all sides were the "curtain walls," composed of wide split-cedar planks. They overlapped horizontally and were cinched tightly between pairs of slender uprights with cedar withes.

Roof boards were also of split cedar, which sometimes was gouged on one side to overlap like roofing tile. Rocks helped hold them in place during storms. In marked contrast to the prominently decorated entryways of

Salish shed houses

One of the first photographs taken on the Northwest Coast *(top left),* shows shed houses in Quamichan, Puget Sound, Washington, ca. 1866. The interior of a large shed house *(above)* was painted ca. 1850 by Paul Kane at Esquimalt, a Klallam Salish village on the southeast tip of Vancouver Island.

Abandoned frame of a Salish shed-roofed house *(bottom left)* at Lummi, Washington.

northern Indian houses, the shed house doors were inconspicuously tucked away in one corner of the main facade and consisted of planks swinging from the transom on cedar ties. Another door usually was cut out at the rear.

Just inside the entryway, plank barricades were positioned to block cold drafts, and bark sheets were sometimes fastened to the walls to provide added insulation. Rush hangings or plank dividers often partitioned the interior into living chambers, and bark or rush mats softened the 3-foot-wide sleeping benches that lined the chamber walls. In the larger buildings each "apartment" had its own hearth, while occupants of smaller structures used a common fireplace.

As Charles Jones, a hereditary chief of the Pacheenaht, recalls from his boyhood, the fire in a traditional house "was built in a circle of rocks and sand, which would help to retain the heat." His home, which sheltered six related families, was built with tightly overlapping side planks. "When they put this kind of siding on a house," he recalls in his autobiography, "they would start at the bottom of the house and work up, lapping each new plank over the one below. The walls were up off the ground just a bit, a few inches or so, so that the hot fire could pull the air in around the bottom of the house, which would help to keep the dirt floor dry." Provisions and tools were stored on racks suspended from the ceiling or under the sleeping platforms.

When choosing sites for their villages that could be defended, the coastal Indians exploited natural sea or rock barriers. In the Puget Sound region, many communities were surrounded by 14-foot-high log palisades piled with rocks that could be used as ammunition against attacking warriors. Secret tunnels led beneath some of the house floors into the forest, linking subterranean hideaways that contained bunks and emergency provisions.

When the families migrated to upriver fishing camps for the summer, tribes like the Nanaimo, Cowichan, and Sanetch stripped their winter houses of their curtain-wall planks. The villagers transported the dismantled walls lashed between their canoes and then used them to cover their summer fishing houses. Captain Vancouver noticed their seminomadic architecture in 1792, when he came upon "skeletons of houses" in what he at first took to be abandoned villages.

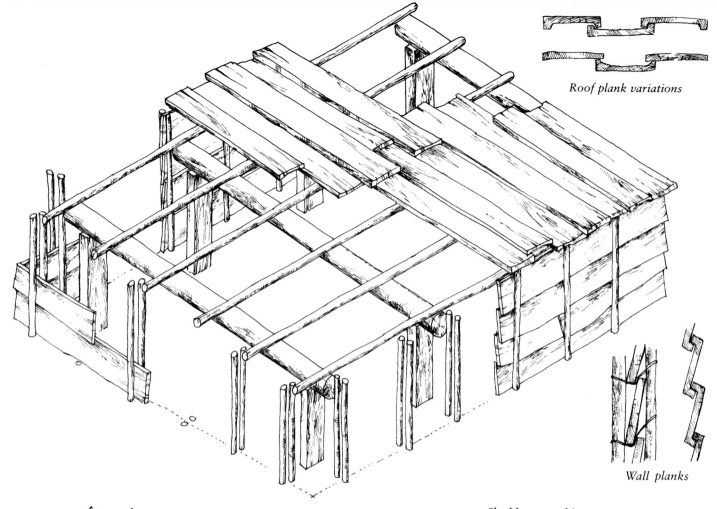

Roof plank variations

Wall planks

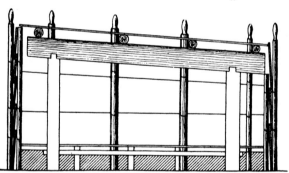

Section

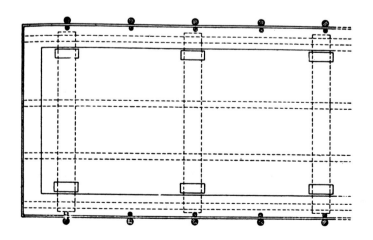

Salish house plan

Shed house architecture

A Salish house, as described by anthropologist Franz Boas *(top and bottom left)*, had a frame that consisted of two rows of posts, 2 to 3 feet wide and 6 to 8 inches thick. The posts were placed 12 to 14 feet apart, with the smaller ones at the rear of the house (the higher side faced the beach). Beams, often more than 2 feet in diameter, spanned the width of the house, which varied from 25 to 50 feet. Roof planks about 3 feet wide were laid overlapping the rows of rafters and were bound to them with cedar bark ties. Wall planks were similarly tied between pairs of poles, and would be removed from the frame and transported by canoe to standing frames at summer fishing camps.

The major house type among the Quinault *(top right)* had a gable roof. Slender poles framed the structure, and roof and wall boards were lashed to the frame. Quinault houses stood parallel to a river bank with their oval doors generally facing downstream. Each house had a plank porch with a bench built on the front. Tillamook houses *(middle right)* were shed-roofed.

At the mouth of the Columbia River, the Chinook built gable-roofed houses *(bottom right)* with plank-lined floor pits. Lewis and Clark traveled among the Chinook from 1804 to 1806; they described dwellings 14 to 20 feet wide and 20 to 60 feet long, with single ridgepoles that sometimes projected beyond the gable end walls.

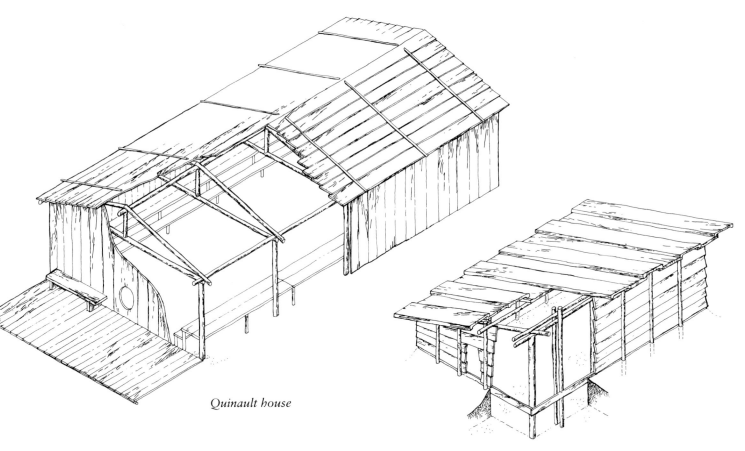

Quinault house

Tillamook house

Chinook house

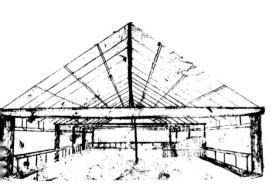

Salish houses

Salish-speaking peoples built a variety of styles of large houses after European contact. The posts of a "potlatch house" *(top left)* on the Quamichan Reservation were carved with guardian spirit figures along the board-and-bat wall. Photographed ca. 1935. A 40- by 200-foot feast house *(middle left)*, built on the Skokomish Reservation in 1875 in Washington state, was photographed by missionary Myron Eells. He sketched the interior *(above)* as well.

The mansard-roofed potlatch house *(bottom left)* on Whidbey Island near Couperville, Washington, was photographed ca. 1899.

A Salish shed-roofed house with adjacent fish-drying racks *(top)* was photographed near Port Angeles, Washington.

After the establishment of European settlements nearby, gable-roofed houses became popular with wealthier or more prestigious Indian families. They were often framed like the old shed-roof houses but with a gabled superstructure of poles resting upon the heavier posts and beams. The Comox and Pentlatch tribes, reputedly the most accomplished gable house builders, moderately excavated their house floors and used eight roof posts. Southern Indian villages freely mixed shed and board-and-bat walled gable buildings: while the Nanaimo Indians came to use gable houses exclusively, a village of Sanetch Indians not far away contained seven large shed houses with one gable house parallel to them. In some communities, however, the old style shed-roof domestic form was retained and converted into a festival or "potlatch" house.

Facades were covered with less symbolic artwork than that found further north. In the mythology of some Salish people, a "thunder house" owned by supernatural beings is described, but even such folklore references to architecture are few. One Klallum house owner perforated his roof boards so that during the day the ceiling would resemble the night sky, but there is no indication this was a common practice. When southern buildings did exhibit painted or carved house posts, the designs usually represented the "spirit guardian" of the head of the household.

A third building type of the Southern region, which in later years accommodated immense crowds of potlatch guests, was the mansard or hip-roofed building. The "old potlatch house" constructed at Whidbey Island shortly after 1800, for example, had an almost level central roof, steeply pitched eaves on all four sides, and metal stove pipes sticking through its enormous plank roof. By 1900, however, most coastal Salish traditional houses of the shed-, gable-, or hip-roofed variety had been burned or abandoned. Indians were occupying what they called the white man's style "Boston houses," or they lived in shantytowns built of cast-off lumber on the outskirts of Seattle, Victoria, and Vancouver.

TODAY

Nowhere on the southern Northwest Coast have any original plank houses survived the ravages of the damp climate and the cultural clash between Indian and European societies. However, on the western tip of the Olympic Peninsula, one old Makah Indian whaling village was rescued from time. About four and a half centuries ago, a sudden mud slide from a storm or an earthquake covered a settlement known today as Ozette. Preserved like a Native American Pompeii under 8 feet of earth were six shed-roofed houses, including their furnishings. Whaling gear, toys, and baskets were among the thousands of artifacts unearthed, along with a killer whale fin carved from wood and inlaid with over seven hundred sea otter teeth.

On the last day of our visit to the Northwest we took the three-and-a-half-mile plank trail through the forest to Ozette, after we had inspected the 30- by 70-foot house reconstruction at the Makah Museum in nearby Neah Bay. With furnishings and cooking utensils realistically placed in the living room, it was clear how the major house posts effectively marked individual family quarters.

One of the six Ozette structures uncovered by Dr. Richard D. Daugherty's excavators had whale bones strewn in trenches just outside the house walls and under their floors. Interpretations, as often is the case in architectural archeology, divide along pragmatic and symbolic lines: the bone rubble was used in a whale-hunting ritual, or buried to assist rain runoff. The cedar planks used on the curtain walls in Ozette were up to 2½ feet wide, their flat surfaces were smoothly adzed, and some retaining planks were incised with whale, thunderbird, and wolf motifs. Study of the architectural remains suggested that the upright posts had been reset frequently to accommodate the varying lengths of the wall boards since the curtain walls were seasonally dismantled and reconstructed over the years. To release smoke and to let in light, the occupants of the houses merely pushed aside some roof boards. Analysis of alder and twinberry leaves preserved on the house floors seemed to pinpoint the disastrous mud slide occurred around June.

Off the beach, we were told, whales pass closer to land than anywhere along the coast, making it a prime home for a whaling community. At the archeological dig itself we touched the corner of a cedar wall plank that protruded from the dirt. We turned to the ocean, imagining these Makah seamen launching their canoes on their last hunt before the earth buried their village.

Roofs and ceilings

During ceremonies and potlatches, the Coast Salish rooftops were crowded with spectators, as in Songhees village *(above)*, Victoria, British Columbia. Inside *(right)*, the roofs were hung with dried fish, masts, boating gear, and chains that suspended kettles over fireplaces on the floor.

Central Northwest Coast architecture

House carvings and paintings faced the water so visitors could be impressed by their imagery. At the Kwakiutl village of Blundens Harbor *(below)* a "main street" of planks on pilings fronted the water, and wooden stairs led past family totems down to canoes. At another Kwakiutl village, Tsadsisnukwomi, a housefront *(right)* painted with the "devouring mouth" motif suggests the Northwest Coast belief in the house as a living being. Photographed ca. 1900.

CENTRAL

In spring 1788, a fur trader named John Meares approached a Nootka chief's stately house in a village just north of where Cook had anchored ten years earlier. "The door," Meares wrote, "was the mouth of one of these huge images ... We ascended by a few steps on the outside, and after passing this extraordinary kind of portal, descended down the chin into the house ..." Meares found eight hundred guests inside, awaiting a feast. He estimated that "the trees that supported the roof were of a size which would render the mast of a first rate man-of-war diminutive." About twenty feet up, at the ceiling, "three enormous trees, rudely carved and painted, formed the rafters, which were supported at the ends and in the middle by gigantic images, carved out of huge blocks of timber."

The Kwakiutl, Nootka, and Bella Coola—each of which was divided into numerous, autonomous subgroups—were the major tribes of the Central region. Cook visited one of the largest villages of the Nootka, a tribe of roughly six thousand people who held sway along the 280-mile edge of Vancouver Island from Cape Scott to the Juan de Fuca Strait. The villages were loosely organized into political groups of four or five, and each village was under the control of a chief whose noble house proclaimed his influence.

Like Cook, Meares recorded two striking architectural characteristics common to these family houses: massive-scale construction and iconography representing supernatural beings from the mythical history of the lineage occupying the house.

KWAKIUTL

The most populous and powerful of the Central people were the linguistic group known as Kwakiutl, whose thirteen subtribes inhabited the northeastern shores of Vancouver Island and the mainland across from the Queen Charlotte Islands. Their typical village contained at least a dozen large gable-roofed structures and a population ranging from fifty to one thousand. The buildings lined the beach in rows two or three deep, with the highest ranking families nearest the ocean. Built around a central, rectangular excavation, these structures could not be expanded by adding modules boxcar-fashion as was done in the south. Generally their pole-framed gable roofs and curtain walls were lashed onto a massive frame of two major beams resting upon four great posts.

The mural-like paintings on Kwakiutl house facades sparked European admiration as early as 1790, but details about their architectural artistry were not collected until 1885, when Franz Boas began recording the tribe's culture. Named "He Who Says the Right Thing" by the Kwakiutl, Boas made his final field trip there in 1932. In the intervening half-century he documented the last of their traditional village ways and watched the population center of Kwakiutl society shift from Fort Rupert, where he first encountered them, to Alert Bay, which remains their capital.

It was through his Indian collaborators George Hunt (for the Kwakiutl) and Henry W. Tate (for the Tsimshian) that Boas learned that the prominent, permanent winter houses were not considered the property of their occupants but rather of family lines or lineages the Kwakiutl called *numema*. A house was considered a "spiritual associate" of the current lineage chief. With each successive generation, ceremonial names and design motifs or "crests" representing supernatural beings also became the property of these numema, to be carved and painted onto architectural elements. Occupants, every one of whom had what was known as a "seat" in the house, were responsible for safeguarding and adding to their lineage's wealth, which included crafted wood, textiles, and copper; slaves taken from other tribes; and the supernatural property and prestige embodied by the crests.

Kwakiutl villages

Villages were sited on coves or inland waterways along the eastern coast of Vancouver Island and the mainland. The houses were closely grouped in rows. Where the site sloped, the houses were built on an earth embankment, with plank steps leading to the beach. Plank platforms, parallel to the facades, served as gathering places.

The village of Gwayasdums, Gilford Island (*above*), faced Kincome Inlet. The house with the painted front was owned by Chief Johnny Scow. Photographed ca. 1900. The village of Kalokwis (*left*) ca. 1900. The drawing (*right*) of Xumtaspi-Nawittl village shows the construction of a plank deck projecting over the water.

The Kwakiutl regarded red cedar and its products as living substances. Its reddish hue was equated with blood, lending the tree what the Kwakiutl called *nawalak*, or supernatural force. They believed this spirit coursed through its three vital parts, which they used in various ways. The inner bark was shredded and woven into blankets, ceremonial paraphernalia, seats, and ropes; the outer wood was split into planks, each of which retained its spiritual power; and the tree's heart was sometimes trimmed into a pole used in the winter season's ceremonies. Planted in the middle of the sunken house floor and jutting 40 feet through the smoke hole, the pole was climbed by shamans during highly dramatic performances. It symbolically linked the three layers of Kwakiutl cosmology: the underworld (the house pit), this world (the house and its occupants), and the sky world (through the smoke hole).

Boas learned that in earlier days planks had been split from driftwood cedar logs, but it had become more common to harvest them from standing or felled trees. Cedars were tested by "feeling into the tree," as the Kwakiutl said. They gouged a hole with a long-handled chisel to assure the soundness of the wood. Coarse-grained wood was preferred for roof beams because it resisted fire best; house posts, rafters, and sea-going canoes called for the dense-grained wood found in aged trees with moss-covered trunks.

Large lineages usually owned their own stands of timber, which could be some distance by canoe from the winter towns. Before cutting into a standing tree the Kwakiutl prayed and offered gifts to its spirit. Edward Curtis learned that when the Kwakiutl cut a tree down it was considered "killed," but a standing tree from which boards were taken had been "begged from." The straight-grained trunk was notched 3 feet above the ground, then further up

Harvesting planks

To make wall and roof boards, planks were split from a living "begged from" tree *(above)*, or from felled timbers *(right)*.

to the length of the desired boards. As the top notch was widened, yew wood wedges were pounded into the gap and down the sides, then a lever was worked from the upper split to the bottom, freeing the new board without killing the tree. If whole trees were felled, their bases were cut slowly with hammer and chisel, sometimes aided by controlled burning in the notch.

When a house-building expedition had collected enough trunks or boards—most about 20 feet long (except for the massive framing timbers)—they were bundled up and towed home by canoe. Warped planks were countertwisted and held firmly in place by angled stakes. Both vertical-and slash-grained planks were used, but vertical-grain surfaces from the tree's center were favored for decorative facing. Kwakiutl carvers used short "elbow-adzes" on this wood, chopping with the grain for a fluted texture. The chiefs prized house boards that were adzed to under an inch in thickness yet were as wide as possible. Slices across the grain produced triangle, band, and diamond patterns. To join two planks, or to fill developing splits as the wood dried, yellow cedar bark was driven into the crack, then the sides were sewn together with twisted cedar twigs tied through drilled holes so neatly that the welded boards seemed to be one piece.

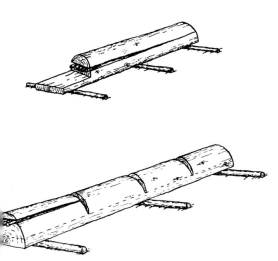

Construction of a major Kwakiutl house was governed by elaborate protocol. Between the first feast announcing the project and the actual move three years might elapse. It would require of the host-builder a substantial outlay of gifts and periodic feasts. Boas recorded one instance of a Kwakiutl chief overseeing construction of such a house to seal an arranged marriage. The chief invited representatives from three major Kwakiutl subtribes to witness his vow to erect this "inviting house." Once messengers had summoned and fed the visitors, blankets were given to the men chosen to provide the two cedar trees for main beams. Other participants were named to deliver the remaining beams, the major house posts, the rafters, and the planks that lined the recessed fire pit. Once cut and roughed to size by a fourteen-member work party, the timbers were floated to the construction site. This work took four days and was punctuated with speech-making, feasting, and public presentation of gifts.

Before artisans began carving the pieces to be assembled, the chief's spokesman proclaimed: "Indeed, truly long ago it was said by the creator of the ancestors of all the tribes that we should do it this way when we build houses . . . Do not be too quick, when you build a new house . . . for you will bring disgrace upon yourself if the property [to pay the participants] gives out before you finish the house."

After the house dimensions were carefully staked out on the site with bark ropes, four more days were devoted to adzing the two main beams and digging the four major post holes to a depth about equal to that from a man's foot to his navel. On house-raising day, the heavy posts were maneuvered into the holes so they extended 15 feet above ground. With the help of levers and pivots the huge roof beams were hoisted onto the posts as work crews chanted in unison. Then the gable roof was framed and the building was covered with roof and wall planks. In general the northern Kwakiutl tied their wall boards on horizontally, the southern tribes vertically. The nearly square floor pit was lined with carved retaining planks. The floor was bare tamped earth. The walls were hung with mats to block drifting snow. Sometimes the families living in a great house each had their own fireplace near a corner.

Upon completion of the building a participating Kwakiutl headman announced to his host: "The great house is finished for all the different tribes. My tribe has treated you as a chief, with split boards for your feasting house. Go and sing in the house tomorrow evening, and let the inviting canoes go to all the different tribes that they may come."

The place of honor was in the middle rear of the building, and in descending order ranking family members occupied the right side, left side, and door side. Slaves slept around the fire. Dried olachen fish, so oily that they burned like candles if a wick was run through them, might be burned for additional illumination. The finest cedar boards were owned by the higher-ranking occupants and walled their inner sleeping alcoves, which occasionally had their own gable roofs; other compartments were merely pole frames hung with mats for privacy. Owners of the most prestigious Kwakiutl houses boasted that "one did not hear the rain, the house was so high." Such houses increased in stature with each generation. Franz Boas recorded the speech of one Kwakiutl chief to his guests: "This is the house of my great-great-grandfather Mahwa who invited you here. This is the house of my great-grandfather Mahwa who invited you to Sandy Beach. This is the house of my grandfather Mahwa who invited you at Crooked Beach. This is the feasting house of my father who invited you at Tide Beach. Now I have taken the place of my father. I invited you, tribes, that you should come and see my house here."

In summer, the secular time of year, Kwakiutl households followed the Northwest Indians' seasonal pattern of moving to family-owned hunting and foraging grounds. In autumn, when everyone returned to the coastal settlements, the houses were cleaned and interior hanging mats were replaced. For special ritual performances, house screens of thin painted planks or hide hangings formed an interior backdrop and converted the center of the house into an arena. Drummers pounded on the long hollow-log drums in front of the screen and spectators thronged on all three sides.

Prestigious houses

Houses with prominent poles or paintings were the property of high-ranking chiefs, who increased their status by holding periodic feasts, or "potlatches," at which they gave presents to the guests. Blankets were the primary gift, as can be seen in the photograph (left) of a potlatch in progress. The Kwakiutl village of Xumtaspi-Nawittl (below), on Hope Island, ca. 1884, had totem poles, a painting of a "displayed figure" crouching over a doorway, and signs with advertising to attract Anglo-American seamen. One reads, "CHEAP. The home of the head chief of all tribes in this country. Whiteman can gaet (sic) information." The other says, "BOSTON. He is true and honest. He don't give no trouble to no white man."

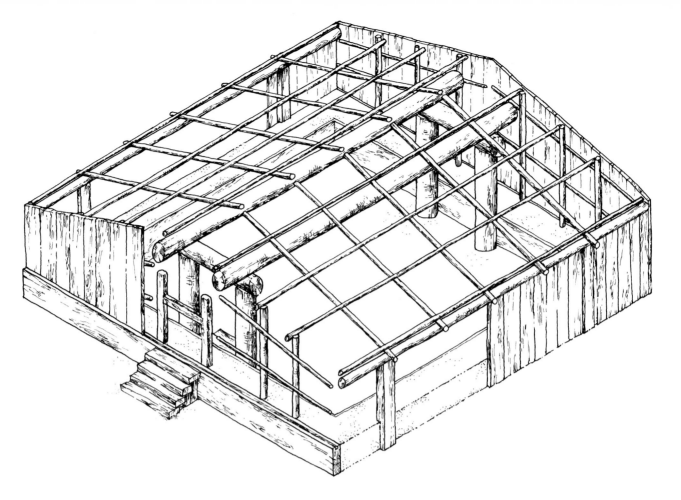

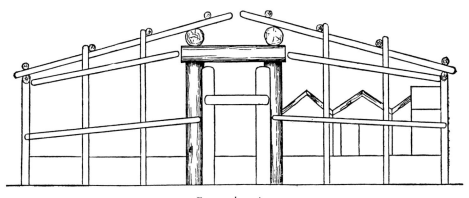

Front elevation

Kwakiutl architecture

Kwakiutl houses were essentially square, with sides 40 to 60 feet long *(top left and right)*. To lay them out, a cedar-bark rope was used to measure and stake off a line from the front door to the rear of the house. To establish the facade's width, the rope was halved and staked at roughly right angles to the first line at the front of the house. Then the distance from these front corner stakes to the rear center was measured and made equal to triangulate and thereby square the building lines.

The following construction sequence is compiled from notes and drawings by Franz Boas. The gable roof was formed by a heavy post and beam frame on which a lighter framework of poles, each about 3 inches in diameter, was tied (or, later, nailed). After the post and beam framework was up, long, heavy planks, 4 to 5 inches thick by 2 ½ to 3 feet wide, were set on edge at floor level at the front and back of the house as bottom wall plates. Next, the wall planks were inserted vertically into a groove in the front and back edge-set planks, and into the ground at the sides. An interior plank was then set on edge (sometimes at an angle as a back post) parallel to the house walls, and the space between was filled with earth. This created a raised platform all around the house interior upon which small gable-roofed bedroom structures might be placed, sometimes with separate floors and fireplaces. The lighter poles were then set in the earth fill to brace the walls.

The roof planks were set on the purlins, running from ridge to side, and were channeled and overlapped like tiles. There were no smoke holes; planks were pushed aside from within by a pole to vent excess smoke. Midspan posts sometimes helped to support the two main heavy beams, as shown in Boas's drawings *(right)*.

A house frame with carved rear posts was photographed at Gwayasdums village *(left)* in 1955.

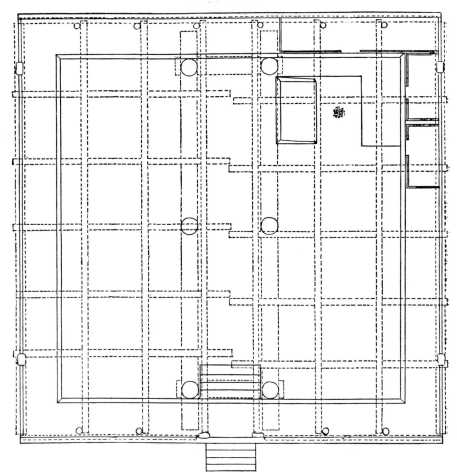

Plan

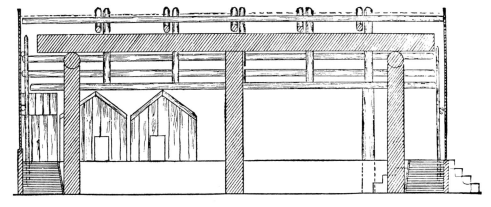

Longitudinal section

House frames

A Kwakiutl house frame *(above)* with milled wall boards, Memquimlees village, Vancouver Island, ca. 1917. The remains of a carved post and beam house frame *(left)* at Quatsino Sound, 1955.

Thunderbird

Raven

Raven

Kwakiutl iconography

The facades of important Kwakiutl houses often bore dramatic paintings of mythical animals and beings. They were family "crests," and belonged to the family that owned the house. Related to the sacred lineage ancestry of the house, they portrayed mythic events, and signified the tranformation of the house into a symbolic being during the winter ceremonials.

The drawing *(top)* depicts the painted housefront shown in the photograph on page 249. The central figure inside the circle is an example of the "displayed figure" motif, typically a figure crouched in a frontal position over the entrance passage. Death and rebirth were symbolized by passage through the entrance. The central circle symbolized the moon. At the sides are two grizzly bears representing other house ancestors.

The six animal figures by Franz Boas on this page are a gallery of crests drawn from housefront paintings in the late nineteenth century. The figures were usually painted directly on the planks, with no preliminary bas-relief carving. The colors were primarily black and red, symbolizing death and rebirth, respectively. Some blue was used, and sometimes whitewash for background. After commercial paints became available, however, muralists became extravagant; their favorite color was orange.

Thunderbird

Whale

Killer whale

254

Kwakiutl iconography

The snapping door *(top left)* is from the Vancouver Island village of Gwayasums, photographed ca. 1917. It is a variation on the "devouring mouth," motif, which dramatizes the warning that only worthy people can enter without harm. During ceremonial occasions, the lower beak dropped to form a ramp for people to enter the building or to snap threateningly at them. The facade of a house *(bottom right)* at Xumptaspi-Nawittl Village on Hope Island shows the doorway as a gaping mouth.

The mythological Sisiutl, a double-headed serpent with a central human face, was considered a dangerous creature. Representing in one image the sky and sea, or the upperworld and underworld, it was able to change from sky into lightning, or from fish into canoe, which lent it great power. A symbol found also in China and Mexico, it is thought to symbolize a dragon-monster belonging to and capable of passage between the three cosmic zones: sky, earth, and sea. It is seen on the roofline of a house at Tsadsisnukwomi village *(bottom left)*. Photographed ca. 1910.

Frequently found on Kwakiutl facades, bird and fish motifs are symbols of the tribal cosmos, the thunderbird representing the sky and upperworld; the whale, the sea and underworld. After a mythic combat, the bird consumes the fish, symbolizing the dominance of the upperworld. The housefront painting at Koskimo village *(above right)* represents the thunderbird lifting a whale.

255

Ceremonial space

During winter, the sacred part of the year, masked dances and initiation rites were held in decorated Kwakiutl house interiors, as shown *(below)* in a diorama in New York's American Museum of Natural History.

During these ceremonies, the Kwakiutl secret societies inducted new members in dramatic displays that involved symbolic rebirth, enacted through circular openings in the rear screens. Some Kwakiutl buildings were altered for the elaborate theatrical performances of masked dancers. Tunnels were dug beneath the flooring for dancers to disappear into through false-bottomed chests, and tubes made of kelp were used to make the house posts speak or sing. The audience lost sight of shamans as they climbed the sacred pole through the smoke hole, while wooden puppets swooped from the roof on strings. Goose down was blown through the mouths of wooden statuary. Performers with special costumes handled fire. Dancers wearing carved masks, which were hinged to split open and reveal inner masks with moveable facial parts, cast wild shadows against the walls; the deeply carved eyes and protruding mouths on the house posts seemed alive. It was at these times that the Kwakiutl saying, "The house holds the tribes in its hand," seemed literal.

Raven House

Special houses, such as the Raven House
(*above*) on Deer Island belonging to Chief
Wakyas of Alert Bay, were refurbished for
guests, dancers, and feasting for the winter
ceremonial season.

NOOTKA AND BELLA COOLA

Of all the Central tribes, the Nootka lived closest to the southern Salish people, so it is not surprising that they built both shed-roofed structures and the single-ridgepole gable house. The monumental residence that impressed the trader John Meares was a gable building, and, although he obtained no dimensions, fifteen years later another American seaman named John Jewitt estimated the size of a similar Nootka house. Its 100-foot ridgepole rested on central posts at front and back. Sidewall boards were held up by four corner posts. At the peak, its gable roof stood 14 feet high, while the earthen floor only sunk a foot below ground level.

The Nootka prepared for building a house by measuring the site and angling the four corner post-holes to steady the bulky posts as they were being put in. Already carved and painted, the posts themselves were set at a 45-degree angle, leaning outward. Then everyone rested while the chief sang a blessing and dropped offerings in the cavities. Another collective effort heaved the posts into a vertical position, whereupon they were twisted into exact alignment and the holes were rammed tight with rubble and dirt. Raising the roof beams and ridgepole was harder. A long lever helped to rock them up a steadily ascending crib-work pillar. Using wedges and ropes, they were fitted into precut notches in the four corner posts and, if the house used a ridgepole, in the two central pillars.

Meares, among the earliest observers to realize that these solid-looking structures served a seminomadic residence pattern, wrote that one day, "as if by enchantment, the greater part of the houses disappeared . . . The manner in which the houses of the Nootka are constructed, renders the embarkations as well as the debarkations a work of little time and ready execution, so that a large and populous village is entirely removed to a different station with as much ease as any other water carriage."

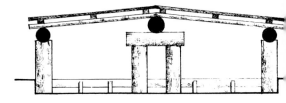

Nootka house frame

Nootka architecture

The Nootka built both shed-roof and gable-roofed structures. The gable roof of a Nootka house *(above)* at Friendly Cove is supported by a central ridgepole resting on cross beams at each end. The projecting ridgepole of this particular house was carved into a serpent's head.

Nootka whale house

The Nootka harpooners relied on a special hunting shrine *(below)* a gable-roofed structure containing masks, skulls, carved effigies of past whalers, and carved wooden images of whales. In rituals that used statues of successful hunters, shamans would attempt to entice whales up to the beach to be killed.

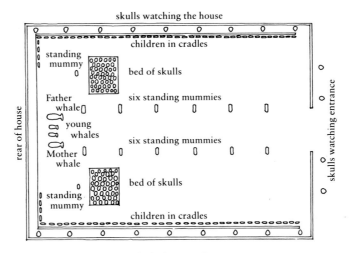

Whale house plan

Just north of Nootka and Kwakiutl territory lived the Bella Coola tribes, whose villages were along the upper reaches of the Dean and Burke channels and the Bella Coola River. Captain Vancouver learned that Bella Coola villages were deliberately situated in hard-to-reach spots when he was led to a village on Channel Island between the mainland and Vancouver Island. He was guided along "a very narrow path winding diagonally up the cliff, estimated by us to be about a hundred feet in height, and within a few degrees of being perpendicular. Close to the edge of this precipice stood the village, the houses of which were built after the fashion of the Nootka...."

Vancouver also found some dwellings which were elevated on 6- to 8-foot pilings. At another Bella Coola village, which the fur trader Alexander Mackenzie visited in 1793, the six houses were all "erected on palisades, rising twenty-five feet above ground."

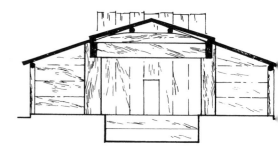

Bella Coola house frame

TODAY

When we boarded a ferry for the old Kwakiutl trading center of Fort Rupert we were aware that no old-style lineage houses were still standing, but Indian carver Tony Hunt soon showed us where the village's largest building apparently had been. Stakes in the ground indicated its dimensions—90 by 75 feet—and Hunt hoped to reconstruct it someday in the traditional fashion.

We already had seen some excellent replicas of classic Kwakiutl houses. At the British Columbia Provincial Museum's Thunderbird Park on Victoria Island, the late Kwakiutl artist Mungo Martin had constructed a half-size version of his own family's house, which had once graced the Fort Rupert

Bella Coola building

A house *(above)* in Kimsquit village, ca. 1881, with the unique Bella Coola tripartite facade. The roof was framed with two central roof beams that divided the interior into three equal bays. Sunk well below floor level was a large central fireplace. The side bays were partitioned into bedrooms.

beachfront. At the Seattle Science Park, scholar and artist Bill Holm incorporated authentic Kwakiutl house posts and beams into his recreation of a lineage house. Other original frames have been covered with newly made facades at Indian centers in the Gilford Island, Kingcome Inlet, and Comox native communities. More recently, Hunt supervised the construction of a permanent architectural exhibit at Chicago's Field Museum that displays the old-style Kwakiutl house in both its secular and sacred aspects.

We rode another ferry to Alert Bay, the hub of Kwakiutl community life today. We just missed a children's dance that day at the village "longhouse"; the forbidding "Devouring Mouth" or "Snapping Door" motif painted on its facade seemed to reinforce warnings we had received about photographing the building, but local custodians graciously recorded the facade with our cameras. Perched on a hill overlooking Comorant Island, the 75- by 55-foot building stood about 20 feet from dirt floor to the peak of its gable. The two main house beams were adzed in slender rows; each groove represented a tribal ancestor, we were told. The sculpted ends of the rafters did not quite meet at the ridge.

Against the rear wall stood two carved and painted Thunderbird house posts, their wings outstretched as if they were lifting the building into the air. The smoke-aged cedar beams and planks glowed warmly in the light filtering through the smoke hole. The milled lumber, frame doors, and glazing on some of the windows represented the changes that had been increasing for more than a century. Yet some old functions of the building, and its interior arrangement around a central fire pit on the bare dirt floor, remained; the Canadian government's edict that had once outlawed potlatches in such traditional-style buildings had not eradicated the practice nor its architectural setting.

Alert Bay longhouse

The interior of the community "longhouse" *(below)* at Alert Bay has carved houseposts replicating the symbolic Thunderbird. The grimacing face on the central panel is reminiscent of the building's painted facade.

Northern architecture

Villages of the Haida, Tsimshian, and Tlingit featured totem poles and houses with tightly fitted plank walls. One of the most important Haida villages was Skidegate *(below)*, photographed in 1878. The Haida were known for their carving; the Tsimshian for their painting. The bold, sculptural carving of the Haida is shown on an interior house post *(right)* depicting the Bear Mother and her cub. The house post is from a two-beam house on Prince of Wales Island.

NORTH

Northwest Coast Indian carpentry reached its technical and artistic climax in the northern region. The three principal Indian nations there—the Haida, Tlingit, and to some extent the Tsimshian—responded to the harsher winters by building smaller, more tightly fitted houses than those found down the coast. Generally about 40 feet square, they stood shoulder to shoulder on the upper beach, usually behind a lofty screen of the crest columns popularly called totem poles.

The Tlingit and the Tsimshian used a version of two-beam house construction similar to that of the Kwakiutl. The Haida's innovation was the unique six-beam house. The Tlingit lived north of the Haida, along the coves and river channels of the southeastern Alaska mainland. Their houses were usually built of locally available yellow cedar, spruce, and hemlock, although sometimes they traded with their neighbors for red cedar. Tsimshian territory extended south of the Haida islands and up the Nass and Skeena river basins. It is unfortunate that documentation on their architecture is so meager, for reputedly they were the master house carvers and painters on the Northwest Coast.

HAIDA

In 1792, the French explorer Etienne Marchand was awestruck by the Haida buildings he visited in the northern Queen Charlotte Islands. "Is not our astonishment increased," he wrote, "when we consider the progress these people have made in architecture? What instinct, or, rather, what genius, it has required to conceive and execute solidly . . . those edifices, those heavy frames of buildings of fifty feet in extent by eleven in elevation?"

Marchand noted the 4-foot-wide planks, the tight joinery of mortise and tenons that was a hallmark of Haida carpentry, the interior pit lined with retaining planks, and the underground "cellar" used in extremely cold weather. He described the elliptical doorway that "imitates the form of a gaping human mouth, or rather that of a beast, and . . . is surmounted by a hooked nose about two feet in length proportioned in point of size to the monstrous face."

Of the estimated thirty-four Haida villages strung along the island coast-lines when Europeans first appeared in 1774, only two would survive epidemics and the reconsolidation of their remnant population. In their heyday, Haida islanders usually occupied their winter villages from November through February, the season for feasting, recreation, and tasks such as preparing cedar logs for trade. March and April were times for hunting sea lions and refurbishing canoes for trading expeditions. From June through fall the men pulled their fishing gear from storage and moved to their summer camps, where women gathered berries. Salmon runs lasted from September to November, after which the Indians returned to their coastal homes.

The unique six-beam house found only on the Queen Charlotte Islands intrigued the early photographer George M. Dawson when he visited the Haida in the late 1800s. In these buildings, he observed, the roofs were not supported on central posts as in the more widespread two-beam construction system. They rested on the angled gable plates, the slotted corner posts, and "three stout beams flattened on the lower side," which protruded beyond the plate beams on either side of the gable. Dawson's photographs show how the vertical wall planks fit neatly into slots in both these gable plates and the base plates that ran along the ground. Sometimes they were bent by steaming and forced to overlap to produce a weather-tight wall. The six-beam system opened up the interior, making its use more flexible, because free-standing house posts were no longer necessary.

Haida houses also were distinguished by their unpainted facades. Instead, the occupying families' crests and myths were portrayed on prominent doorway poles, on screens and retaining planks inside, or on the free-standing poles—which early on were not painted—that rose before the buildings like proud genealogies.

Dating the phases of Haida monumental art has prompted considerable speculation. Northwest Coast art forms were firmly established before the influx of traders, metal tools, and European paints in the early 1800s, but the fur trade certainly increased their quantity and probably their quality. Carved inside screens and house doorway poles were sketched by early European artist John Barlett and described by Marchand in the 1790s, but there is only one brief reference in 1794 to a free-standing "totem pole." Only a century later, however, these ceremonial and mortuary poles were dominating Haida village-scapes.

Haida two-beam houses

The Haida built both two-beam and six-beam houses. Houses in the more northerly Haida villages were two-beam structures, such as the Goose House *(top right)* in Kayang village, famous for its beautiful frontal pole. At Kasaan village *(bottom right)*, on Prince of Wales Island in southern Alaska, most of the houses were also of the two-beam style. One of the earliest drawings of Haida architecture *(below)* was made during John Barlett's visit to the village of Kiusta, Graham Island, in 1791. "The door was made like a man's head," wrote the fur trader Barlett, "and the passage into the house was between his teeth and was built before they knew the use of iron."

The birthplace and relative age of the distinctive Haida six-beam house is also unclear. That it was a recent innovation is suggested by the fact that a group of Haida who reportedly left the Queen Charlotte people over two centuries ago for Prince of Wales Island farther north constructed only the two-beam house. Because the six-beam house was built most commonly in southerly Queen Charlotte settlements, the Anthony Island region has been identified as its place of origin. Perhaps this anomalous architectural contribution was stimulated by trading with European seamen, when new wealth enhanced artistic inventiveness among the Haida.

In the northern Queen Charlottes, the village of Masset, or "White Slope," was the site of the largest recorded Haida house, the "Neuwons" or "Monster House," built around 1850. Even under ordinary conditions, building a Haida house was a major financial undertaking, but it was especially difficult at Masset, where the builders were far from suitable timber.

The grand building had been envisioned by a chief named Weah to commemorate an advantageous marriage which had been negotiated between his son and the daughter of a wealthy nearby chief. As with the Kwakiutl, etiquette required that the builders be reimbursed during each construction stage. Planks were harvested from standing trees only after complex negotiations with the appropriate chief who owned them. Cedar beams had to be dragged behind canoes for many miles. An estimated two thousand people worked on this legendary building, and the 55-square-foot structure required eight beams instead of the customary six.

Chief Weah's "Monster House"

The six-beam house was typically found in the Haida's principal territory, the Queen Charlotte Islands. Chief Weah's house *(above)* was of the six-beam type but required two extra beams because of its size. This house of the wealthy chief of Masset was said to be the greatest of all Haida homes; it was at least 55 feet square.

An interior photograph *(right)* shows a three-level floor with a central fireplace. The pit was lined with wide, horizontal planks. After the house disintegrated, its dimensions were reconstructed working from this photograph, which showed items such as the captain's chair whose exact measurements were known.

The Haida villages of Ninstints and Skedans

The remote village of Ninstints *(left)*, on Anthony Island has been named a World Heritage Site, a monument of historical and architectural significance. The houses stood around the rim of a secluded bay *(map, lower left)*. Houses 1-12 were sited on a terrace about 20 feet high; a second row, houses 13-17, was built on a lower and somewhat swampy area. The houses were on the average about 35 feet square (house 3 was the largest, 47 feet wide by 49 feet deep) and were spaced only 2 to 7 feet apart. Three two-beam structures were found; the others were six-beam. Raven and Eagle clans occupied the village, and in winter several lineages of each moiety lived in the houses. Photographed ca. 1901.

The village of Skedans *(bottom right)* had an unusual "double-bay" site. House 1 *(map, below)*, at the heart of the village, was the chief's house, which was over 50 feet square and had six beams. Its name was "Clouds Sound Against It (as They Pass Over)." The floor had three terraces. Small houses were grave houses.

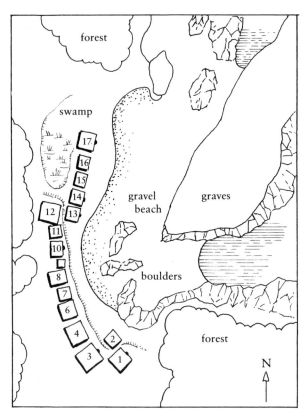

Ninstints village plan

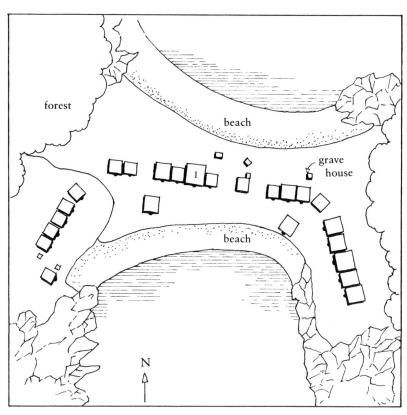

Skedans village plan

One of the best-preserved old Haida village sites is Ninstints, situated on an isolated, sheltered cove along the eastern shore of the mile-and-a-half-long Anthony Island. In the 1830s it was known as Red Cod Island Town, a thriving hunting and fishing village of about twenty houses, each with a formal name, which was occupied by more than three hundred people. As in most Haida towns, the lineage houses belonged to either the Eagle or Raven moieties of the community.

When Ninstints was abandoned in the 1880s, its survivors moved eighty-five miles north to Skidegate, a village the Haida knew as "Place of Stones." Skidegate received refugees from another well-documented Haida town, the village of Koona, also known as Skedans. In the 1830s this, too, had been a thriving community of 471 people living in twenty-seven cedar houses. But by the late 1880s the last of its people paddled thirty miles south to settle in Skidegate.

When the Canadian artist Emily Carr visited the abandoned village of Skedans in 1907, only a few six-beam Haida house frames were still standing, but nearly all of the free-standing crest poles were there. She wrote that they stood "in a long straggling row the entire length of the bay and pointed this way and that, but no matter how drunken their tilt, the old poles never lost their dignity ... They were bleached to a pinkish silver color and cracked by the sun, but nothing could make them mean or poor."

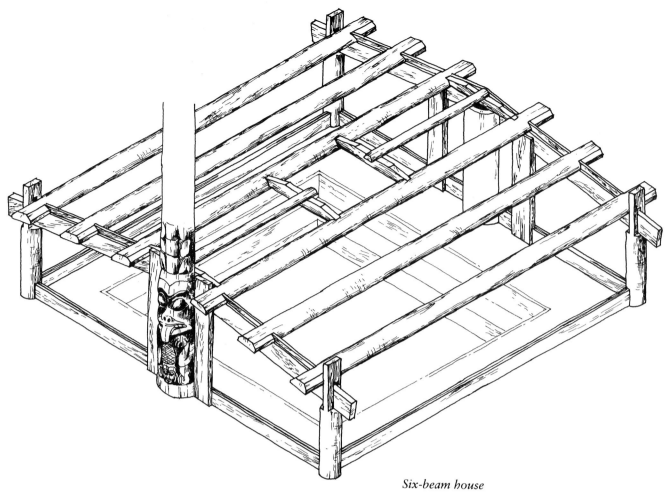

Six-beam house

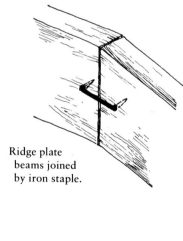

Ridge plate
beams joined
by iron staple.

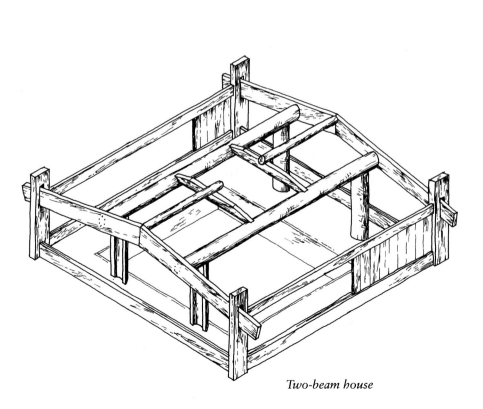

Two-beam house

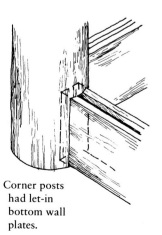

Corner posts
had let-in
bottom wall
plates.

Haida architecture

Of the Haida's two different structural systems, the most common was the six-beam; the two-beam house was evidently an earlier type.

The drawing of the six-beam house *(left)* is based on a reconstruction of the structure of house 12 at Ninstints and on additional information from Haida artist Bill Reid. The plan was basically 45 feet square. Four slotted and notched corner posts received a bottom plank wall plate and a sloping roof plate beam. The plates were up to 30 by 6 inches in size and were made from the most carefully selected planks in the house. The sloping roof plates extended through corner post slots. Two central six-sided posts spaced 3 to 4 feet apart supported the plate beams, and the frontal pole abutted the post fronts. Roof supports were six large, equally spaced beams that rested on the plate beams, the larger end at the front. While the wall boards were fit together with battens, the roof planks were randomly set and were held down with stones.

Roof beam plates were sometimes fastened together by an iron staple, as at Tanu village *(top right)*. Photographed in 1901. Vertical wall boards fit into grooves in a bottom wall plate, as at an abandoned Tlingit village *(middle right)*. In the completed Haida house frame, faceted beams protruded beyond the gable plate, as in this frame in Cumshewa village *(bottom right)*. Photographed in 1901.

Haida iconography

Carved frontal poles were the dominant symbol associated with Haida houses but interior screens and house posts were also carved. Frontal poles combined sculpted crests from the clans of both husband and wife. Images on posts and poles were interconnected, producing an abbreviated and stylized narrative history. The rear post of the Skidegate Raven House *(above)* had a raven flanked by frogs, stacked on top of the Thunderbird. The beam ends of the Eagle House *(top right)* in Tanu village were carved into sea lion heads, and its carved door post had an eagle and baleen whale. Chief Gold's Moon House at Skidegate village *(bottom right)*, with a moon mask over the door, was one of the few painted house fronts noted among the Haida.

TODAY

In the summer of 1979, we flew in a seaplane to see the Haida community house in Masset. It was under construction, the stud frame walls inside still uncovered. Early missionaries had persuaded the extended-family Haida households to splinter into nuclear families and move into cottage-style dwellings. During these transition years, the exteriors had combined white man's materials with native art. But behind their milled-siding facades, mail-order trim, and often extravagant use of glazed windows, Indians still cooked over central fires and stored their potlatch valuables in the rear of the house. This Masset building would continue that synthesis of architectural customs.

Next we drove south to Skidegate through Moresby Island's logged landscape of silted creeks and second-growth forests. We hoped for tribal permission to board a fishing boat to the old Skedans and Tanu townsites. Even though the forest had reclaimed the lineage houses, we wanted to see their settings.

Good fishing had emptied the harbor of boats, so we rented a seaplane. The surf was too choppy to land, but as we dropped over Skedans we made out a lone house post leaning toward the ground. The loss of Haida architectural art to climate and museums has left few remains, but by correlating historic photographs, museum collections, and interviews with the Indian descendants, many Haida town histories have been reconstructed.

Historical photography is accepted as "direct evidence" of the criteria which permits special places to be placed on the UNESCO roster of World Heritage Sites. Ninstints on Anthony Island won that designation in 1981,

Haida architecture today

Contemporary Haida communities use the old lineage house form for their community buildings. The Masset town center *(left)* features painted bas-relief crests. The recently built council house at Skidegate *(above and right)* is glazed on the side of the building facing the beach. Inside, a central fireplace is capped by a black hood suspended from the ceiling.

thanks to the photographic coverage of George M. Dawson, Richard and Hannah Maynard, and other pioneer British Columbia photographers. The year 1875 was chosen to mark the period when Ninstints was in its prime, when the community raised its last crest poles.

Haida artist Bill Reid told us that the Haida band council had just built an "interpretation" of a traditional six-beam house at Skidegate, which we decided to see. The building stood alone, its rear facade of unpainted, aged cedar weathering into a silvery patina. A glassed front wall faced the beach, divided in the center by the hollowed back of a frontal crest pole. Since the plate beams forming the traditional gable did not bear on the wall planks, the glazing seemed remarkably harmonious with the building's weight. Inside, a metal lighting hood was suspended over a depressed central rectangle where a polished wood conference table stood in place of the old-time hearth. Viewed from the beach, the sea rippling in the reflecting glass and Bill Reid's deeply sculpted crest pole on the facade, it seemed the most successful fusion of traditional and modern aesthetics we had encountered.

TLINGIT

The Tlingit nation consisted of about forty winter towns spread along the Alaskan panhandle and offshore islands. Each Tlingit town was divided into halves, generally known as the Raven and Wolf sides of the community—with an Eagle division added in some northerly villages. Tlingit towns ranged from one row of a few houses to sixty plank buildings clustered by clan and arranged in two rows paralleling the coast. Each clan-lineage house displayed the crests associated with its house ancestor.

While the lower Northwest Coast nations were largely dominated by British regimes, the Tlingit came under Russian religious and commercial influence. By 1806, their winter village at the Russian trading depot of Sitka was protected by a double palisade of tree trunks 15 feet high. The Chilkat, a Tlingit subgroup, had a "mother town" called Klukwan on the north bank of the Chilkat River. When the scholar George Emmons visited in 1882, much of old Klukwan was intact; the houses were propped up on their front pilings for three quarters of a mile and faced a shore busy with smokehouses, fish-drying frames, and canoe shelters. Emmons took special interest in the "Whale House," a structure that had gained fame for its carvings since it was built in about 1835.

Tlingit architecture

A Tlingit painted house front *(left)* featuring a bear, Cape Fox village, Alaska, 1899.

Tlingit Indians Louis and Florence Shotridge provided information for the drawing *(right)* of a house whose main roof beams are 44½ feet long and 2 feet in diameter. In the old days houses were larger and were built without nails or spikes; all the parts fitted together to support one another and boards were tightly overlapped for weatherproofing. As units of measurement, the builders used the thickness of their fingers, the span of their hands, and the distance between the joints of their arms.

The house interior had two floor levels, the lower of which was sunken about 2 feet and covered with plank flooring.

The door (not shown) was raised to be above the average winter snow level. A smoke hole in the roof (which was composed of heavy split shingles) was directly over the fireplace and was sometimes protected by chimneylike windbreaks with shutters. Space on the upper floor level was divided according to the number of people living in the house. Sleeping places were sometimes enclosed by screens and occasionally even had an upper bunk.

Chief Shake's house compound at Wrangell, Alaska *(below)*, ca. 1890. The structures have been reconstructed and can be visited today.

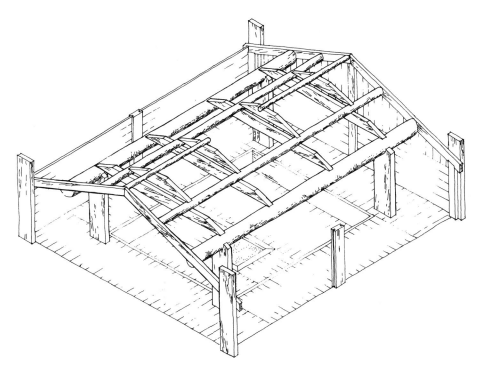

Tlingit house frame

Like most Tlingit winter houses, the Whale House was nearly square. Its facade was about 50 feet wide, and its side walls were 53 feet deep. The corner and intermediate posts were vertically grooved to accept a stack of horizontal spruce wall planks. Large top and bottom facade plates were mortised into the corner posts and grooved so the vertical front planks could slide into them. To shingle the roof, spruce planks and bark slabs were held fast by spars running the length of the house and weighted down by boulders at each end. The central smoke hole, which offered the only light, had a movable shutter balanced on a cross bar so it could be adjusted from inside by a pole.

Outside, the building was beautifully proportioned but unadorned, lacking even a crest pole. Inside, its four carved house posts and painted rear screen of thin cedar planks featured the finest artwork in the Tlingit world. Two years after the old Whale House was dismantled in 1899, a modern two-story replacement structure that inherited its title and crests was consecrated in a grand potlatch. But the resident new chief died before he could reinstall the house's posts and rear screen. They were guarded for years by Klukwan's residents, who resisted many efforts by major museums to buy them. The Tlingit preferred their treasures to remain, even rotting and unseen, where their spirits were at home.

The Whale House

One of the most renowned Tlingit houses was the Whale House of Klukwan village, belonging to the family of Chief Klart-Reech *(below)*, photographed ca. 1895. Built in 1835, it was nearly square, measuring 49 feet, 10 inches wide by 53 feet long. In contrast to its plain facade, its interior posts and rear screen *(right)*, known as the "Rainwall screen" were exquisitely crafted. Early Northwest Coast observer George Emmons said that the central figure in this screen represented the rain spirit, and that the small border figures were called "rain-drops splash up."

Interior screens usually were carved or painted on thin cedar planks and set up for winter ceremonies. They were pierced by an inner doorway, marking a transition zone between the communal part of the house and the chief's compartment.

TSIMSHIAN

Esteemed by neighboring tribes for their architectural craftsmen, the Tsimshian occupied the mainland between Kwakiutl and Tlingit country. One Tsimshian tale describes a wanderer's arrival at an "artisan's town" in which every house boasts a painted facade. In the chief's house he is instructed to memorize all the housefront motifs because "they will tell you about a medicine." Such references suggest the special connection between building symbolism and Tsimshian talents.

The Tsimshian nation was divided between groups who dwelt along the ocean and the Gitskan Tsimshian who occupied the Upper Skeena and Nass river valleys. Their mythology suggests, however, that they originated from the interior, where, like groups of Bella Coola who lived inland, they probably once built plateau-style pit houses. All nine of the coastal Tsimshian winter villages moved to the mouth of the Nass River after the Hudson Bay Co. established its Port Simpson trading post there in 1834.

Around 1862 their culture underwent a radical change, however, when forceful Scottish missionary William Duncan oversaw construction of a "model" Christian Indian settlement at Metlakatla. Duncan discouraged native festivals and potlatches and the display of family crests on poles and house fronts. His parishioners were pressured to move into identical, undecorated wood frame houses built on the beach like barracks, and to work collectively in the community sawmill, boat-building plant, and printing press. Duncan died in 1918, but his legacy of imposed assimilation lingers in Metlakatla today. In Tsimshian communities beyond the reach of Duncan's influence, native houses also changed with the times as milled siding, the number of windows, and hinged doors replaced painted facades as signs of the owner's prestige.

The Tsimshian region

The inland Gitksan Tsimshian occupied the upper Skeena and Nass river valleys. Smoke houses and a trussed bridge (*above*) were photographed in a fishing village near the Skeena River in 1920.

On the coast at Fort Simpson, British Columbia, a large housefront (*right*) was photographed ca. 1900, with its Standing Beaver frontal pole. A mid-nineteenth-century trading center, Fort Simpson thrived under the protection of the Hudson Bay Company. In this town, Tsimshian chiefs competed for prestige by commissioning elaborately painted housefronts and interior screens. Tsimshian artwork was considered the finest and most complex on the Northwest Coast.

Tsimshian houses (*drawing top right*) were of moderate size, probably about 30 feet square, and typical of the northern gable-roof, two-beam style, with a two-level deep pit lined with planks. Although the Haida and Tlingit usually floored their buildings with smooth planks, the Tsimshian often left their earthen floors uncovered. Finely adzed wall planks were carefully fitted into notched wall plates.

280

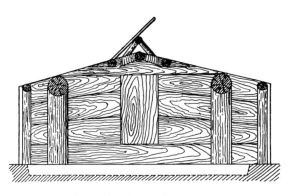

Tsimshian house frame

Laboratory analysis of early Tsimshian architectural paintings has brought some of their traditional artistry to light. Around the turn of the century, two faded house screens, believed to date from as early as 1830 and originating near Port Simpson, were added to the University of British Columbia collections. Recent studies of Tsimshian symbols and Northwest Coast cosmology by anthropologist Dr. George MacDonald indicate that only chiefs' residences of the four Port Simpson clans would have been entitled to display such paintings. MacDonald used infrared photography to conduct microscopic pigment analysis and to reconstruct the barely perceptible designs. Large acetate tracings at half-scale were tinted to recover the iconographic detail and coloration of the original facades.

In the Smithsonian Institution in Washington, D.C., is another house screen, in good condition, which was acquired in 1875 at Port Simpson. The design is believed to depict aspects of a myth first recorded by Franz Boas and later intrepreted by MacDonald in terms of studies of Northwest Coast mythology by anthropologist Claude Lévi-Strauss. Many of these myths, according to Lévi-Strauss, were about a "... complicated network of chiefs and chieftainesses who control game, fish, and other forms of wealth, and to whom the human shamans and chiefs had to pay homage through songs and rituals...."

MacDonald believes that the screen portrays the legend of *Nagunaks*, a mythical Tsimshian sea chief who lives at the bottom of the ocean. When his

Painted screen

A Tsimshian ceremonial screen *(below)* acquired by the Smithsonian Institution in 1875. It is believed to illustrate the myth of *Nagunaks*, a mythical chief who controlled the plentitude of food and other material wealth of the tribe. The facade is 38 feet wide and 12 feet high.

clansman, Chief Dragging-along-the-Shore, and his men drop an anchor on his roof, Nagunaks brings them down, feasts them, and presents his guest with a house front painting and an interior house decoration. He also wishes him good luck in hunting, but adds that he must never again hurt any fish. MacDonald writes, "On the one hand, Nagunaks is the master of great wealth who assures the fortunes of those he favors, but on the other hand, he places his favors under very severe conditions."

Nagunaks is depicted in the center of the screen with a crown of small human heads, and is flanked on either side by killer whales, who symbolize his alter ego. The whales's dorsal fins rise through the upper border design, becoming, as MacDonald speculates, "... visual thresholds between different zones of the design. There is little doubt that the extreme extension of the dorsal fins beyond the design field emphasizes the symbolic attribute of the dorsal fin of the killer whale as a world axis...." The killer whales are therefore indicated as beings who can cross between worlds.

Human figures are depicted in the blowholes of the whales. Apparently they represent the men about to return to the surface after Nagunaks' feast. In the myth one of them kills a fish, violating Nagunaks' request. The men perish in a whirlpool, and Dragging-along-the-Shore must dwell forever in the house of Nagunaks. MacDonald concludes, "The doorway of the house is through the abdomen of Nagunaks as part of an equation in which the whole house structure becomes the body of Nagunaks as the chief of wealth, or as Dragging-along-the-Shore as primary ancestor...."

TODAY

Since the 1950s, a renaissance of native arts has been under way along the Northwest Coast. We witnessed it at K'SAN, a museum and craft complex in Hazelton in the heartland of the Tsimshian-speaking Gitskan people. On a grassy plain at the confluence of the Skeena and Buckley rivers stands a "village" of reconstructed plank houses mixing various architectural styles.

The Tsimshian-style "Skeena Treasure House" was first erected in 1958. Six buildings now blend facade motifs and construction methods from as many different tribes. In 1970, K'SAN also opened a center for young Indian artists to learn the traditional artistry of masks, blankets, rattles, and carved house posts.

Anthropologist Polly Sargent was a prime mover behind the K'SAN revival. Gathering detailed information on Tsimshian house-building traditions has been difficult, she told us, because elders contradict each other on construction points. At one time each house displayed only the crests it owned; these days the only buildings that could be labeled "traditional" in Northwest Coast native villages are communal meeting halls which often display crests and symbols assembled from all of the town clans.

Tsimshian architecture today

K'SAN, the reconstructed Gitksan village *(above)* in Hazelton, British Columbia, has a museum and houses that are open to the public. Tours describe early Gitksan life and arts.

The government school building *(right)* at Kispiox, near Hazelton, features traditional crests.

We admired artist Vernon Stephens's eagle-and-ship mural on the facade of the K'SAN woodworking shop. Inside, on a plank screen made of aged cedar boards, Nootka artist Ron Hamilton had painted one of the classic Northwest Coast scenes for house fronts—the mythic combat of Thunderbird and Whale, lords of the upper and lower realms. Inside the Frog, Wolf, and Fireweed houses at K'SAN, electric lights illuminated the blankets and woodworking tools of life-size dioramas. Not far from K'SAN we visited the old village site of Kitwancool. Here stands the "Hole in the Sky" totem pole, believed to be the only crest pole still in its original spot. Once, guests entered a mansion of cedar through its oval opening; today only the sky shows through the door.

As we drove back to the coast we noticed huge heraldic figures in red, black, and white on the government school building in the settlement of Kispiox. There was one on each wall, representing the inherited crests owned by the community's six major lineages. As Polly Sargent had explained, the underlying ideas of Northwest Coast Indian architecture would last as long as its societies felt the ancient compulsion to turn their buildings into their autobiographies.

NORTH

CENTRAL

SOUTH

Tolowa
Yurok
Karok
Hupa
Achumawi
Wintu
Nomlaki
Maidu
Chico
Pomo
Clear Lake •
Patwin
Fort Ross
San Francisco
Miwok
Monache
Yokuts

Pacific Ocean

Sierra Nevada Mtns

Lake Tahoe

GREAT BASIN

Paiute

• *Yosemite Valley*

Chemehuevi

Chumash
Santa Barbara
Gabrielino
Mohave
Needles
Serrano
Los Angeles
Cahuilla
Luiseño
COLORADO
RIVER
Diegueño
Quechan
Cocopa

7 WOOD, EARTH, and FIBER

CALIFORNIA

California diversity

The California region contained the widest variety of native languages, ecological settings, and house types of any North American culture area. The oldest illustration *(above)* of California Indian life, engraved by Theodore de Bry in 1599, depicts a conical lodge of the coastal Miwok, with a central fire and earth banking. The Wintu Indian pit house village *(below)* with its acorn caches was located near Redding, was drawn by Henry B. Brown in 1852.

In June 1579, Sir Francis Drake landed just north of present-day San Francisco and visited an Indian encampment believed to have been occupied by a coastal branch of Miwok speakers. "Their houses are digged round with earth," wrote Drake's chaplain, "and they have from the uttermost brims of the circle cliffs of wood set upon them, joining together at the top like a spire steeple, which by reasons of that closeness are very warm."

Dugout floors and earth banking were insulating techniques used by many Indian groups in California. Twenty years after Drake's visit, the Dutch engraver Theodore de Bry illustrated this Miwok domicile. He depicted five adults and one child sitting on fiber mats, together with the grass pillows the Miwok called *hawi*. The building, or *kotca*, "place where real people live," is framed with two interlocking forked poles into which poles lean from around a circular floor. The covering material resembles slabs of redwood bark rather than the grass or tule thatching tied with lupine-root cord that ethnographic accounts of later coastal Miwok groups describe. The engraver emphasized the banking of earth insulation—probably fill taken from the slightly excavated floor—that extends part way up the outside walls.

Despite California's generally temperate climate, the Indians were forced to shelter themselves from chilling fogs along the coast and sweltering summer heat in the valleys to the incessant winter rains of the foothills and the heavy snows of the high Sierra Nevada. These variations in local climate and habitat are reflected in the wide diversity of Indian house types found throughout aboriginal California.

For at least ten thousand years, California became home to a swelling population of emigrant tribes that ventured down the coast or entered from the north and east through mountain passes. On the eve of Drake's appearance the region held more than 300,000 people—perhaps thirteen percent of the entire continent's native population. It was also a culturally diverse population—six of native North America's seven major language groups were represented in California, divided into more than one hundred dialects.

The Indian cultures of California have been subdivided by the region's leading anthropologist, Alfred L. Kroeber, into four cultural "provinces," each with representative forms of architecture. Located just below the present-day Oregon state line, tribes of the Northern province lived up and down the Klamath and Trinity River valleys and fished for salmon, hunted deer in the Siskiyou Mountains, dug clams along the Pacific tide line, and gathered plants. Here groups like the Yurok and Hupa built semisubterranean plank houses of redwood or cedar. To the southeast, on the eastern flank of the southern Cascade range, were tribes like the Modoc and Achumawi, who constructed earth-roofed, semisubterranean dwellings.

In the Central area, between the Pacific Ocean and eastward to the Great Basin, lived what Kroeber called "tribelets"—small autonomous groups of Miwok, Maidu, and Pomo speakers. Near the sea, their houses were made of brush or redwood bark. In the valleys, they usually built small pit houses. In the foothills they used more carefully constructed conical frames with redwood bark covering.

In the Southern province, bounded on the north by the Chumash tribal territories near Santa Barbara and to the south by today's Mexico-United States border, simple dome-shaped brush structures were built before the

Spanish arrived. Cooking windbreaks, large ceremonial arbors, and mud-plastered sweat baths often were found in their camps. After contact with the Spanish, however, form-molded adobe bricks became prevalent, which were mud-mortared into one-room thatched homes that resembled the Mexican peasant house known as a *jacal*.

The fourth province stretched along the lower Colorado River basin, and in many respects seemed a world apart. The ways of its people—the Mohave, Quechan, Cocopa, and others—resembled Arizona Indian cultures as much as they did Southern California Indians. This collection of linguistically related tribes grew corn, squash, and beans in the silt-rich Colorado basin in the spring. But they also were fishermen, bird hunters, and proficient gatherers of nutritious mesquite and screw beans. In traditional times these tribes built four-post, sand-roofed houses. Like the smaller groups of the Southern province, however, they eventually adopted the Mexican jacal but walled them with arrowweed-and-daub rather than adobe brick.

Scholars categorize the rich array of California Indians on the basis of their language families and dialect groups. However, the linguistic approach fails to reflect the tribelet's sense of identity, which was determined more by geographic, family, and local group affiliations. For most California Indians, "home" was the local hamlet and surroundings of one's tribelet; it was the "central place," in current archeological terminology, from which one ventured out in quest of seasonal foods.

Part of this collective identity was also the tribelet's house type. In California, structures included a variety of summer and winter house types, open-air assembly arenas, earth-roofed dance chambers, sweat baths or "sudatories," menstrual retreats, and a host of spaces reserved for processing and storing food.

California Indians regarded their environment as not only animate but ready to intercede in human affairs, an attitude that probably grew out of an intense awareness of their immediate surroundings. "The boundaries of all tribes," the amateur ethnographer Stephen Powers wrote in 1877, "are marked with the greatest precision, being defined by certain creeks, canons, bowlders, conspicuous trees, springs, etc., each of which objects has its own individual name . . . If an Indian knows but little of this great world, he knows his own small fighting ground intimately better than any topographical engineer."

NORTH

Origin stories of the Yurok Indians of the Klamath and Trinity Rivers area describe a supernatural race known as the *Woge* who dug the first rectangular house pits and passed onto their Yurok successors the annual cycle of ceremonies known as the World Renewal rituals. The Woge also had them build a special men's sweathouse every six years as an earthly replica of the sacred sweathouse believed by the Yurok to stand at the center of their cosmos. Semisubterranean family houses and men's sweathouses, erected around rectangular excavations with redwood or cedar planks, remained the characteristic house forms for the Yurok and their neighbors, and when the Spanish landed on Trinidad Bay in the eighteenth century, the Indians were

California plank house

The Yurok, Karok, Hupa, Tolowa, and other tribes that inhabited the forested river valleys of northwest California built redwood or cedar split-plank houses with two- or three-pitch roofs. This Hupa three-pitch family house *(above)* of split cedar planks was surrounded by a low wall of river boulders. Photographed ca. 1920. The early sketch of the Yurok village of Tsauri *(left)* shows redwood plank dwellings and sweathouses, at Trinidad Bay, California, ca. 1850. These villages rarely had more than five or six family houses, and one or two sweathouses.

still constructing their buildings as the Woge had taught them. An early description of Yurok architecture comes from a Spanish captain who visited the southernmost of the Yurok's fifty-four villages in 1775, a community known as Tsauri, or "Mountain:" "The native houses are square, subterranean huts, well-constructed of thick planks, with roofs which touch the ground and circular entrances barely the width of a human body. The floor is very flat and clean and in the middle there is a square hole, one vara deep, for making and keeping a fire, which heats the entire inside of the house." Until the last Tsauri resident died in 1914, more than a dozen chroniclers would make this community the best-documented architectural complex in native California.

Yurok family homes, usually with three-pitched roofs and gabled sweathouses, were constructed of redwood, which was sacred to the Yurok. (The Hupa preferred cedar.) Redwood was naturally resistant to infestation and rot, and its straight-grained trunks produced large, even boards when split with elkhorn wedges and basalt mauls. Large rectangular family houses might be as much as 35 feet long by 25 feet wide, but dwellings about 18 by 20 feet

were more common. Built around a 3-foot-deep pit, their thick wallboards were planted upright in the ground a few feet back from the pits to form a storage shelf running around the cellarlike sleeping and cooking pit. Below ground level, the earth was held back by horizontal planks locked behind vertical posts.

Yurok homes stood no more than 8 feet high. The Hupa dug their sleeping areas more deeply but raised the dwellings only about 4 or 5 feet above ground. Thick, notched corner boards held the long side plate beams, which in turn supported the lower end of the long roof boards. They were overlapped and left unfinished so that their natural grooves channeled rain runoff. The three-pitch Yurok houses had an asymmetrical profile, achieved by resting three sections of roof boards on two pole rafters that ran the length of the building. They were supported by notches in the front and back wallboards. Outer poles of willow or hazel were lashed to the frame on walls and roof to fasten the roofing.

Another feature peculiar to Northwest California dwellings was the circular doorway. Various interpretations have suggested that it was meant to simulate a woodpecker's hole, to force enemies into a helpless posture, or to symbolize rebirth. The openings were only about 2 feet wide. Just inside, a round door plug—or a sliding door that rode on the curved gunwales from an

Sweathouse and family house

Sweathouses were an important center of male activity among Northwestern California Indians. Here they smoked, counseled, and prepared for social and religious events. The structures had well-swept polished-board or hard earth floors, careful stonework on their retaining walls and sunning porch, and sooty ceilings. Some sweathouses were considered very sacred. This Karok example *(above left)* stood near the Klamath River. The drawings *(vertical row, far right)* show a Yurok sweathouse, which stood at the village of Pekwan, twenty miles up the Klamath River. The interior *(above)* is from the last remaining Yurok family house, located at Rekwoi. The drawings *(vertical row, right)* are based on a family house at Pekwan.

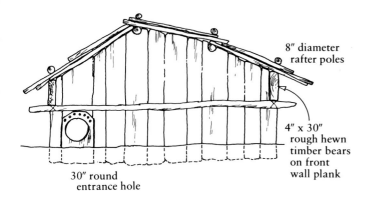

8" diameter
rafter poles

4" x 30"
rough hewn
timber bears
on front
wall plank

30" round
entrance hole

Front elevation

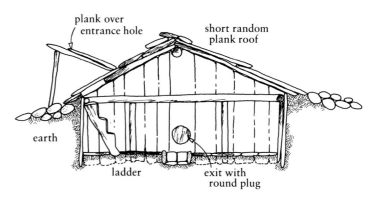

plank over
entrance hole

short random
plank roof

earth

ladder

exit with
round plug

Cross section

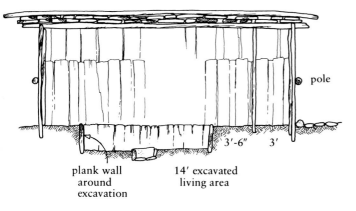

pole

plank wall
around
excavation

14' excavated
living area

3'-6"   3'

Longitudinal section

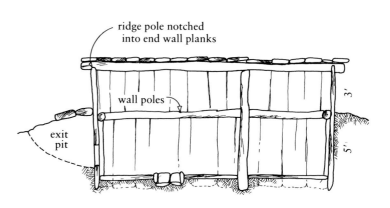

ridge pole notched
into end wall planks

wall poles

exit
pit

5'   3'

Longitudinal section

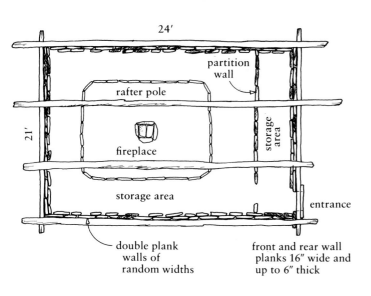

24'

partition
wall

rafter pole

storage
area

fireplace

21'

storage area

double plank
walls of
random widths

entrance

front and rear wall
planks 16" wide and
up to 6" thick

Plan

Yurok family house

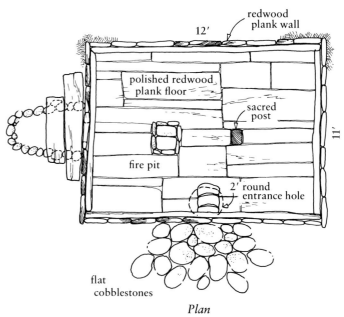

12'

redwood
plank wall

polished redwood
plank floor

sacred
post

fire pit

2' round
entrance hole

11'

flat
cobblestones

Plan

Yurok sweathouse

old redwood canoe—shielded the inhabitants from drafts, as did an interior screen of planks. A notched log ladder descended to a sleeping pit with sleeping mats and carved wooden headrests. Wooden stools surrounded the cooking fire, often ringed by five serpentine boulders, and drying fish and garments hung from poles overhead. Just outside the low, round doorway were rocks from the river that served as handgrips to haul oneself out. A well-worn threshold boulder often stood before the entrance, and the ground around the house might be paved with river cobbles. Houses were sometimes sited beneath a pepper tree, revealing a concern with landscaping that was unusual in Indian architecture.

Every Yurok settlement also contained one or two gable-roofed subterranean sweathouses where men socialized, cleansed and purified themselves, deliberated, smoked, prayed, and trained boys in sacred matters. From the outside, they looked like roofs that had collapsed on the ground. One entered through a rectangular door in the roof but left at one end through a circular opening in a trench below ground. Often an old, overturned canoe was used as a raincap over the ridge where the roofboards met.

Most of the Klamath and Trinity River people built special sacred sweathouses in preparation for spectacular group ceremonies. Before their New Year's ceremony, the Karok built a sweathouse following the guidelines in their mythology, keeping a sacred stone beside its fire to "make the world firm." For rituals to bless the arrival of the salmon, on which their lives depended, the Tolowa, neighbors of the Karok, constructed a sacred sweathouse near the mouth of the Smith River. They believed this was the spot where the first redwood tree had grown, at the center of their world. Wood scraps from the building were believed to have rain-making power. As it was built, its parts were renamed: the ridgepole was referred to as the "salmon's backbone," its roofboards the "salmon's ribs," and its front wall the "salmon's head." Before their fishing expeditions the men would climb into the metaphoric body of the salmon to pray for a healthy catch.

Rebuilding the Yurok sacred sweathouse was a major ritual performed every six years. It opened with an address to the hallowed redwood tree: "I will cut you because we are going to have you for holding up the sky." After extending offerings to the tree, the builders cut the sacred center post, the four major plates "which reach the ends of the world," and the ridgepole. These six pieces were then "killed," treated as royal funerary corpses, and resurrected through the World Renewal rite. To the Yurok, such reverence was due the sweathouse because it was the "purest of buildings."

TODAY

We visited a complete Northern California architectural ensemble at the Hupa Indian "rancheria" known as Takimitlding. Three family houses had been assembled recently from split cedar planks around a 3-foot sleeping pit. We entered the sweathouse the wrong way, through its sunken, circular exit. The sunning patio, formed of hundreds of smooth boulders that had been hauled up from the riverbed, curved around the building's south side. The family structures featured both two- and three-pitch roofs.

Later, on a steep hillside at the old Yurok town of Rekwoi, we crawled into

House identity

This round doorway (right) leads into a Yurok family house at Rekwoi. Carved from a redwood plank four feet wide and a foot thick, it is one of the structure's most precious heirlooms. As anthropologist Thomas Buckley explains, "The inhabitants of most villages considered themselves relatives, but one's identity and loyalty seem to have been primarily to one's own house. If the house was a prosperous one it was accompanied by a sweathouse for its men and sometimes a second family house, which bore the name of the first. Important members of strong descent groups used the house name as their own, public name. Many such houses were the sites of rituals; their roofs and sidewalls set aside; their open pits became arenas for the world-renewing Jump Dance and for the child-curing Brush Dance."

the tribe's last standing traditional house. Around 1900, the old Yurok term for "house" was supplanted by the English word "family" among the tribespeople, marking a significant change in Yurok society. No longer was the house considered a "person" with its own property rights and reputation. Given the name of *Lye-eck,* this building represented that bygone time when social and architectural identity were one. Its weathered boards, salvaged from the original structure and used on this building in the 1950s, were considered a community keepsake until one family claimed ancestral rights to them. Its unusually wide door board was decoratively indented around the entrance hole. Inside, the cooking hearth was bordered by five stone slabs and surrounded by hourglass-shaped wooden stools and sleeping mats. Stooping low to leave through the portholelike door, our groping fingers fell naturally onto the hand-grip rocks. We heaved ourselves out to admire the Klamath River pouring into the Pacific surf below us.

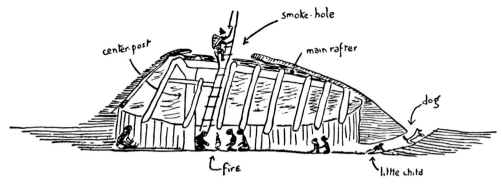

center-post

smoke-hole

main rafter

dog

fire

little child

To explain a winter-house of the large communal type
dug partly underground

CENTRAL

In 1869, an adventurer-journalist named Stephen Powers hiked and rode through much of Central California and recorded native food-gathering techniques, religious practices, and the diverse ways the Indians' available materials and social constraints shaped the production of their houses. Unfortunately, much of the architecture Powers illustrated soon became obsolete, such as a large communal lodge thatched by its Pomo builders with grass and shaped like a giant letter L, and a huge arbor built by the Yokuts over an entire village. Powers pioneered the idea that one could estimate the population of prehistoric Indian villages by counting the number of old pit house depressions found throughout Central California, then multiplying that by the number of people in the families he encountered living in pit houses. Powers was struck by the relation between house types and climate across California. He also distinguished the influence upon the architecture of California Indians of three basic building materials: earth, wood, and fiber.

The pit house was a preferred winter shelter among Central people such as the Maidu and Miwok, for whom sun-drenched valleys were home. These semisubterranean houses, resembling simpler versions of northern Plateau pit houses, usually were strung along low shelves above streams and rivers, maximizing southern exposure to the sun wherever possible. When suitable sites safely above the level of the spring floods were found, everyone hauled dirt for a week to raise the village foundation. A village might comprise from six to forty pit houses interspersed with acorn granaries built on stilts to deter rot and varmits; high poles brandished stuffed-bird decoys to lure passing wildfowl.

EARTH

Pit house floors usually were excavated in spring before the summer sun hardened the ground. Maidu and Miwok pits were generally 10 to 15 feet across, but tribelets of the Patwin dug them somewhat wider. Posts and radiating beams framed the ceiling, then tule mats or bunched grass were laid above smaller sticks. Packed earth from the original excavation finished the roof. One usually entered and left through the smoke hole by a notched log ladder, but people also crawled out through the side shafts used for ventilation. Sleeping pallets decked with willows were supported by stakes driven into the floor. Mattresses were made of fine twigs, pine needles, and tule mats.

Among the Pomo, influential men such as hunting or war leaders, lucky gamblers, or medicine men sometimes hired builders to construct oversized homes. Their floors, which could be 15 feet below ground, were entered by short tunnels that led through extra storage chambers. Their roofs were

California earthlodges

Central California tribes built earthlodges for dwellings and ceremonial halls. The linguist Jaime de Angulo made this sketch (*above*) of an Achumawi domestic pit house in the 1920s. He wrote, "From the outside, at a distance, the whole thing was hardly visible. It was just a large mound of earth with grass growing over it; except that you might notice a plume of smoke coming out of it, and the ladder sticking out. You walked to the top, and peered down the hatchway, and it was like looking down into a cavern. You saw the fire, and then you could make out the shapes of people sitting around against the wall, or sprawling in the straw, or walking about, stepping over people lying down."

The Nomlaki village plan (*below*) shows pit houses oriented around a larger chief's earthlodge, and the dance hall to one side. The painted center pole of a Pomo dance house (*far right*) was photographed at Sulphur Bank, ca. 1902.

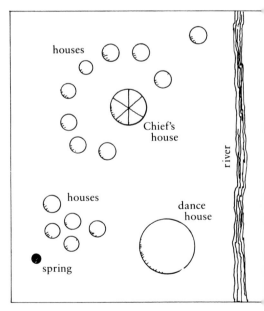

houses

Chief's house

houses

dance house

river

spring

Nomlaki village plan

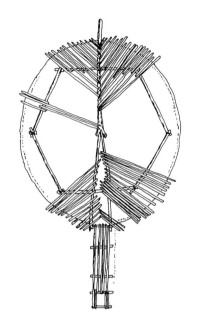

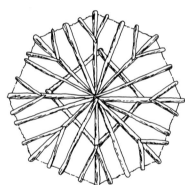

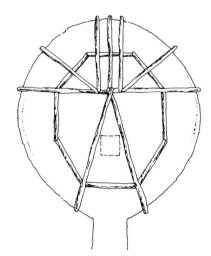

Dance house roof framing plan variations

framed of radiating poles carefully layered with brush, grass, and mats under the 3 to 4 inches of earthen covering. A final plastering with wet clay was smoothed by hand over the exterior and allowed to set.

Among the Miwok, men's sweathouses were simply reduced versions of their domestic pit houses. From 6 to 15 feet in diameter, they were usually the height of a man bent over. Dry rather than steam heat from a central fire was used; the small smoke hole helped to retain warmth. In most Pomo settlements, both sexes and all ages used communal sweathouses. Between 15 and 20 feet across, they were built much like their earth-covered dance house, but they were accorded little sacred significance.

Religious life focused around community dance houses built by the Pomo, Maidu, Miwok, Patwin, Nomlaki, and Wintu. According to California Indian scholar Robert F. Heizer, they represented aboriginal California's most "complex architectural achievement." Among the Pomo these earthen assembly halls extended from 40 to 60 feet in diameter. They featured one or two long tunnel entrances, a smoke hole, and a hollowed-log drum in the rear that was played by men wielding 5-foot-long drumsticks. One or more painted hardwood posts stood in the middle of the floor—the sacred center of these buildings. The Pomo even outfitted their elaborate halls with trapezes from which performers would swing during certain dances.

A Nomlaki account describes the ritualized construction of such a ceremonial chamber. Harvesting the poles took a full month, with special care given to finding the central oak post, which was chopped down last. Every piece had its name, and all joints were prefitted so the entire building could be erected in a daylong celebration. Participating groups excavated the side of the

pit closest to their own hamlets—breaking up the earth with digging sticks and removing it in conelike baskets—as if to make the building a microcosm of the wider Nomlaki world. When, after about three hours, they had dug a 4- to 7-foot hole, six to eight men, singing together, carried in the sacred center pole on a grapevine litter. Once it was raised, two "brother" poles, all the side posts, and the entire frame of rafters were lashed with green grapevine, which hardened as it dried. Wormwood was laid atop the rafters, and the crevices were stuffed with moss. Finally the 3- to 4-inch earthen roof layer was tamped down by foot.

After the 1870s, the use of these ceremonial buildings was revived when the so-called Earthlodge Cult, often described as a California form of the Plains Ghost Dance, attempted to reaffirm Indian identity in the face of Anglo-American oppression. Central tribes flocked to these rituals; the halls, which reached 70 feet in diameter, held over three hundred celebrants. The Maidu and Miwok, whose dances with elaborate costumes were held between October and April, developed a variety of ways to support their roofs using two and four central-post frames and extending the sloping vestibules. The Central Miwok decorated the interior walls and posts of their *lamma*, or ceremonial dance house, with horizontal black and white stripes and cushioned the clay floor during their ceremonies with willow branches. They believed that as the blazing central fire projected the shadows of the costumed dancers, the central posts became conduits for communicating directly with the spirit world and for transmitting dream songs to the participants, such as this Wintu lyric from the Earthlodge Cult period:

There above, there above.
At the mystical earthlodge of the south.
Spirits are wafted along the roof and fall.
There above, there above,
Spirits are wafted along the roof and fall.
Flowers bend heavily on their stems.

Assembly earthlodges

Earth-roofed ceremonial halls became increasingly important as Indians sought to shield their ceremonies from outside interference in the late nineteenth century. The section of a Patwin dance house *(below)* was probably based upon the dance house which stood west of Yuba City.

The largest earthlodge in California *(bottom right)* was built by Maidu who migrated to the Bidwell Rancheria in Chico. Known as Mechoopda Village, the community erected the building in the 1870s. It could hold 250 guests, and was an active cultural center into the twentieth century. This northern Miwok dance house *(top right)*, in Amador County had a log roof.

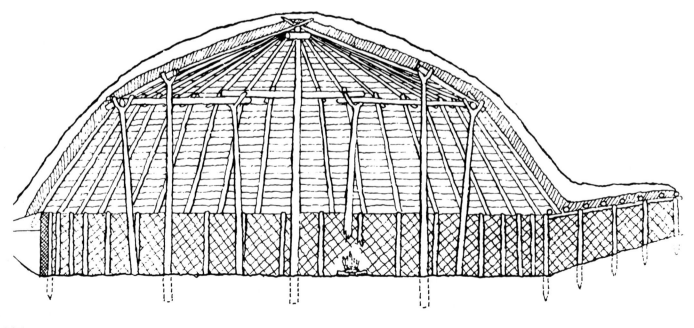

BRUSH

The Pomo to the north of the Central California province and the Yokuts in the south constructed Native America's largest grass and reed-thatched buildings. Along the grassy valleys of the Russian and Eel Rivers and throughout their tule-fringed lake territory, with its abundant plant life, the Pomo developed their expertise in crafting fiber. From roots, reeds, shoots, and barks, they produced baskets, skirts and capes, boats, granaries, and houses. Each season, they rebuilt circular or rectangular structures for their thatched camp shelters. Supple side poles were embedded in the ground about 2 feet apart, then bent and lashed to a ridgepole with grapevine. After saplings were woven into a weblike superstructure, courses of thatching were overlapped up to the smoke opening at the crest.

The valley Pomo also built larger, elliptical houses, averaging 20 by 40 feet, from stout tule stalks. Inside were five fires, and five doorways opened into five separate family sleeping areas. The unusual L-shaped Pomo valley house that Powers described in the 1870s also was covered with tule. Occupied by six related families, the house had three small round doorways and three cooking hearths. There were no partitions in the interior, probably to maximize the air flow. Pomo groups who lived close to the lakes had an abundant supply of rushes for the roofs of their sizable multifamily houses. Their average building measured 35 by 15 feet and stood about 12 feet high. Eighty framing saplings were bent to a 25-foot-long ridgepole from either side to form forty arches which were supported by interior poles. Then the bulky tule cover was fastened over this framework.

Fiber buildings

The Pomo and Yokuts of the Central Valley inhabited large grass and reed structures along the interior lakes and rivers. This Pomo multi-family tule-thatched house *(left)* stood on the east side of Clear Lake, 1927. An earlier tule-covered structure *(below)* stood in the Pomo village of Elem in Lake County, ca. 1870. The plan shows the interior arrangement of one of these multifamily dwellings.

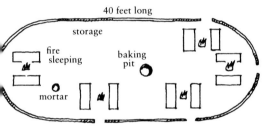

Eastern Pomo multifamily house plan

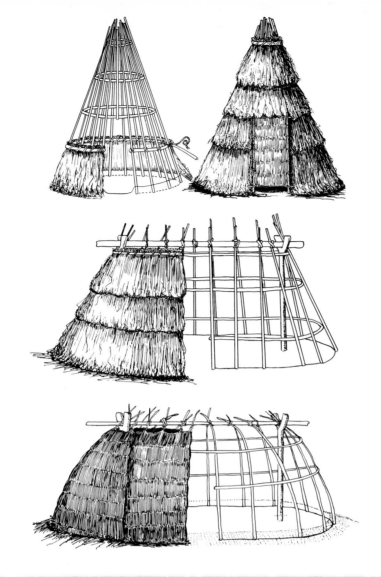

Yokuts architecture

The Yokuts groups who occupied the San Joaquin Valley and surrounding foothills, built houses with grass, tule, and wood. Their fiber buildings, however, are the most distinctive. In the 1860s a village (above) was described by journalist Stephen Powers. The entire community was shaded by an arbor. Such villages were generally positioned on raised ground near major watercourses to avoid spring flooding. The drawings (top left) of grass-covered Yokuts dwellings from the central foothills are similar structures. Another Yokuts house type (left, bottom drawing and photograph) was the oval dwelling, 1903. Built by the valley and central foothill groups, it featured a ridgepole supported by two posts. The Monache Indians, who lived near the Yokuts, used thatch instead of mats (center drawing).

The Yokuts, who lived in the San Joaquin Valley and the nearby foothills farther south, built four kinds of fiber-covered houses. The largest were the mat-covered, wedge-shaped structures that bordered a main village pathway. Up to ten people might live in each house. Each family was responsible for the construction of its portion of the multifamily buildings, but inside, as in the Pomo houses, no partitions were needed to establish family spaces. Domestic etiquette called for behaving as if physical dividers did exist. Usually the chief's house was in the middle, while his "messengers' houses" were at both ends of the house row. In one of Powers's illustrations of these settlements, a mammoth arbor shades the entire community. Dance and assembly buildings were positioned just outside this living area, while special arbors for hosting visitors stood a safe mile away.

The Yokuts also constructed smaller tule houses. They were covered with tall mohya stalks clamped in place by outside battens, or with tule mats sewn together with bone needles and fiber cord. They had rounded ends and were framed by five bent-pole ribs on either side that met at a ridgepole held up by two crotched posts. The Yokuts' cone-shaped houses, which were large enough to contain two fireplaces, were framed with poles tied firmly to a hoop and then covered with bunches of tule or grass. Some were built with doorway overhangs for shade.

Two types of fiber dwellings appear to have been unique to the Yokuts. For an overnight shelter, a clearing was cut from a thick patch of tule along the lakeshore, then the encircling reeds were drawn together and bound overhead. This living roof kept growing, but the marshy floor was often very damp. The other unusual home was built by Yokuts from the foothills who found the lakeshore camping sites already overcrowded. They lashed floating platforms together, which they could move around, fish from, and sleep on. Fifty feet long or more, the decks of these "house rafts" supported mud cooking hearths and sleeping areas that were assigned to families.

Great Basin fiber houses

The Great Basin of Nevada and western Utah is a hot, barren, desert that was first explored by John C. Fremont in 1843. The resourceful, seminomadic Paiute inhabited the upland regions, where survival depended on wise use of scarce resources. An encampment of forked-stick brush structures *(right)* was photographed on the Kaibab Plateau in southwestern Utah during the expedition led by Major John W. Powell, ca. 1873. After this northern Paiute winter-house frame *(left)* at Pyramid Lake is covered with thatch, it will resemble the building shown below, photographed by C. Hart Merriam in 1903, along the Truckee River.

BARK

Cone-shaped bark slab houses were built by the Pomo, Wintu, Miwok, and Maidu on both the seaward and mountain sides of the dry, hot valleys. In the coastal redwood belt, the Pomo split off rough bark slabs and placed them around a forked center post until all cracks were covered. In the rugged Sierra Nevada, the inland Maidu and Miwok built better-insulated bark lodges for the winter. In the foothills, their doorways faced north or east, and fires often remained outside. At higher elevations, however, fires were built indoors, and the eastern side of the cone sloped steeply to help shed snow.

These lodges, called *ho-be* by the Maidu, were framed with 12-foot pine poles and had floors 8 to 15 feet in diameter. Long slabs of incense cedar, pine, or redwood bark were stripped from dead trees and placed on the frame in three or four overlapping layers. Some slabs were cut shorter to allow smoke to escape. The Maidu partly excavated their floors, but the Sierra Miwok built directly on the ground; both used pine needles to complete the lodge floor. While the Maidu added layers of branches, pine needles, and leaves on the outside, and sometimes put a roof over the entrance, the Miwok insulated the interior of their walls with pine needles and left the entry uncovered.

Within Yosemite Valley, which was known to the Sierra Miwok as the "Place of the Gaping Mouth," there were settlements of conical bark houses clustered on both sides of the Merced River. At the time of the arrival of the white man in the 1830s there were perhaps ten such villages, containing an estimated 450 residents. Their pattern of distribution followed the Miwok belief that all living beings—people, plants, and animals—belonged to either the Land or the Water sides of the world. Miwok villagers on the southern side of the Merced were members of the Water moiety, and their chief totem was the coyote. Villages to the north of the river were known as Land villages, whose major totem was the grizzly bear. Individuals from one moiety married into the other, and conjugal ties, ceremonies, and tournaments bound the two halves of the Miwok world tightly together.

Bark dwellings

California Indians who inhabited the upper foothills of the Sierra Nevada and coastal ranges built conical bark lodges for winter habitation. A camp of Miwok bark houses, painted by Thomas Hill about 1876 *(left)* borders the Merced River in Yosemite Valley. Eight to 15 feet in diameter, their tipi-like frames *(sketch above)* supported overlapping slabs of redwood or incense cedar bark. The bark-covered house *(top)* was built by North-fork Mono Indians. Its slightly excavated floor was 6 to 12 feet in diameter, and outer bark slabs and brush were fastened by encircling willow withes.

ROUNDHOUSE

By the late 1800s, metal nails and split shingles had replaced the earthen roofs of most traditional assembly halls. The Indians of Central California may have been introduced to European building methods and materials by the Russians, who during the construction of their trading post, Fort Ross, in the early 1800s taught carpentry to Pomo Indian conscripts. Before the end of the century, Pomo ceremonial enclosures were no longer sunk into the ground, and eventually they incorporated vertical redwood plank walls, shake roofs, and gabled entrances.

Earthlodge cult adherents and new California Indian nativistic movements also converted to plank roundhouses for their dances and rituals. Round, shingled roofs were adopted by the Wintu, Nomlaki, Maidu, Miwok, and Pomo. The ethnographer C. Hart Merriam visited one northern Miwok roundhouse near Railroad Flat in Calaveras County in 1906 and discovered roof shingles and sawn vertical wall boards nailed to the twelve-sided building. Inside he found a 7-foot plank that had been set up as a foot drum at the rear of the building. It was laid over a 4-foot hole to make it resound deeply when performers stomped on it. He noticed that the dance hall was floored with fresh pine needles in preparation for an upcoming ceremony.

Roundhouse architecture

Around the turn of the century, ceremonial earthlodges were replaced by round wooden structures built above ground. They had pole frames and were roofed and sided with split planks or shakes. The Miwok roundhouse, photographed in 1901 *(left),* was located in Calaveras County. The Maidu roundhouse *(below)* was photographed at the Bald Rock Rancheria, near Mooretown in Butte County, 1924.

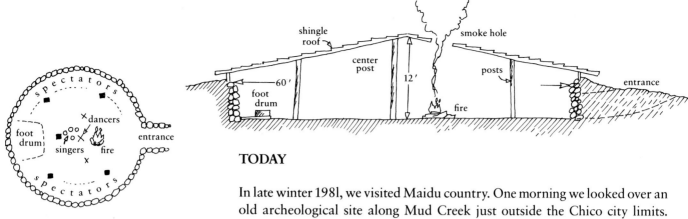

Dance houses

This large Pomo roundhouse *(top left)* was built before 1900 a few miles north of Ukiah. The frame for this Miwok dance house *(bottom left)* was erected at Murphys in preparation for a ceremony on September 1, 1901. The sketch of a Pomo dance house *(above)* shows the building as it stood at Sulphur Bank Rancheria in the 1940s. The roundhouse *(below)* at the Nomlaki community of Grindstone northeast of Sacramento remains an active ceremonial building.

TODAY

In late winter 1981, we visited Maidu country. One morning we looked over an old archeological site along Mud Creek just outside the Chico city limits. Although archeologists cannot date the village, and anthropologists can find no living Maidu to name it, the positioning of the remains of its pit house is the same as that described by early visitors. Twelve or so house depressions faced a rushing creek; nearby, large boulders had been hollowed out to serve as bedrock mortars for grinding acorns. One oversized pit probably served as the community's dance house, known to the valley Maidu as the *kum*.

A few hours later we were forty miles farther west, hunting for the Grindstone Creek Rancheria in Glenn County, where the Nomlaki Indians have lived since the 1870s. As we parked beside a basketball court set amid small, government-built houses and trailer homes, we noticed the earth-walled, shingle-roofed roundhouse. The tunnel of the structure led down into a dark interior. Under the low-lying circular eave the outer wall was banked with dirt tinted green by fresh grass. Probably the oldest roundhouse still in use in California, the building was half old-time earthlodge, half transition-period wooden dance house. It was where the midsummer ceremonies still drew dispersed Central California tribespeople to watch masked dancers, known as Big Heads, and to conduct curing rituals.

SOUTH

When the Spanish explorer Juan Cabrillo first met the Chumash Indians near present-day Santa Barbara in 1542, all he recorded of their dwellings was that they were "round and very well covered clear to the ground. They say that in each house there are fifty persons." Subsequent travelers compared Chumash grass-thatched dwellings to "half-oranges," but no construction details were provided until the ethnographer John Harrington persuaded a Chumash to build one for him.

The major mainland Chumash dwelling was a taller version of the domed grass or brush house used by native groups farther south. Harrington's example was framed with green willows thick as a man's arm (sycamore also was used), which were debarked with flint knives. Cut 18 to 20 feet high, these uprights were planted a step apart in a circle from 15 to 20 feet in diameter and lashed together at the top. One rib was left higher than the others to prop open the smoke-hole cover.

Horizontal stringers were then lashed in tiers, followed by the tule, carrizo, brush or grass roof fastened all around in overlapping rows. On the bottom course, the thick ends of the stems rested on the ground to help keep animals or enemies out. The rest were turned upside down, with the stems lashed to the stringers and the grass fringing down. Then the thatch was trimmed to "square it off like bangs," Harrington noted. More artful house-builders first covered their frames with woven tule mats, then tied on the tule or carrizo and

Southern California

Domical grass houses were used throughout much of Southern California. This painting, done in 1832 by Ferdinand Deppein (*above*) shows the characteristically tall form built by the Chumash and Gabrielino Indians at San Gabriel Mission, 1832. It resembles the tall structure (*bottom right*) which Chumash Jose Romero built at the Ventura County Fair in 1924. A grass house (*top right*) was constructed by a Tipai man, Angel Quilpe, for the anthropologist John Peabody Harrington in 1925.

Gabled brush houses

The brush buildings built toward the end of the nineteenth century in Southern California reflected Mexican influence. Some had their fiber walls lashed onto a gabled, pole frame. This house (*top left*) of the Luiseño Indians was built similarly. A stone foundation supported the thatch-roofed brush house (*above*) built by Ipai Indians in northern San Diego County, photographed by Edward S. Curtis, ca. 1924. At the Cupeño village (*bottom left*) near Warner Springs, however, adobe walls supported the thatch and ramadas were attached to the houses.

battened down the padded covering with horizontal stringers tied to the frame with willow bark. On occasion the thatch was plastered. The smoke hole was large; often side holes were left for windows. The door was a hanging tule mat, and interior mats were draped to create partitions. The floor was hardened by sprinkling it with water and then pounding it; a ditch outside the entrance carried away roof drainage. As a finishing touch, Harrington learned, the Chumash often fashioned a little "door bell" of limpet shells with a tie dangling outside the door.

Southeast of Chumash territory lived the Cahuilla, whose buildings resembled those of their Luiseño, Diegueño, and Serrano neighbors. Their traditional old-style house, the *kish,* appeared to be a squatter version of Chumash homes, except that an inner support ring of posts helped to brace the slighter, bent-willow ribs. Arrowweed was used for the stringers, native California palm for the thatching, and the floor was slightly scooped out.

Later Cahuilla homes reflected Mexican influence. Like the rural peasant jacals south of the border, they were rectangular, gabled, and framed with straight poles. Their walls were formed of forked corner posts and interlaced arrowweed, willow, or brush wattling, and they were solidified with thick adobe daub that was plastered smooth. Their roofs were thatched with palms or reeds. Adjoining these houses were arbors, or ramadas, made of stout mesquite uprights and flat thatch roofs for shade through the summer.

313

Perched on both ramadas and house roofs were huge, spiral-woven basket granaries where seeds, acorns, or mesquite beans were stored. Whenever they could buy or make them, Southern California Indians would also wall their houses with Spanish-style uniformly sized adobe bricks, which were formed in wooden molds and left to dry in the sun. Usually the houses were roofed with carrizo thatch, but wealthier or more acculturated Indians sometimes preferred to use red Spanish roofing tiles.

Prominent in most Southern Indian settlements were ceremonial buildings and enclosed sacred arenas. Brush fences enclosed the oval or rectangular grounds of special houses where ritual paraphernalia were kept for the worship of a late cult deity known as Chingichngish and the ritual ingestion of hallucinogenic datura, or *toalache*. The ritual house of the Cahuilla, known as the *kishumnawat*, also served as living quarters for the local clan *net*—the religious and civic leader. Usually circular, its floor was slightly sunken; its steeply pitched roof of arrowweed, palm fronds, or tule rested upon 5-foot-high walls and was also supported by interior uprights.

The so-called Mission tribes, such as the Luiseño and Diegueño, enclosed their open-air sacred spaces with brush fencing and arbors. Once the ethnographer Harrington watched a Luiseño head man named Juan Calac prepare a holy ground for Chingichngish worship. It was 38 feet wide from north to south and 58 feet long from east to west, with a 4-foot-wide fire pit in the middle. When these elliptical or rectangular spaces were the scene of male initiation rites, sand paintings depicting the tribal cosmos were created on the floors of the sacred houses.

Nearly every Indian hamlet had its cone-shaped, mud-plastered sweat bath, known by the Mexican Indian word *temescal*, which resembled the Navajo sweathouses further east in Arizona. Chumash sweathouses were reportedly the largest, up to 12 feet in diameter. Like most traditional California Indian sudatories, they used the dry heat of a relatively smokeless fire fed with willow twigs. Either the entrance was through a side door, or, more commonly, a pole ladder descended through the smoke hole.

TODAY

While we found no traditional Indian dwellings in Southern California that are still occupied, the Cahuilla hold summer ceremonies in open arenas rimmed with palm-roofed arbors, and use some of the transition-period wattle-and-daub jacals to store gardening equipment. We did hike to an old Chumash rock shelter deep in the Kern County hills. Scholars claim its polychrome wall paintings are the finest in North America. The site is not far from Point Pinos, which Harrington believed was the spiritual heart of the Chumash universe. As we approached we could make out a shadowy crevice below the crest of a sandstone butte. Soon we saw the brightly painted panels in five different colors spanning the ceiling. During the period of Spanish oppression, the cave was probably as much a safe house for Chumash deities as for the Indians themselves. Rock art specialist Georgia Lee has theorized that the location was possibly the last refuge of Chumash rebels who defied the Spanish in 1824, and that these gesso-backed paintings may have functioned as war magic. The renegade artists were using mural techniques learned from the Spanish to cast spells against their oppressors.

Ritual places

Arenas for festivities and ceremonies in the south were often enclosed by arbors, although some groups also set aside structures for initiating the young, curing, and councils. This ceremonial quadrangle *(below)* contained a courtyard for summer ceremonies and games at the Cupeño village of Warner Springs, along Agua Caliente Creek. All Indian groups in the region used the mud-plastered sweatbath, or *temescal*, such as the Luiseño example *(left)*, Soboba Rancheria, photographed in 1885.

Food

This Pomo fishing shelter *(left)* could be constructed in half an hour, and shaded a fisherman all day. Photographed ca. 1924.

Acorns were a staple of Indian life. After the harvest, the acorns were stored in elevated granaries to protect them from ground moisture and animals. These Yosemite granaries *(right)* were built with grass and brush, and raised on 12-foot poles. After grinding and leaching the acorns in water (to remove acids), the nutritious flour was cooked in various ways. Here Mono women *(above)* break up nuts in bedrock mortars, scooping the meal into special baskets.

COLORADO RIVER

The Mohave Indians who farmed and fished along the floodplain of the lower Colorado River ascribe the origin of their architecture to their mythic hero, Matavilya. Born of the union of the Earth and Sky, Matavilya chose the center of the world—the Colorado River Valley, and the sacred mountain Avikwame in particular—as the site for the first sand-roofed house. As it was constructed, he named each supporting post and beam so his Mohave Indian children would know how to shelter themselves properly.

Early historical accounts suggest that Colorado River houses were quite big. In 1699 Juan Mateo Mange, a Spanish soldier, visited some Quechan hamlets east of the major river which, he wrote in his diary, "reduce themselves to one or two houses, with flat roofs, erected upon many poles for pillars with small beams between them, and they are so low that they can only live inside them sitting or lying down; they have no sections for single persons or families, and they are so large that they are capable of containing more than one hundred families." This sounds like the *ava'cope't* or "closed house" for winter use. Mange also mentioned a ramada near the door, "the same size as the house and low in order to sleep in the summer;" it was known as the "sunshade," or *ava'metkya'l*.

When Lieutenant A.W. Whipple visited Mohave homesteads in 1854, he recorded that "their favorite resort seems to be the roof, where usually could be counted from twenty to thirty persons, all apparently at home." Whipple arrived when cylindrical granaries around the houses were stocked with mesquite beans and corn, and earthen pots inside were full of flour and beans from their floodplain gardens. The Mohave were but one of the Yuman-speaking tribes—including the Cocopa and Quechan—whose rancherias of two or three houses were found along both shores of the Colorado River. The traditional flat-domed, hip-roofed winter house was C-shaped and measured about 20 by 25 feet, with the side facing south left open. The frame consisted of stout center posts and a ridgepole with rafters rising up on all four sides

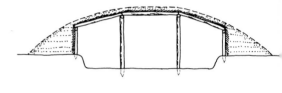

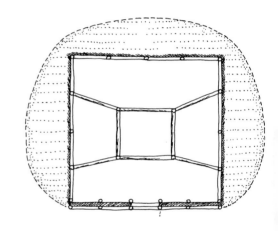

Colorado River architecture

Sand-roofed houses were constructed by Yuman-speaking tribes like the Mohave and Quechan who inhabited the terraces along the lower Colorado River. The roof provided a place for storage and socializing. The plan and section *(above)* show construction of a traditional Yuman home. The center posts were 8 feet high, the side posts about 4 feet. The front wall was arrowweed packed between uprights, as shown in this old photograph *(left)* of a Quechan dwelling.

Old and new houses

The front walls of earlier Quechan houses were left open, as in this sand-roofed dwelling *(right)*, photographed ca. 1900. The change from open to closed dwellings is illustrated in a Mohave camp scene *(below)*. At the far left is a summer ramada supporting granaries of woven arrowweed. In the middle stands an old-style sand-roofed dwelling with the horizontal arrowweed front, while to the right is a more recent *jacal*, or rectangular Mexican peasant-style house with a hinged wooden door. Photographed by Ben Wittick, 1883.

layered with slender stalks of arrowweed. Sandy mud from the riverbank then filled all crevices so that, except for the front, the structure became indistinguishable from the surrounding dunes. Since there was no smoke hole, the door provided the only ventilation, and cooking was generally done outside.

South and east of Mohave country lived the Quechan (also known as the Yuma proper) in small hamlets of similar sand-roofed, circular "closed houses." Situated in sandy swales and excavated to 2 feet or more, they used four 8-foot center posts. Their wall posts were only 4 to 5 feet high, and the sides and rear were heaped with sand. The front was sometimes extended with a single hip, producing an egg-shaped floor plan with the side to the prevailing wind sloped toward the ground. A blanket or skin hung over the door. In summertime both the Mohave and Quechan spent most of their time under outdoor arbors.

Most of the inhabitants of the 200-mile stretch of the lower Colorado River held cremation rites when a tribesperson died and observed an annual memorial ceremony for the dead. Known as the *Keruk*, it required that special enclosures be built for mourning and remembering the relatives who had died the previous year. After a narrative had been recited relating how the first death house was built by their creator, the Quechan and Cocopa would erect a special Keruk arbor. To the Cocopa, the structure represented a man's body. Its six posts stood for legs, the top of a front post was his head, a central beam running between the two center posts was his backbone, and the beams running between pairs of side posts were the ribs. The shade faced east, toward the land of the departed. When the Quechan constructed their Keruk house, they sang songs describing the construction of their prototypical mourning shelter by a mythic badger. At the climax of the ceremony, the Keruk structures were burned to provide a haven for the dead in the next life.

TODAY

When we visited the Colorado River Tribes Museum north of Blythe, California, director Chuck Lamb told us that the sand-roofed dwellings were long gone. Using a museum model, however, he showed how its placement, sand roof, and excavated floor provided radiated heat and insulation in winter; in summer everyone slept outdoors. The roofs were also excellent platforms for Indian criers, Lamb said, because the still, layered desert air carried messages for more than a mile.

Lamb showed us the museum's replica of the later-period, Mexican-influenced Mohave house. A thatched gable roof protected its four walls of arrowweed lattice and packed mud.

Mohave country

The Mohave house with sand roof, attached ramada, and granaries (*above*) was drawn by Heinrich Balduin Möllhausen during his visit to the lower Colorado in 1854. While no examples of these old-style structures have survived, larger Colorado Indian constructions can be seen today. This pattern of winding, parallel furrows (*right*) is known as the Mohave or Topock Maze. It is the largest of many gigantic earthworks produced by these early Indians, almost certainly for religious purposes, on the middle terraces of the river.

Later, we walked along a 65-foot depiction of a rattlesnake scraped into desert rock, one of the enormous pieces of environmental art, created by Mohave ancestors, for which this region is known. Its eyes were two boulders that are said to glow at night. Then we saw the largest of the "geoglyphs" that archeologists have identified in the 165-mile strip from Needles, California, to Yuma, Arizona, known as the Mohave or Topock Maze. Except for the swath cut by Interstate 40 and the railroad line, every yard of this 18-acre expanse is mantled with parallel, twisting furrows, resembling an Andean agricultural landscape. Actually it is not a true maze; from an airplane its winding rows of scraped-away surface stones suggest an anthropomorphic figure. In the 1920s, the photographer Edward S. Curtis described the Mohave's use of the earthwork for purification. The participants began in the center of the site. It was believed that after running every mile of its criss-crossing pathways, they were physically and spiritually restored. When we asked Lamb how contemporary Mohaves regarded it, he said that they would not talk with outsiders about it or about cremation rituals the Mohave, Quechan, and Cocopa still practiced in their "cry houses." A resident of nearby Needles told us that in the 1960s, his local history club drove an old Mohave basketmaker to the site in the hope that she would divulge its meaning. As they entered the maze the old woman darted away from them and ran brokenly down the furrows. She reached into the pockets of her long dress and scattered corn seeds in all directions as she went. Then she turned back and sat in the back seat of the car that had brought her, refusing to say a word.

8 HOGAN, KI, and RAMADA
SOUTHWEST I

When Francisco de Coronado's expedition crossed the Southwest in 1540, its mesas, deserts, and canyons were home to three different architectural traditions: the condominiumlike complexes of the Pueblo groups, the single-family *ki* of the Pima and Papago communities, and the *wikiup* and *hogan* used seasonally by far-flung bands of Apache and Navajo. These traditions emerged from at least four major pre-Columbian cultural groups: the Mogollon of south-central Arizona and southwestern New Mexico; the Hohokam of southwestern Arizona; the Anasazi of north-central Arizona and northwestern New Mexico; and bands of latecomers who are believed to have migrated from the Subarctic.

The adobe-and-sandstone villages Coronado observed along the Rio Grande Valley and on the Colorado plateau belonged to Indians the Spanish called Pueblos because the large, white-washed buildings situated around plazas reminded the visitors of their Iberian homeland. The ancestry of these Indian villages has been traced to archeological sites attributed to both the Anasazi and Mogollon pre-Columbian traditions.

In Arizona, the Spanish encountered Indians whose simpler architecture and way of life made their society appear less complex than the civic-minded Pueblos. Yet the Pima and Papago groups, who lived along the Salt River, are thought to be descendants of an older cultural world that archeologists call Hohokam. Their modest brush-and-mud shelters bore little trace of the canal systems, courts for playing ritual ball games, and stepped-earth pyramids that their Hohokam forbears apparently developed from Mexican prototypes.

In our next and final chapter we study the architecture of these pre-Columbian cultures and the historic Pueblo peoples. Here, however, we focus on the two less monumental building traditions of the Southwest, one imported from the north by the Athabaskan-speaking Apachean and Navajo bands, and the second, belonging to the Piman-speaking peoples, which developed out of the older Hohokam culture.

Attempts to reconstruct the architectural evolution of these Southwestern groups remain conjectural since the ethnographic record of building styles only begins in the 1880s, when they already had undergone hundreds of years of Spanish influence. What we do know about the diverse housing approaches across the aboriginal Southwest, however, underscores the influence of culture on architecture. Indeed, for more than a century the stark contrast between Navajo and Pueblo architectural principles has been a favorite example for scholars who emphasize social over environmental determinants of built form.

The land that supplied raw materials for these buildings embraces the present-day states of Arizona and New Mexico. Bordering it on the east and west are two river systems, the Rio Grande and the Colorado. Beyond reach of their watersheds, water became a precious commodity. In the east, the arid flatland rises gradually from the Texas plains into the Sangre de Cristo Mountains. As one continues west, evergreen forest gives way to highland desert and scenic tablelands. From the north, the land slopes southward from the Colorado plateau to deeply cut canyons and volcanic ridges before it blends into the baking Sonoran Desert.

In pre-Columbian times, the Sonoran region supported the Hohokam, who built up thick-walled, fortresslike compounds from hand-shaped loaves of

damp adobe and practiced a sophisticated form of large-area irrigation. Some of their farming techniques were still in practice in the sixteenth century when their monumental house compounds, exemplified by the imposing sites of Casa Grande and Snaketown in central Arizona, were abandoned for unknown reasons. In their place, the Spanish explorers found instead modest hamlets of farming Indians called Pima and Papago who lived in small, partly excavated structures known as ki during the winter. Over the hot summer months they spent most of their time under arbors, which soon acquired the Spanish name *ramada.*

Unlike the Pima and Papago, the Athabaskan-speakers were relative newcomers to the Southwest. Their lifeways also contrasted with the Piman-speaking people in that they proved unreceptive to Christianity. The skimpy record of the early interaction of the Navajo and Apache with the Spanish testifies to their distaste for settling in any sort of large community and for any gods but their own.

The Navajo hogan

In the Navajo language, the word *hogan* means "home place."

Shown on the preceding page are a hogan and summer ramada frame, probably in Canyon de Chelly above the mouth of Wild Cherry Canyon. Photographed ca. 1930.

Navajo women pose in front of a conical forked-pole hogan *(above).*

conical forked-pole hogan (male)

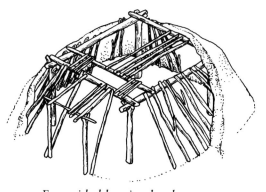

Four-sided leaning log hogan

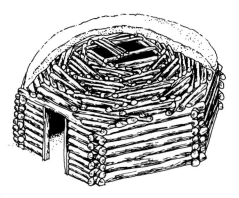

Corbeled log roof hogan (female)

HOGAN

In 1788, a Spanish soldier named Vicente Troncosco was escorted by a Navajo headman to his home on Big Bead Mesa, near Chaco Canyon in New Mexico. The Indian lived within his mother's homestead, consisting of five houses, "one of which resembles a cone-shaped military tent with a square vestibule." This is our first description of what we know as a "forked-stick" or "male" hogan. A ramada was also part of the family compound.

Years later, in 1851, a cannoneer named Josiah Rice who was assigned to duty in Navajo country noted a much different house type in his journal. "These huts," he wrote, "are comprised of the green bows of the abounding pinon tree, piled one bough on top of another in a circle similar to a pig pen, with a gap in the front to go in and out at . . ." This was evidently the earliest observation of what we know as a "corbeled-log" or "female" hogan. Scholars and Indians give different accounts of the origins of these houses, but both agree that they have always been critical emblems of Navajo identity.

Perhaps as early as the eleventh century the Athabaskan-speaking ancestors of the Navajo and Apache began their migration south from western Canada, venturing down the mountain corridors, probably in small extended-family bands. They are believed to have brought with them the basic design of cone-shaped structures framed with interlocking poles and covered with brush. Among the Athabaskan-speaking Sekani and Beaver tribes of the Canadian Subarctic, tipilike shelters built around a tripod of three forked posts were found up to the late 1800s.

By the fourteenth century, these loosely organized hunting groups were spreading across the region, and two hundred years later they had claimed various territories within the highland deserts of the Southwest's heartland. Navajo religion, architecture, and means of subsistence soon incorporated traits of Pueblo Indian culture. They learned to weave and farm, they were attracted to new rituals, and their architecture changed as well. Now their brush lodges were covered with adobe; they learned to make sacred ground paintings with colored sand. The Navajos' readiness to incorporate new ideas spawned more changes in their architecture as Spanish, Mexican, and other European settlers entered their territory.

Meanwhile, their linguistic relatives, the Apache, had adapted to two different habitats. The Eastern Apache, who had grown attached to hunting on the Plains, cloaked their old conical frames in sewn-together buffalo skins instead of brush and mud. The Western Apache, who established themselves in present-day Arizona and western New Mexico, continued to construct simple brush shelters. Before long, non-Indians gave these structures the name "wikiups," from an Algonquian rather than an Apache word.

In the Navajo tongue the word hogan means "home place." Since the arrival of the Navajo in their homeland, the term has come to refer to a proliferating collection of buildings, all of which share essential characteristics: they are single-room, roughly circular structures, heated by a central floor fireplace or wood-burning stove, with a hole in the roof—or a stove pipe—to release smoke; the door always faces east, toward the rising sun; and they are generally built by their occupants.

To the Navajo, the architectural origins of their hogan is bound up in their mythology. The building's forms were originally a divine gift to the *Dineh*—the "People," as the Navajo call themselves. Their Blessingway myth is the body of tales and songs that explains how the Dineh were created and how they should live with themselves and the world around them. In one of the many versions of the Blessingway, First Man and First Woman complete an upward migration through three underworlds to be greeted by the supernatural being, Talking God. This deity thereupon creates the first hogan, sometimes referred to as the "male" hogan, modeling it after a promontory on Gobernador Knob Mountain in New Mexico, which the Navajo called the "heart of the Earth." Talking God framed this mythic prototype with forked posts made of the four sacred minerals, white shell, turquoise, abalone, and obsidian.

Talking God also gave the Navajo a second type of hogan, the dome-roofed "female" hogan, whose shape he copied after Huerfano Mountain, a butte in New Mexico that the Navajo called the "lungs of the Earth." This was said to be Changing Woman's home, the wife of the sun. When Talking God's first hogan proved too small, he blew upon its jeweled posts to expand them. Until recently, whenever a new forked-stick hogan was built, pieces of shell or turquoise were placed beneath the door, symbolically linking it to that perfect model of hogans. Today, as Talking God instructed, hogans are considered "alive" and must be periodically purified and fed. After the initial construction, they are consecrated by the male head of the family, special hogan songs are sung, oak sprigs are stuck in the roof, and corn pollen or white corn meal is sprinkled on the east, west, south, and north posts. Navajo house-blessing songs, of which there are hundreds, ensure that the buildings will provide harmony, beauty, and protection for their occupants. As this excerpt suggests, they also affirmed the woman's dominion over the house.

Beauty extends from the rear corner of my hogan,
    it extends from the woman,
Beauty extends from the center of my room,
    it extends from the woman,
Beauty extends from the fireside of my hogan,
    it extends from the woman,
Beauty extends from the side corners of my hogan,
    it extends from the woman,
Beauty extends from the doorway of my hogan,
    it extends from the woman,
Beauty extends from the surroundings of my hogan,
    it extends from the woman,
Beauty radiates from it in every direction, so it does.

Life in and around the hogan also was guided by tradition. The floor area was divided into male (south) and female (north) sides. Dishes and food were stored on the women's side, while men stowed their gear on the south side. During ritual occasions, seating was sexually segregated. The pervasive Navajo worry about ill fortune extended to the hogan. Knocking on the doorpost was forbidden because it was believed that the sound was suggestive of the tapping made by malevolent wind spirits. If a premature or violent death occurred inside a hogan the building would usually be abandoned. Its fire would be quenched, the smoke hole blocked up, and the north wall opened

The Navajo homestead

An old-style conical forked-stick hogan stands in the middle of this typical Navajo homestead of the 1930s. It includes ramadas and storage places. Dinnehotso area, Arizona.

The hogan was constructed with five major poles, following Talking God's instructions. First 2 poles came from east and west, next 2 from south and north, the fifth from northeast. The mountains inhabited by Talking God were the first homes; after the blessing rites, they became hogans.

Southern Pole

'Mountain World's Leg' place turquoise under

The East pole is set first, South second, West third, North last. The builder asks permission for them to be set willingly in position.

The structural pole's 'Worlds' or realms are personified as women.

The floor inside was covered with jewels of the 4 kinds that made the posts. The door was curtained with dawn, the blue sky, evening twilight, and darkness.

Prototype hogan covered with sunbeams and rainbows

Western Pole

'Water World's Leg' place abalone under

mask recess

seat of honor

western recess

sunwise course

Day

Farther center (Sky)

Night

southern recess

northern recess

Hearth

male side

female side

Ceremonial Fireside

eastern recess

small northern recess

hogan

premises

entry

Eastern Pole

'White Bead Pole'

Entry Poles

Ch'é'etundęę náá'ál 'slender ribbed objects'

Earth world's recess . . .

entry poles rested on stone slabs

the 'without' of the Hogan is a transitional space

East

Conical forked pole hogan symbolism

First man and First woman requested the hogan be blessed with white and yellow cornmeal, with pollen and powder from prayer sticks. Blessingway songs are addressed to Sky, Earth, Rain. With four songs, the hogan is blessed by marking the four directions with the cornmeal and powder.

Northern Pole

'Corn World's Leg' place obsidian under

On the roof, where they placed the end of the east pole, they put a white shell. Under the poles, the put white bead, turquoise, abalone, obsidian. Under the fifth pole, they put jewels from all the directions.

Where poles came together at the roof top, they tied feathers of different birds. The log tips are thought to be the 'eyes' of the hogan.

Conical hogan construction sequence

After the poles are gathered and cut to length *(top left)*, the north and south poles are placed first, the west pole next. The east-facing door poles are placed last *(middle left)*. The poles are usually juniper, 8 to 10 inches in diameter and 10 to 12 feet long. A long sapling is used to determine measurements, and the circle (from 12 to 30 feet in diameter) is laid out by eye. The floor is excavated enough to provide an earth bench around the perimeter. Leaning poles are laid on the tripod frame to form the wall *(bottom left)*, and the cracks are chinked with pieces of bark. The frame is then covered with 6 inches of damp earth, which is tamped and smoothed by hand or with a piece of bark to complete the structure *(below)*. Photographed in St. Michael's, Arizona, ca. 1905.

to remove the corpse. Occupants then packed up hastily, condemning it as a "dead" building, a "no fireplace home" in Navajo phraseology, and travelers would avoid it.

While Navajo myth describes the origin of these house forms as a revelation, scholars have noted that, in architecture as in other forms of Navajo culture, foreign materials were readily appropriated. As neighbors of the Pueblo villages, the Navajo began excavating their hogan floors like the early Pueblo pit houses. Hogan doorways faced east, and the walls were layered in a sequence of poles, cedar bark chinking, and adobe—the Pueblo method of constructing a roof. Two upright door posts standing on stone slabs upheld a protruding entryway. Archeologists argue that some Navajo hogan sites dating from this early period even betray evidence of clusters of connected adobe rooms, which they classify as "pueblitos."

However, archeologist David M. Brugge has suggested that around the mid-eighteenth century the Navajo consciously began limiting the degree of Pueblo cultural influence they absorbed. Some scholars believe a new synthesis of what it meant to be Navajo was achieved through the Blessingway myth and its accompanying ceremony. Part of this revised cultural charter discouraged the use of pueblitos, especially the communal social life they represented. According to Brugge, it was then that the earth-covered, cone-shaped hogan was sanctioned as the proper Navajo residence and key emblem of tribal identity.

Around the same time, two other structures joined the hogan family. One was the "female" or round-roofed hogan, framed of horizontal rings of logs that were corbeled from the ground up to approximate a dome, and then covered with bark and packed with wet earth. It is conceivable that the Navajo picked up the method of corbeling from early Pueblo ruins, because that was how some of the more elaborate circular kiva chambers were roofed. Later, another Pueblo building technique was adopted, the corbeled roofs built upon

Stacked-log hogan

The typical stacked-log hogan (above) was hexagonal, with walls of cribbed logs and a roof framework of corbeled logs (above right). The origins of the stacked-log hogan are not clear. There is little evidence of Athapaskan origin, although cribbed roofs are found among the Inuit Eskimo and Ingalik Athapaskan in western Alaska. Corbeled log kiva roofs have been found at various archeological sites in the Southwest.

The early hogan form had unnotched logs corbeling up directly from the ground, the walls slightly tilting in. After steel axes became available around 1900, the walls were cribbed, with logs notched at the corners. The roof remained a structure of unnotched, corbeled logs, producing the "whirling log" effect on the ceiling (right).

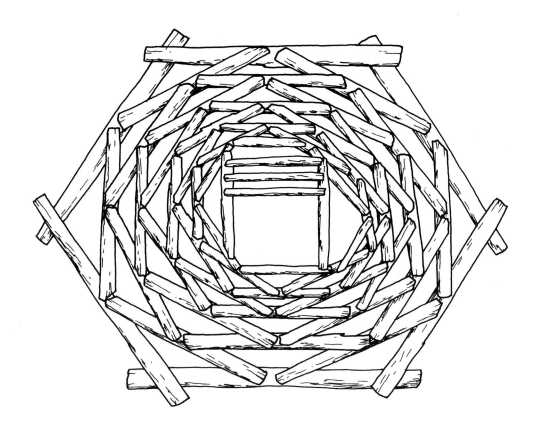

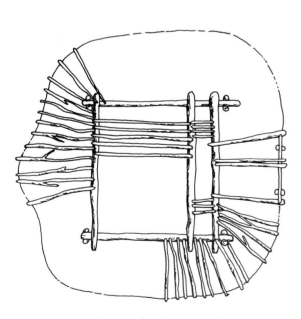

Leaning log hogan roof plan

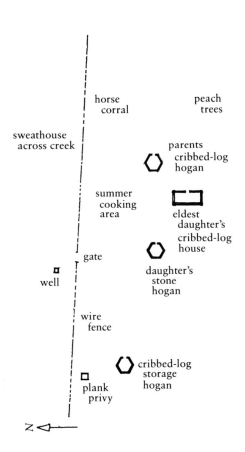

Summer-farm homestead plan, 1978

In the image:
horse corral
peach trees
sweathouse across creek
parents cribbed-log hogan
summer cooking area
eldest daughter's cribbed-log house
gate
daughter's stone hogan
well
wire fence
cribbed-log storage hogan
plank privy
N

Leaning wall structures

The leaning bough summer shade *(above left)* resembles the bare frame shown in the plan and photograph *(bottom left),* ca. 1935, of the leaning log winter hogan. It appears to be a four-post, four-beamed structure enclosed with vertical leaning log walls, then plastered over with adobe mix.

stone-and-adobe walls. The other type of hogan to come into use was a flat-roofed, earth-covered structure with leaning-log sidewalls. Used mainly for special ceremonies, it could extend 30 feet in length.

In the late eighteenth and early nineteenth centuries, certain economic and architectural practices of the Hispanic homesteaders began to attract the Navajo. They acquired a passion for horses and raising sheep from these herders. It was possibly at this time that they began raising their corbeled roof hogans on upright cedar logs similar to the walls of Hispanic ranch cabins. But they never relinquished the traditional pattern of dispersed seasonal camps in favor of Hispanic-style plaza-centered towns.

The household "camp," composed of a few families related through the female line, each of which lived in a separate hogan, remained the basic Navajo domestic and architectural unit. Their annual pattern involved farming at lower elevations in the summer, then migrating to the foothills to pasture their sheep over the winter. Sometimes they switched the cycle, spending winter in the lowlands, then taking their livestock to mountain meadows where they raised short-term crops. These seasonal sites were chosen for their available water, pinon and juniper firewood, and grassy, tillable land.

In the summer camps, the Navajo spent much of their time under cool arbors. Simply framed with upright, crotched pinon posts and cross pieces, they had three sloping sides of leaning poles or cornstalks to break the driving wind and dust. The roof was laid with green juniper boughs. During certain rituals, such as the War or Squaw dance, guests were fed in bough-shrouded ramadas that extended a hundred feet or more. The Navajo also improvised structures for storing food and housing their stock, and they fenced their animals in corrals made of entwined scrub juniper. Alongside many camps were sweat baths, miniature versions of conical hogans, with mud-plastered roofs that were sometimes painted with lightning and rainbow symbols. They used dry heat from a fire instead of steam from water on heated rocks. After a session of prayer and perspiration, the participants rolled in dry sand outside, which brushed off, leaving them cool and clean.

As Anglo ranches, towns, and prospectors encroached upon their home-lands, the Navajo were ordered by United States authorities to cease raiding white and Hispanic settlers and stockmen and to stay within territorial boundaries. When they refused, a harsh campaign to subdue them was launched in 1864. Within a short period, virtually the entire Navajo nation was confined at Fort Sumner in eastern New Mexico. By the time they were released four years later, the Navajo had lost a quarter of their population to disease and malnutrition. At that time, they were granted the largest Indian reservation in North America, comprising some 16 million acres today in New Mexico and Arizona.

By the late 1800s, with the availability of European-American tools and materials, the hogan form diversified further. With steel axes the Navajo could easily notch their juniper and pinon trunks to create "stacked" or crib-work walls. Only their roofs were capped with reddish earth. Other walling materials included railroad ties, rough sawn planking, boulder and adobe mortar, and shaped sandstone. A hanging blanket or handmade door of milled lumber covered the entrance.

Hogan variations

Travelers in Navajo country are likely to see hogans constructed of almost any possible building material. The cribbed log hogan *(above)*, has stacked walls of raw juniper; in another setting, a hogan might have upright posts, or walls of stacked railroad ties. Cinder blocks or stone *(bottom right)* produce a more perfectly circular plan. In the oldest style of female hogan *(above right)* the corbeling begins at ground level and the wooden hemisphere is completely covered with adobe—which is seen here eroding away. The woven wool rugs for which the Navajo are renowned appear in these photographs.

TODY

Navajo homesteads today can seem like architectural museums, containing dwellings whose styles and materials span a century of change. At any one camp one will often notice a single, forked-stick hogan. It might be a stroll away from two or more polygonal-walled "female" hogans, one with crib-work walls and an open smoke hole, another completely covered with red earth and sporting a stovepipe, with corbeling starting from the ground. A third might have stud framing and a red and green tarpaper roof. Only yards away a trailer home might be parked beside a recently built government-subsidized house of concrete blocks. Corrals, a hay shed, a four-post summer arbor, and a sweat bath behind some shrubbery often complete the compound.

In the summer of 1982, we were driving out of Chinle, Arizona, along the Navajo reservation's eastern boundary, when we chanced upon a hogan under construction. We were allowed to photograph the builder chopping the bark off the scrub juniper posts that would complete the rounded wall. The roof of two-by-fours pointing up to a hexagonal smoke hole apparently was the latest hogan style officially endorsed by the tribal council.

True to Navajo custom, it would house one family. The builder also was observing traditional taboos during construction. His hogan was being built on ground where lightning had not been known to strike. It was situated far away from a box canyon or ridge so that the Wind People would not inflict bad dreams or face and neck pains on its occupants. Nor was it near a river, which they thought might arouse the jealousy of the Water spirits. To the best of the builder's knowledge, the house was not in danger of being contaminated by the presence of an old corral where antelope had once been slaughtered, and it was a safe distance away from prehistoric ruins where the ghosts of the ancestral Pueblo people, the Anasazi, still roamed.

Hogan today

This modern hogan *(above)* was built near Chinle, Arizona in 1982. With juniper log-post walls and a roof frame of two-by-fours, it was a type officially approved by the tribal council in Window Rock. In a corbeled-wall hogan *(right)*, a Navajo woman cards wool while sitting in the northern or "female" zone of the house.

WIKIUP

As the Apache entered the Southwest, they split into nine different tribes who used two major house types. The buffalo-hunting Apaches, like the Mescalero and Jicarilla groups who established themselves to the east along the New Mexico-Texas border, adapted the hide-covered tipis of the Plains Indians but retained the pattern in which men moved into their wife's family homestead. They never grouped their tipis into the socially complex circular encampments of most Plains tribes, and their tipis were smaller and less intricately constructed.

The Apaches who settled further west, such as the central Chiricahua and the White Mountain groups, refined the old brush shelter that was part of their Subarctic heritage. Unlike the matriarchal clans of the Navajo, which linked up widespread homesteads, the basic social unit of these western Apaches was usually the compact, traveling band under the leadership of a single headman. As their hunting and raiding threatened settlers in the southwest borderlands, they remained in highly mobile units to outmaneuver the Mexican and U.S. troops pursuing them. Smaller versions of their grass-and-brush houses—they called them *kowas* but Europeans knew them as wikiups—could be assembled in an hour and were ideal for this hit-and-run existence. As Apaches started to settle on reservations, however, wikiups were built larger for more permanence. A typical homestead would contain several wikiups and a *dasdah*, or arbor, where families spent most of their summer days.

Wikiup construction began with the selection of the most level and well-drained site. A shallow trench about 12 feet in diameter was dug. Four framing saplings of juniper or mesquite were set in the ground, curved to a central meeting point, and lashed together, producing a pointed roof, or they were twisted around each other for a rounder profile. Other uprights were bent

Apache wikiups

Two variations of the Western Apache wikiup are the domed and pointed roof. The Mescalero Apache wikiup frame *(below)* was a light branch skeleton, which was covered with a thatch of weeds or bear grass and sometimes canvas. An archeological analysis conducted in 1965 *(near right)* of the floor remains of a historic period Western Apache wikiup confirmed that specific places in the wikiup were designated for storage, sleeping, and cooking.

The wikiup was a temporary structure that could be built quickly. A more permanent White Mountain Apache summer camp *(above right)*, ca. 1919, included an outdoor cooking hearth and ramadas for shade and sleeping. Some pointed roof wikiups also had entryway porticos.

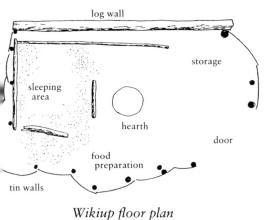

Wikiup floor plan

Labels on floor plan: log wall, storage, sleeping area, hearth, door, food preparation, tin walls

around this basic frame. When tough tamarisk saplings were used, the four framing poles were not necessary. Stringers of cottonwood, oak, sumac, or willow with leaves left on were tied horizontally up to the peak.

Material for the roof thatch depended on the locale. Yucca leaves or scrub, or rushes from the dry river bottoms, were used in the desert. If a band was in the transition zone, they selected bear grass. To make sure it stayed fresh and supple, the women pulled the bear grass up with the bulb attached. Spiky yucca leaves were cut green, dried until their needle-sharp tips could be pulled off, then shredded and rolled into cord. The first course of bear grass was stitched onto the ribbed structure with the yucca fiber so the bulb ends lay in the trench. Thereafter the ascending layers of thatching were sewn with the bulbs up and grass fronds facing down. The uppermost course was made of a thin layer of grass to permit smoke to filter through. The outer base was banked with dirt, and a hide covered the east-facing door. In the late nineteenth century, Apaches began to stretch canvas "skirts" around the side of the wikiup that faced prevailing winds. Bailing wire or cloth strips replaced the yucca fiber ties, and homemade doors with hinges and padlocks protected their furnishings.

The Apache also erected one special ceremonial tipi with extreme care and reverence during their *Nah-ih-es* ritual, the elaborate puberty ceremony for girls. The young women undergoing this life-passage festival are temporarily likened to the sacred epitome of Apache femininity, White-Painted Woman. Much of the ceremony takes place inside a symbolic representation of White-Painted Woman's sacred home, represented by an immense tipi frame built of four long logs with branches left green at the top. Upon completion the structure is sanctified with eagle feathers tied overhead.

KI and RAMADA

To the southwest of Navajo and Apache territory live the Pima and Papago Indians. The Spaniards found the Pima along the Gila and Salt Rivers, major tributaries of the Colorado River. Their age-old dependence upon streams for irrigation gained them the name "river people"; they were able to grow up to sixty percent of their food supply, which was supplemented by wild foods. Pima communities were situated near their fields, and often supported several hundred people. Their building materials were arrowweed, willow, and cottonwood, which require a moderate amount of rain.

The Papago lived to the south. They traveled in hunting and gathering bands close to today's Mexican border and called themselves "desert people." Surviving in one of North America's hottest climates, the Papago were forced to "follow the water," as they called their seasonal traveling. Family groups customarily spent July and August in so-called field villages, where they took advantage of the brief rainy season to plant tepary and lima beans, cotton and corn. After harvest, they wintered at "well villages," near familiar watering holes in the rugged uplands where they foraged for wild foods and hunted. They built with desert plants such as ocotillo, saguaro cactus, grease wood, and sacaton grass.

Both tribes used the ki during the winter and arbors, or ramadas, in the summer. The ki often measured up to 10 feet in diameter, although a headman's might be almost twice that size. Large settlements often boasted a ki 25 feet in diameter that could accommodate up to eighty tribal members for village council meetings. An extremely strong structure, the ki could withstand fierce windstorms.

Pima and Papago dwellings

In the nineteenth century both the Pima and Papago built forms of the ki, a brush and mud-covered structure. The Pima version *(below)* was slightly excavated and banked with earth, with a domed adobe-plastered roof. It was often accompanied by a ramada, as shown *(below right)* in an early drawing of a Pima encampment.

The later-period Papago house was a rectangular flat-roofed structure with a post and beam frame covered with arrowweed and mud *(above right)*. A ramada stood alongside it, shading an outdoor area for summer living.

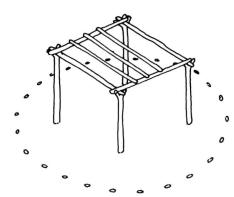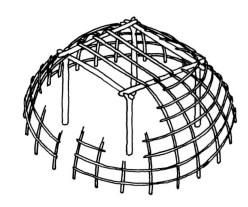

Pima ki construction sequence

The Pima began by scooping out an 18-inch excavation for the floor. Four crotched posts of cottonwood were erected and joined by cross beams to create a boxlike foundation measuring 7 by 8 feet. Parallel sticks were laid side by side on top to form a flat ceiling; sometimes a second perpendicular layer was added. Willow ribs were placed in the earth around the sunken floor and then bent to the cross beams in a domelike form. Woven in and out of the frame was a padding of arrowweed, cornstalks, wheat straw, and brush, all tightly bound to form insulating walls. A mud sealant was smeared on the roof, and the outer base was thickly banked with earth.

Before the Pima rainmaking ceremony, an orator would recite the myth of the original ki. The assembled crowd heard how a Black Measuring Worm broke its length into the four crotched posts. Then the Blue Measuring Worm divided itself up to become the joists, the White Measuring Worm became the flat-roof cross pieces, and the Reddish Measuring Worm segmented its body for the curved side ribs. A Blue Gopher covered the First House with brush, "covering it as with thin clouds." Then he layered it with earth from four gopher hills, "as snow covers the ground." Finally, with a puff of a prayer cigarette and a scattering of seed, the Blue Gopher magically spread the first grasslands and corn fields from the door of the first ki.

The Pima stored the community's food in flat-roofed storage buildings. Unlike the ki, their ceiling beams were made from dried and split saguaro cactus trunks. Cylindrical granaries woven of straw and caulked with mud were placed on top of the brush-and-earth roof coverings. For most of the summer Pimas lived under their shade arbors, "every inch of whose floors is purified by a burning sun," noted the ethnographer Frank Russell. "The arbor is kept well swept and clean, as is the entire yard about the house, so that a more healthful habitation could not be devised."

The Papago's ki were constructed of mesquite rather than cottonwood, and slender ocotillo cactus stalks were used instead of willow. Their camps were smaller than the Pima villages, containing no more than four shelters and usually inhabited by a set of parents with their married sons. When a man died, it was customary for his house rafters to be dismantled and arranged over his grave.

Papago house-life

The rectangular house of the Papago *(below right)* often featured a round granary on the roof, as at the San Xavier Indian reservation in Arizona, ca. 1894. A cooking windbreak can be seen behind the house. They were often framed of cornstalks *(above right)* or light brush, ca. 1916.

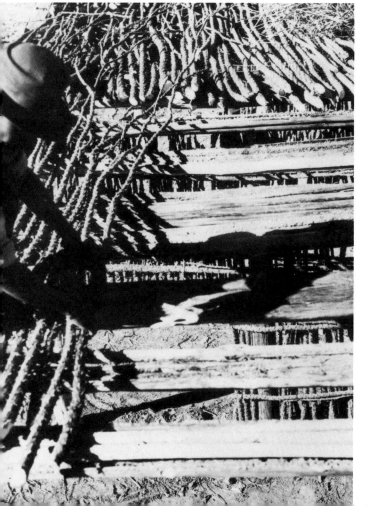

Papago construction

Late-period flat-roofed buildings are shown here *(below)* at San Xavier Reservation, with Black Mountain in the background. Their construction *(sequence at left)* began with a crotched post-and-beam frame overlaid with split saguaro cactus rafters. A layer of willow or ocotillo thatch then held a mud and straw plaster outer skin. The lath which held the adobe mixture could be installed either vertically or horizontally *(upper right)*.

Papago today

The "sandwich house" adapted the lath-and-mud construction to new materials, as adobe was wadded between one-by-fours *(left)*.

TODAY

In the 1880s, the U.S. Indian Bureau began to pressure the Pima and Papago to change their way of life. Indian householders were offered free wagons if they would cut their hair, build homes of adobe brick, and abandon their arbors. In the same period, the Indians adapted their old ocotillo-and-mud walling technique to gabled structures. Before long, milled lath replaced ocotillo in the so-called sandwich house. These owner-built homes featured posts at the corners and along the four walls, with uniform strips of ocotillo or thin lumber nailed at intervals horizontally on all sides. Adobe mud was packed in as wall fill, and the house was finished with plaster inside and out. Later, the sandwiching technique was adopted to build the walls of staggered, horizontal squared-logs or railroad ties, with mud packing in between.

However, the traditional ki did not die out. While the rain-melted remnants of a few old-time dwellings can only be found in outlying corners of Papago country, the ki form of construction was preserved in the sacred "Rain House" structures. They protect the jars of fermenting saguaro cactus pulp used during the Papago wine festival held every summer.

In June 1983, archeologist Jeff King drove us along the sandy roads of the Big Fields settlement near the eastern side of the Papago reservation and stopped at the local Rain House. (It also was sometimes referred to as "smoking house" or "round house.") The building was supported by four mesquite posts and had almost vertical brush walls; dry earth was spread over the flattened roof to keep the interior cool. The Indians store jars of fermenting saguaro cactus fruit pulp here for the festive rain ceremony. This is said to encourage rainfall on their fields. East of the Rain House stood a *watto*, the arbor that accompanies the sacred building. As we entered the ceremonial dance ground, the crooked mesquite posts of the arbor framed the Rain House. In the distance loomed Boboquiviri Mountain, where the Papago believe their creator-hero, I'itoi, still watches over them.

Papago Rain House

The old ki house type has not died out. Among the Papago, it was known aṣ the *vahki*, or Rain House, and one or more could be found in most Papago communities, such as this example at Big Fields, Arizona, 1983. Here wine made from saguaro cactus fruit was fermented in anticipation of annual rain-making ceremonies. The sacred Rain House is always accompanied by a ramada, known as the *watto*.

9 PUEBLO
SOUTHWEST II

"We came in sight of Cibola," wrote Father Marcus de Niza in the spring of 1539, "which lies in a plain on the slope of a round height. Its appearance is very good for settlement, the handsomest I have seen in these parts." Assessing the region's rumoured riches on behalf of the Spanish viceroy in Mexico City, the Franciscan friar never actually set foot in this Southwestern Indian community, located along a tributary of the Little Colorado River in present-day western New Mexico. He had already dispatched his black slave, Estevan, to do that. But the residents, who were probably Zuni Indians belonging to the village of Hawikuh, one of seven early Zuni towns, killed Estevan at the entrance to their village.

What Father Marcus glimpsed from a mesa away was an example of a distinctively Southwestern Indian architectural creation: a cluster of contiguous rooms constructed up to several stories which the Spanish quickly classified as a "Pueblo." Since that time, the natives belonging to a number of different language groups, who for over a thousand years have continued to farm and occupy these housing complexes, have been known collectively as "Pueblo Indians." Over the decade preceding Father Marcus's arrival, Spanish greed had been aroused by extravagant reports that the pueblo walls were inlaid with precious jewels and their alleyway-like streets lined with silversmith shops. When Father Marcus's own exaggerations about the village of Hawikuh reached Spain, the court was excited again to learn that this "city" was larger than the Aztec capital of Mexico and could "encompass two Sevilles."

A glance at an archeological map of the American Southwest reveals that the priest was exploring near the heart of a pre-Columbian cultural region that had witnessed a succession of architectural traditions, leaving behind a large number of stunning and intact building remains. To early visitors, the American Southwest was perhaps the most spectacular corner of the continent. Its arid isolation, high desert panoramas, and gorgeous light were reminiscent of mythological holy lands and ancient civilizations. Its northern rim begins as the tail end of the Rocky Mountains gives way to the Colorado Plateau with its sandstone mesas, outstretched valleys, and hardy upland forests, which are watered mainly by the Colorado River and its tributaries. The air is dry and clear, the winters are cold, topsoil is meager, and life-giving rains fall only occasionally in late summer.

Toward the Mogollon highlands of eastern Arizona the topography grows increasingly rugged where the Gila and Salt River systems penetrate the mesquite and cactus desert. Continuing down into northern Mexico, the withering Basin and Range country lifts into the Sierra Madre wall. The great pre-Columbian Pueblo cultures of the Southwest were invigorated by traders and emissaries from the civilizations of Mesoamerica, who made their way through the natural passes and corridors of this rough terrain.

The earliest Spaniards to see the American Southwest and its Indian housing tended to regard architectural size and apparent permanence as reflections of cultural development. Initially they admired these communal stone and adobe towns with their clusters of multistoried and specialized rooms, their connecting rooftops and interior passageways, their spaces for storing water and processing the produce of agricultural fields, their bustling

Emergence

The emergence of human beings from the underworld is a fundamental theme in Pueblo Indian myth, ritual, and architecture. The emergence design *(above)* is from a bowl made by the Mimbres people, southwestern New Mexico, A.D. 900-1200. This wide view *(bottom)* of the rooftops of Zuni Pueblo, New Mexico, looks toward the sacred mountain, Dowa Yalanne. Photographed ca. 1880.

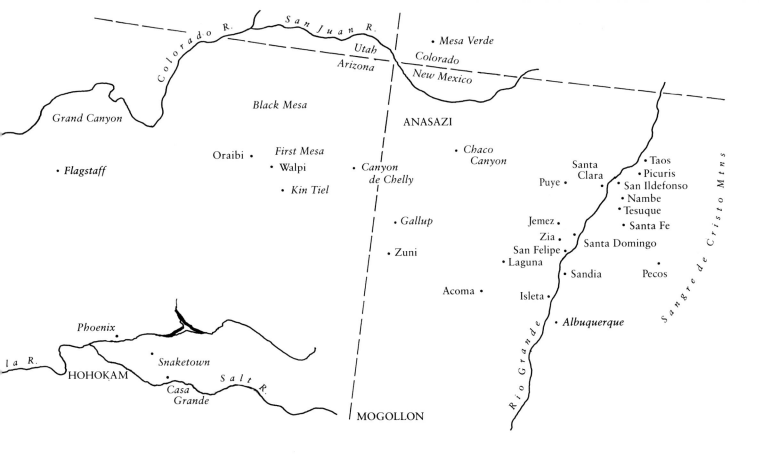

Grand Canyon

Flagstaff

Oraibi • • *First Mesa*
• *Walpi*

• *Kin Tiel*

Colorado R. *San Juan R.*

Utah
Arizona

Black Mesa

• *Canyon
de Chelly*

• *Gallup*

• Zuni

Mesa Verde •

Colorado
New Mexico

ANASAZI

• *Chaco
Canyon*

Puye •

Jemez •

Zia •
San Felipe •
• Laguna

Acoma •

Santa
Clara

• Taos
• Picuris
• San Ildefonso
• Nambe
• Tesuque
• Santa Fe

Santa Domingo

• Sandia

Isleta •

• *Albuquerque*

Pecos •

Sangre de Cristo Mtns

la R.

Phoenix
•

HOHOKAM

• *Snaketown*

*Casa
Grande*

Salt R.

MOGOLLON

Rio Grande

work terraces, and their public plazas and underground religious chambers (which we now call by the Hopi term *kivas,* but which the Spanish called *estufas,* or stoves, because of their overheated interiors). In this architectural ensemble the Spanish sensed a familiar civic impulse. Furthermore, the developed look of the towns, the manpower and level of social organization needed to maintain them, and the pieces of turquoise and coral jewelry they found, suggested to the Spanish the sort of byproducts of civilization they had exploited among the Aztecs and Incas: a native labor force and natural riches.

Fourteen months after Father Marcus's visit, however, the humble, mud-plastered town of Hawikuh was demoted in Francisco Coronado's eyewitness report to "a little crowded village, looking as if it had been cramped together." Yet if the houses were "not decorated with turquoises, nor made of lime nor of good bricks" as the priest had implied, "nevertheless they are very good houses, with three and four and five stories, while there are very good apartments and good rooms with corridors, and some very good rooms underground." As for deducing wider cultural development from architectural evidence, Coronado expressed disbelief that the Zuni occupants could produce even these structures. "I do not think they have the judgement and

Hopi food room

Most of the space within a typical southwestern pueblo was given over to the storage and preparation of food. People lived in the upper rooms, and stored dried corn, vegetables, and other food in chambers deep within the houseblock. This Hopi food room *(above)* shows stacked corn cobs to the left, fresh melons, and a row of milling basins to the right. The basins hold grinding stones, or *metates,* of varying degrees of roughness for grinding corn from coarse to medium to a fine meal.

intelligence needed to be able to build those houses in the way in which they are built, for most of them are entirely naked...."

Of course Coronado was as misled about the sophistication of Zuni society as he was about the durability of their architecture. The size of their mortared-stone buildings belied their relatively impermanent construction. Unlike the great buildings of the Anasazi period whose primary structures often were built in one organized construction campaign, these Zuni house-blocks were actually fragile honeycombs of plastered and whitewashed cell-like rooms which had been stacked up somewhat haphazardly over time. Relatively little attention was paid to bonding together the rooms, which themselves were often hastily dismantled to provide building material for a new unit somewhere else.

The country of the Zuni people, or "Cibola" to the Spanish, was one of three Indian "kingdoms"—containing nearly eighty Indian Pueblos altogether—that were identified by the Coronado expedition. To seven other native villages in the province of Tusayan, the Painted Desert homeland of the Hopi Indians, Coronado dispatched Pedro de Tovar. He sent Hernando de Alvarado to the third province of Tiguex, which included a dozen or more villages along the banks of the Rio Grande to the east. En route, Alvarado passed beneath the site of Acoma Pueblo, perched atop an impregnable sandstone mesa. Finally he reached the easternmost Indian town, a large settlement named Cicuique, which today is the archeological site of Pecos Pueblo.

Alvarado's description of this village offers a checklist of features that would typify Pueblo architecture over the next three centuries: "... it is square ... situated on a rock with a courtyard in the middle, containing the estufas. The houses are all alike, four stories high.... There are corridors going all around it at the first two stories, by which one can go around the whole village.... The houses do not have doors below, but they use ladders, which can be lifted like a draw bridge.... The village is enclosed by a low wall of stone."

Such sketchy glimpses are all that Spanish sources yield of late-period Pueblo architecture, whose built forms had undergone six centuries of change and decline. The Spanish also tell us little of the impressive archeological sites for which the region is renowned today. Before Coronado ever reached Hawikuh he had noted a massive ruin along the Gila River south of present-day Phoenix, Arizona, which almost certainly was the adobe citadel of Casa Grande. But Spain was uninterested in scientific or cultural exploration, and further disclosures of the region's architectural heritage would not come for almost three hundred years.

In the mid-nineteenth century, the United States took over the Southwest from Mexico and sent its own military emissaries to learn about its people and natural resources. Their reports included drawings and descriptions of the native buildings they found everywhere—recently abandoned, long in ruins, or occupied by surviving Pueblo societies. As ranchers began chasing stray stock into unexplored canyons, other ancient settlements came to light. In the 1870s and '80s, pioneer archeologists and anthropologists began discovering old rooms that seemed frozen in time: fresh murals were on the walls, fiber sandals lay on the floor, and cooking pots rested on cold fire pits.

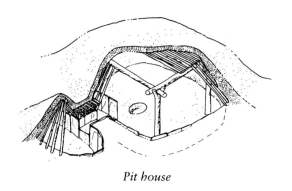

Pit house

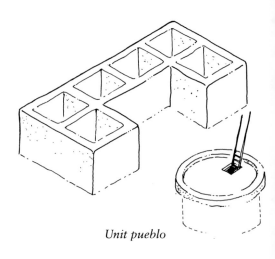

Unit pueblo

THE PREHISTORIC SOUTHWEST

The earliest excavators of old Pueblo ruins tried to reconstruct the chronology of their pre-Columbian societies by making general correlations between painted designs on old pots and architectural features. With the refinement of this approach, the first major effort to establish the sequence of early Southwestern cultures occurred in 1927 during a symposium at Pecos Pueblo, which by then had been excavated and restored. The best scholars in the field hammered out a broad timeline which, with important additions, remains the most developed chronology for the cultural prehistory, and architectural evolution, of the central American Southwest.

According to the Pecos schema, early Indian groups, which shared what has been labeled the Basketmaker culture, occupied caves in the Four Corners heartland around 200 B.C. Five centuries later, agriculture was well-established and the Basketmakers were living in villages composed of one- or two-family, circular pit houses.

The culture known as prehistoric Pueblo emerged around this time, identified architecturally by the Indians' gradual move into above-ground "unit pueblos." From then on the techniques for building monumental houseblocks and separate ceremonial chambers, for organizing sophisticated regional food production networks and communication systems among many towns, developed with unparalleled rapidity. During the classic period of Pueblo architecture, from roughly 1100 to 1300 A.D., extensive cliff dwellings were constructed in the northwestern plateaus, and an even more elaborate regional network of agricultural townships appeared in western New Mexico: the "Great House" architectural system centered in Chaco Canyon. Toward the close of the thirteenth century, however, environmental or social troubles seem to have precipitated the relatively sudden abandonment of these magnificent stone-and-adobe city-states. For the next two and half centuries, the Pueblo Indians' descendants periodically regrouped and resettled, migrating gradually ever eastward.

By the mid-twentieth century, further archeological work and refined dating techniques, including counting tree-rings on old Pueblo house beams and comparing the annual growth cycles against a master chronology to pinpoint the year the beam was cut, made it clear that the Southwest's prehistory involved more traditions than could be embraced by one architectural chronology. The Pecos timeline remained basically sound for the widespread cultural world known since 1936 as *Anasazi*, from a Navajo word meaning "enemy ancestors," which had produced spectacular cliff dwellings such as Mesa Verde and the even more impressive buildings of Chaco Canyon. But it largely ignored the architectural and cultural achievements of the great

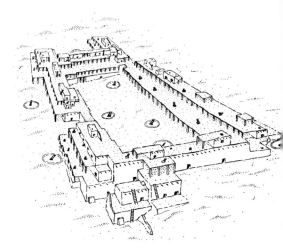

Pecos Pueblo

Pre-Hispanic building

These drawings trace major stages in the evolution of Pueblo architecture. Pit houses, the earliest house type, were built in various ways. The reconstruction of an early Basketmaker form *(above left)* is based on archeological work at Shabik'eshchee Village in San Juan County, New Mexico. After A.D. 850, early Pueblo period builders began constructing rectangular rooms above ground of stone and adobe, roofed with timbers, branches, grass, and adobe mud. Combined to share walls, and with a kiva (a vestigial pit house) close by, these are called "unit pueblos" by archeologists *(above right)*. A fully developed early example of this construction is Pecos Pueblo in central New Mexico, as it appeared ca 1700.

Mogollon pit houses *(right)* are drawn from excavations at Harris Village in southwestern New Mexico.

Mogollon and Hohokam cultures found further to the southwest.

When the Spanish encountered the native descendants of all of these cultures, nearly a thousand years of migration, cultural interaction, ecological adaptation, and climactic shift had already taken place. Despite the harsh program of Spanish colonialism, including military conquest, Catholic missionization, and conscripted labor, the Pueblo Indians and their architectural traditions remained remarkably resilient. Although the Indians incorporated new architectural ideas, they did not forswear their construction practices or abandon their traditional spatial concepts. Today the Pueblos still represent the most persistent architectural heritage in North America.

MOGOLLON

Mogollon culture is named for the rugged plateau and mountains of central Arizona and southwestern New Mexico, where archeologists have found remains of another distinctive prehistoric Southwestern tradition. Dating from shortly before 300 B.C. and generally found in villages built on defensible mesa crests, the early Mogollon habitations had floors excavated quite deep, up to three feet. The sides of the pit formed the walls; the roof was supported by heavy posts and the principal rafters which held a layer of smaller sticks and a final mat of brush capped with wet earth. One entered through the smoke hole by a ladder or down a ramp, which was usually oriented south-southeast, and near the entryway stood a square, stone-rimmed hearth. Otherwise the construction and shape of Mogollon structures varied: the interior posts could be positioned near the center of the room or stand closer to the walls; the buildings could be built upon a D-shaped, ovoid, or rectangular plan.

Mogollon settlements contained from five to fifty of these semisubterranean structures and were fortified on their exposed sides by simple masonry walls. The dwellings had plank-lined food storage cysts and cooking pits inside and out. Additional heat for the house was sometimes generated from rocks that were warmed in outside fires; then carried inside. Nearby were garden plots, where Mogollon farmers raised the corn, beans, and squash that augmented what they hunted and gathered.

For ceremonies a special pit house was built either in the midst of the settlement or on its periphery. As Mogollon society grew more agriculturally competent around A.D. 800, members began to move down into the valleys. There they reinforced their pit house walls with masonry linings and expanded the single "Great Kiva" to serve larger communities. Built on a rectangular plan, these religious structures sometimes extended 40 feet.

After A.D. 1000, Mogollon architecture seems to have reflected Anasazi influence as rooms were joined and walls composed of cobbles held together with mud mortar were raised to two stories. These apartment-style room clusters, facing central plazas, could multiply into sizable communities, such as the 500-room Grasshopper Ruin found in western Arizona. Scholars cannot agree on what precipitated the population decline of Mogollon society in the 1100s, but it left their villages utterly deserted by A.D. 1450. Some suggest that their survivors were among the founders of the Zuni pueblo of Hawikuh seen by Father Marcus de Niza.

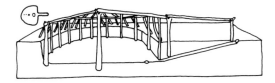
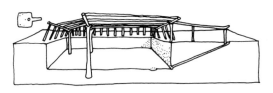
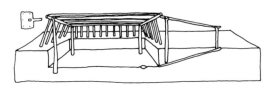

*Mogollon pit houses,
section and plans*

HOHOKAM

A different set of architectural forms belonged to the nearby Hohokam people, some of whose extensive ruins along the Gila and Salt Rivers were noticed by the early Spanish conquistadors. The word *Hohokam* does not mean "those who have vanished" as is commonly thought, but originates from the Pima Indian phrase meaning "all used up." Some archeologists argue that their culture came under Mesoamerican influence rather rapidly, pointing out that by the time the Hohokam archeological record begins—about 2,300 years ago—their settlements already exhibited a fairly integrated "cultural kit," including a knowledge of canal irrigation agriculture, techniques for building imposing adobe walls, and rituals that required flat-topped, pyramidal earth mounds. The ovoid-shaped ball courts for playing ritual games, characteristic of many Hohokam sites, were introduced later.

Snaketown, a sizable archeological site in Pinal County, Arizona, is the most extensively studied Hohokam community. It was occupied continually for nearly seven hundred years. Beginning around A.D. 300, during the period known as Pioneer, two house types were built: shallow-dug pit houses with

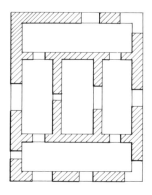

Casa Grande plan

Hohokam archeology

Spanish conquistadors passed by this massive, mud-walled ruin *(below)*, constructed by the Hohokam people after A.D. 1300. This is an early photo of Casa Grande, near Florence, Arizona. Adobe castles such as this possibly represented an abrupt change in political organization, with centralized leadership.

The most extensive Hohokam site is Snaketown *(below)*, in Pinal County, Arizona. Seen in this partial view are 50 house floors excavated by archeological teams led by Emil Haury. In his words this photograph represents "1000 years of architectural history."

rectangular floors and roof posts pressed near the walls, and dwellings with squarer floors, rounded corners, and ceilings supported by four central uprights. No common orientation of the houses prevailed, and from studying floor post holes archeologists conclude that dwellings were often rebuilt on the same site.

In the sixth century, the Hohokam began deepening, narrowing, and lengthening their irrigation canals. Over the next five hundred years they extended the system until their plastered trenches were 30 feet wide and up to 10 feet deep to lessen water loss from surface evaporation. The system branched 30 miles into the desert east of the Gila River, so that the vegetable gardens of the large communities of Casa Grande and Pueblo de los Muertos were watered by rivers 6 miles away.

Hohokam spaces for play, worship, and defense were unique in the ancient Southwest. Leveling over their trash dumps and plastering them with clay, the Hohokam created pyramidal foundations for temporary temples and dance grounds. They also introduced two types of game fields for playing the semiritualistic sport that used raw rubber balls imported from Mexico. The Snaketown-style courts were relatively large, oriented east to west, and featured bulbous end fields. At Casa Grande they were smaller, more egg-shaped, and oriented north to south.

At Casa Grande today, one can walk around the most original and durable Hohokam architectural contribution—the monumental compound. Shaded beneath a metal roof a few miles from Phoenix stands a castlelike structure with 5-foot-thick adobe walls believed to have been built in one great effort around A.D. 1300. It was once thought that these walls were piled in stages, using a rammed-earth technique in which preprepared mud was pressed into wattle-and-daub forms. But careful study reported by David Wilcox in 1975-76 found that the stiff mud actually had been piled up by hand, tier by tier, up to four stories, without forms or internal reinforcing beams. To frame the ceilings, more than six hundred juniper, pine, and fir beams were cut on mountainsides 50 miles from the site.

The use and meaning of these unusual Hohokam structures have been harder to decipher than their construction. The massive walls and elaborate room networks suggest they were bastions against attack. Apertures in upper rooms, however, have been discovered to be aligned to equinoctial and solsticial positions of the sun, and other observation holes might be sited to record the longer lunar cycles. To archeologist Frank H. Cushing, the interior room arrangement at Casa Grande conformed to the cosmographic layout of Zuni Indian altars that paid homage to the "houses" of the six sacred directions. Sometimes these Hohokam strongholds were grouped together, such as at the Los Muertos site, where twenty-five compounds once stood inside a mile-long enclosure.

Hohokam society faded less quickly than its neighboring cultures. The metropolis of Snaketown declined around A.D. 1100, but Casa Grande was built later, perhaps by an offshoot or replacement group. By the time the Europeans arrived, there remained an inexplicable contrast between the grand architectural legacy of the Hohokam ruins and the dispersed, humble dwellings occupied by their probable descendants, the historic Pima and Papago Indians.

355

ANASAZI

Without question the most elaborate native architecture in North America was produced by the cultural world we identify by the name Anasazi. Nestled beneath sandstone cliffs or positioned along valley floors, their compact apartmentlike town clusters integrated the most advanced inventory of building types, special-use rooms, construction methods, and road and water management systems in the continent.

Constructed with only the available materials of earth, stone, and sunlight, these proto-urban settlements still appear strikingly harmonious with their high desert surroundings. As archeologists Michael P. Marshall and David E. Doyel have written of what is popularly labeled the "Chaco Phenomenon" of the southeastern Anasazi, "The buildings often appear as extensions of pinnacle spires, mesa cliffs, and canyon walls . . . A sense of place is clearly a very important aspect of Bonito-style architecture, especially in the outlying districts. It is as if the environment were personified with attributes of mythological character, and the placement of the structures were dictated by Chacoan cosmography and sacred geography, balanced by certain economic considerations."

As with the Mogollon and Hohokam architectural heritages, Anasazi house building started with semi-subterranean structures. About the time of Christ, their forebears were digging 4-foot-deep house floors in the Mesa Verde region of southern Colorado. These shelters contained sunken hearths and sandstone slabs to deflect drafts that blew through their tunneled entryways. Gradually these rooms expanded, and ladders through the smoke hole replaced the doorway, which shrank into a ventilation shaft. Sometimes pit house floors contained a fist-sized pit later called a *sipapu,* from the Hopi word for the mythic place of emergence. Some archeologists believe that this floor shrine stands for the opening in the earth from which, according to Pueblo myth, human beings emerge after their ascent through a succession of underworlds.

A change occurred around A.D. 700, however, when people began to live for part of the year in small "unit" structures above ground. Constructed of easily chipped sandstone rock set in masonry, their walls lacked windows or doors and were roofed like pit houses with main rafters, smaller closing material, and earth. These cubicles were combined so that adjoining units shared walls, and eventually the linear arrangement of rooms embraced irregular plazas, usually with the rear facade toward the prevailing northerly wind or backed against a cliff. The front facade and terracelike roofs faced south. During the winter the adobe soaked up solar heat throughout the day and radiated it into the domestic rooms at night. With small, relatively smokeless fires burning in the rooms during very cold weather, and the smoke hole shuttered for the night, the warm walls kept the interior comfortable.

In colder reaches of Anasazi land, pit houses, which probably kept family groups warmer than the multiroom pueblos, continued to be used for awhile for shelter and storage. But by about 950, as an increasing population depended more extensively upon agriculture and new, efficient practices of processing and food storing, most of the multiroom pueblos were occupied year-round. Also around this time, the pit house form appears to have gradually transformed into the circular sacred or social kiva. Over the next thousand years it became the most symbolic Pueblo built-form, an architec-

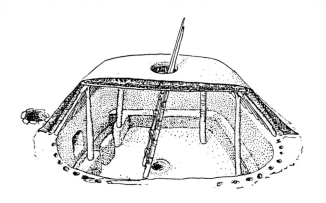

Section

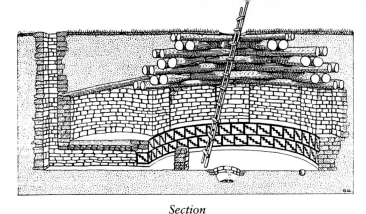

Section

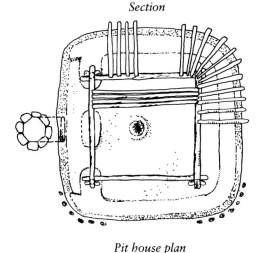

Pit house plan

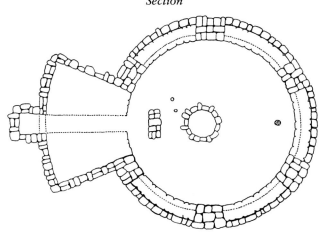

Kiva plan

Prehistoric change

Buildings used exclusively for sacred and social purposes, known as kivas, evolved from domestic pit houses. The pit house drawing, *(top left)* is based on remains from the La Plata district in southern Colorado. It was built between between A.D. 500 and 700, and has a bench around the interior, a small air vent and a stone to deflect incoming drafts, a central hearth and ladder for entering through the roof.

In the generalized drawing of a Anasazi "keyhole" kiva *(top right)*, which was fully developed in the same region by the twelfth century, the ventilator shaft has been lengthened, the structure is sunk deeper within the ground, the bench has become more elaborate—with paintings and often with pilasters—and the roof is composed of corbeled logs. Behind the firepit is the small cavity known as the *sipapu*.

tural embodiment of the collective, insular, and spiritual nature of Pueblo theocracy. Anasazi kiva interiors were often covered with multicolored murals and ringed with adobe-plastered benches on which rested pilasters or embedded posts that supported corbelled-log ceilings. These San Juan kivas featured ventilation shafts and fire pits, and sometimes included sipapu shrines and floor basins for ritual activities.

To shelter their growing population, the Anasazi added second stories to their unit pueblos. Families slept in the upper, front units where sunlight peered through the smoke hole, and the passive-solar heating properties of adobe were most effective. During late fall and early spring the inhabitants worked or socialized on the outdoor roof terraces. In the cooler, darkened interior rooms they processed and stored dried corn, squash, and other produce. Over time, archeologists now believe, the more organized Anasazi villages used the interiors as storage depots for a regional food supply; a remarkable number of rooms are devoid of any sign of domestic life.

By the time of the florescence of the Anasazi culture, between about 1100 and 1300, kivas—tightly inserted between recent building additions—were proliferating. At settlements in the Mesa Verde region, for example, they fit snugly amid concentric walls, unusual D-shaped buildings known as "horse-shoe" houses, and ceremonial towers to which some are connected by underground tunnels. Scholars have suggested that this plentitude of kivas is evidence of the emergence of a clan form of social organization, with larger kin groups starting to favor "suites" of rooms, each with their own meeting chamber or kiva. It is conceivable that such ensembles actually comprised neighborhoods, with tribal rules dictating the interdependent work, worship, and recreation of the pueblo as a whole. It has also been proposed that the community at large convened in the expanded circular structures that archeologists call "Great Kivas," over twenty of which have been found throughout Anasazi territory.

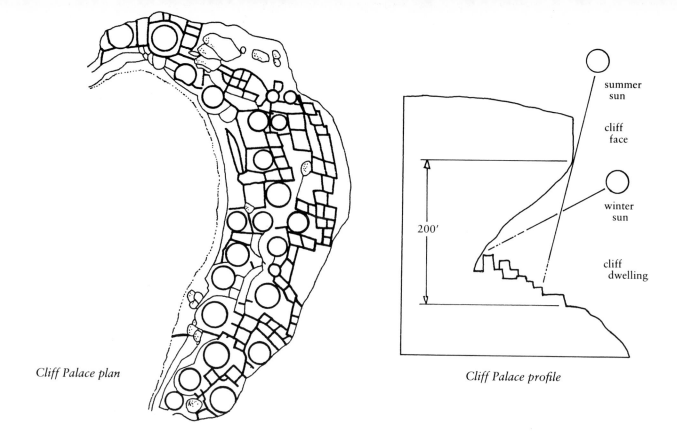

Cliff Palace plan

summer
sun

cliff
face

winter
sun

200'

cliff
dwelling

Cliff Palace profile

Mesa Verde

In the southwestern corner of Colorado, at Mesa Verde National Park, are preserved many spectacular Anasazi cliff dwellings from the period A.D. 1100 to 1275. Cliff Palace *(left)* had plazas, 220 rooms in buildings up to three stories, 23 kivas, and ceremonial towers.

Spruce Tree House *(above)* is another large cliff dwelling. The walls have been restored and the kiva ladder reconstructed. The upper-level T-shaped doorways would have been entered from roof terraces which no longer exist. Food was probably prepared and cooked outdoors in front of the rooms. The small plazas were actually the roofs of kivas buried below, which were framed as shown to the right.

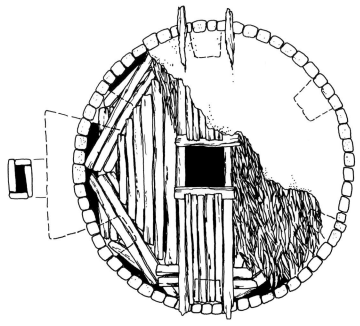

Kiva roof framing plan

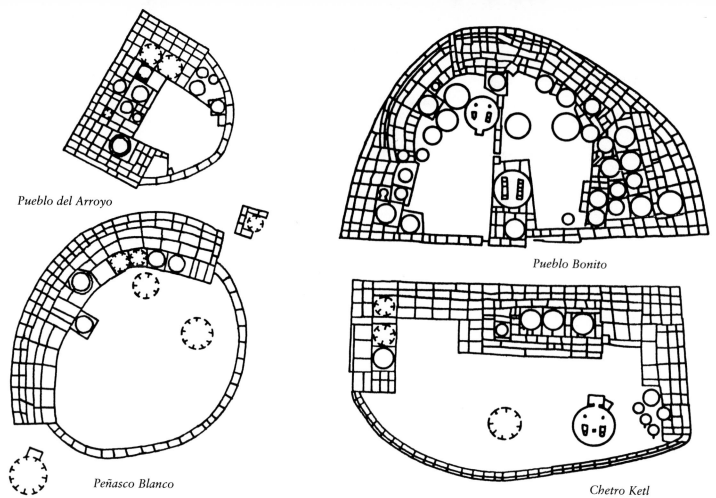

Pueblo del Arroyo

Pueblo Bonito

Peñasco Blanco

Chetro Ketl

Chaco Canyon Great House plans

Chaco Canyon

Most of the Great House complexes of Chaco Canyon *(above, looking east)* were built by the Anasazi along a seven-mile stretch of Chaco Wash. Entering the canyon from the west, Peñasco Blanco is encountered first. It is the only town complex situated to the south of the wash, and was built between A.D. 900 and 1120. When architect Victor Mindeleff visited this pueblo in 1888, some rooms still retained their original wood plank roofs. Further into the canyon three major towns are side by side: Pueblo del Arroyo, built between A.D. 1065 and 1110, Pueblo Bonito, (920 to 1085), and Chetro Ketl (1010 to 1105). At the eastern end of the canyon, La Fajada Butte can be seen; its pictographs and stone alignments possibly functioned as a solar observatory, marking the solstices and equinoxes.

The reconstruction drawing of Pueblo Bonito in its prime *(bottom left)* was by the photographer William H. Jackson, who visited the canyon in 1877.

It was during this period that Mesa Verde and Chaco Canyon appear to have become the command centers of the Anasazi Southwest. While the extent of Mesa Verdian influence is harder to identify, Chaco Canyon, according to archeologist Stephen H. Lekson of the National Park Service, held sway over a regional system "only slightly smaller than Ireland." A shared religious worldview and sociopolitical system probably created a certain unity among the inhabitants of the northerly and southern Anasazi regions. A communication network of straight roads and fire beacon signals extended for hundreds of miles, linking smaller outlying pueblos, and long-distance trade relations brought prized goods such as macaw feathers and copper bells from hundreds of miles away.

By the eleventh century, undoubtedly the most skilled builders were in Chaco Canyon, where at least nine major "Great Houses," highly integrated assemblages of rooms, kivas, plazas, towers, and terraces, lined the valley floor. Unlike the gradual process of room accretion which the Spanish were to witness among the historic Pueblos, the construction of these immense houseblocks was not piecemeal. According to Lekson, "Complete blocks of up to 50 rooms or more were built as single planned structures. Clearly, the design of Chacoan Great Houses was not a committee affair; not all of the occupants or users had a say in how the finished building would look. Design was centralized, and the role of architect was at least rudimentally present." Also present must have been the role of contractor, for Lekson emphasizes the amount of material and sweat which went into the building phase in Chaco Canyon in the 900s: "Construction of a typical room required 45,000 kilograms of stone, 15,000 kilograms of clay, and 4,100 liters of water. The massively timbered roof or ceiling of a typical room required 40 beams, each a separate pine or fir tree obtained from forests up to 60 kilometers from the desert canyon."

The apparent "capital" of Chaco Canyon was Pueblo Bonito, a D-shaped Great House which grew in successive stages from a kernel arc of about one hundred rooms in the early tenth century to a garrison town covering almost two acres by 1070. By then it stood at least four stories high at the rear, which backed against a sheer sandstone cliff, and contained 800 rooms, 37 kivas, and a divided plazalike open area which held two Great Kivas.

From ground-level footings, which rested upon trenched foundations filled with rubble and clay mortar to prevent the walls from settling, the curved back of Pueblo Bonito was about 35 feet high. At its widest point, where the central rooms faced the low-lying winter sun, the living area was six rooms deep. The tapering of the outer walls from a thickness of about 3 feet at the base to 1 foot at the uppermost story supports the supposition that the central section was conceived as a total unit. As in most Chaco Canyon constructions, it was the unparalleled craftmanship of these walls, which, unlike abutted historic period pueblo walls, were often bonded together by interlocking the stone in adjoining walls, that makes Chacoan architecture so outstanding. As described by archeologist Linda S. Cordell, "The Bonito sites were constructed of cored, veneered masonry in which the load-bearing wall core was composed of rough flat stones set in ample mortar with each stone oriented to only one face of the wall and overlapping or abutting the stone on the reverse face, creating a structurally sound wall. The wall core was then covered on both sides with veneer of coursed ashlar, often in alternating bands of thick and thin stones, forming various patterns. The strikingly decorative veneers were then covered with adobe plaster or matting."

Chacoan kivas

Near Pueblo Bonito are the remains of Casa Rinconada (above), a Great Kiva 63 feet in diameter. It included a masonry box for the fire, trunk-like vaults possibly for foot drums, and a subfloor passage which might have been used for theatrical effects during rituals.

The overview photograph of Pueblo Bonito (right) shows round kivas amongst the rectangular rooms.

By contemporary standards, the rooms at Pueblo Bonito were cramped, averaging 9 by 14 feet and under 8 feet in height. They were entered by ladders, as was the walled town itself. Within the darkened rooms, doorways and trap doors opened on to storage rooms, units with rows of milling basins for grinding corn, and chambers with carefully oriented observation windows so ritualists could mark key moments in the solar and lunar calendars that governed agricultural and ceremonial life.

To maintain this dense population and highly organized way of life, the canyon and upper mesa rim around Pueblo Bonito and its sister towns had been converted into a major water management enterprise. Residents tilled the garden plots that lined the valley bottom's trickling stream. They also cooperated on the upkeep of an intricate system of dams, floodgates, and ditches. As the thunderstorms of July and August brought rain, virtually all of the water that fell in the immediate vicinity was channeled down spillways and troughs to feed their gardens and replenish their reservoirs.

DECLINE

What led to the abrupt end of Anasazi society in the late thirteenth century remains a mystery. There is no convincing evidence that some "invading horde" of aggressive hunters, Athapaskans or otherwise, wiped them out. Theories of social or religious schism remain speculative. A period of threatening droughts is known to have occurred between 1276 and 1329, but its full ramifications remain unclear. Whatever the combination of likely causes, after 1300 all the major Southwestern cultures experienced disarray, migration, and reconsolidation.

It is believed that in the wake of these upheavals the upper Rio Grande basin eventually became a refuge for Anasazi survivors who abandoned the San Juan basin and adjoining areas in increasing numbers. Their hastily built, oversized settlements—many hidden in mountain pockets—are found along a 150-mile stretch of the Rio Grande. Other Anasazi offshoots, perhaps migrating as intact clans, coalesced as the incipient Hopi around the Black Mesa terrain of northeastern Arizona.

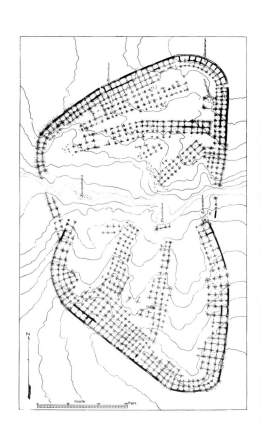

Although during this unsettled period the Anasazi resettlers continued to use traditional building methods, masonry at the new sites was not up to former standards. Some of the large communities, such as the briefly occupied Kin Tiel site north of present-day Holbrook, Arizona, seem little more than refugee camps. Covering 30 acres, Kin Tiel seems to have been built with defense in mind around 1275. While its house blocks were split into two sections in a town plan remarkably similar to present-day Taos Pueblo in northern New Mexico, square kivas are found here, too, more in keeping with the rectangular kiva tradition found among the Western Pueblos of historic times.

Late Anasazi settlements

About A.D. 1300, Anasazi migrants from the Mesa Verde and Chaco areas moved east and south. They resettled in large communities such as Kin Tiel *(bottom left)*. Another important pueblo built between A.D. 1300 and Spanish arrival is Puŷe; this view *(top left)* shows the grid of rooms atop the Parajito Plateau; other dwellings were carved into the soft tufa rock at the base of the mesa. About a thousand rooms are estimated to have housed some 2,000 people. Among the kivas at Puŷe is this solitary kiva *(below)*, which overlooks Frijoles Canyon 150 feet below.

As the emigrants continued eastward, two forms of settlement predominated. At sites like Tyuonyi in Frijoles Canyon in present-day Bandelier National Park, single-story structures were the norm, arranged linearly around plazas. In other transitional communities rooms were massed into irregular pyramids. These towns were laid out in a circular or rectangular shape, walling in an enclosed courtyard or, as at Tsirege, Otowi, and Tsankawi, merely establishing house blocks on three sides of a plaza with openings generally to the south. The new Rio Grande communities seemed to prefer the rounded, San Juan style of kiva, and in a few of their plazas the old Great Kiva reappeared.

Some of these settlements withered, while others flourished and developed new construction techniques. Along the Rio Grande, where usable stone was at a premium, Indian builders formed squat wet bricks known as "turtle backs," slapped and shaped them atop each other, then smoothed the surface over with plaster. We will never know, however, what architectural forms might have been produced during this time of reorientation, for the arrival of the Spanish in the mid-sixteenth century abruptly ended that natural evolution.

SPANISH INFLUENCE

The Spanish campaign to dominate the Pueblos had an impact on Indian culture and architecture for the next 140 years. The roofline of many Pueblo villages betrayed one highly symbolic modification: The harmonious planes of pueblo terraces and mesas were now pierced by the bell towers of Franciscan missions. Other innovations were less obvious. Spanish interior corner fireplaces, known as *fogon,* were gradually adopted by the Indians, who added flues and chimney pots to release the smoke. In replacing their old center-floor hearths with the Spanish molded fireplaces, however, they improvised ways to suspend smoke hoods over the raised burn area that still allowed them to fit pre-Spanish granite griddles over the fire. The stone pans were used to toast unleavened *piki* bread, made from thin corn batter. Beehive-shaped outdoor ovens, known as *horno* to the Spanish, were added to roof terraces. The ovens were fired up with burning juniper, and held heat long enough to bake yeast bread and pastries and to roast game and unhusked corn.

In regions with sufficient water to make adobe, the Spanish wooden forms for molding the bricks made raising walls somewhat easier. But the Indians' bricks and the walls they built were not as thick as those preferred by the Spanish, perhaps because the Indians were less preoccupied with the permanence of their constructions. Nor did the Pueblo Indians alter greatly the dimensions of their diminutive rooms or adopt such Hispanic adobe features

as wrap-around porticos, carved lintels, or corbels. For their part, Spanish homesteaders appear to have been equally influenced by Indian building patterns and customs. Soon they were forming their northern New Mexico ranchos protectively around plazas, and Spanish women took charge of the fresh plastering each year as if imitating Pueblo Indian custom.

From 1600 to 1680, as Spanish oppression intensified, the Pueblo Indian population dropped an estimated 50 percent from forced labor, execution, and epidemics. In 1680, however, the Pueblos of Hopi country, the Rio Grande villages, and the Indian communities in between staged the most successful multitribal uprising in American history. Its architectural consequence was the destruction of most of the Catholic chapels. Indeed, among the Hopi, church beams were salvaged as rafters for their traditional kivas. After the city of Santa Fe was liberated by the Indian rebels, a kiva was built in the downtown plaza as if to declare their triumph in architectural terms.

The all-Pueblo rebellion of 1680 surprised the victors as much as the vanquished. Perhaps fearing retaliation, or to exorcise spiritual contamination after so much bloodshed, a reshuffling of Pueblo sites took place. The Hopis rebuilt their villages atop three secluded stems of Black Mesa, where they still live today. The Anglo-American visitors of the late nineteenth century were recording the lifeways and architecture of Indians who wanted little to do with the white man again.

PUEBLO

In few tribal regions are the culture and architecture so closely identified as they are among the southwestern Indian village peoples. Yet technological and social variations distinguished Pueblo traditions from one another. In the Western Pueblo villages of the Acoma, the Hopi, and to some extent the Zuni, water was scarcer than in the eastern or Rio Grande communities. Wet adobe was used more often as mortar and plaster than as masonry. The western methods of walling included using a rubble core faced with split sandstone slabs. When the wall was chinked with stone fragments, the surface took adobe plaster more economically. The social customs reflected in village patterns also varied. In the Western Pueblos, where clan organizations were politically prominent, residence patterns were dictated by relationships in the extended family. Hopi and Zuni villages, for instance, were not divided into halves, or moieties. Clans and members of the many kivas, who felt a sense of mutual dependency, lived together in adjoining rooms and spaces. Garden plots also were inherited through the female line. Most of the rituals in the Western villages were devoted to inducing rainfall, and the well-being of crops was a constant concern.

In the Eastern Pueblos, where access to the flowing Rio Grande alleviated worries about irrigation, form-molded adobe bricks were used. Rituals involving social solidarity seem to have taken precedence over ceremonial attention to fertility and rainfall. Communities often were divided into moieties named for vegetables and minerals, such as Squash and Turquoise, whose members convened in one of the two kivas found in each community. Extended family groups owned the house sites and garden plots, and agricultural work was delegated among them.

Spanish influence

Catholic churches were built within the Pueblo. As suggested by the church at San Felipe *(left)*, they often combined Spanish and Indian elements. Although pre-Hispanic Indians did use hand-molded adobe bricks, the Spanish brought the idea of the form-molded brick to the Southwest. A Zuni woman is shown forming bricks *(above)*.

All Pueblo Indians inherited a common cosmology with a distinctive spatial organization which emphasized motifs of ascent, descent, and the four directions. Their origin myths told of underworld migrations that led upward to the earthly plain of the present "fourth world." Higher still lay the powerful, life-giving "houses" of the sun and rain spirits. Hence emergence motifs and shrines and symbols of a celestial nadir and zenith recur in Pueblo folklore and rituals. On the horizontal plane, an idealized schema of Pueblo spatial concepts might show zones of sacredness radiating out from such a "center" shrine toward the "houses" of the four cardinal directions.

The "heart" of a pueblo was sometimes architecturally represented in a modest rock shrine or by an offering beneath the central plaza. In striking contrast to the uninhabited ceremonial centers of Mesoamerica, the plaza itself seemed to incarnate this idea of a sacred, shared center space, with domestic rooms where people actually lived piled protectively around it. Beyond the village walls were the gardens and encampments, and still farther into the countryside lay sacred springs and cave shrines—the entire matrix of special places enclosed by four holy mountains that usually bounded and nurtured each Pueblo territory.

Pueblo planning

Open areas within the pueblos are used for sacred and festive occasions. In the "plaza type" pueblo such as San Felipe (above), the houses define the center space, the kivas and the church (upper left in the photograph) are off the plaza.

Santo Domingo is a "street type" pueblo (bottom right) organized on a linear plan, the widest middle street used as a dance ground. The elongated street-type plaza of Zia (top right) is a combination of the two. Its small mesa-top site does not allow room for other streets parallel to the central plaza.

368

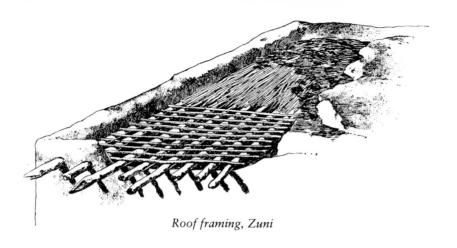

Roof framing, Zuni

Canale (roof drain), Hopi

ROOM

In northern New Mexico, the phrase of the Tewa-speaking Pueblos for building an adobe house translates as "raising" a house, in the sense of bringing a dwelling out of the earth much as one "raises" crops, or children. Among all Pueblo Indians building a house is an undertaking of the entire extended family, in which men and women have distinct roles.

The primary building unit—the rectangular room—was perhaps 12 feet wide, 14 feet long, and no more than 7 feet from hard-packed floor to ceiling rafters. Construction was generally done in early spring or late summer when agricultural work slackened and there was enough water to mix adobe. Men who had recently married traditionally moved into a place near their wife's mother, often building an adjoining room if necessary.

Adding on new rooms was a collective affair. Among the Hopi, a man's clan mates helped measure the area, gather and haul earth, and collect the rock, timber, brush, and water. At intervals the work was halted to pray that the house would have a firm foundation, that its walls would remain strong, and that its inhabitants would prosper. Prayer sticks, little offerings of feathers and other sacred items, were placed in the walls as embodiments of these wishes and blessings. Hopi women took over once the foundation had set, reaching from ladders to build their walls with fitted sandstone shaped by the men. Then they plastered or chinked the rocks with wads of adobe as they worked upward. Thereafter the walls were freshly layered with adobe plaster each year, generally in late summer when the cisterns were fullest.

To construct the roof the men first put peeled ponderosa pine or fir beams, known by the Spanish term *vigas*, in place. Wood was a precious resource in the arid Southwest and had to be cut in distant forests, packed on mules, then trimmed and aged for a year. Rarely thicker than a foot, the beams were staggered about 2 feet apart by means of spacing stones. A second layer of lighter, peeled poles called *latillas* came next, followed by twigs or brush. Then a blanket of grass or hay held the wet adobe, which was spread smooth by the women and left to dry. A final skin of dry earth was raked so that it tilted slightly toward the drains to avoid losing earth during downpours.

Pueblo buildings were most vulnerable at drainage points on the roof and at ground level. To divert water from the roofs and the walls, Zuni and Acoma builders raised a low parapet, or coping wall, around the edge of the roof, capping the spots where roof beams jutted beyond the wall. This parapet was pierced by drainspouts, or *canales,* devised from broken pottery, pieces of old metates, gourds, and, in modern times, old cans or discarded stovepipe. Then "splash rocks" were positioned below them to deflect the water as it spilled off the roof.

Splash blocks under Canale, Zuni

Pueblo architecture and details

Adobe construction began with first-story walls of adobe-packed rubble, often set on a rock foundation to deter the capillary action of ground moisture. In the Rio Grande area, upper-story walls were constructed with mud-packed adobe brick or crudely worked sandstone and adobe mortar. Floors were smooth adobe mud.

To frame the roof, round beams, *(vigas)* were then laid atop the walls and small poles *(latillas)* were placed over the vigas. Grass packing, adobe, and a final layer of dry earth sealed the roof structure. Women smoothed mud plaster by hand over outer and inner surfaces. An interior layer of whitewash completed the finished walls.

The detail drawings on these pages are by architect Victor Mindeleff, who visited Zuni and Hopi Pueblos in the 1880s.

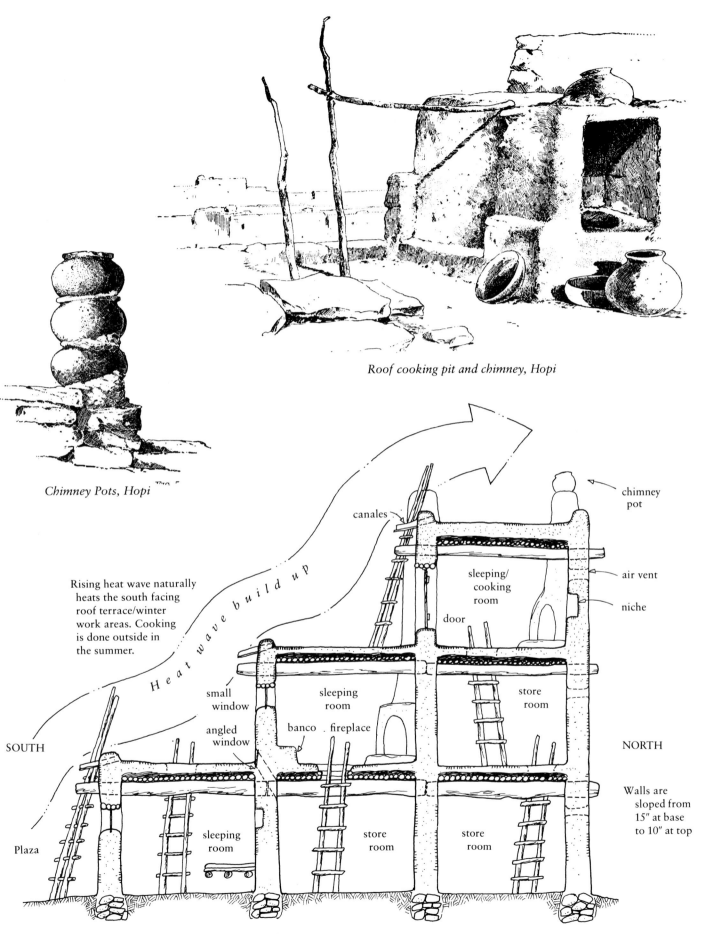

Roof cooking pit and chimney, Hopi

Chimney Pots, Hopi

canales

chimney pot

Rising heat wave naturally heats the south facing roof terrace/winter work areas. Cooking is done outside in the summer.

Heat wave build up

sleeping/ cooking room

air vent

niche

door

small window

sleeping room

store room

angled window

banco

fireplace

SOUTH

NORTH

Plaza

sleeping room

store room

store room

Walls are sloped from 15" at base to 10" at top

Idealized Pueblo cross section

371

Interior of a Zuni dwelling.

Wall opening, Hopi

Fireplace, Hopi

372

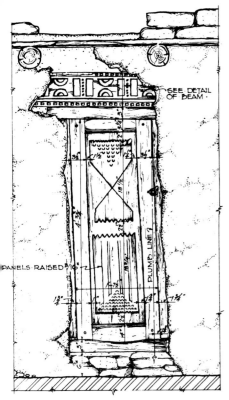

ELEVATION
SCALE · 1" = 1'-0"

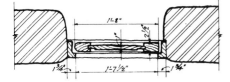

PLAN
DETAIL · OF · EXTERIOR · DOOR
SCALE · 1" · 1'-0"

*Detail of exterior door, from
Historic American Buildings
Survey drawings, Acoma*

Log ladder, Hopi

Pueblo details

To enter a traditional Pueblo, one climbed up
ladders to the lower rooftops. Smaller ladders
(above right), led to the upper rooms. The
T-shaped doorway *(above)*, still found in Hopi
structures in the late nineteenth century,
resembled prehistoric Pueblo door forms. The
Zuni interior *(above left)* shows non-Indian
influence in room furnishings, but is still
illuminated through skylights as in older times.
Flagstones made sturdy treads on this Acoma
stairway *(right)*. Sometimes Pueblo builders
incorporated carved elements from non-Indian
buildings into their own homes. The Spanish
beam *(above)*, from a church or convent, has
been recycled as a door lintel.

Building elements

Vigas were set on top of the walls, then held in place with stones or adobe set between and on top of them *(top left)*. Adobe bricks set with mud mortar formed the wall, *(far left)*, which were plastered with adobe by the women *(near left)*. Inside a completed room *(above)*, which has a built-in corner fireplace, or *fogon*, women prepare bread dough for baking in an outdoor oven, or *horno*.

Since Spanish times a traditional way to enhance light in the rooms was to glaże small, circular windows or skylights with selenite—a form of crystallized gypsum. To enter or leave the house, one went "up the ladder and down the ladder," as the Zuni people used to say. But sometimes T-shaped front entrances resembling those of prehistoric buildings were used on upper terraces. From the Spanish the Indians borrowed the idea for small wooden trapdoors, crafted without nails, which they placed within the houseblocks for access to rooms below the floor.

As in prehistoric times, people usually unrolled their blankets on adobe or wood pallets in upper rooms that faced inward toward the plaza. Each room had its terrace space overhead—an elevated "front yard." Their roofs offered this important domain for working and socializing, which were reached by ladders until milled lumber doors were introduced with the railroad. The rooms benefited from the southern exposure, as the walls absorbed the sun's heat. Innermost rooms were used for storage. Some cooking rooms held a bank of three or four corn-grinding stones, or metates, which were cured with spruce gum and blessed prior to use.

Furnishings in domestic rooms were spare. Wooden poles hanging from the ceiling beams were used to store bedding after a night's sleep. Other personal items were stored in trunks or hide containers against the wall. Niches held religious items; in Hopi rooms, kachina dolls carved from cottonwood root hung from the walls. On the upper terraces stood chimneys made of stacked broken pots held together with mortar; the higher they stood, the better they drew. In case of rain, sandstone slab covers were kept beside the ladder hatchways. The terraces were strewn with drying strings of chilis, skins on which corn was drying, hides being processed, and tools for various domestic activities.

375

KIVA

As religious and social havens of Pueblo Indians everywhere, kivas are the oldest type of religious building in continuous use in the Western hemisphere. Their location—often sunk halfway into the earth like their pit house prototype—intentionally suggested a link between this world and the ancestral underworld with its manifold benevolent powers. In many kivas the old sipapu shrine was maintained; among the Hopi it was covered by a cottonwood board that dancers could stomp upon to send messages to the spirits below.

Kivas have many forms and functions. What is known about them is mostly conjectural, however, due to the cloak of secrecy around Pueblo religious beliefs and practices. It is often difficult to distinguish kivas from fetish rooms or the meeting chambers used by special sacred societies or by separate clans. Kivas of the Western Pueblos are almost invariably rectangular, as if stemming from the Mogollon prehistoric tradition, while those of the Eastern Pueblos are more often circular. Some rectangular rooms were reserved by Eastern Pueblos for special sacred purposes, however. Hopi kivas are generally about 25 feet long, 15 feet wide, and 10 feet high, with a third of the floor space raised half a foot or more so that an audience can watch performances from behind the leaning entry ladder. Wood stoves near the ladder warm the rooms, and nearby is the covered sipapu hole. In most Hopi communities, each of the village clans and religious societies has its own kiva. At Old Oraibi, for instance, there are thirteen. Wherever possible they are oriented north-south, although some mesa-top sites are too narrow.

Among the Hopi, each clan traditionally renovated its kiva on the winter solstice. In anticipation of this job, a "kiva chief" chanted a "house song." Only the choicest beams were used in kivas. At Old Oraibi a few have been in place for over 300 years. Consecration rites performed at the sipapu shrine were so hallowed in the Hopi village of Mishongnovi that onlookers were warned to avert their eyes. Feathered prayer sticks, color-coded for the cardinal directions, zenith and nadir were strung along the roof so it would not fall. During the annual replastering, Hopi workers left white hand smears on kiva beams to represent their prayers for rain.

At Acoma Pueblo, west of present-day Albuquerque, New Mexico, an origin myth tells of the First Kiva. A culture hero declares, "We have no sacred place.... This is the way I emerged, so I guess we will make a house in the ground ... this will be a sacred place for the kachina when they come." The first Acomans learned how to design this circular kiva so that it resembled their emergence place, but it also symbolized the entire world. Four of its beams were drawn from the first four trees to stand on Earth, and its roof stood for the Milky Way. The walls were "the sky," and four hollows in the walls stood for the "doors" of Acoma's four sacred mountains. Encircling the chamber was a bench, or *banco,* which stood for the fog where their rain-giving kachina spirits dwelled. When descending the tilting ladder, which represented a rainbow, one faced the rungs, because to look down shortened life.

By historic times, the circular kiva described in the origin story had been absorbed into rectangular house blocks, as at Jemez Pueblo, where they also originally were round. One explanation for this conversion is that the Indians began camouflaging their places of worship as domestic units to avoid persecution by Catholic priests.

376

The kiva

For more than a millenium Pueblo peoples have constructed various forms of social-ceremonial meeting chambers known as kivas. These special multipurpose buildings, sometimes free-standing, sometimes embedded within the larger houseblocks, are primarily used by men. In the kiva, men discuss the governing of their community, decide when to plant and harvest crops, plan seasonal rituals and rehearse dances, build altars and repair kachina costumes, train the young, smoke, and pray. During major ceremonies, however, both men and women dancers use these rooms for rest and costume changes. The photograph shows a dancer descending the steps of the communal kiva at San Ildefonso Pueblo.

Among the Eastern Pueblos, kivas are less associated with clans than with the theocratic divisions that administer everyday work and life. At Taos and Picuris Pueblos, which have six kivas each, the kivas are divided into two groups—three on the north side of town and three on the south. In other Rio Grande settlements farther down the river, the "summer" half of the community is generally associated with a Squash kiva, while the "winter" moiety belongs to the Turquoise kiva. In some places, as at San Ildefonso, there is an additional kiva, possibly the legacy of the Great Kivas of Anasazi times, which serves the entire village during festivals in which both moieties participate.

Kivas can easily be identified by the presence of ladder poles reaching into the sky. Some are topped by ladder braces ornamented with terraced "cloud" symbols. Often a wooden stairway leads to the kiva roof where people descended into the interior by ladder. Nearly all of these sacred structures are off-limits to nonresidents, and many a tourist has been sternly reproached, even by young children, for failing to observe the prohibition against taking photographs or trespassing. They remain the most potent architectural reminder of the abiding gulf between Pueblo and Anglo-American worldviews.

Roof is built with beams of four different trees, said to be from the underworld, planted for the people to climb on.

Placed under the foundation is yellow turquoise to the north, blue to the west, red to the south, and white to the east. Prayer sticks are also placed there.

The ladder is invariably made of pine.

Above the hatchway is the fourth world, the occupied world.

Upper room area is the third world, where animals were created.

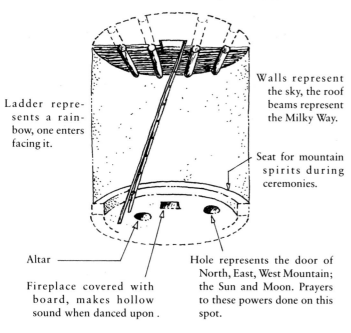

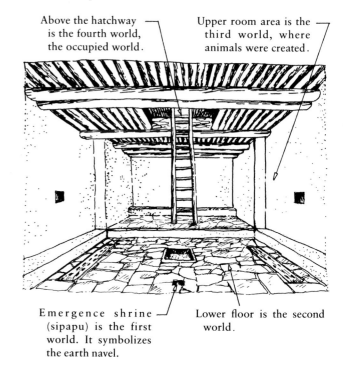

Ladder represents a rainbow, one enters facing it.

Walls represent the sky, the roof beams represent the Milky Way.

Seat for mountain spirits during ceremonies.

Altar

Fireplace covered with board, makes hollow sound when danced upon.

Hole represents the door of North, East, West Mountain; the Sun and Moon. Prayers to these powers done on this spot.

Emergence shrine (sipapu) is the first world. It symbolizes the earth navel.

Lower floor is the second world.

Mythic Acoma Kiva

Hopi kiva

Kiva symbolism

All kivas are used for ritual or private activities. Hence it is usually inappropriate for nonresidents to press for information about what occurs inside them. However, anthropologist Alfonso Ortiz, himself a member of San Juan Pueblo, has discussed generally the underlying meanings of contemporary kivas among Tewa-speaking villages: "... the contemporary Tewa kiva, whether circular or rectangular, subterranean or entirely aboveground, set apart or incorporated into a houseblock, is regarded, when in use, as a symbolic representation of the primordial underworld home from which the Tewa believe they emerged to this world. The term used for the kiva when the gods [kachinas] are impersonated, *Sipofene,* is the same name used for the primordial home. The impersonation of the gods is itself a reenactment of the original act of emergence from the underworld. Therefore, although there may be numerous sacred centers, the kiva itself is the center of centers, or the navel of navels...." Kiva architecture is more conservative than that of domestic units.

Whether kivas are rectangular, as among the Western Pueblos, or circular, as in most Eastern Pueblos, one usually descends into them as into an ancient Pueblo room, by means of a ladder, simulating a return to an earlier, mythic realm.

These drawings offer symbolic interpretations, from published sources, for a circular kiva *(above left)* from Acoma Pueblo, and a rectangular kiva *(above right)* from the Hopi. Acoma information derives from a portion of their origin myth which tells of the First Kiva. What is curious about this description of a mythic round kiva is that the kivas at Acoma today are rectangular and built into the first story of a houseblock. It has been suggested that this architectural transformation was a conscious effort by the Acoma people to disguise their traditional places of worship from Spanish eyes. The speculation that the rectangular kiva of the Hopi symbolized former underworlds of Hopi existence comes from Victor and Cosmos Mindeleff, who authored a major study of Pueblo architecture in 1891.

TODAY

With the extension of railroads through the Southwest in the 1880s, imported building materials began to open up the solidity of pueblo facades. Frame doors, windows, and commercial colors on trim were innovations that the conservative Pueblos gradually adopted. New demands on their lives—9-to-5 jobs, mandatory schooling for the young, and a growing sense of individualism—also were reflected in their buildings and spaces. In certain communities, nuclear families withdrew from kinship groups, either migrating or resettling in single-family houses beyond the old Pueblo perimeter. With factionalism, new plazas were built and old kivas abandoned, which disrupted the architectural ideal of residential unity around a common center. Tract housing built by the U.S. government in the 1960s further changed residence patterns.

Most of the families that once occupied old Acoma Pueblo, for instance, have descended over the years from the mesa, resettling in housing developments in Acomita and McCarty's, which are closer to the highway, the railroad, plumbing, and the job market. Yet most of them also retain strong emotional and proprietary ties to the stacked rooms on the mesa, where they return for traditional feast days. A skeleton crew of rotating "war chiefs" and their families, appointed by the tribe's *caciques,* or religious leaders, guard the deserted community year-round and guide tourists. It is as if these narrow sandstone streets, the crumbling house blocks, the kivas, and the graveyards of the old Keresan-speaking town have been transformed into a vast architectural shrine.

Hopi kiva interior

This kiva at Mishongnovi Village on Second Mesa *(below)* shows the flagstone floor and planks along both wall's sides with sockets for loom frames on which men weave home-spun cotton cloth. During theatrical rituals, the audience stands on the raised platform behind the square fire pit and ladder base. Plaster hand smears barely visible on the rear roof beam represent prayers for rain, ca. 1902.

TAOS

In 1540, when Hernando de Alavarado visited Taos Pueblo, the village probably had been expanding for at least a century. Seventy miles up the Rio Grande from Santa Fe, New Mexico, situated in the shadow of Taos Mountain and straddling the principal trade route between the Rio Grande Valley and the Great Plains, Taos remains the exemplar of traditional Pueblo construction. Entering the village for the first time, one is reminded of what Alavarado recorded more than three and a half centuries ago: "The houses are very close together and have five or six stories." More than any Eastern Pueblo, Taos epitomizes the pre-Hispanic imperative to concentrate and cluster. Described as the only Anasazi-style community still occupied, Taos possibly was founded by Chaco Canyon refugees who had intermixed with Plains Indian migrants.

The aesthetic link between Taos and any possible Chacoan heritage is the pyramidal massing of living units. Taos features major house blocks on its north and south sides, the village's social and architectural divisions. Classified as a "plaza" rather than a "street" type of pueblo, its irregular, semipublic plaza is bisected by Red Willow Creek, the community's main source of drinking and washing water. Like an artery, it also connects the village to its sacred Blue Lake, hidden from view behind the mountain. Surrounding the north and south sides of the village is an eroding five-sided adobe wall. Although ineffective as a physical barrier, it functions well as a psychological and cultural barricade. Electricity is banned within the low wall, and architectural change is governed by stringent rules. Even adding a window requires a council's consensus. As the Taos people have expressed their sense of architectural integrity, "We are in one nest."

380

Early Taos

Situated on the valley floor below its sacred mountains, the plaza of walled Taos Pueblo is split by Red Willow Creek. The north block of houses *(below)* rises five stories. Photographed ca. 1880.

Change at Taos

The kivas at Taos closely resemble those of Anasazi times, as seen in this photograph by W.H. Jackson *(bottom)*. The houseblocks, however, have been slowly changing for decades. This was the conclusion of scholar William Reynolds who recently studied a half-century of historical photographs and visited the community.

Change in the massing of room blocks *(right)* was due as much to interpersonal relations and housing customs as to residents quitting the village for lives in the outside world.

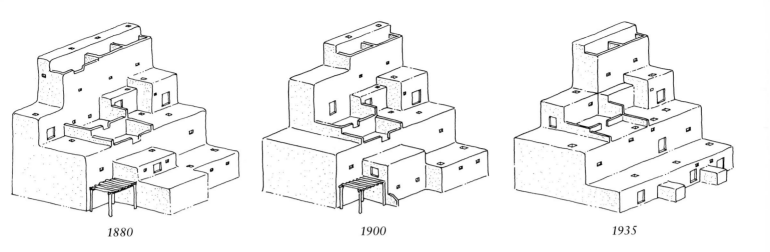

1880   1900   1935

Four hemispherical mounds known as "ash piles" stand just outside this perimeter. They function as more than refuse dumps, as archeologist Florence H. Ellis has clarified after excavating similar heaps in Chaco Canyon: "They put with the ashes the broken shards, the broken implements and everything that comes sweeping out of their houses . . . it all goes back to nature and this is the Pueblo idea of what is good in the world . . . they put prayer offerings on top of the dumps, periodically, on ceremonial occasions."

Beyond the immediate village are sacred shrines, springs, and caves that play a part in religious observances. Most notable is the Taos pilgrimage to Blue Lake every August. Songs are sung and prayer sticks are planted where the Indians believe human beings first emerged. Another sacred space linking Taos to the wider cosmos is an unmarked east-to-west racetrack. Running for a quarter-mile from the plaza through a break in the adobe wall, it is known as the Sun Road. For Taos and most Rio Grande Pueblos farther south, these racecourses symbolize the path the sun follows through the sky each winter. Each fall and spring, ceremonial runners initiate relay races to lend their strength to the sun so that it will make it through the season. These spaces can be overlooked by planners anxious to upgrade Indian communities. When a road was proposed from nearby Ranchos de Taos to the Indian village, Taos leaders refused permission because it would have desecrated an ancient "sun road."

In addition to the racetrack, ash piles, and shrine and pilgrimage sites, the central plaza also is regarded as sanctified space. Its earthen floor is crossed every day as families draw their water from the common creek, but on feast days it becomes the stage for ceremonial dances. Set back from direct view, but detected from the plaza by their towering ladder poles, are Taos' six active kivas. Lacking the clan or strict moiety organization found among most Eastern Pueblos, Taos Pueblo's political and social organization appears to be based on kiva allegiance. Each child is "given" to one of these kivas at adolescence and is introduced by priests to the religious and civic responsibilities of being a Taoseño.

The only Eastern kivas that are almost entirely underground, Taos' round kivas are evocative of Anasazi architecture. Within the community wall, northside kivas feature unusual wood fences encircling the ladder housing, while the three southside kivas are found outside the wall with masonry enclosing their hatchways. Rising perhaps 15 feet into the air, the older ladders have rungs still fastened with buffalo thongs. Utmost secrecy surrounds the kiva. "People want to find out about this pueblo," a Taos man once told anthropologist Elsie Clews Parsons, "but they can't. Our ways would lose their power if they were known."

It is not clear when the Taos people adopted wooden frames for making adobe bricks, or when the cubist lines of their rooms were offset by domed cedar-burning adobe ovens. Today, sundried mud bricks are set in masonry that is mixed by Taos laborers who twirl their characteristic flannel cowls into makeshift turbans for the task. Bricks for the hornos, the beehive-shaped outdoor ovens, are molded into a triangular shape to form the oven dome—often over a metal rebar support.

The greater height and breadth of the north house block, rising up a full five stories, maximizes southern exposure during the cold winter. One cannot know whether the lower-story walls are substantially thicker—as at Pueblo Bonito—because Taoseños refuse to let outsiders inspect their buildings. Traditionally, the north block, eleven rooms wide, would have storage rooms in its innermost recesses. Upstairs one might find corn-milling rooms, used today only in preparing ritual meals.

When the north house block was photographed by Adam Clark Vroman in 1899, many families still climbed ladders from ground level to the first terrace. The tiny windows, placed high, were still glazed with selenite. Around the turn of the century, factory-made doors were painted a bright turquoise. In the 1930s, after considerable discussion, the Taos elders allowed windows to be enlarged with glass and sashes.

Near the houses are racks of stout juniper posts for drying firewood and corn and storing hay. During trade fairs or public dances they became bough-roofed concession booths. Plastered enclosures beside the doorways hold split pinon kindling. Each family also owns one or more hornos; over a hundred of them turn out prune pies and steaming loaves of bread before the Taos feast day of San Geronimo.

Building renewal

With a steady source of water close to every home, the adobe brickwork of the buildings is kept thickly coated with adobe plaster mixed with straw. In this photograph *(left)* a Taos man swathed in flannel blanket piles pumpkins from his garden on the first terrace. The upper terraces are reached by ladders, and turquoise colored door frames lead into living units.

On the feast day of San Geronimo, September 30th, the terraces serve as bleachers *(below)* for visitors to view the sacred relay races, ceremonial dances, and clown performances. House and oven replastering occurs just before the Fiesta.

Early fall, before the equinox, is the customary time for house renewal, when rooms and dance grounds are swept clean and women apply fresh plaster to their house walls and ovens. This traditional architectural facelift anticipates the San Geronimo Fiesta, when visitors arrive to watch the sacred relay races. Another rare occasion when Taos hosts outsiders is Christmas eve, when drummers and dancers fill their tiny church, and hundreds of lighted candles on terraces and rooftops outline the architecture against the night sky.

Following Christmas, however, the community goes into retreat. During this private period, Taoseños who live far from home often return to their tribal roots, and tribe members who have built homes just outside the walls visit relatives more often. What the anthropologist M.E. Smith observed of Taos' acculturation can be said of its architectural evolution: "... it is this dance with time—two steps forward, one step back—which allows the Taos to gradually adapt to the new while retaining (or even inventing when necessary) the past."

SANTA CLARA

Santa Clara Pueblo, one of five Tewa-speaking Pueblos of northern New Mexico, stands on the west bank of the Rio Grande almost equidistant from Santa Fe and Taos. It is noteworthy that its architectural history has been investigated by a resident, art historian Rina Swentzel. A member of Santa Clara's Naranjo family, she was raised by her grandmother, who was a medicine woman. "I would join with her," Dr. Swentzel remembers, "when she went through the ceremonies for blessing a house. She would make prayers before the building went up and at the various stages of construction, and then before people moved in." Dr. Swentzel's 1973 study of Santa Clara highlights the influences which have altered Pueblo building traditions throughout the Southwest.

A plaza-type village that serves as the capital of a 45,742-acre reservation, Santa Clara probably was founded in the fourteenth century. A hundred years later, the Spaniards discovered it. Today Santa Clara is known for its wealth and progressive attitude, due in part to the proximity of Los Alamos scientific laboratories, where some tribespeople have found work, and its endorsement of tourism. Among its attractions are the Puye Cliffs in Santa Clara Canyon.

In Dr. Swentzel's view, Santa Clara's spatial heritage began to deteriorate in the early eighteenth century. By 1720 the Catholic church that was burned down during the 1680 rebellion had been rebuilt and drew townspeople from the plaza toward the northeast part of town. A half-century later, the first separate family houses were built outside the old village's protective fold. By 1900, a second plaza and new kiva had been established, probably indicating a lessening emphasis on work in communal fields based on cooperative irrigation. Families began staking off their own garden plots. A series of dry years left irrigation ditches empty, people were growing more wheat than corn, and government boarding school returnees introduced new notions of family autonomy. There were Santa Clarans who "would be in the Pueblo but not of it," an attitude that held architectural implications.

As family homes became scattered, the unused second stories of house blocks around the old plaza began to crumble apart without their annual replastering. A factional dispute isolated the village's west side winter moiety, prompting it to build its own kiva, and a third plaza grew around it. At the same time the defense tower southwest of town—Santa Clara's last architectural link to prehistoric times—disintegrated.

In 1900 the U.S. government stepped up its program of alloting village lands to individual families, further weakening the sense of community responsibility. During the early 1900s three pitched-roof houses appeared just outside the pueblo center, and another rose within the second plaza. In 1905, even the Catholic church was given a shiny tin roof. Metal chimneys sprouted from every rooftop, while the houses under them had hinged wooden doors and glass windows. Hand-wound coffee mills made the old corn-grinding milling basins obsolete.

Outside forces penetrated Pueblo privacy in other ways. After the railroad was laid near the west side of town in the 1880s, the fenced grid of separate family ranches began to sprawl in that direction. Construction of a Bureau of Indian Affairs school in 1915 required arteries north of the Pueblo that fed into the paved highway. The two L-shaped house blocks that had enclosed the old plaza were broken up by three new alleys. And the customary entry into the

Santa Clara in transition

Santa Clara, which was probably established in the fourteenth century, is a plaza-type pueblo which has undergone considerable change. Unlike Taos, it had no wall around its two L-shaped houseblocks. From the traditional multiunit building which protectively encloses a plaza, the settlement has dispersed *(as shown in the plans at right)* because of outside influences.

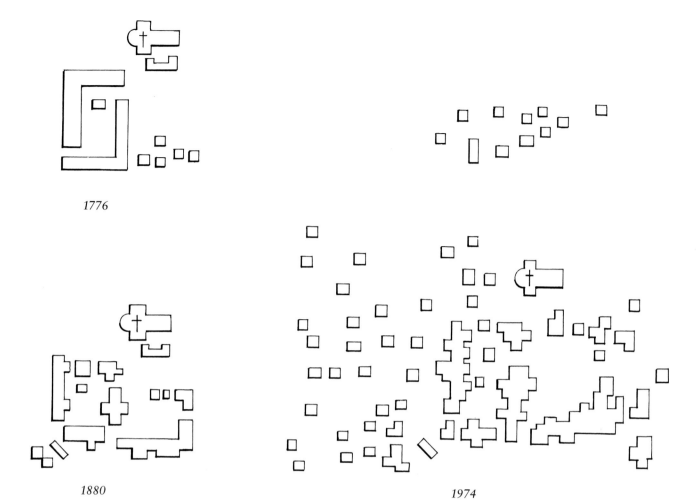

1776

1880

1974

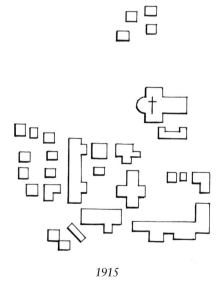

1915

plaza's southwestern corner was summarily sealed by a family who claimed the spot as its own. What had been common ground was being subdivided into individual sections, each with its own well, oven, and private orchard.

Within the houses separate rooms for sleeping, watching TV, and cooking became more common. Open spaces were crowded with basketball backboards, electrical poles, water tanks and a forest of television antennas. In the 1970s, the irregular scheme of casually fenced farmlands was replaced by a grid of uniform plots. "After four hundred years the center-oriented Pueblo form has almost totally disintegrated," says Dr. Swentzel. Despite her sense that "individualism has a firm grip" at Santa Clara, however, she emphasizes that other patterns emerged to stave off total assimilation. Some people who lived outside of the Pueblo retained room rights in the old town, where they lived for short periods. The ancient footrace path—serving the same function as the Taos Sun Road—was preserved. Santa Clara's large, rectangular kiva still houses costumed dancers from both moieties during feast day celebrations. It has been suggested by Pueblo novelist Leslie Marmon Silko, in fact, that it is only non-Indian romantics who think a medicine man must occupy a decrepit adobe house near the plaza in order to fulfill his office; he can serve just as effectively from a trailer home provided by the U.S. Department of Housing and Urban Development.

Santa Clara 1879

Santa Clara 1899

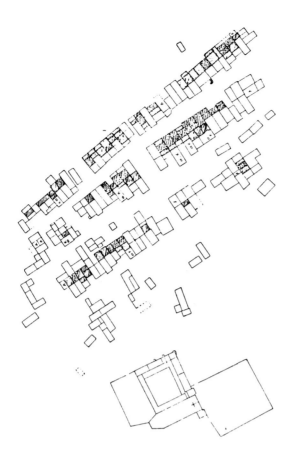

Located between the Eastern and Western Pueblos, Acoma shares features of both building styles. It is a street-type village like Santo Domingo further east, but it contains rectangular kivas — six in number — like those to the west. Its mesa-top cisterns hold water for drinking, washing, and mixing adobe. The water supply also makes Acoma self-sufficient, as suggested by one of their names for the village, "place of preparedness."

This is an early aerial photograph of Acoma *(right)*, while below is a view of the mesa and pueblo from the valley below *(bottom)*.

ACOMA

Acoma is a "street"-type pueblo built by Keresan-speaking Indians and placed dramatically on the summit of a craggy 375-foot sandstone mesa west of Albuquerque, New Mexico. Vying with the Hopi Pueblo of Old Oraibi as the oldest continuously occupied village in the United States, Acoma is believed to have been a cultural—and architectural—bridge between the Eastern and Western Pueblos for a thousand years. Over the centuries its parallel corridors, with plazas tucked between house rows, have undergone significant alterations.

In 1540 Alvarado wrote of Acoma, "The village was very strong, because it was up on a rock out of reach.... There was only one entrance by stairway ... no army could possibly be strong enough to capture the village. On the top they had room to sow and store a large amount of corn, and cisterns to collect snow and water." Acoma resisted the invading Spanish until 1598, when troops led by Don Juan de Oñate scaled the mesa and their cannons destroyed Acoma's buildings and kivas. Oñate executed one-tenth of the residents of Acoma, amputated the right foot of every man over twenty-five, and sentenced the rest to twenty years of slavery.

During the early seventeenth century, a friendly priest helped the Acomans reconstruct their Pueblo and its church, San Estevan. This may have been the rebuilding program that an Acoma man described to linguist Wick R. Miller in the 1930s. First, a row of houses on the north side was erected, then a middle row, and finally a south row. "Everybody helped with each building," the Indian said. "The building materials were carried up from down below, things like fine sand being carried on the back to be used for plaster.... Bark, sticks and ashes were mixed together. Then they mixed the adobe with this, and the bricks were made. And I believe they used to haul pine and oak from Pine Mountain for beams (forty miles away, across the San Jose River basin and into the San Mateo mountains)."

Documenting Acoma

In the spring of 1934, draftsmen produced eighty-three drawings of the entire Acoma Pueblo for the government's Historic American Buildings Survey. The drawings *(right)* are of a representative three-story section, from the westernmost houseblock of the north row of buildings. The second floor is for food production, with storage in the rear. One room contains corn-grinding *metates*; another a hooded fireplace. A oven for baking is on the terrace.

The same house was photographed *(below)* by Forman Hanna, ca. 1930. A larger-than-average Acoma interior *(left)* shows furnishings of European origin, and traditional pottery, for which the pueblo is noted, ca. 1900.

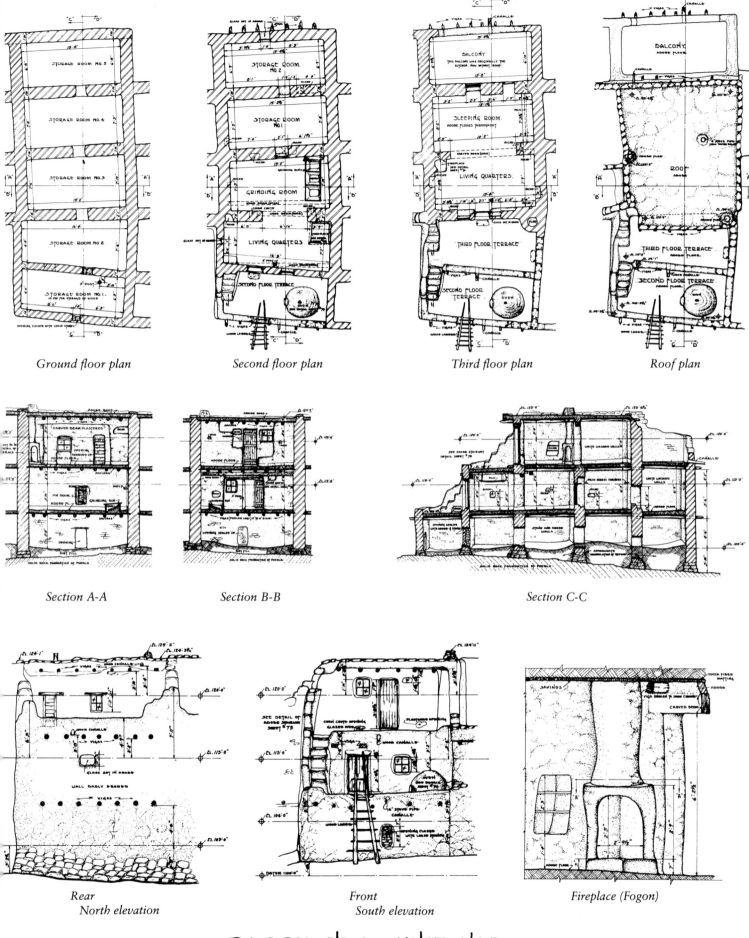

Ground floor plan

Second floor plan

Third floor plan

Roof plan

Section A-A

Section B-B

Section C-C

Rear
North elevation

Front
South elevation

Fireplace (Fogon)

← BLOCK № 1 ← UNIT №3 ←
· OLD · ACOMA · PUEBLO ·

As work proceeded across the seventeen-acre mesa, nine separate house block units were arranged into three rows facing two principal thoroughfares, portions of which served as community dance plazas. Facing southward, the houses were set back on the upper stories, forming a sort of raised patio where people could prepare food and enjoy being outside in fall and spring. Inside might be stored enough food to supply the Pueblo for three years, and the mesa-top cisterns contained fresh, cool water all year round.

Walls were composed of the thin Indian brick, or mud mortar and rock, rising from a foundation layer of fieldstone. They were rarely more than 2 feet thick, and they customarily were not bonded. Partition walls never bore loads; the weight of the roof and upper stories was carried on cross walls, which were usually continuous from grade up through three or four stories. Men completed heavier tasks, from leveling and mortaring the sandstone at ground level to laying the major cedar beams. Skylights on the roof or selenite portholes high in the walls illuminated the rooms.

Roofing methods changed little from pit house times. Shorter pieces of cedar were laid above the major vigas, followed by a mat of willow or yucca fiber and a final 6-inch layer of earth. The floors were hardened by wetting and tamping, with animal blood sometimes used as a sealer. Plastering, flooring, and building the inside and outdoor fireplaces were the women's responsibility. They baked ground gypsum and dung chips to make whitewash for the walls and collected yellowish clay for a wash that protected the baseboard area from dirt. At Acoma, the season for renewing buildings was August, when enough water had collected in the washing cisterns for the women to replaster the walls and ovens.

In August 1980, we joined members of the community on a kiva rooftop—one of six at Acoma—as tribal runners darted into the village in a symbolic re-enactment of the secret courier mission that set up the Pueblo rebellion three hundred years before. Northward was the Enchanted Mesa, a stony column once occupied by Acoma ancestors. Below us the skeleton crew of families who serve as custodians of the pueblo greeted the runners, handing them ears of blessed, boiled corn.

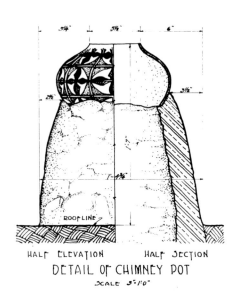

HALF ELEVATION   HALF SECTION
DETAIL OF CHIMNEY POT
SCALE 3"=1'-0"

Acoma street scene

Houseblocks at Acoma face south-southeast, for protection from winds that come from the west, and to expose the living areas to solar heating. This early view of the northernmost row shows meat and vegetables drying in the sun, bread ovens, and stacks of firewood which have been packed up the mesa on burros. Photographed ca. 1890.

The Middle Place

The older portion of present-day Zuni is shown *(below)* in a photograph taken around 1880, and *(right)* in plan. On the rooftops are ladder hatchways and skylight and air vent openings. Walls are both plain and whitewashed, and windows are made of selenite fragments.

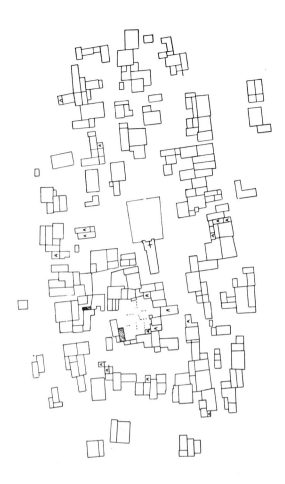

ZUNI

The Pueblo of Zuni, about 40 miles south of present-day Gallup, New Mexico, was established shortly after the 1680 rebellion. After the war, fear of retaliation made the Zuni abandon their seven towns; when they returned from hiding on their sacred Corn Mountain, only one of the old homesites, Halona, or "Red Ant Place," was reoccupied—the Pueblo of Zuni. After living in the Pueblo during the early 1880s, the ethnographer Frank Hamilton Cushing vividly described its housing: "Imagine numberless long, box-shaped, adobe ranches, connected with one another in extended rows and squares, with others, less and less numerous, piled up on them lengthwise and crosswise, in two, three, even six stories, each receding from the one below it like the steps of a broken stairflight—as it were, a gigantic pyramidal mud honey-comb with far outstretching base,—and you can gain a fair conception of the architecture of Zuni."

The art historian Bainbridge Bunting chose Zuni for his case study of architectural change because it is considered a classic example of late pre-Hispanic Pueblo architecture, and because it has been well-documented by photographers and scholars since the 1880s. Bunting surmised that living units in the eighteenth and early nineteenth centuries were built above lower walls that were not originally planned to support them.

Cushing had traced the origin of certain architectural words in Zuni to support his theory that Zuni terracing did not originate from building rooms directly on top of each other but was a function of seating successive tiers of adobe cubicles into a natural slope. In fact, in early photographs of Zuni taken by John K. Hillers, shot against the background of the community's incline, there do appear to be more stories than actually exist.

Rooms and gardens

Ceremonial interiors at Zuni were often larger than the domestic rooms. These special chambers were photographed by Adam Clark Vroman in 1899: the "Animal Room" *(top left)* had a procession of sacred creatures painted around the walls; the "spirit lines" from mouth to organs indicate their supernatural power. Another room *(bottom left)* was decorated with symbols associated with the Macaw Clan. Its orientation and carefully positioned window allowed the morning sun to strike an altar.

The pueblo was surrounded by "waffle gardens" *(above)*, possibly for special crops like peppers, cotton, and tobacco, which were protected by adobe-and-rubble walls. Photographed during the George M. Wheeler expedition, ca. 1873.

From the center of Zuni proper, wings of terraced rooms extended on a north-south axis to shield occupants from sandstorms, winter winds, and the hot afternoon glare. Capstones on the roofs protected the raised coping walls from erosion, while drain spouts and splash stones prevented rainfall from undermining the foundations. As at Acoma, upper terraces were divided by stepped wall extensions, which functioned as stairs and provided shade. Chimney pots drew smoke from many small interior fireplaces, whose plastered hoods either swung from the ceiling or were supported by beams that ran the length of the room and were fixed into the walls at either end.

As the town's population increased in the late nineteenth century, the inclination to cluster around a centralized plaza for rituals and defense diminished. Southeast of the "old city," new house blocks initiated this settlement sprawl. By the 1880s the Catholic church was the centerpiece for this expanding neighborhood. In 1881, the railroad reached Gallup, and Zuni builders began using carpentry tools to add doors and windows. When first-floor walls buckled from the weight of upper story loads, the occupants simply relocated toward the periphery of town. After the turn of the century, easily worked blocks of purple ashlar had largely replaced adobe as the popular building material, and nearly every house was reduced to a single story.

Today only a few complete rooms and walls remain from the Zuni documented a century ago. Over the past forty years stone has given way to concrete block—often camouflaged with earth-colored cement stucco. Many of the pueblo's six hundred residents actually live in government subsidized suburbs containing two- or three-bedroom houses with aluminum windows. Most are situated on half-acre lots and face paved, straight streets. Nevertheless, the crumbling town core remains the Zuni people's revered "middle place" and the focus of a thriving ceremonial life. Somewhere near the old center lies the community's modest rock center shrine, which the Zuni people say contains the beating heart of the world.

Bunting's emphasis on the loss of Zuni's old architectural practices concentrates only on material form. Other aspects of their building tradition, however—those related to the inner spirit of the buildings and the Pueblo—remain alive. In the Pueblo's grandest ceremony, known as the "Coming of the Shalako," buildings are blessed by the Zuni gods. On the forty-ninth day of the ceremony, outsiders are welcome to witness the all-night climax. The central characters are six dancers portraying gods (kachinas), called Shalako. They wear masks that make them 10 feet tall. The Shalako and other masked dancers, known collectively as the Council of the Gods, arrive accompanied by a cadre of sacred clowns known as Mudheads.

In the months before the festival eight concrete-block houses are either built or remodeled to host the sacred beings and receive their prayers. At the new or renovated houses the kachina leader known as Long Horn, head of the Council of the Gods, arrives first to offer his formal house-blessing prayer:

Then my father's rain-filled room
I rooted at the north,
I rooted at the west,
I rooted at the south,
I rooted at the east,
I rooted above,
Then in the middle of my father's roof,
With two plume wands joined together,
I consecrated his roof.
This is well;
In order that my father's offspring may increase,
I consecrated the center of his roof.
And then also, the center of my father's floor,
With seeds of all kinds,
I consecrated the center of his floor.
This is well;
In order that my father's fourth room
May be bursting with corn,
That even in his doorway,
The shelled corn may be scattered before the door,
The beans may be scattered before the door,
That his house may be full of little boys,
And little girls,
And people grown to maturity;
That in his house
Children may jostle one another in the doorway,
In order that it may be thus,
I have consecrated the rain-filled room
Of my daylight father,
My daylight mother.

The new walls are marked with corn meal, and corn and squash seeds are deposited on the earthen floor. Then the six towering Shalako themselves appear, first praying at the six rectangular kivas at Zuni, each dedicated to a

House ritual

The high point of the Zuni year is the annual house-blessing ceremony which brings tall masked dancers called Shalako, who represent supernatural beings. In the photograph, *(below)* Shalako with attendant priests leave the pueblo following their long night of dance, song, and prayer, ca. 1885. During the ceremony, recently built or remodeled buildings are specially prepared so that Kachina impersonators and dancers can perform before altars while outsiders look on from protected rooms to the side *(as shown in floor plans, right)*.

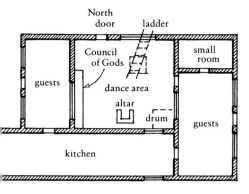

North
door — ladder

Council
of Gods

dance area

altar

drum

guests

small
room

guests

kitchen

Council of the Gods house plan

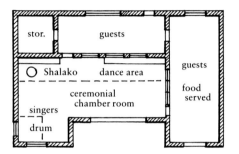

stor.

guests

Shalako — dance area

ceremonial
chamber room

singers

drum

guests

guests

food
served

Shalako house plan

cardinal direction, before trotting to the appointed houses, where they offer their own threshold prayers before entering.

Troughs in the earthen floors of the brilliantly lit homes allow the tall Shalako to perform without snapping their headdress eagle feathers. Bright shawls and striped blankets are abundantly displayed, silver jewelry hangs conspicuously from the unfinished walls, and stuffed deerhead antlers are adorned with turquoise necklaces. Long myths are recited, teams of unannounced masked dancers roam from house to house, and dancing and miming delight the audience of Zuni families, Navajo onlookers, and other guests. To everyone the Zuni serve gallons of coffee, steaming tubs of mutton stew and chili, and piles of fry bread.

During the long night, we were treated to seeing the Comanche dancers, who mocked high-pitched Plains Indian singing, wore wildly stylized war bonnets, and were teased by the visiting Mudhead clowns. Long past midnight, in the house dedicated to the Council of the Gods, it seemed as if the structure momentarily reverted to the days of prehistoric pit houses. For over a thousand years Pueblo priests have revered the sun, timing rituals and work by solar observations made from their house roofs. The masked figure of Long Horn, dressed in the most ancient-appearing costume and acting in character as a stiff-jointed elder, slowly ascended a ladder in the middle of the room. Everyone grew quiet as he reached the roof, outlined against the stars, and greeted the rising sun with a chanted prayer. Then, as Long Horn descended the ladder, the Zuni world was reborn.

First Mesa

The pueblos of Walpi, Sichomovi, and Hano are situated in the most dramatic landscape of Hopi Indian country. This view *(bottom)* of the southeastern side of First Mesa shows Walpi linked to the rest of the mesa by a natural stone ledge wide enough for a cart to cross. Photographed in 1895.

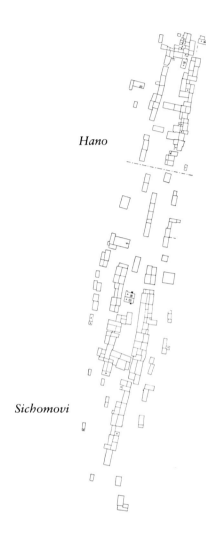

Hano

Sichomovi

Walpi

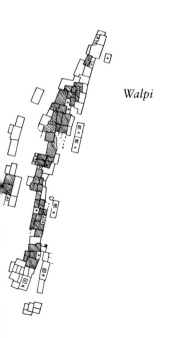

HOPI

The Hopi Indians live in twelve Pueblos, most of them positioned on three mesas that stem southward from Black Mesa in central Arizona. The three villages on the narrow summit of First Mesa were not established until after the Pueblo rebellion of 1680. By 1700, Walpi, the "place of the notch," which looked down on the Painted Desert from three sheer sides, already had been built on the mesa's prow. It is First Mesa's "mother" village.

When a band of Tewa-speaking refugees appeared from the Rio Grande region shortly thereafter, the Walpi residents let them build on the mesa's northern side, figuring they could defend the foot trail leading up to the precipice. Hano, still in that strategic "guard" village position, is the first settlement one encounters on the winding uphill drive from Polacca on the desert floor. Sichomovi, or "place of the mound where wild currant bushes grow," was a "colony" village constructed nearby in the mid-eighteenth century by Walpi residents and other Eastern Pueblo arrivals. Finally, at road's end stands Walpi, whose land base is only 150 feet at its widest. Before the rebellion, its houses stood on the rocky terrace below. Whenever Pueblos rebuilt their villages, they recycled rocks and beams from the older sites. After the rebellion, for instance, vigas from the destroyed San Bartolome Mission were carried up the mesa for Hopi houses and kivas.

Hopi house-building customs emphasize the sanctity of the domicile and its materials. When the tribe recently petitioned the U.S. government to safeguard their territory, one reason they gave was, "It is from this land that we obtained the timbers and stone for our homes and kiva." After marriage a woman was expected to bring her new mate into her family's house block. If that called for a new room, house-building preparations and rites began. Men cut and dragged the mountain pine beams and juniper poles from the San Francisco peaks and then let them age. They split off sandstone building blocks, then raised and chinked the primary walls and layered the roof. Women supervised and clan members pitched in.

From his study of the relationship between Hopi vocabulary and architecture, the linguist Benjamin Whorf believed that the Hopi did not classify their buildings into types and lacked words for "room" or "interior." What was of concern to them, however, as revealed in their architectural phraseology, was the activity that occurred in their built spaces, or the objects that should be kept and protected there. According to Whorf, it was also those activities which called for their architecture to receive spiritual attention. Prayer sticks or *pahos* were stuck in the corners of the walls so they would "take good roof hold" and "stand firm and secure." Before the chimneys were built, cactus slices were offered to nourish the "roots" of the house.

Then the village chief tied raw cotton strings to bits of eagle down, sprinkled them with blessed corn meal, and placed them under large stones in the corner of the room. The first was for the sun, the second for fertile land, the third for rain, and the fourth for many strong children. At most First Mesa towns the threshold also was marked by small offerings—food crumbs, tobacco, etc.—to appease the spirits and ward off evil. Today in the Hopi ceilings one can find feathers attached to willow sticks inserted into the central roof beam to "feed" the structure and protect its occupants from premature death.

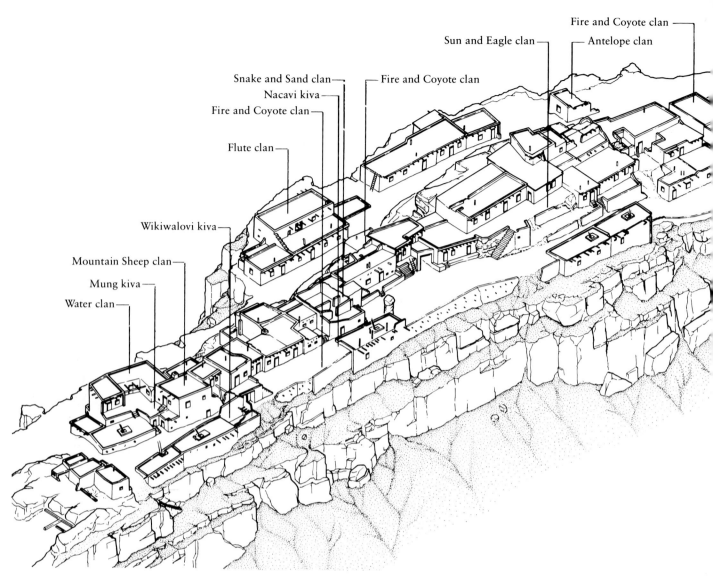

Water clan
Mung kiva
Mountain Sheep clan
Wikiwalovi kiva
Flute clan
Fire and Coyote clan
Nacavi kiva
Snake and Sand clan
Fire and Coyote clan
Sun and Eagle clan
Antelope clan
Fire and Coyote clan

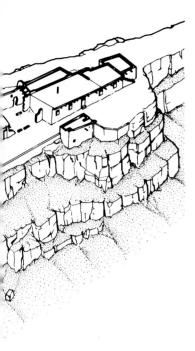

Walpi

The drawing of Walpi *(above left)* identifies locations for clan houses and kivas; the photograph *(below)* shows the same part of the village. Hopi social organization is complex, community members belong simultaneously to religious kivas, villages, housegroups, lineages, clans, and the clan groups known as phratries. All five of the Walpi kivas are dug into the sandstone rim.

A typical room at Sichomovi *(right)* holds milling basins on the left, a pole for airing bedding, and prayer feathers hanging from the roof beams.

Inside the house, women framed the fireplaces and vents with lightweight sunflower stalks, supervised the mixing of mortar, and applied plaster with bare hands or raw wool pads, producing a scalloped-shell texture. Hopi hearths burned a blend of sagebrush, grease-wood, corn stalks and cobs, as well as piñon and cedar. Cooking was done inside. Their unleavened piki bread made from blue corn floor was toasted on seasoned stone slabs that fit over a wood fire. In older days, furnishings were meager. Milling rooms contained the three or four grinding metates in basins; sleeping quarters had poles hung from the ceiling to air bedding and sandstone stools with handholds so they could be lifted easily.

The nine semisubterranean kivas and the clan houses of First Mesa were used for the men's deliberating, prayer and meditation, for initiating the young and storytelling, for kachina dancers' costume changes, and for male clan members' social gatherings. At one time, young and old males spent the better part of their winters in the kivas, spinning cotton and weaving cloth on vertical looms, making weapons and repairing ritual paraphernalia. Because of its constrained land base, First Mesa kivas generally were dug into the bedrock along the mesa's edge. Walpi has five kivas; Sichomovi and Hano have two each.

In 1975, Walpi was restored by the Hopi tribe in collaboration with specialists from the Museum of Northern Arizona. The trend toward depopulation that followed World War II seemed to be turning around, and its people needed more space. Like the citizens of Taos and Acoma to the east, they regarded their village as a cultural sanctuary. Three-storied house blocks were shored up, more than seventy rooms were rehabilitated, kivas were restored and replastered, and textiles, pottery shards, and plant and seed remains were exhumed from rooms that had been shut for centuries.

Walpi plaza

Snake Rock is one of Walpi's most sacred places. Near this eroding sandstone pillar Hopi dancers offered to snakes their prayers for rain; in its crevices they placed bead, plume, and cornmeal offerings. On the small plaza ground they drew with cornmeal the four-quartered world and its rainclouds. A kiva hatchway and ladder is to the left of the rock. Photographed ca. 1895.

In mid-February 1980, we had a rare opportunity to watch the Hopi kivas serve their ancient function as theaters for sacred performances. The sole occasion when outsiders can enter these charged chambers occurs during the Bean Dance, a segment of the great *Powamuy* festival which takes place in mid-winter. The ritual begins as the rain-bringing kachinas, impersonated by Kachina Society members costumed in brilliantly theatrical masks and dress, are believed to have just taken up their half-year residence among the Hopi. Throughout this period the kivas acquire heightened importance as the kachinas' temporary home away from their traditional home among the clouds in the San Francisco Mountains.

The public events of the Bean Dance include a parade by more than a hundred kachinas through the Pueblo streets and alleys, with kachina dancing and intricately staged puppet ceremonies in the kivas throughout the night. It is only on the last night of the sixteen-day festival, we were told, that nonresidents are permitted to witness the kiva rituals.

When we ascended First Mesa in late afternoon, we learned that each of its nine kivas was responsible for producing one "act," which circulated from kiva to kiva. If we found a good berth in one kiva we could enjoy all nine of the mesa's performances. The parts of the ceremony that we knew were off-limits included the indoctrination of Hopi youth into the kachina cult and the forced germination of bean seeds in the kivas. In a piece of winter magic, intended to prefigure and stimulate the bountiful crops the Hopi yearn to cultivate in the coming spring, semisubterranean rooms are filled with steamy heat until green bean shoots emerge from seeding beds.

At first we tried to get a good seat in a Walpi kiva, but its townsfolk were anxious that their own women and children might not have enough standing room in their exceedingly small kivas, so we huddled in the sleet and rain around a Sichomovi ladder well, which looked down as if into a well-lit cave. On the roof beams we noticed fresh hand smears indicating the last plasterers' prayers for rain. The audience packed into the viewing area behind the ladder, and the ceremonies began.

In six of the acts, teams of kachina dancers wearing identical animal masks filled the stage floor, singing and shuffling in time to shaking rattles. Between their performances, three classic puppet acts were presented. During intermissions, the Coleman lanterns were turned low and hooded, and we were brusquely whisked away from the kiva hatchways by masked *Wuyataywas*, or Angry Guard Kachinas. Under cover of darkness the staging for the next act was dropped into the kiva and made ready. At a signal, illumination flooded the interior once more, accompanied by renewed singing, drumming, and whirling colors. Each puppet show, which dramatized folkoristic figures and stories primarily meant to entertain and teach the women and children, opened against a screen vividly painted with cloud, lightning, and rain symbols, and bordered by young fir trees which had recently been harvested from a sacred grove.

In the first puppet ceremony, 3-foot-long water serpents, known as *Paaloloqangw*, slowly pushed aside round flaps depicted as blazing suns. Their red gaping mouths yawned wide as they emerged from behind the screen, writhing with increasing ferocity, their wild swings sometimes betraying the arms of the puppeteers manipulating them from behind the screen, on top of which a wooden sandpiper puppet scooted back and forth. As vibrating sound effects reached a crescendo, the serpents thrashed a miniature "corn field" which we had just noticed on the kiva floor before them, symbolized by green bean shoots sprouting from little red mud cakes. Thus, according to anthropologist Mischa Titiev, who witnessed a performance in 1934, the serpents "signify that they are harvesting the crops which they produce and own."

The second puppet performance featured a *Kooyemsi,* a little masked clown kachina believed to have been modeled after the Mudhead Kachinas more commonly associated with Zuni ritualism. Once his stagecraft was in place and the lights rose again, this marvelously articulated puppet, about a foot high, seemed to prance magically behind his miniature proscenium without apparent strings or hand manipulation. To the eerie drone of a bull-roarer, a humming instrument whirled by a soundmaker hidden behind the screen, he cavorted to everyone's delight. To the Hopi all these puppets are considered alive, this Kooyemsi being a "naughty little boy" who is "always ridiculing us" but who is dearly loved by his indulgent Hopi parents. It is said that anyone who wants a son should pray to this little being, and that each year the Hopi insert a new "heart," consisting of a little leather pouch holding corn meal, a prayer stick, and a quartz crystal, into these puppets.

The last kiva performance was a piece of puppetry which, we were told, had not been enacted on First Mesa for decades. It depicted the *Sa'lak-wmanawyat,* or Corn Grinding Maidens, two figures beloved to the Hopi. When the kiva lights flared on, the little girls seemed merely painted on a screen which stretched from wall to wall of the kiva, flanked by fir trees. Then their little arms stuck out from the backdrop and began swaying in rhythm to music by means of strings pulled by their invisible puppeteers.

Suddenly the masked chorus of kachina dancers on either side thronged towards the girls, momentarily blocking them from our view. When they drew back the girls seemed alive, their tablita headdresses tipping forward as they knelt over miniature stone metates and began to grind corn. According to historian of religions Armin W. Geertz, the Hopi hold these dolls in considerable awe; the two puppets, who are said to weep if they are separated, are believed to bless with female offspring the Hopi who pray to them.

White-daubed clown-like kachinas, who gleefully clapped their hands and adoringly attended to the little girls, squatted on the kiva floor and took pinches of their newly ground corn meal to sprinkle on the heads of recently initiated youngsters in the front row of the audience. Then the kiva was sunk in darkness. When the lights reappeared, only the clowns lay curled on the dirt floor, apparently heartbroken at the loss of the dolls. Comforted by the children, they hobbled up the kiva ladder. Without fanfare, the show abruptly ended there, and the lanterns were doused for the last time.

Our final glance was into a murky interior, where kiva members with headbands and flashlights were shooing out visitors and breaking down the set. Steam from departing bodies lingered over the ladder well. Then a kiva official ordered us out of the way as he tugged at the wood-and-tarpaper hatchcover and sealed the kiva.

Old Oraibi kiva

The Pueblo of Old Oraibi, near First Mesa, is believed to have been continuously occupied since 1150. In this photograph, taken in 1900, men emerge from their Snake Society kiva to embark upon a snake-hunting expedition in preparation for the annual rain-making ceremony.

BIBLIOGRAPHY

Since this book is for the general reader, we have chosen to avoid footnotes and to withhold references until this section. First we review the history of the interest in Native American architecture; then we offer key references chapter by chapter. Throughout the record of early exploration of North America, most accounts of Indian life begin with descriptions of dwellings and settlement patterns—that is, architecture. It is perhaps only natural to consider houses and human spaces as the most immediate evidence of culture, not only because they are the most visible, but also because around notions of "house," "home," and "community" gravitate central ideas about what it means to be a human being, to belong to a family and a larger social organization, and to be part of an encompassing sacred universe.

As the most prominent and symbol-charged of the handmade products which anthropologists classify as "material culture," American Indian houses also were used by Europeans as a yardstick for assessing the general degree of "civilization" of tribal societies. At first the Spanish believed that the monumentality of Southwestern pueblos suggested that here were town-dwellers of substance with whom they might deal profitably. When they learned that the buildings were actually quite simple in construction, their estimation of the sophistication of the occupants began to drop. Later Anglo visitors often likened Indians who dug their buildings out of the earth—to escape from the heat or to insulate themselves from the cold—to burrowing animals, and treated them accordingly.

Some early architectural descriptions were objective and thorough, such as material on Iroquois bark houses by the Jesuit priest J-F Lafiteau in the 1720s, documentation on Southeastern Indian settlements by the botanist William Bartram in the 1770s, accounts of Northwest Coast plank houses by Captain James Cook and Etienne Marchand in the 1770s and 1780s, coverage of Middle Missouri earthlodge towns by Prince Maximilian of Wied-Neuwied in the 1830s, and descriptions of California Indian houses by journalist Stephen Powers in the 1860s.

But most Western visitors did not usually settle into Indian life long enough to learn how the Indians used their architecture. Rarely did they help to build one of these dwellings. Few of them investigated the pattern of social life in and around the homes. Thus they missed the "annual architectural round," or pattern of seasonal building, which provided different spaces for shelter, work, and special gatherings throughout the economic year. Also, the early European observers did not learn about the symbolic encoding of many of these buildings, which could make house construction a ritual act. Aside from information gleaned from archeology or teased out of Indian oral traditions, however, their often biased and fragmentary observations are still the only primary information we have on Native American architectural traditions before they were altered by white contact. As Indian and Western societies became more exposed to each other, the ensuing clash of values and interests resulted in disease, warfare, population decline, land loss, relocation, forced assimilation, and economic dependency for Indians across North America. Architectural change directly reflected this sequence of experiences, yet in many cases the tenacity of traditional Indian house-life was remarkable, as if architecture was absolutely central to the sense of identity which many tribes struggled to safeguard as they came under outside domination.

Not until the late nineteenth century did anyone attempt to synthesize those travelers' accounts and elevate the subject of Indian houses to a field of study. Formal analysis of Native American architecture was launched in 1881 by a book so precocious in theory and wide-ranging in evidence that it still overshadows others on the topic. That year a lawyer and Indian-rights advocate from upper New York State named Lewis Henry Morgan—deemed the "father of American anthropology"—completed on his deathbed *Houses and House-Life of the American Aborigines* (U.S. Geographical and Geological Survey of the Rocky Mountain Region: Contributions to North American Ethnology, V. 4, Washington, D.C., 1881). Morgan believed that "All forms of this architecture sprang from a common mind, and exhibit, as a consequence, different stages of development of the same conceptions...." Thus, he argued, "If we enter the great problem of Indian life with a determination to make it intelligible, their house life and domestic institutions must furnish the key...." Morgan's work boldly applied information on the built-forms of Indian groups across North America to support his grand theory of social evolution.

In an appendix to his first book, written thirty years earlier about the Iroquois tribe, Morgan amassed every scrap of available information on the elm-bark covered "longhouses," which played such an important part in the Iroquois worldview. The intimate link between the Iroquois' social organization and their use of these buildings—where everyone under one extendable roof was related through the female line—sparked his lifelong curiosity about other Indian building traditions. Morgan's exposure to Iroquois customs also influenced many of his notions about how societies developed. An evolutionist of his time, he believed that on a rising scale from savagery through barbarism to civilization, American Indian cultures could be slotted within the three "intermediate periods" of barbarism because of their adherence to two cultural "laws" that he believed were directly reflected in their use of their buildings. For one, within the communal Iroquois longhouse was found the principle of "adaptation to communism in living"; all clan members related through the female line lived together. For another, this principle was coupled with what Morgan called the "law of hospitality," which dictated that hunger was not known at one end of a village if plenty existed at the other end. Morgan's approach was revolutionary in that it sought to interpret material culture in terms of social organization.

Morgan's functional-evolutionary ideas have proved to be a limiting framework for interpreting Indian buildings, but his research did consolidate the best ethnographic sources of his day. He included the elegant surveys completed from 1845 to 1847 by E.G. Squier and E.H. Davis of giant earthworks in the Midwest. Their drawings and descriptions in *Ancient Monuments of the Mississippi Valley: Comprising the Results of Extensive Original Survey and Exploration* (Washington, D.C., 1848) made Indian architecture the inaugural topic of the new Smithsonian Institution's publishing program. Morgan also appropriated illustrations and accounts from recent articles by Stephen Powers, who had ventured into little-known byways of native California in 1871 and 1872, and he reprinted drawings and data John L. Stephens and Frederick Catherwood had collected among the ruined Mayan cities of Yucatan between 1839 and 1842.

Morgan's handwritten draft for his last book featured the word "architecture" in its title. It is unclear what prompted Morgan to shift to "houses" in the published version. However, his lesser-known contemporary, a Presbyterian scholar named Stephen D. Peet, had no hesitation using "architecture" for the numerous articles he wrote about Indian buildings between 1878 and 1908, largely for the journal he founded, *American Antiquarian* (later *American Antiquity*). Peet's concern was to detect in indigenous structures of the Pueblo Southwest and pre-conquest Mexico "the primordial germs of the different kinds of architecture" throughout the world, as well as prototypes for the "orders" of classical architecture.

While Morgan and Peet were advancing grand theories regarding Indian architecture, the first wave of pioneer ethnographers began recording it on a more modest scale. In 1879 the geologist and explorer John Wesley Powell took over the fledgling Bureau of American Ethnology in the Smithsonian Institution. Among the eight categories of information he wanted from his fieldworkers was data on "houses with reference to domestic life"—a reflection of Morgan's influence. Until 1933 the Bureau published annual reports and bulletins which still contain much of what we know about Indian architectural systems.

In 1895 the German scholar Franz Boas began his long tenure as America's most influential anthropologist. From his work among the Central Eskimo of the Arctic and the Kwakiutl tribe of the Northwest

Coast, Boas gained an appreciation of the role of houses in native social life. Together with his prize student, Alfred Kroeber, who shortly thereafter dominated the scholarship about California Indians, Boas was concerned about "salvage ethnography"—the urgent program to record the lifeways of Indian tribes before the last elders and their knowledge was lost forever. Over the next fifty years, facts about Indian architecture were collected by a host of ethnographers across North America as part of large checklists of traditional "traits" of authentic Indian life—with housing high on the agenda. At the same time, "ethnohistorians" began looking anew into early historical documentation on tribes, turning up in the archives drawings and descriptions of Indian houses and towns which were by then a thing of the past.

When it came to fresh ideas about what all these data actually said about these cultures, however, there were few American trailblazers to challenge Morgan. Twice, the California scholar Thomas T. Waterman submitted sweeping generalizations about the evolution of Indian house forms. His claim (in "North American Indian Dwellings," *Geographical Review*, V. 14, 1924) that circular houses were also "found among more primitive and backward tribes," while rectangular houses as a rule succeeded them and were built by more progressive groups, would be invalidated by archeological evidence from the Northwest Coast, the Great Plains, and the Southwest. Waterman's other notion (in "Native Houses of Western North America," *Museum of the American Indian, Heye Foundation, Indian Notes and Monographs,* Misc. 11, 1921), that the semisubterranean "pithouse" had a family tree which extended back to northeastern Asia, was a probable supposition, but his research never pieced together details of construction so as to prove historical diffusion rather than common-sense independent invention. This did not end speculation about the origin of the pithouse, however, as W. Jochelson ("Past and Present Subterranean Dwellings of Northeastern Asia and Northwestern America," *International Congress of Americanists,* 15th Session, Quebec, 1906), Ralph Linton ("The Origin of the Plains Earth Lodge," *American Anthropologist,* V. 26, 1924), and Hiroshi Daifuku ("The Pit House in the Old World and in Native North America," *American Antiquity,* V. 17, N. 1, July 1952) continued to emphasize interesting parallels but offered no firm diagnostics for ascertaining a direct connection between Southwestern kivas, Eskimo pit houses, semisubterranean structures in California and the Plateau, northern Plains earthlodges, and town houses in the Southeast.

The only other early scholars to venture a synoptic overview of Indian architecture at this time were Cyrus Thomas, whose classification of thirty-three Indian house types ("Habitations," in *Handbook of American Indians North of Mexico,* Smithsonian Institution, Bureau of American Ethnology, Bulletin 30, 1912) was an arbitrary blurring of geographical and technological criteria, and the German architect Ernest Sarfert, whose "Haus und Dorf bei den Eingeborenen Nordamerikas" (*Archiv fur Anthropologie* [Brunswick], V. 35, 1909) presented a typology based on such distinctions as "round styles" and "four-corner" styles in order to fix centers of architectural diffusion; these very general architectural characteristics had little bearing, however, on cultural affinities or contrasts among the tribes. Only a few maverick ethnographers, such as Frank Hamilton Cushing and French scholars of the L'Année Sociologique school in the first decade of this century, suggested a deeper reading of Indian architecture. Close examination of Eskimo house-life yielded evidence for Marcel Mauss's theory of the influence of the environment upon Eskimo behavior and symbolism (*Seasonal Variations of the Eskimo,* London: Routledge and Kegan Paul, 1976 [1906]). Mauss and Emile Durkheim used Cushing's material on the Zuni Indians' spatial principles and George Dorsey's early material on the Plains Indians' settlement patterns to demonstrate how "primitive" people mentally organized the world around them (*Primitive Classification,* Chicago: University of Chicago Press, 1963 [1903]).

With few exceptions, however, "primitive" or "tribal" houses had so far been the property of anthropological discourse, and even then were rarely dignified as "architecture." As Clark Wissler wrote in 1917, "The only regions in which building rises to the level of architecture are those occupied by the higher cultures of Mexico and Peru" ("Types of Dwellings and Their Distribution in Central North America," *16th International Congress of Americanists,* Vienna and Leipzig: A. Hartleben Verlag, 1910). This opinion was echoed in 1957 by Dr. Harold Driver: "Although some would like to dignify the building skill of the Pueblo Indian with the label architecture, we have reserved this term for the much more spectacular achievements of the peoples of Meso-America" (*Indians of North America,* 2nd Edition, Chicago: University of Chicago Press, 1970).

When indigenous buildings were discussed in architecture schools, it was only to illustrate the impact of environment upon construction and design. (This deterministic emphasis is exemplified in James Marston Fitch and Daniel P. Branch, "Primitive Architecture and Climate," *Scientific American,* V. 203, N. 6, 1960 and Alan H. Broderick, "Grass Roots: Huts, Igloos, Wigwams and Other Sources of the Functional Tradition," *Architectural Review,* V. 115, Feb. 1954). For studio projects it became common to have students model a shelter using only available materials from a designated eco-zone in a particular region. Subsequent comparison with the region's actual vernacular tradition was a way to assess the multiple solutions which might work in a given environment. But this exercise did not set the stage for exploring the wider range of factors—social, economic, religious, historical—which might have contributed to the indigenous built-forms. Folk builders, in this approach, were viewed largely as what environmental scholar Christopher Williams calls "craftsmen of necessity," their creations shaped principally by geography, natural building materials, and climate.

Even when Bernard Rudovsky's notorious exhibit of photographs and text, "Architecture Without Architects," opened at the Museum of Modern Art in the fall of 1964, environmental and functional determinism still held sway. In its highly influential and polemical attack on the pretensions of modern architecture, Rudovsky's exhibition catalog (*Architecture Without Architects,* New York: Doubleday and Co., 1964) brought "nonpedigreed" architecture to the attention of the world. Unfortunately, his only Native American entry was the prehistoric Anasazi pueblo of Cliff Palace, which he erroneously attributed to "Mongolian hunters" of 12,000 years ago. Moreover, in his lengthy captions to the exhibit, Rudovsky talked little of social organization, cosmological encoding, or the importance of history. Rather, he saw the buildings as inventive responses to territory and climate whose organic designs unintentionally surpassed the most avant-garde or self-conscious of contemporary design.

About the same time, however, some scholars began to explore larger implications of tribal spatial systems around the world. As French sociologist Pierre Bordieu emphasized, it is "inhabited space—above all the house" which socializes human beings into becoming members of their culture. For Claude Lévi-Strauss the organization of the house and spatial domains offered important clues to indigenous principles of both social organization and cosmology. Criticizing scholars, for example, who claimed that Northern California Indians had minimal social organization, Lévi-Strauss pointed out that rather than being "mere buildings," the dwellings of tribes like the Yurok were given personal names and considered "the actual bearers of rights and duties." "The fault" with most scholarship, Lévi-Strauss wrote, "lies in the disregard of the concept of 'house' as a moral person possessing a domain, perpetuated by transmission of its name, wealth and titles through a real or fictitious descent line."

From the field of architecture, Amos Rapoport, an Australian scholar with architectural and anthropological training, produced an important little treatise, *House Form and Culture* (Englewood Cliffs, N.J.: Prentice-Hall, 1969), which reviewed prevailing theories of what did affect building forms in non-Western, non-"designed" traditions. Rapoport promoted no single determinant, but argued that the house must be considered within its full cultural context. Drawing upon examples from diverse cultures to assess the many reasons a given house looked and functioned as it did, Rapoport argued that sociocultural factors were actually more significant than environmental-technological ones in the development and variation of vernacular dwellings. Neither Rudovsky nor Rapoport, however, produced a working distinction between "folk" and "tribal" traditions, between, that is, the architecture of peasant or rural peoples which has been influenced by wider political developments and economic changes, and the architecture of indigenous groups such as those in this book, whose buildings expressed, and in some cases, still express, ties to their old languages, social organizations, and subsistence and religious systems.

Under the qualifying names of "folk," "vernacular," "indigenous," and "primitive" architecture, the study of tribal buildings, including, to some degree, those of North America, has been taken up over the last twenty years by cultural geographers, anthropologists, folklorists, and architectural historians. In our chapters we have sought to incorporate these recent studies and interpretations.

Our chapters are developed from the following sources. The founding work remains *Houses and House-Life of the American Aborigines* by Lewis Henry Morgan (Chicago: University of Chicago Press, 1965 [1881]). Other standard references containing material on Indian housing include the still-emerging volumes of the Smithsonian Institution's *Handbook of North American Indians,* with twenty volumes envisaged, and the series by Edward S. Curtis, *The American Indian* (reprint, New York: The Johnson Reprint Co., 1970). While Curtis occasionally paid to have ceremonies staged in front of the examples of Indian house types he photographed, were it not for his visual archive and writings (edited by Smithsonian Institution scholar Frederick Webb Hodge) we could not see such buildings as the last Arikara sacred earthlodge at Beaver Creek, North Dakota, a host of structures on the British Columbia coast, Eskimo winter houses at Hooper Bay, and so forth.

Among the article-length attempts to give an overview of Indian house types are Cosmos Mindeleff, "Aboriginal Architecture in the United States" (*Journal of the American Geographical Society,* V. 30, N. 5, 1898); Frederick S. Dellenbaugh, "Shelter, Dwellings, and Architecture," in *The North-Americans of Yesterday* (New York: G.P. Putnam's Sons, 1901); R.I. Geare, "Typical Homes of American Indians" (*Out West,* V. 27, N. 2, 1907); Clark Wissler, "Types of Dwellings and Their Distribution in Central North America" (*16th International Congress of Americanists,* Vienna and Leipzig: A. Hartleben Verlag, 1908); T.T. Waterman, "The Architecture of the American Indian" (*American Anthropologist,* V. 29, 1927); John P. Harrington, "Buildings of Native Americans" (*The Pan American Magazine,* August 1930); Harold Madison, "Indian Homes" (Cleveland Museum of Natural History, *Pocket Natural History,* N. 2, Anthropological Series, N. 1, 1925); J.M. Butree, "Habitations of the Indians" (*The Totem Board,* V. 2, N. 2, 1932); Pliny Earle Goddard, "Native Dwellings of North America" (*Natural History,* V. 28, N. 2, 1928); the Indian Leaflet Series of the Denver Art Museum, under the guidance of curator Frederic H. Douglas; the chapter on "Housing and Architecture," in Harold E. Driver and William C. Massey, "Comparative Studies of North American Indians" (*Transactions of the American Philosophical Society,* V. 47, N. 2, 1957); chapters in *Prehistoric Settlement Patterns in the New World,* edited by Gordon R. Willey (Viking Fund Publications in Anthropology, N. 23, 1956); and Peter Nabokov and Robert Easton, "North American Indians," in *Roots: America's Vernacular Heritage* (Washington, D.C.: American Heritage Press, 1986). We are grateful for access to materials from the graduate seminar conducted in 1978 by Dr. Raymond D. Fogelson at the University of Chicago, Department of Anthropology, which studied traditional Native American buildings: among the papers most useful for this book have been those on the Tlingit (Sergei Kan), Delaware (Polly Strong), Creek (Amelia Walker), Navajo (Karen M. Art),

Miwok (Barrick Van Winkle), Netsilik Eskimo (Linda Gould), Oglala Sioux (Josette Gosella), Hisinai-Wichita (Bradley R. Leftwich), Zuni (David D. Newman), and Yurok (Thomas Buckley). While our work does not engage contemporary housing, David Stea introduces the topic in "Indian Reservation Housing: Progress Since the 'Stanton Report'" (*American Indian Culture and Research Journal,* V. 66, N. 3, 1982).

1 WIGWAM and LONGHOUSE

The best collection of historical writings and pictures on Indian architecture east of the Mississippi is by David I. Bushnell, Jr., *Native Villages and Village Sites East of the Mississippi* (Smithsonian Institution, Bureau of American Ethnology, Bulletin 60, Washington, D.C., 1908). For overviews of eastern seaboard Algonquian architecture, see C.C. Willoughby, "Houses and Gardens of the New England Indians" (*American Anthropologist,* V. 8, 1906); Regina Flannery, *An Analysis of Coastal Algonquian Culture* (Catholic University of America, Anthropological Series, N. 7, 1939); Howard S. Russell, *Indian New England Before the Mayflower* (Hanover, N.H.: University Press of New England, 1980); and Dean R. Snow, *Archeology of New England* (New York: Academic Press, 1980).

One of the oldest New England wigwam sites is reported in Maurice Robbins, *Wapanucket #6, An Archaic Village in Middleboro, Mass.* (Cohasset Chapter, Massachusetts Archeological Society, Inc., 1960) and *An Archaic Ceremonial Complex at Assawompsett* (Attleboro: The Massachusetts Archeological Society, 1968). Errett H. Callahan describes an interesting effort to reconstruct Virginia Algonquian longhouses in his dissertation, *Pamunkey Housebuilding: An Experimental Study of Late Woodland Construction Technology in the Powhatan Confederacy* (The Catholic University of America, 1981; Ann Arbor, Mich.: University Microfilms). In both *The Grant Oneota Village* (Report 4, Office of the State Archeologist; Iowa City: University of Iowa Press, 1973) and "Reconstructing the Longhouse Village Settlement Patterns" (*Plains Anthropologist,* V. 19, N. 65, 1974), Marshall McKusick blends archeology and ethnohistory to speculate on early longhouses on the woodland/prairie borderlands.

In "Plantagenet's Wigwam" (*Journal of the Society of Architectural Historians,* V. 27, N. 4, 1958), G. Carroll Lindsay looks at early graphics for historic period house-types, while William C. Sturtevant uses early documentation on Niantic wigwams in "Two 1761 Wigwams at Niantic, Connecticut" (*American Antiquity,* V. 40, N. 4, 1975) to call for clearer architectural typologies. Abenaki houses are discussed by Wilson D. Wallis and Ruth Sawtell Wallis in *The Micmac Indians of Eastern Canada* (Minneapolis: University of Minnesota Press, 1955) and also by William C. Orchard in "Penobscot Houses" (*American Anthropologist,* V. 4, N. 2, 1909). Frank Speck, *A Study of the Delaware Indian Big House Ceremony,* V. 2, (Harrisburg: The Pennsylvania Historical Commission, 1931) offers construction details and discusses the architectural symbolism of the building which represented the continuity of the Delaware culture into the twentieth century, also discussed in Mark R. Harrington, *Religion and Ceremonies of the Lenape* (Indian Notes and Monographs, misc. pub. 19, Museum of the American Indian, Heye Foundation, 1921).

Lewis H. Morgan combined information from the Seneca, Ely S. Parker, and the early ethnographer J-F Lafitau on Iroquois longhouses in his *League of the Ho-de-no-sau-nee, or Iroquois* (New York: Dodd, Mead & Co., 1904 [1851]). A prehistoric Iroquois longhouse is reported in James Tuck, "The Howlett Hill Site: An Early Iroquois Village in Central New York," in *Iroquois Culture, History, and Prehistory,* edited by Elizabeth Tooker (Albany: New York State Museum and Science Service, 1967). Additional material on Iroquois buildings can be found in W.M. Beauchamp, "Aboriginal Use of Wood in New York" (*New York State Museum Bulletin,* V. 139, 1905) and William Starna et al., "Northern

Iroquoian Horticulture and Insect Infestation: A Cause for Village Removal" (*Ethnology*, V. 31, N. 3, 1984). On continuity and change in Iroquoian architecture, see Tooker, ed., *Iroquois Culture, History and Prehistory*, especially William N. Fenton's contribution, "From Longhouse to Ranch-Type House: The Second Housing Revolution of the Seneca Nation"; also helpful is Fenton's work on Iroquois cosmology, "This Island, the World on the Turtle's Back" (*Journal of American Folklore*, V. 25, 1962), and on contemporary longhouse ritual activities, *An Outline of Seneca Ceremonies at Coldspring Longhouse* (Yale University Publications in Anthropology, N. 9, 1936). For material on Iroquois architecture and identity, see Harold Blau, "Mythology, Prestige and Politics: A Case for Onondaga Cultural Persistence" (*New York Folklore Quarterly*, V. 23, N. 1, 1967) and the entire issue of *Recherches Amerindiennes au Quebec*, V. 10, N. 3, 1980. For Huron architecture, the basic source is Conrad Heidenreich, *Huronia: A History and Geography of the Huron Indians, 1600-1650* (Toronto: McClelland and Stewart Ltd., 1971). For a mixture of architecture, archeology, and experimental reconstruction, see the work James V. Wright supervised in Ontario, *The Nodwell Site* (Archeological Survey of Canada, Paper No. 16, Ottawa: National Museum of Canada, 1974).

For general works on Great Lakes Indian dwellings, see the chapter on dwellings in Ronald J. Mason, *Great Lakes Archeology* (New York: Academic Press, 1981) and William J. Kubiak, *Great Lakes Indians: A Pictorial Guide* (Grand Rapids, Mich.: Baker Book House, 1970). For Chippewa house types, see David I. Bushnell, Jr., "Ojibway Habitations and Other Structures" (Smithsonian Institution, Annual Report of the Board of Regents, 1916/1917, 1919); Frances Densmore, "Chippewa Customs" (Smithsonian Institution, Bureau of American Ethnology, Bulletin 86, 1929); and Karen Daniels Peterson, "Chippewa Mat-Weaving Techniques" (Smithsonian Institution, Bureau of American Ethnology, Bulletin 186, Anthropological Paper N. 67, 1963). Paul Radin discusses dwellings in *The Winnebago Tribe* (Smithsonian Institution, Bureau of American Ethnology, 37th Annual Report, 1923). On Menominee housing, see Alanson Skinner, *Material Culture of the Menominee* (Museum of the American Indian, Heye Foundation: Notes and Monographs, 1921), while Kickapoo building practices are covered in Robert E. Ritzenthaler and Frederick A. Peterson, *The Mexican Kickapoo Indians* (Milwaukee Public Museum, Publications in Anthropology, N. 2, 1956); Felipe A. Latorre and Dolores L. Latorre, *The Mexican Kickapoo* (Austin: University of Texas Press, 1976); and Peter Nabokov, "Kickapoo Houses," in *Shelter II*, edited by Lloyd Kahn, Jr. (Bolinas, Calif., Shelter Publications, 1978).

Religious architecture of the Great Lakes is discussed in Werner Muller, *Die Blaue Hutte* (Wiesbaden: Franz Steiner Verlag GMBH, 1954) which focuses on Midewiwin ritualism and its enclosure, the "Midewegun." Additional material is found in Ruth Landes, *Ojibwa Religion and the Midewiwin* (Madison: University of Wisconsin Press, 1968); Selwyn Dewdney, *The Sacred Scrolls of the Southern Ojibway* (Toronto and Buffalo: University of Toronto Press, 1975); Joan M. and Ramon K. Vastokas, *Sacred Art of the Algonkians* (Peterborough: Mansard Press, 1973); Basil Johnston, *Ojibway Heritage* (New York: Columbia University Press, 1976); and Ivar Paulson, "The Seat of Honor in Aboriginal Dwellings," in *Indian Tribes of Aboriginal America*, edited by Sol Tax (Chicago: University of Chicago Press, 1952). Spatial symbolism in the Dream Drum religion is discussed in Thomas Vennum, Jr., *The Ojibwa Dance Drum: Its History and Construction* (Washington, D.C.: Smithsonian Institution Press, 1982), while the shamanic "shaking tent" is interpreted in A. Irving Hallowell, *The Role of Conjuring in Saulteaux Society* (Publications of the Philadelphia Anthropological Society, N. 2, 1942), and Sylvie Vincent, "Structure du rituel: le tente tremblante et le concept de Mista. pe. w (*Recherches Amerindiennes au Quebec*, V. 3, N. 11–12, 1973).

2 MOUND, TOWN, and CHICKEE

For an overview of the complex archeological record on structures, mounds, and ceremonial spaces, see *Archeology of the Eastern United States*, edited by James B. Griffin (Chicago: University of Chicago Press, 1952). For more specific information, see architect William Morgan's renderings in *Prehistoric Architecture of the Eastern United States* (Cambridge: MIT Press, 1980), based in part upon documentation in E.G. Squier and E.H. Davis, *Ancient Monuments of the Mississippi Valley* (Smithsonian Institution, Smithsonian Contributions to Knowledge, V. 1, 1848). Architecture of Mississippian times is addressed in Thomas M.N. Lewis and Madeline Kneberg, *Hiwasee Island: An Archeological Account of Four Tennessee Indian Peoples* (Knoxville: University of Tennessee Press, 1946), "The Southern Cult and Muskhogean Ceremonial," in *The Collected Works of Antonio J. Waring Jr.*, edited by Stephen Williams (Cambridge: Peabody Museum Papers, 1969) and in *Mississippian Settlement Patterns*, edited by Bruce D. Smith (New York: Academic Press, 1980), while J. A. Brown offers a different view in "The Southern Cult Reconsidered" (*Mid-continental Journal of Archeology*, V. 1, N. 2, 1976). Continuity in the Southeastern Indians' ritual use of space is discussed in James Howard, *The Southeastern Ceremonial Complex and Its Interpretation* (Missouri Archeological Society, N. 6, University of Missouri, 1968) and "Bringing Back the Fire: The Revival of a Natchez-Cherokee Ceremonial Ground" (*American Indian Crafts and Culture*, December 1969).

In the debate over interpretation of Poverty Point—covered generally in C.H. Webb, "The Poverty Point Culture" (*Geoscience and Man*, V. 17, 1977)—K. Brecher and W.G. Haag, "The Poverty Point Octagon: World's Largest Prehistoric Solstice Marker?" (*Bulletin of the American Astronomical Society*, V. 12, N. 4, 1980) are pitted against Robert D. Purrington, "Supposed Solar Alignments at Poverty Point" (*American Antiquity*, V. 48, N. 1, 1983). An astronomical interpretation for Hopewell spaces is given in Ray Hively and Robert Horn, "Geometry and Astronomy in Prehistoric Ohio" (*Journal for the History of Astronomy*, V. 13, Supplement 4, 1982). Adena houses are discussed in William S. Webb and Charles E. Snow, *The Adena People* (Knoxville: University of Tennessee Press, 1974). Ceremonial structures are discussed in Charles R. Wicke, "Pyramids and Temple Mounds: MesoAmerican Ceremonial Architecture in Eastern North America" (*American Antiquity*, V. 30, N. 4, 1965), and in Charles H. Fairbank, "The Macon Earth Lodge" (*American Antiquity*, V. 2, 1946), while James E. Price examines common dwellings in "A Middle Mississippian House" (Museum Briefs, N. 1, Museum of Anthropology, University of Missouri, 1969), as does Dennis E. Harvey, "Reporting House Structures: Towards an Analysis of Living Units" (*Missouri Archaeological Society Newsletter*, N. 268, 1973).

For the historic period, most of William Bartram, *Observations on the Creek and Cherokee Indians* (Transactions of the American Ethnological Society, V. 3, N. 1, 1853) is in an area summary by John R. Swanton, "Housing," in *The Indians of the Southeastern United States* (Smithsonian Institution, Bureau of American Ethnology, Bulletin 137, 1946). For specific tribal studies from the historic period, see John R. Swanton, *Organization and Social Usages of the Indians of the Creek Confederacy* (Smithsonian Institution, Bureau of American Ethnology, 42nd Annual Report, 1928), which covers much architectural material, while his brief "The Creeks as Mound Builders" (*American Anthropologist*, V. 14, N. 2, 1912) underscores the continuity between early and late Creek spatial traditions. For later Creek material, see John R. Swanton, "Modern Square Grounds of the Creek Indians" (*Smithsonian Miscellaneous Collections*, V. 85, N. 8, 1931); Frank G. Speck, "The Creek Indians of Taskigi Town" (*Memoirs of the American Anthropological Association*, N. 2, 1907); Mary R. Haas, "Creek Inter-Town Relationships (*American Anthropologist*, V. 42, 1940); and Morris E. Opler, "The Creek Indian Towns in Oklahoma in 1937" (Department of Anthropology Papers, V. 13, N. 1, University of Oklahoma, 1972). Of recent scholars, William C.

Sturtevant, "Notes on the Creek Hothouse" (*Southern Indian Studies, V. 20, 1968*), revisits the older traditions, while Amelia Bell Walker has done advanced symbolic interpretation in "Symbolic Space and the Creek Square Ground" (presented at "Spaces and Places: Cultural Perspectives on Native North American Structures," Central States Anthropological Society Meeting, March 29, 1979, Milwaukee, Wisconsin) and "Tribal Towns, Stomp Grounds, and Land: Oklahoma Creeks After Removal," in *Native American Land* (Chicago: Department of Anthropology, University of Chicago, Chicago Anthropology Exchange, V. 14, N. 1–2, 1981).

For Cherokee architecture, see James Mooney, "Cherokee Mound-Building" (*American Anthropologist, V. 11, 1889*), which discusses architectural links to the pre-contact past, while *Tellico Archeology: 12,000 Years of Native American History* by Jefferson Chapman (Knoxville: University of Tennessee Press, 1987) summarizes recent excavations in Tennessee with sketches reconstructing early Cherokee mounds and buildings. Charles H. Faulkner, "Origin and Evolution of the Cherokee Winter House" (*Journal of Cherokee Studies, V. 3, N. 2, 1978*), and William C. Sturtevant, "Louis-Philippe on Cherokee Architecture and Clothing in 1797" (*Journal of Cherokee Studies, V. 3, N. 4, 1978*) and "The Cherokee Hothouse" (*Tennessee Archeologist, V. 9, N. 1, 1953*) focus on the communal winter structure. Robert K. Thomas, *The Redbird Smith Movement* (Smithsonian Institution, Bureau of American Ethnology, Bulletin 180, 1961), on the Cherokee revitalization movement, contains background on Cherokee sacred grounds.

For Yuchi material, see Frank G. Speck, *Ethnology of the Yuchi Indians* (Philadelphia: University of Pennsylvania Museum, Anthropological Publications, V. 1, N. 1, 1909) and W. L. Ballard, *The Yuchi Green Corn Ceremonial: Form and Meaning* (Los Angeles: University of California, American Indian Studies Center, 1978). Seminole architecture is covered in Clay MacCauley, *The Seminole Indians of Florida* (Smithsonian Institution, Bureau of American Ethnology, 5th Annual Report, 1884); Louis Capron, "The Medicine Bundles of the Florida Seminole and the Green Corn Dance" (Smithsonian Institution, Bureau of American Ethnology, Bulletin 151, Anthropological Paper N. 35, 1952); Alexander Spoehr, "Camp, Clan and Kin among the Cow Creek Seminole of Florida" and "The Florida Seminole Camp" (Field Museum of Natural History, Anthropological Series, V. 33, Nos. 1 and 3, 1941 and 1944); and William C. Sturtevant, "Creek into Seminole," in *North American Indians in Historical Perspective*, edited by Eleanor B. Leacock and Nancy O. Lurie (New York: Random House, 1971). Useful, too, is William T. Arnett, "Seminole Indian Clues for Contemporary House Form in Florida" (*Florida Anthropologist*, December 1953), but more detailed data come from Ormond H. Loomis of the Florida Folklife Program and William C. Sturtevant's unpublished field notes at the Smithsonian Institution, "Seminole Housing: Research and Fieldwork Notes," from work conducted in the 1950s.

3 EARTHLODGE, GRASS HOUSE, and TIPI
4 PIT HOUSE and EXTENDED TIPI

For early reports and drawings of western Indian architecture, see the compilation by David I. Bushnell, Jr., *Villages of the Algonquian, Siouan and Caddoan Tribes West of the Mississippi* (Smithsonian Institution, Bureau of American Ethnology, Bulletin 77, 1922). Material on the archeology of the Missouri is rich: Donald J. Lehmer, *Introduction to Middle Missouri Archeology* (Anthropological Papers, N. 1, National Park Service, 1971) surveys the entire region and relies heavily on *River Basin Survey Papers* (printed in various Bulletins of the Bureau of American Ethnology, Smithsonian Institution), while Waldo R. Wedel, *Central Plains Prehistory* (Lincoln: University of Nebraska Press, 1986), summarizes prehistoric architecture farther south. For a single house study, see D.J. Lehmer, K. Meston, and C.L. Dill on "Structural Details of

a Middle Missouri House" (*Plains Anthropologist, V. 18, N. 60, 1973*). Wedel analyzes earthlodge remains farther south in both "House Floors and Native Settlement Populations in the Central Plains" (*Plains Anthropologist, V. 24, N. 84, 1979*) and "Two House Sites in the Central Plains: An Experiment in Archeology" (*Nebraska History, V. 15, N. 490, 1970*).

Tipi ring sites are summarized in J. Jacob Hoffmann, "Comments on the Use and Distribution of Tipi Rings in Montana, North Dakota, South Dakota, and Wyoming" (Anthropology and Sociology Papers, N. 14, Missoula: Montana State University, 1953), and Leslie B. Davis, "From Microcosm to Macrocosm: Advances in Tipi Ring Investigation and Interpretation" (*Plains Anthropologist*, Memoir 19, pt. 2, 1983). The excavation of a Pawnee earthlodge site whose remains seem to verify ethnographic accounts of Pawnee earthlodge symbolism is discussed in Patricia J. O'Brien, "Prehistoric Evidence for Pawnee Cosmology" (*American Anthropologist, V. 88, N. 4, 1986*). This article also makes special use of materials by Pawnee scholar James Murie, in papers (primarily "The Ceremonial Lodge and Its Symbolism") listed under George A. Dorsey at Chicago's Field Museum of Natural History. Much of this material is summarized by Von Del Chamberlain, *When Stars Came Down to Earth: Cosmology of the Skidi Pawnee Indians of North America* (Los Altos: Ballena Press, 1982). Waldo R. Wedel speculates on Pawnee settlement/cosmological relationships in "Native Astronomy and the Plains Caddoans," in *Native American Astronomy*, edited by Anthony F. Aveni (Austin: University of Texas Press, 1977); Douglas R. Parks looks at "Bands and Villages of the Arikara and Pawnee" (*Nebraska History, V. 60, 1979*), and both Wedel and Parks discuss Pawnee "animal lodges" and religion in "Pawnee Geography: Historical and Sacred" (*Great Plains Quarterly, V. 5, 1985*). Life in Pawnee earthlodges is brought vividly to life in the Gene Weltfish classic, *The Lost Universe* (Lincoln: University of Nebraska Press, 1977). Construction and consecration rituals of a single Arikara earthlodge are covered by Melvin R. Gilmore in "The Arikara Tribal Temple" (*Papers of the Michigan Academy of Sciences, Arts and Letters, V. 14, 1930*).

From Gilbert Wilson's detailed monograph *The Hidatsa Earthlodge*—with basic information from Buffalo Bird Woman and illustrations by his brother Frederick—one can practically build a Missouri earthlodge (Anthropological Papers of the American Museum of Natural History, V. 33, 1934), and additional data is in his *Agriculture of the Hidatsa Indians: An Indian Interpretation* (University of Minnesota, Studies in the Social Sciences, N. 9, 1917). More material on Mandan and Hidatsa earthlodges can be found in George F. Will, "The Mandan Lodge at Bismark" (*North Dakota Historical Quarterly, V. 5, 1930*) and Russell Reid, "The Earth Lodge" (*North Dakota Historical Quarterly, V. 4, 1930*). Hidatsa and Mandan village plans are in O.G. Libby, "Typical Villages of the Mandan, Arikara and Hidatsa in the Missouri Valley" (Collections of the State Historical Society of North Dakota, V. 2, 1908), while Frank L. Stewart discusses their settlement shifts in "Mandan and Hidatsa Villages in the 18th and 19th Centuries" (*Plains Anthropologist, V. 19, N. 66, 1974*).

Detailed material on Southern Plains grass houses is scarce, but G.A. Dorsey has useful references in both his *Wichita Tales* series (*Journal of American Folklore, V. 15, 16, 17, 1902, 1903, 1904*) and *The Mythology of the Wichita* (Carnegie Institute of Washington, Publication N. 21, 1904), while Edward S. Curtis provides the Wichita origin myth in "Wichita" (*The North American Indian, V. 19, 1930*) and F.H. Douglas has some construction data in "The Grass House of the Wichita and Caddo" (Denver Art Museum Leaflet Series, N. 42, 1932).

Along with the popular handbook on tipi making and use by Reginald and Gladys Laubin, *The Indian Tipi: Its History, Construction and Use* (Norman: University of Oklahoma Press, 1971), see more detailed descriptions of the Blackfeet: Walter McClintock, "The Blackfoot Tipi" (Southwest Museum Leaflet, N. 5, 1936) and "Painted Tipis and Picture-Writing of the Blackfoot Indians" (Southwest Museum Leaflet, N. 6,

1936); George B. Grinnell, "The Lodges of the Blackfeet" (*American Anthropologist*, V. 3, N. 4, 1901); Ted J. Brasser, "Tipi Paintings, Blackfoot Style," in *Conceptual Studies of Material Culture* (National Museum of Man, Canadian Ethnology Service, Mercury Series, Paper 43, 1978), "Home, House and Temple Among the Plains Indians" (*Canadian Collector*, V. 11, N. 1, 1976), and "The Pedigree of the Hugging Bear Tipi" (*American Indian Arts Magazine*, Winter, 1979) and the exquisite portfolio edited by John C. Ewers, *Blackfoot Indian Tipis: Design and Legend* (Bozeman: Museum of the Rockies, 1976). Other tribal studies include Donald A. Cadzow, "The Prairie Cree Tipi" (Museum of American Indian, Heye Foundation, Indian Notes, V. 3, 1926); Stanley Campbell, "The Cheyenne Tipi" (*American Anthropologist*, V. 17, N. 4, 1915) and "The Tipis of the Crow Indians" (*American Anthropologist*, V. 29, N. 1, 1927). Sioux tipis are examined in Charles R. Corum, "A Teton Tipi Cover Depiction of the Sacred Pipe Myth" (*South Dakota History*, V. 5, 1975); Sam Reynolds, "A Dakota Tipi" (*North Dakota History*, V. 40, 1973); Alice H. Poatgietter, "The Sioux Tipi" (*Gopher Historian*, V. 22, 1967-68). Kiowa and Kiowa-Apache tipi covers and stories collected by James Mooney are in John C. Ewers, *Murals in the Round* (Washington: Smithsonian Institution Press, 1978).

The most sophisticated speculation about the origin of an Indian house type is offered for the tipi in Ted C. Brasser, "The Tipi as an Element in the Emergence of Historic Plains Indian Nomadism" (*Plains Anthropologist*, V. 27, N. 98, Pt. 1, 1982). For studies of tipi encampments, and socio-religious rules underlying their arrangement, see J. Owen Dorsey, *Siouan Sociology* (Smithsonian Institution, Bureau of American Ethnology, 15th Annual Report, 1896), *Omaha Sociology* (Smithsonian Institution, Bureau of American Ethnology, 3rd Annual Report, 1884) and *A Study of Siouan Cults* (Smithsonian Institution, Bureau of American Ethnology, 11th Annual Report, 1896). For revitalization of tipi art see Myles Libhart and Rosemary Ellison, *Painted Tipis by Contemporary Plains Indian Artists* (catalogue of an exhibition organized by the Indian Arts and Crafts Board, U.S. Department of the Interior, Anadarko, Oklahoma: Oklahoma Indian Arts and Crafts Cooperative, 1973).

Unusual shelters on the Eastern Plains are described by J.H. Howard, "New Notes on the Dakota Earth Lodge" (Plains Archeological Conference Newsletter, V. 4, 1951) and W. R. Hurt, "House Types of the Santee Indians" (Museum Notes, University of South Dakota, V. 14, 1953). Studies of nondomestic structures include the sweatbath as built form and ritual: W. Kickeberg, "The Indian Sweatbath" (*Ciba Symposia*, V. 1, 1939); for specific tribal studies see George Bird Grinnell, "A Buffalo Sweatlodge" (*American Anthropologist*, V. 21, N. 4, 1919), on the Blackfeet; V. Dusenberry, "Ceremonial Sweat Lodges of the Gros Ventres Indians" (*Ethnos*, V. 28, 1963); Deward Walker, "Nez Perce Sweatbath Complex" (*Southwest Journal of Anthropology*, V. 22, N. 2, 1966); and Eric D. Sismey, "Ouil'sten: Okanagon Steam Bath" (*The Beaver*, Summer, 1966). Sun shades are discussed in Peter Nabokov, "Native American Arbors" (*East West Journal*, V. 14, N. 12, 1984). Among other special religious structures, the Sun Dance lodge is studied by George B. Grinnell, "The Cheyenne Medicine Lodge (*American Anthropologist*, V. 16, N. 2, 1914); Ake Hultkrantz, "The Traditional Symbolism of the Sun Dance Lodge among the Wind River Shoshoni" in *Religious Symbols and their Functions*, edited by H. Biezais (Stockholm: Scripta Instituti Donneriani Aboensis 10, 1979); and Joseph G. Jorgenson, *The Sun Dance Religion* (Chicago: University of Chicago Press, 1972).

Verne F. Ray provides the sole overview of Plateau buildings in *Cultural Relations in the Plateau of Northwestern America* (Publications of the Frederick Webb Hodge Anniversary Publication Fund, V. 2, Los Angeles, 1939). For the border between Plateau and Northwest Coast, see Marian W. Smith, "House Types of the Middle Fraser River" (*American Antiquity*, V. 12, N. 4, 1947). Monographs by James A. Teit contain first-hand house descriptions: "The Thompson Indians of British Columbia" (*Memoirs of the American Museum of Natural History*, V. 2, 1900); "The Lillooet Indians" (*Memoirs of the American Museum of Natural*

History, V. 1, N. 4, 1906); "The Salishan Tribes of the Western Plateau" (Bureau of American Ethnology, Annual Report 45, 1930); and "The Shuswap" (*Memoirs of the American Museum of Natural History*, V. 4, 1909). In "Building a Winter Dwelling" (*Kelowna Centennial Museum Booklet*, V. 2, Kelowna: Lamong-Surtees, 1975), some Shuswap discuss their own building practices and houses.

5 WINTER HOUSE, IGLU, and TENT

Overviews of Eskimo house types are found in Kaj Birket-Smith, *The Eskimos* (London: Methuen &. Co., 1936); Nelson Graburn et al.; *Circumpolar Peoples* (Pacific Palisades: Goodyear Publishing Co., 1973); C.D. Forde, *Habitat, Economy and Society* (London: Methuen, 1963); Edward M. Weyer, *The Eskimos: Their Environment and Folkways* (New Haven: Yale University Press, 1932). In *Eskimos and Explorers* (Novato, Calif.: Chandler and Sharp, 1979), Wendell Oswalt collects early travelers' accounts for the entire circumpolar region. Among recent scholarly overviews are Gregory Allen Reinhardt, *The Dwelling as Artifact: Analysis of Ethnographic Eskimo Dwellings, With Archeological Implications* (Ph.D. Thesis, Department of Anthropology, UCLA, 1986, University Microfilms International, Ann Arbor) and *Maqiuq: The Eskimo Sweatbath*, by John Marpessa (University of Munich, Contribution to American Studies, N. 17, 1986). For a popular summary see Dorothy J. Ray, "The Eskimo Dwelling" (*Alaska Sportsman*, V. 26, N. 8, 1960); on tents see Jean Gabus, "La Maison des Esquimaux," in *Aspects de la Maison dans le Monde* (Brussels: Centre Internationale de la Maison dans le Monde, 1961). Duration of occupancy organizes Eskimo settlements for Kwang-Chih Chang in "A Typology of Settlement and Community Patterns in Some Circumpolar Societies" (*Arctic Anthropology*, V. 1, N. 1, 1962). Edmund Carpenter discusses Eskimo spatial aesthetics in *Eskimo Realities* (New York: Holt, Rinehart and Winston, 1973) and "Eskimo Space Concepts" (*Explorations* V. 5, 1955). For contemporary Canadian Eskimo and Indian housing see "Le Logement Amerindien," a special issue of *Recherches amerindiennes au Québec* (V. 5, N. 4-5, 1975).

Prehistoric housing of the Thule period is cited throughout the general works listed above, but Peter Schledermann reported on late Dorset "longhouses" first in "Preliminary Results of Archeological Investigations in the Bache Peninsula Region, Ellesmere Island, N.W.T." (*Arctic*, V. 31, N. 1, 1978), and later in "Eskimo and Viking Finds in the High Arctic" (*National Geographic*, V. 159, N. 5, 1981). Moreau S. Maxwell reports on one early structure in "The House on the Ruggles" (*The Beaver*, Autumn, 1962).

The principle sources of Alaskan Eskimo house types, especially the variety of winter houses, remain Robert F. Spencer, *The North Alaskan Eskimo: A Study in Ecology and Society* (Smithsonian Institution, Bulletin 171, 1959) and Wendell H. Oswalt, *Alaskan Eskimos* (San Francisco: Chandler Publishing Co., 1967). On the all-men's house, the kashim, see Margaret Lantis, *Alaskan Eskimo Ceremonialism* (New York: J.J. Augustin, 1947). Good early documentation on western Eskimo structures is in V. 20 of Edward S. Curtis, *The American Indian* (reprint, New York: The Johnson Reprint Co., 1970); Edward W. Nelson, *The Eskimo About Bering Sea* (Bureau of American Ethnology, 18th Annual Report, 1899); Dorothy J. Ray, *The Eskimos of Bering Strait* (Seattle: University of Washington Press, 1975); and Riley D. Moore, "Social Life of the Eskimo of St. Lawrence Island" (*American Anthropologist*, V. 23, N. 3, 1923). Aleutian *barabara* dwellings are discussed in William S. Laughlin, *Aleuts: Survivors of the Bering Land Bridge* (New York: Holt, Rinehart and Winston, 1980) and "Barabara" (*Cuttle-Fish One*, Unalaska High School, Fall and Winter, 1977).

On housing of specific central Arctic peoples, see Franz Boas, who first documented the winter house, snow house, and summer tents in *The Central Eskimo* (Bureau of American Ethnology, 6th Annual Report,

Washington, 1888). Among many group-specific studies with significant material on housing are Elmer W. Ekblaw, *The Material Response of the Polar Eskimo to their Far Arctic Environment* (Annals of the Association of American Geographers, V. 17, N. 4, 1927); Erik Holtved, *Contributions to Polar Eskimo Ethnography* (Meddelelser om Gronland, V. 182, N. 2, 1967); Diamond Jenness, *The Life of the Copper Eskimo* (Report of the Canadian Arctic Expedition, V. 12, Ottawa, 1922); Kaj Birket-Smith, *The Caribou Eskimos: Material and Social Life and Their Cultural Position,* 5th Thule Expedition, V. 5, Copenhagen, 1929); Nicholas J. Gubsner, *The Nunamiut Eskimos* (New Haven: Yale University Press, 1965); Therkel Mathiassen, *Material Culture of the Iglulik Eskimos* (5th Thule Expedition, V. 6, Copenhagen, 1928); Knud Rasmussen, *Intellectual Culture of the Iglulik Eskimos* (Fifth Thule Expedition, V. 7, N. 1, Copenhagen, 1929); Cornelius Osgood, *Ingalik Material Culture* (Yale Publications in Anthropology, N. 22, 1940); and Asen Balikci, *The Netsilik Eskimo* (Garden City: The Natural History Press, 1970). Balikci's work is the basis of *The Netsilik Eskimos on the Sea Ice* (Workbook 7, *Man: A Course of Study,* Education Development Center, Inc., 1970).

On eastern Eskimo dwellings and house-use, see William Thalbitzer, *The Ammassaalik Eskimo* (Meddelelser om Gronland, V. 39, N. 1, 1914); Kaj Birket-Smith, *Ethnography of the Egedesminde District with Aspects of the Culture of West Greenland* (Meddelesler om Gronland V. 66, N. 1, 1924); Ernest W. Hawkes, *The Labrador Eskimo* (Canada Department of Mines Geographical Survey, Memoir 91, 1916).

The snow-block house is featured in Vilhjalmur Steffansson, *Arctic Manual* (New York, Macmillan, 1944); Richard L. Handy, "The Igloo and the Natural Bridge as Ultimate Structures" (*Artic,* V. 26, N. 4, 1973); Graham Rowley, "Snow-House Building" (*Polar Record,* V. 16, 1938); A. F. Buckham, "Indian Engineering" (*Canadian Geographical Journal,* V. 40, 1950); J. Gabus, "La construction des Iglous chez les Padleirmiut" (La Société Neuchâteloise de Geographie, Bulletin 47, 1940); Bernard Saladin d'Anglure, "Recherches sur le symbolisme Inuit" (*Recherches amerindiennes au Québec,* V. 5, N. 3, 1975). Life in Eskimo dwellings and modern adaptations is discussed in John D. Leechman, "Igloo and Tupik" (*The Beaver,* V. 4, March, 1945).

Subarctic architectural patterns are underreported. Those who offer some material are Cornelius Osgood, *The Ethnography of the Taniana* (Yale University Publications in Anthropology, V. 16, 1937); John Honigmann, *Ethnography and Acculturation of the Fort Nelson Slave* (Yale University Publications in Anthropology, V. 33, 1946) and *The Kaska Indians: An Ethnographic Reconstruction* (Yale University Publications in Anthropology, V. 51, 1954). Frederica de Laguna includes material on Tena housing in *The Prehistory of Northern North America as Seen from the Yukon* (Memoirs of the Society for American Archeology, V. 12, N. 3, 1947). Kutchin tents are described in Robert McKennan, *The Chandalar Kutchin* (Arctic Institute of North America, Technical Paper N. 17, 1965) and Cornelius Osgood, *Contributions to the Ethnography of the Kutchin* (Yale University Publications in Anthropology, N. 14, 1936). In *Bringing Home Animals* (New York: St. Martin's Press, 1979), Adrian Tanner provides explanatory graphics to clarify Cree spatial principles.

6 PLANK HOUSE

The incomparable architectural guide remains Joan Vastokas, *Architecture of the Northwest Coast Indians of America* (Ph.D. Thesis, Department of Art, Columbia University, 1966, University Microfilm International, Ann Arbor). Architecture is also featured in such general Northwest Coast surveys as Erna Gunther, *Indian Life on the Northwest Coast of North America* (Chicago: University of Chicago Press, 1972); Ruth Underhill, *Indians of the Pacific Northwest* (Lawrence: Indian Life and Customs Pamphlets, U.S. Indian Bureau, 1944); Phillip Drucker, *Cultures of the North Pacific Coast* (San Francisco: Chandler Publishing Co., 1965), while Daniel J. Joyce offers a general introduction in "Houses

of the Maritime Peoples of the Northwest Coast" (*Field Museum of Natural History Bulletin,* March, 1982). George F. MacDonald underscores the cosmological basis of Northwest Coast architecture and art in "Cosmic Equations in Northwest Coast Indian Art" in *The World is Sharp as a Knife: An Anthology in Honor of Wilson Duff,* edited by Donald N. Abbott (Victoria, British Columbia: University of British Columbia Press, 1981).

For the Southern region little has been synthesized since Thomas T. Waterman and Ruth Greiner, "Indian Houses of Puget Sound" (*Indian Notes and Monographs,* Museum of the American Indian, Heye Foundation, New York, 1921) and Ronald Olson, *Adze, Canoe and House Types* (University of Washington Publications in Anthropology, V. 2, N. 1, 1927). Useful short pieces include Homer G. Barnett, "Underground Houses on the British Columbia Coast" (*American Antiquity,* V. 9, 1944) and his discussion of dwellings in *The Coast Salish of British Columbia* (University of Oregon Studies in Anthropology, N. 4, 1955) and Thomas Newman, "Native Peoples and Shelters" in *Space, Style and Structure: Building in Northwest America,* edited by Thomas Vaughan (Portland: Oregon Historical Society, 1974). Personal reminiscences of house life are in Chief Charles Jones with Stephen Busnow, *Queesto, Pacheenaht Chief by Birthright* (Nanaimo, B.C.: They thus, 1981).

For the Central zone, many of Franz Boas's publications are rich with house descriptions and construction protocol provided by his native collaborators, George Hunt and Henry W. Tate. A detailed guide to Boas's work is Leslie A. White, *The Ethnography and Ethnology of Franz Boas* (Texas Memorial Museum, Bulletin 6, University of Texas, 1963). Boas focuses on architecture in "Houses of the Kwakiutl Indians" (*Proceedings of the U. S. National Museum,* V. 11, 1888) and "The Houses of the Tsimshian and Nisk'a" (*Report of the British Association for the Advancement of Science,* V. 66, 1896). A useful breakdown of the Boas data is also presented by Irving Goldman in *The Mouth of Heaven: An Introduction to Kwakiutl Religious Thought* (New York: John Wiley & Sons, 1975). A single community is described in *The Totem Poles and Monuments of Gitwangak Village* (Studies in Archeology, Architecture and History, Ottawa, National Historic Parks and Sites Branch, 1984). On Nootka housing see Peter Drucker, *The Northern and Central Nootkan Tribes* (Bureau of American Ethnology, Bulletin 144, Washington, D.C., 1951). For a symbolic interpretation of Tsimshian architecture see George F. McDonald, "Painted Houses and Woven Blankets: Symbols of Wealth in Tsimshian Art and Ceremony" in *The Tsimshian and Their Neighbors,* edited by Jay Miller and Carol M. Eastman (Seattle: University of Washington Press, 1984). The restoration of Tsimshian house-front art is chronicled by Robert D. Forrest in "Recovering a Masterpiece" (*Heritage West,* V. 6, N. 3, 1982).

The most lavish summary of Haida architecture, by Museum of Man director George F. MacDonald, is *Haida Monumental Art: Villages of the Queen Charlotte Islands* (Vancouver: University of British Columbia Press, 1983), which includes village plans, individual house histories, and historical photographs. John and Carolyn Smyly examine a single Haida village in detail in *Those Born at Koona* (Saanichton, B.C.: Hancock House, 1973) as do Wilson Duff and Michael Kew in "Anthony Island: A Home of the Haidas" (*British Columbia Museum of Natural History and Anthropology,* Report for 1957, 1958). Margaret B. Blackman focuses on single houses in "Hatna—The Haida Longhouse" (*The Charlottes: A Journal of the Queen Charlotte Islands,* V. 3, Queen Charlotte Islands Museum Society, 1975) and in her photogrammetric study of the most famous of Haida buildings, "Neiwans, the 'Monster' House of Chief Wiha: An Exercise in Ethnohistorical, Archeological, and Ethnological Reasoning" (*Syesis,* V. 5, 1972). She discusses Haida architectural change in "Creativity in Acculturation: Art, Architecture and Ceremony from the Northwest Coast" (*Ethnohistory,* V. 23, N. 4, 1976).

Architecture of the northernmost people, the Tlingit, is the subject of G.F. Emmons, "The Whale House of the Chilkat" (*Anthropological Papers of the American Museum of Natural History,* V. 19, 1916) and

Louis Shotridge, "Chilkat Houses" (*University of Pennsylvania Museum Journal*, V. 4, 1913). Tlingit house culture is summarized by Frederica De Laguna in V. 5 of *Under Mount St. Elias* (Smithsonian Contributions to Anthropology, Washington: Smithsonian Institution Press, 1972).

7 WOOD, EARTH, and FIBER

House types are discussed throughout Alfred C. Kroeber, *Handbook of California Indians* (Smithsonian Institution, Bureau of American Ethnology, Bulletin 78, Washington, D.C., 1925), as they are in Stephen Powers's early overview, *Tribes of California* (reprint, Berkeley: University of California Press, 1976). For illustrations of a range of central California house types, see C. Hart Merriam, "Native Dwellings and Ceremonial Structures," in *Studies of California Indians* (Berkeley: University of California Press, 1955). Josef Haeckel, *Das Mannerhaus in Nordlichen Kalifornien* (Berlin: Stiftung Verlag, 1940) typologizes men's ceremonial and sweat structures from the California region. Lynn Gamble discusses the literature with emphasis on social organization in "California Indian Houses" (paper delivered at Second Annual California Indian Conference, University of California at Berkeley, October 1986). For traditional structures still in use, see Dolan H. Eargle, Jr., *The Earth Is Our Mother, A Guide to the Indians of California, Their Locales and Historic Sites* (San Francisco: Trees Company Press, 1986).

On northwestern California see Alfred C. Kroeber, *Karok Towns* (University of California Publications in American Archeology and Ethnology, V. 25, 1936). T.T. Waterman adds to regional documentation in both "Yurok Geography" (University of California Publications in American Archeology and Ethnology, N. 16, N. 5, 1920) and "The Village Sites in Tolowa and Neighboring Areas in Northwestern California" (*American Anthropologist*, V. 27, 1925). Tolowa buildings are also discussed in Philip Drucker, *The Tolowa and Their Southwest Oregon Kin* (University of California Publications in Archeology and Ethnology, V. 36, N. 4, 1936), while Hupa houses are in Pliny E. Goddard: *Life and Culture of the Hupa* (University of California Publications in American Archeology and Ethnology, V. 1, 1903). Robert Heizer and John E. Mills, *The Four Ages of Tsauri: A Documentary History of the Indian Village at Trinidad Bay* (Berkeley: University of California Press, 1952), traces the history of Yurok buildings by focusing on one town site. C.H. Merriam offers "Data Pertaining to Various Indian Ceremonial Houses in Northern California" (*University of California Archeological Survey*, Report N. 50, 1960). For Yurok buildings see Thomas Buckley, "Yurok Houses" (*News from Native California*, V. 1, N. 3, July/August 1987), while drawings of a Yurok sweat house and a family house are in *Report on a Study of a Yurok Indian Village* (House Resolution No. 327, Statues of 1963, Department of Parks and Recreation, State of California, 1964). Alfred Kroeber and E.W. Gifford provide a deeper analysis of the relation between Yurok religion and architecture in *World Renewal: A Cult System of Native North-west California*, Anthropological Records. V. 13, N. 1. (Berkeley: University of California Press, 1949). Thomas Buckley updates much of their material in *Structure and Meaning in Yurok World View: An Exploration in Religious Epistemology* (M.A. thesis, University of Chicago, 1977).

Central California houses are described in *Seven Early Accounts of the Pomo Indians and their Culture*, edited by Robert F. Heizer (Berkeley: University of California Archeological Research Facility, 1975); Samuel A. Barrett, "Pomo Buildings" (*Holmes Anniversary Volume*, Washington, D.C.: J.W. Bryan Press, 1916) and Barrett and E.W. Gifford, "Miwok Houses" in *The California Indians, A Source Book*, edited by Robert F. Heizer and M.A. Whipple (Berkeley: University of California Press, 1971). E.W. Gifford looks at settlement organization in "Miwok Moieties" (University of California Publications in American Archeology and Ethnology, V. 12, N. 4, 1916); C.A. Harwell also describes Miwok houses in "Building an Indian Chuck-A" (*Yosemite Nature Notes*, 1933), while Will C. McKern examines "Patwin Houses" (University of California Publications in American Archeology and Ethnology, V. 20, 1923).

Southern California structures are reviewed in William Duncan Strong, *Aboriginal Society in Southern California* (Banning: Malki Museum Press, 1972). Ritual spaces are discussed in C.G. Dubois, *Religion of the Luiseño Indians of Southern California* (University of California Publications in American Archeology and Ethnology, V. 8, 1908), and in John P. Harrington, "Researches on the Archeology of Southern California" (*Smithsonian Miscellaneous Collections*, V. 78, N. 1, 1925) and "Fieldwork Among the Mission Indians of California" (*Explorations and Fieldwork of the Smithsonian Institution in 1932*, Washington, D.C., 1933). Travis Hudson and Thomas Blackburn have edited Harrington's material on Chumash houses in *The Material Culture of the Chumash Interaction Sphere* V. 2 (Palo Alto: Ballena Press, 1983). In William Duncan Strong, "Analysis of Southwestern Society" (*American Anthropologist*, V. 29, 1927) links between women and house ownership are surveyed for southern California and the Southwest.

Of the Great Basin structures, Paiute houses are described in Margaret M. Wheat; *Survival Arts of the Primitive Paiute* (Reno: University of Nevada Press, 1967), C.T. Hurst, "A Ute Shelter" (*Southwestern Lore*, Colorado Archeological Society V. 5, 1939) and in Frances E. Watkins, "Moapa Paiute Winter Wickiup" (*The Masterkey*, V. 18, N. 6, 1944). A basic work on Colorado River house types is Leslie Spier, *Yuman Tribes of the Gila River* (Chicago: University of Chicago Press, 1933). Details are given in J.G. Bourke, "Notes on the Cosmogony and Theogony of Mohave Indians" (*Journal of American Folklore*, V. 2, 1889); A.L. Kroeber, *Seven Mohave Myths* Anthropological Records, V. 11 (Berkeley: University of California Press, 1948); C. Daryll Forde, *Ethnography of the Yuma Indians* (University of California Publications in American Archeology and Ethnology, V. 28, N. 4, 1931); E.F. Castetter and W.H. Bell, *Yuman Agriculture* (Albuquerque: University of New Mexico Press, 1951).

8 HOGAN, KI, and RAMADA

The best early source, Cosmos Mindeleff's "Navaho Houses" (Smithsonian Institution, Bureau of American Ethnology, 17th Annual Report, 1898) does not divorce technology from social-ceremonial aspects of architecture, unlike the chapter on shelter in Clyde Kluckholn et al., *Navaho Material Culture* (Cambridge: Harvard University Press, 1971). The emphasis in Berard Haile "Why the Navajo Hogan" (*Primitive Man*, V. 15, N. 34, 1942), and in Edwin N. Wilson, "The House of the Navaho" (*Landscape*, V. 10, Fall, 1960) is also holistic.

In a more recent study, geographer Stephen C. Jett and Virginia Spencer offer an illustrated typology of the inventive variety of Navajo housing forms in *Navajo Architecture: Forms, History, Distribution* (Tucson: University of Arizona Press, 1981). Jett in "Origins of Navajo Settlement Patterns" (*Annals of the Association of American Geographers*, V. 68, N. 3, 1978) and his more recent "Cultural Fusion in Native-American Folk Architecture: The Navajo Hogan," in *A Cultural Geography of North American Indians*, edited by Thomas E. Ross and Tyrel G. Moore (Boulder: Westview Press, 1987) presents a historical reconstruction of hogan development, a subject also discussed in David M. Brugge, "Pueblo Influence on Navajo Architecture" (*El Palacio*, V. 75, N. 3, 1968). For a Navajo perspective see Chester D. Hubbard, "The learning of that which pertains to the home" (Many Farms: Navajo Community College Press, 1977) and the mythological section in *Navajo History*, edited by E. Yazzie for the Navajo Curriculum Center (Many Farms: Navajo Community College Press, 1971).

Navajo beliefs and concepts regarding built space are covered in Louise Lamphere, "Symbolic Elements in Navajo Ritual" (*Southwestern Journal of Anthropology*, V. 25, 1969); Franc Newcomb, *Navajo Omens* and *Taboos* (Santa Fe: Rydal Press, 1940); Gary Witherspoon, "The Central Concepts of Navajo World View (1)" (*Linguistics*, V. 119, 1974); and Susan Kent, "Hogans, Sacred Circles and Symbols—The Navajo Use of Space," in *Navajo Religion and Culture: Selected Views*, edited by David M. Brugge and Charlotte Frisbie (Santa Fe: Museum of New Mexico Press, 1982). Ethnomusicologist David McAllester explores hogan blessing songs in *Hogans: Navajo Houses and House Songs* (Middletown: Wesleyan University Press, 1980), while the presentation of the major Navajo myth, *Blessingway*, by Leland C. Wyman (Tucson: University of Arizona Press, 1957) clarifies the tie between Navajo myth and architecture. For another sacred/secular built form, see David M. Brugge, "Navaho Sweat Houses" (*El Palacio*, V. 63, N. 4, 1959). A linguistic study of spatial concepts is in Rick Pinxton, et al., *The Anthropology of Space: Explorations into the Natural Philosophy and Semantics of the Navajo* (Philadelphia: University of Pennsylvania Press, 1983).

Charlotte J. Frisbie summarizes her Ph.D. thesis on house consecration ritual in "The Navajo House Blessing Ceremonial" (*El Palacio*, V. 75, N. 3, 1968), while architectural change is the subject of Susan Kent, *Analyzing Activity Areas* (Albuquerque: University of New Mexico Press, 1984). Change is also the topic of C. Lockett in "Hogans vs. Houses" *For the Dean, Essays in Anthropology in Honor of Byron Cummings*, (Tucson: University of Arizona Press, 1952) and Marc A. Tremblay et al., "Navaho Housing in Transition" (*America Indigena*, V. 14, N. 3, 1954). Useful efforts to compare neighboring traditions (in this case Navajo and Pueblo) in order to underscore the importance of sociocultural determinants of house form include R.W. Shufeldt, "A Comparative Study of Some Indian Homes" (*The Popular Science Monthly*, October 1892) and Amos Rapoport, "The Pueblo and the Hogan: A Cross-Cultural Comparison of Two Responses to an Environment" in *Shelter and Society*, edited by Paul Oliver (New York: Praeger, 1971).

A good case study linking archeological remains with ethnographic data is W.A. Longacre and J.E. Ayres, "Archeological Lessons from an Apache Wickiup," *New Perspectives in Archeology*, edited by S.R. and L.R. Binford (Chicago: Aldine, 1968). Other works that discuss Apache housing are Grenville Goodwin, *The Social Organization of the Western Apache* (Tucson: University of Arizona Press, 1969); Morris E. Opler, *Grenville Goodwin Among the Western Apache* (Tucson: University of Arizona Press, 1973), Ales Hrdlicka, "Notes on the San Carlos Apache" (*American Anthropologist*, V. 7, 1905); Morris E. Opler, "A Summary of Jicarilla Apache Culture" (*American Anthropologist*, V. 38, 1936). For more recent material see Margaret Schaeffer, "The Construction of a Wickiup on the Fort Apache Indian Reservation," (*The Kiva*, V. 24, N. 2, 1958), Rex E. Gerald, "Two Wickiups on the San Carlos Indian Reservation, Arizona" (*The Kiva*, V. 23, N. 3, 1958) and Donald R. Tuohy, "Two More Wickiups on the San Carlos Indian Reservation, Arizona" (*The Kiva*, V. 26, N. 2, 1960), while culturally appropriate housing for Apaches is discussed in George S. Esber Jr., "Indian Housing for Indians" (*The Kiva*, V. 37, N. 3, 1971).

The basic source on the Pima is Frank Russell, *The Pima Indians* (Smithsonian Institution, Bureau of American Ethnology, 26th Annual Report, 1908), while John Van Willigen offers an update in "Contemporary Pima Construction Practices" (*The Kiva*, V. 36, N. 1, 1970). Papago housing material is found throughout Ruth Underhill's works, notably *Social Organization of the Papago Indians* (Columbia University Contributions to Anthropology, V. 30, 1939) and *Rainhouse and Ocean: Speeches for the Papago Year* (Flagstaff: Museum of Northern Arizona Press, 1979). Papago housing and settlements are described in Alice Joseph et al., *The Desert People* (Chicago: University of Chicago Press, 1949) and Robert A. Hackenberg: "Aboriginal Land Use and Occupancy," in *American Indian Ethnohistory: Indians of the Southwest* (New York: Garland Publishing Co., 1974). J. Alden Mason, "The Papago Harvest Festival" (*American Anthropologist*, V. 22, 1920) contains material on symbolic use of space, and James S. Griffith, *Papago*

Religious Architecture (Ph.D. Thesis, Department of Anthropology, University of Arizona, 1973), covers Catholic folk chapels of Papagueria.

9 PUEBLO

The most comprehensive text on the subject remains one of the earliest: Victor and Cosmos Mindeleff, *A Study of Pueblo Architecture: Tasayan and Cibola* (Smithsonian Institution, Bureau of American Ethnology, 8th Annual Report, 1891), which emphasizes Zuni and Hopi buildings and construction practices. Other general works for background include: Edward Dozier, *The Pueblo Indians of North America* (New York: Holt, Rinehart and Winston, 1970); Stanley A. Stubbs, *Bird's Eye View of the Pueblos* (Norman: University of Oklahoma Press, 1950); and the impressionistic *Pueblo, Mountain, Village, Dance* (New York: Viking, 1975) by Vincent Scully. Village plans and much data are updated in *Southwest*, Handbook of North American Indians, V. 9, edited by Alfonso Ortiz (Washington, D.C., Smithsonian Institution Press, 1978). Pueblo architecture in general is discussed by Paul Horgan in "Place, Form and Prayer: Prehistoric Human Geography of the Town Indians of the Rio Grande," and J.B. Jackson in "Pueblo Architecture and Our Own" (in *Landscape*, V. 3, Winter, 1953/54). David G. Saile has summarized construction rituals and house symbolism in numerous papers, including "Making a House in the Pueblo Indian World" (*Architectural Association Quarterly*, V. 9, N. 2 & 3, 1977).

Indian architecture in the Southwest has produced considerable architectural theory, from speculations on the relationship between language and architecture, such as Frank. H. Cushing's in "Habitations Affected by Environment" (Smithsonian Institution, Bureau of American Ethnology, 4th Annual Report, 1886) and Benjamin Whorf's in "Linguistic Factors in the Terminology of Hopi Architecture" (*International Journal of American Linguistics*, V. 19, 1953), to considerations of the impact of climate on architecture, such as J. Walter Fewkes, "The Sun's Influence on the Form of Hopi Pueblos" (*American Anthropologist*, V. 8, 1906) to speculations by Elsie Clews Parsons on social organization, "The House-Clan Complex of the Pueblos," in *Essays in Anthropology*, (Berkeley: University of California Press, 1936). The same fascination with pit house and kiva relations found in Paul S. Martin, *The Kiva: Survival of an Ancient House Type* (Ph.D. Dissertation, Department of Anthropology, University of Chicago, 1929), continues as Randall H. McGuire and Michael B. Schiffer theorize about the prehistoric decision-making behind the transition from pit house to pueblo in "A Theory of Architectural Design" (*Journal of Anthropological Archeology*, V. 2, 1983) a popular subject also addressed in Michael E. Whalen, "Cultural-Ecological Aspects of the Pithouse-to-Pueblo Transition in a Portion of the Southwest" (*American Antiquity*, V. 46, N. 1, 1981), in Patricia A. Gilman, "Architecture as Artifact: Pit Structures and Pueblos in the American Southwest" (*American Antiquity*, V. 52, N. 3, 1987), and Robin Y. Farwell, "Pit House: Prehistoric Energy Conservation?" (*El Palacio*, Autumn, 1981). Landscape theorist J.B. Jackson collected a series of unpublished papers generated by his seminar on "Spatial Organization in the Prehistoric Indian Pueblos of the Southwest" (University of New Mexico, Department of Architecture, 1972).

Studies past and present on prehistoric architecture are superbly summarized in Linda S. Cordell, *Prehistory of the Southwest* (New York: Academic Press, 1984). Material on Hohokam construction includes David Wilcox, *The Architecture of Casa Grande and its Interpretation* (Ph.D. Thesis, Department of Anthropology, University of Arizona, 1977, University Microfilms International, Ann Arbor). Much data on Hohokam house types, canals, and ball grounds is in Harold S. Galdwin et al., *Excavations at Snaketown: Material Culture* (reprint, Tucson: University of Arizona Press, 1965). Discussions of Mogollon architecture build upon E.W. Haury, *The Mogollon Culture of Southwestern New Mexico* (Gila Pueblo, Medallion Paper N. 20, Globe, Arizona, 1936), Joe

Ben Wheat, *Mogollon Culture Prior to A.D. 1000* (Memoirs of the American Anthropological Association, V. 57, N. 2, Pt. 3, 1955) and Paul S. Martin et al., "Late Mogollon Communities: Four Sites of the Tularosa Phase, Western New Mexico" (*Fieldiana: Anthropology,* V. 49, N. 1, 1957). A current study is K.G. Lightfoot and G.M. Feinman, "Social Differentiation and Leadership Development in Early Pithouse Villages in the Mogollon Region of the American Southwest" (*American Antiquity,* V. 47, 1982).

A popular survey of Anasazi architecture is William M. Ferguson and Arthur H. Rohn, *Anasazi Ruins of the Southwest in Color* (Albuquerque: University of New Mexico Press, 1987). For interpretation of the architectural "phenomenon" of the Chaco Canyon town clusters built by the Anasazi, no study equals Stephen H. Lekson, *Great Pueblo Architecture of Chaco Canyon, New Mexico* (Albuquerque: University of New Mexico Press, 1986), of which Lekson provides a good popular summary in "Great House Architecture of Chaco Canyon, New Mexico" (*Archeology,* V. 40, N. 3, 1987). The work builds upon such early investigations as Neil M. Judd, *The Architecture of Pueblo Bonito* (Smithsonian Miscellaneous Collections, V. 147, N. 1, 1964). For a focus upon social-ceremonial structures in this canyon, see R. Gordon Vivian and Paul Reiter, *The Great Kivas of Chaco Canyon* (School of American Research, Monograph 22, 1960). Classic studies of other Anasazi period architecture include Earl H. Morris' work at Aztec in northwestern New Mexico (*The Aztec Ruin,* Anthropological Papers of the American Museum of Natural History, V. 26, N. 1, 1919).

For information on the historic period, see William E. Reynolds, *Ethnoarcheology of Pueblo Architecture* (Ph.D. thesis, Arizona State University, 1981, University Microfilms International, Ann Arbor), which discusses Eastern Pueblo architecture, focusing on architectural change at Taos Pueblo. Socio-religious aspects of Taos architecture are looked at in William N. Fenton, "Factionalism at Taos Pueblo, New Mexico" (Smithsonian Institution, Bureau of American Ethnology, Bulletin 164, 1957). Kivas are discussed in Florence H. Ellis, "Big Kivas, Little Kivas, and Moiety Houses in Historical Reconstruction" (*Southwestern Journal of Anthropology,* V. 6, 1950) and "Jemez Kiva Magic and Its Relation to Features of Prehistoric Kivas" (*Southwestern Journal of Anthropology,* V. 8, 1952). Leslie A. White's monographs on Keresan societies contain material on houses: *The Pueblo of Santo Domingo* (Memoirs of the American Anthropological Association, N. 43, 1935), *The Pueblo of Santa Ana* (Memoirs of the American Anthropological Association, No. 60, 1942), *The Acoma Indians* (Smithsonian Institution, Bureau of American Ethnology, 47th Annual Report, 1932), and "The World of the Keresan Pueblo Indians," in *Primitive Views of the World,* edited by Stanley Diamond (New York: Columbia University Press, 1960). Donald N. Brown interprets Eastern Pueblo architecture in "Social Structure as Reflected in Architectural Units at Picuris Pueblo," in *The Human Mirror: Material and Spatial Images of Man,* edited by Miles Richardson (Baton Rouge: Louisiana State University Press, 1974), while change is the subject of an unpublished M.A. dissertation (University of New Mexico, Department of Art, 1975) and later papers by Santa Clara resident-historian Rina Swentzel. Eastern Pueblo spatial concepts are an important topic in *The Tewa World* by Alfonso Ortiz (Chicago: University of Chicago Press, 1969) as well as Ortiz's unpublished paper on kiva symbolism, "A Sacred Symbol Through the Ages."

Western architectural studies include the profile of Zuni Pueblo architectural change by Bainbridge Bunting in *Early Architecture of New Mexico* (Albuquerque: University of New Mexico Press, 1976). T.J. Ferguson and Barbara J. Mills update the material in "Settlement and Growth of Zuni Pueblo: An Architectural History" (*The Kiva,* V. 52, 1987). Ruth Bunzel describes Zuni architectural ceremonialism in both *Zuni Katcinas* and *Zuni Ritual Poetry* (Smithsonian Institution, Bureau of American Ethnology, 47th Annual Report, 1932), following on *Zuni Breadstuff,* the early work on Zuni house-life by Frank Hamilton Cushing (Museum of the American Indian, Heye Foundation, Indian Notes &

Monographs, V. 8, 1920). On Acoma architecture, see Peter Nabokov, *Architecture of Acoma Pueblo: The 1934 Historic American Buildings Survey Project* (Santa Fe: Ancient City Press, 1986).

In addition to Victor and Cosmos Mindeleff's *A Study of Pueblo Architecture,* sources which discuss Hopi buildings and settlements are Cosmos Mindeleff, "Localization of Tusayan Clans" (Smithsonian Institution, Bureau of American Ethnology, 1900); R. Maitland Bradfield, *A Natural History of Associations: A Study in the Meaning of Community* (London: Duckworth, 1973); Mischa Titiev, *Old Oraibi: A Study of the Hopi Indians of Third Mesa* (Papers of the Peabody Museum, V. 22, N. 1, 1944); E.A. Beaglehole, *Notes on Hopi Economic Life* (Yale University Publications in Anthropology, V. 15, 1937) and E.A. Beaglehole and P. Beaglehole, *Hopi of the Second Mesa* (Memoirs of the American Anthropological Association, N. 44, 1935); Elliot G. McIntire, "Changing Patterns of Hopi Indian Settlement" (*Annals of the Association of American Geographers,* V. 61, 1971); E. Charles Adams, "The Architectural Analogue to Hopi Social Organization and Room Use, and Implications for Prehistoric Northern Southwestern Culture" (*American Antiquity,* V. 48, N. 1, 1983). On the Hopi kiva as an arena for ceremonial theatrics, see Armin W. Geertz and Michael Lomatuway'ma, *Children of Cottonwood: Piety and Ceremonialism in Hopi Indian Puppetry* (Lincoln: University of Nebraska Press, 1987).

CREDITS

ABBREVIATIONS

AHS   Arizona Historical Society, Tucson
AMNH   American Museum of Natural History
AMNH.AP   *American Museum of Natural History. Anthropological Papers*
AMNH.M   *American Museum of Natural History. Memoirs*
ASM.UA   Arizona State Museum, University of Arizona
BAE   *Bureau of American Ethnology. Annual Report*
BCPM   British Columbia Provincial Museum
BL.UCB   Bancroft Library. University of California, Berkeley
CHS   Colorado Historical Society
DPL   Denver Public Library, Western History Department
FMNH   Field Museum of Natural History
LC   Library of Congress
LMA.UCB   Lowie Museum of Anthropology. University of California, Berkeley
MAI   Museum of the American Indian, Heye Foundation
MHS   Montana Historical Society
MNM   Museum of New Mexico
MNM.SARC   Museum of New Mexico. School of American Research Collections
MinnHS   Minnesota Historical Society
NMC   National Museums of Canada
PM   Peabody Museum, Harvard University
PN   Peter Nabokov
RE   Robert Easton
SBMNH   Santa Barbara Museum of Natural History
SHSND   State Historical Society of North Dakota
SI   Smithsonian Institution, National Anthropological Archives
SM   Southwest Museum
USNM.P   *United States National Museum. Proceedings*
UW   University of Washington
WHC   Western History Collections, University of Oklahoma Library
YU   Yale University Library

Front cover   Southern Plains Indian Museum and Crafts Center, U.S. Department of the Interior (1973).

Back cover   SBMNH (E.S. Curtis).

Maps   RE (after H.E. Driver, *Indians of North America,* 1969 [1961]; *Encyclopedia Britannica*; Smithsonian Institution, *Handbook of North American Indians,* 1978–).

Introduction   2 William Webb (A.C. Vroman); 5 University of Rochester (L.H. Morgan); 8-9 RE; 10 RE; 13 MHS; 14 SBMNH (E.S. Curtis); 17 SI; RE; 18 *t left* AMNH.M (J. Teit, 1900), *t right* BAE (F. Boas, 1888); 19 *t left* BCPM (C.F. Newcombe), *t right* SHSND, *bottom* SBMNH (E.S. Curtis); 20 *top* National Archives of Canada (R. Harrington), *bottom* SM (James and Pierce); 21 *top* Milwaukee Public Museum, *bottom* SHSND; 22 *top* (W.C. Sturtevant), *middle* SI, *bottom* MHS; 23 *top* NMC, *bottom* SI (W.S. Prettyman); 24 WHC (B. Kent ?); 25 *top* YU, *bottom* SI (W.H. Jackson); 26 *top* SI, *bottom* WHC; 27 SI; 28 *top* R.E. Peary, 1895, *middle* NMC, *bottom* PM (W.H. Pierce, Sr.); 29 SI; 30 (Dick Kent); 31 *top* RE (after W.N. Fenton, 1957), *middle* RE (after L. Standing Bear, *Land of the Spotted Eagle,* 1933), *bottom* P. Radin, 1923; 32 *t* RE (after J.L. Briggs, *Never in Anger,* 1970), *m* RE (after A. Tanner, *Bringing Home Animals,* 1970), *b* RE (after S. Kent, *Ethnology,* 1983); 33 SI; 34 *top* AMNH (E. Dossetter), *bottom* BCPM (F. Dally); 35 W.H. Over State Museum, University of South Dakota; 36 *top* MinnHS (G. Wilson), *bottom* AHS; 37 MNM; 39 *top* (G.F. MacDonald, 1983), *bottom* AMNH; 40 *top* RE (after D. Saile, 1977), *bottom* BCPM; 41 *top* (Dick Kent), *bottom* SI (S.W. Matteson); 42 *top* LC (HABS), *bottom* MNM (J.W. Allen); 43 *top* RE (E.S. Curtis), *bottom* FMNH; 44 *top* BCPM (C.F. Newcombe), *bottom* Vancouver Public Library; 45 *top* SI (O.S. Goff), *bottom* Benson Lanford Coll.; 46 SI; 47 MinnHS (B.F. Upton); 48 AMNH (E.H.H.); 49 *top* Oklahoma Historical Society, *middle* RE, *bottom* Canadian Museum of Civilization; 51 MNM (L.D. Moloney).

Chapter 1   52 LC; 53 *top* RE, *bottom* Oklahoma Historical Society; 54 *top* SI, *b left* New York Public Library, Rare Book Division (T. DeBry), *b right* New York Public Library, Rare Book Division (J. Smith, 1632); 55 *top* RE, *middle* RE (after M. Robbins, 1960); 56 (L.H. Morgan, 1881); 57 Nebraska State Historical Society; 58 *top* SI, *middle* SI; 59 SI; 60 *top* MinnHS (E.A. Bromley), *middle* (W.C. Sturtevant, *American Antiquity,* 1975), *bottom* (W.C. Sturtevant, *American Antiquity,* 1975); 61 *top* MinnHS (E.D. Becker), *bottom* FMNH; 62 *top* DPL, *bottom* DPL; 63 MinnHS (W.H. Illingworth); 65 *top* MinnHS, *bottom* MinnHS (S.C. Sargent); 66 *top* MAI (A.B. Skinner), *bottom* Rasmussen Lee Studio (S. Eastman); 67 *t left* (A.B. Skinner, 1921), *t right* MinnHS (R.O. Sweeny); 68 *top* SI, *bottom* NMC; 69 SI; 70 *top* RE (after A.I. Hallowell, 1942; S. Vincent, 1973), *b left* Manitoba Provincial Archives, *b right* Milwaukee Public Museum; 71 SI, 72 *middle* RE, *bottom* RE; 73 *top* RE (after E. St. Germaine, n.d.), *middle* RE (after N. Lurie); 74 *top* Milwaukee Public Museum, *b right* RE (after F.A. and D.L. Latorre, 1975; PN; R.E. Ritzenthaler and F.A. Peterson, 1956); 75 RE (after F.A. and D.L. Latorre, 1976; PN; R.E. Ritzenthaler and F.A. Peterson, 1956); 76 Newberry Library; 77 *top* Mohawk-Caughnawaga Museum, *middle* Bibliothèque Nationale, *bottom* Bibliothèque Nationale; 78 RE; 79 *middle* (J. Tuck, 1967) *bottom* (J. Tuck, 1967); 80 *top* Museum of Indian Archaeology (London, Ontario (E. Donaldson), *middle* RE (after J.V. Wright, 1974), *bottom* RE (after W.D. Finlayson, *Canadian Studies Report,* 1979); 81 RE (after C. Heidenreich, 1971; H.M. Converse, *New York State Museum Bulletin,* 1908); 82 RE (after L.H. Morgan, 1904 [1851]); 83 *middle* RE, *bottom* SI; 84 RE; 85 *top* RE, *middle* New York State Museum; 86 *top* (L.H. Morgan, 1881), *bottom* New York State Library (J.J. Cornplanter); 88 *top* MAI (E. Spybuck), *bottom* RE (after F.G. Speck, 1931, W.C. Sturtevant [field notes], 1961-62); 89 *top* RE (after F.G. Speck, 1931, W.C. Sturtevant [field notes], 1961-62); 90 (G. Kurath); 91 Peabody Museum of Salem (E.S. Dodge)

Chapter 2   92 *top* RE, *bottom* MAI (M.R. Harrington); 93 SI; 94 (J. Chapman, 1985); 95 (W.H. Morgan, 1980); 96 (W.H. Morgan, 1980); 97 *top* RE (after J. Howard, 1968), *m left* (M.S. Garbarino, 1976), *m right* SI; 98 (W.H. Morgan, 1980); 99 (W.S. Webb and R.S. Baby, 1957); 100 *top* (E.G. Squier and E.H. Davis, 1848), *bottom* SI; 102 *top* (W.H. Morgan, 1980), *bottom* (W.H. Morgan, 1980); 103 SI; 104 SI (Viard); 106 *top* Public Record Office, London, *bottom* (W. Bartram, *American Ethnological Society. Transactions,* 1853); 107 *top* RE (after W. Bartram, 1853), *m left* RE (after W. Bartram, 1853), *m right* RE (after B. Hawkins, 1848); 108 PN; 110 *top* SI, *middle* RE (after A.B. Walker, 1981), *b left* RE, *b right* RE (after W.L. Ballard, 1978), 112 *top* SI, *middle* SI, *bottom* SI (J. Mooney); 113 RE (after J.R. Swanton, 1912, 1931); 114 PN; 115 SI; 116 PM (A.B. Skinner); 117 PM (A.B. Skinner); 118 RE (after W.C. Sturtevant [field notes], 1950s); 119 *t left* RE (after A. Spoehr, 1941), *t right* SI; 120 *top* PN, *bottom* PN; 121 W.C. Sturtevant Coll. (J.M. Goggin)

Chapter 3   122 *top* RE, *bottom* MHS (E.S. Curtis); 123 (M. Beckwith, 1930); 124 RE (after B. Rensberger, *New York Times,* June 10, 1974); 125 *top* RE (after J.L. Livingston in R.A. Krause, *The Leavenworth Site,* 1972), *bottom* (D. Gebhard); 127 *top* SI (F.B. Fiske), *bottom* RE (after G. Metcalf, *River Basin Survey Papers,* N. 26, 1963); 128 (M.A.P. Wied-Neuwied, *People of the First Man,* 1976); 129 *top* New-York Historical Society (K. Bodmer), *bottom* SI; 130 *top* AMNH.AP (G.L. Wilson, 1934), *middle* (G.L. Wilson, 1917), *bottom* RE (after G.L. Wilson, 1934); 131

top AMNH.AP (G.L. Wilson, 1934), *m left* AMNH.AP (G.L. Wilson, 1934), *m right* AMNH.AP (G.L. Wilson, 1934), *b right* AMNH.AP (G.L. Wilson, 1934); **132** *top* SHSND, *bottom* SHSND; **133** *t left* AMNH.AP (G.L. Wilson, 1934), *t right* SHSND, *bottom* SHSND; **134** *top* RE (after D.J. Lehmer, et al., 1973), *m* RE (after W.R. Wood, 1967), *bottom* RE (after W.R. Wood, 1967); **135** *top* Joslyn Art Museum (K. Bodmer), *bottom* New-York Historical Society (G. Catlin); **136** SI (W.H. Jackson); **137** *top* FMNH, *m right* FMNH, *bottom* FMNH; **139** *top* RE (after J. Murie, 1930; G. Weltfish, 1965), *bottom* SI (W.H. Jackson); **140** *top* RE (after A.W. Bowers, Mandan Social and Ceremonial Organization, 1950; G. Will, 1930), *bottom* Smithsonian Institution. National Museum of American Art (G. Catlin); **141** DPL (C. Badger); **142** *top* (M. Beckwith, 1930), *middle* AMNH.AP (G.L. Wilson, 1934); **143** RE; **144** SBMNH (E.S. Curtis); **145** WHC; **146** RE; **147** WHC; **148** *top* SI (J. Mooney), *bottom* SBMNH (E.S. Curtis); **149** *t left* RE, *t right* RE; **150** WHC; **151** SHSND (F.B. Fiske); **152** RE (after R. and G. Laubin, 1971 [1957]); **153** *t left* RE (after S. Campbell, 1927), *t right* RE (after R. and G. Laubin, 1971 [1957]); **154** *t left* NMC, *t right* RE (after R. and G. Laubin, 1971 [1957]), *middle* NMC, *bottom* NMC; **155** *top* WHC, *b left*, *b right* RE (after R. and G. Laubin, 1971 [1957]); **156** CHS; **157** DPL; **158** (Cohoe and K. Peterson [ed.], *A Cheyenne Sketchbook*, 1964); **159** *top* Nebraska State Historical Society (Johnson), *bottom* (D. Fraser, *Village Planning in the Primitive World,* 1968); **160** SI (J. Mooney); **161** YU; **162** YU; **163** RE (after D. Fraser, *Village Planning in the Primitive World,* 1968); **164** *top* RE (after T.J. Brasser, 1977; W. McClintock, 1936), *middle* NMC, *bottom* YU; **165** *t left* Nebraska State Historical Society, *t right* SHSND; **166** *top* SI, *bottom* SI; **167** *top* SI, *bottom* Bildarchiv Preussischer Kulturbesitz, Berlin; **168** *b left* RE (after J.G. Jorgenson, 1972), *b right* (Cohoe and K. Peterson [ed.], *A Cheyenne Sketchbook,* 1964); **169** SI (J. Mooney); **170** *top* MHS (L.A. Huffman), *m left* RE (after J.E. Brown, *The Sacred Pipe,* 1953), *m right* MAI, *bottom* MAI (E. Spybuck); **171** Denver Art Museum; **172** *top* PN, *bottom* PN; **173** Billings [Montana] Gazette.

Chapter 4 174 RE; **175** *top* AMNH, *bottom* SI (L. Moorhouse); **176** RE (after C. Burch, "A Discussion of the Earthlodge ..." [paper], 1977); **177** *top* AMNH.M (J. Teit, 1900), *bottom* AMNH.M (J. Teit, 1900); **178** *top* AMNH, *bottom* AMNH; **179** *top* RE (after M.W. Smith, 1947), *bottom* RE (after C. Burch, "A Discussion of the Earthlodge ..." [paper], 1977); **180** *top* SI (C. Relander), *bottom* SI; **181** BL.UCB (D. Spuler); **182** *top* SBMNH (E.S. Curtis), *bottom* SBMNH (E.S. Curtis); **183** FMNH; **184** *top* PM (J.A. Teit), *bottom* SI (L. Moorhouse); **185** *top* A. Hungry Wolf Coll., *bottom* Yakima Valley Regional Library; **186** *top* National Museums of Canada. National Museum of Man; **187** *top* National Museums of Canada. National Museum of Man, *bottom* SI (C. Clark).

Chapter 5 188 *top* RE, *bottom* NMC; **189** LaFédération des Coopératives du Nouveau Québec (J. Talirunili); **190** *top* SBMNH (E.S. Curtis), *bottom* (M. Maxwell, *The Beaver,* 1962); **192** National Museum of Denmark (T. Thomsen); **193** *top* (O.W. Geist and F.G. Rainey, 1936), *middle* (F.W. Hodge [ed.], BAE Bulletin, v.30, 1907-1910); **194** *top* National Archives of Canada (R. Harrington), *bottom* NMC; **195** BAE (F. Boas, 1888); **196** *top* RE (after A. Balikci, 1970), *m left* BAE (F. Boas, 1888), *m right* BAE (F. Boas, 1888), *bottom* RE (after A. Balikci, 1970); **197** RE (after A. Balikci, 1970; F. Boas, 1888; D. Jenness, 1922; T. Mathiassen, 1928); **198** National Archives of Canada (A.P. Low); **200** *top* AMNH (D.B. MacMillan), *middle* BAE (F.Boas, 1888); **201** *top* BAE (F. Boas, 1888), *middle* NMC (J.D. Soper), *bottom* NMC; **202** *top* West Baffin Coopérative, Cape Dorset, N.W.T. (Pudlo), *middle* RE (after *Netsilik Eskimos at the Inland Camps,* 1968), *bottom* UW; **203** *top* SBMNH (E.S. Curtis), *middle* RE (after F. Boas, 1888); **204** NMC (D. Leechman); **205** SI (J. Webber); **206** SBMNH (E.S. Curtis).

Color 209 RE; **210** *top* SI, *middle* SI, *bottom* SI; **211** Art Gallery of Toronto (P. Kane); **212** RE; **213** Joslyn Art Museum (K. Bodmer); **214** James J. Hill Reference Library (S. Eastman); **215** RE; **216** RE; **217** PN; **218** RE; **219** RE; **220** *top* M. Alquilar Coll. (F. Day), *bottom* MAI (E. Spybuck); **221** PN; **222** *top* PN, *bottom* PN; **223** PN; **224** RE; **225** RE.

Chapter 6 226 *top* RE; *bottom* British Library (J. Webber); **228** SBMNH (E.S. Curtis); **230** BCPM; **232** SBMNH (E.S. Curtis); **234** *top* BCPM (F. Dally), *bottom* AMNH (H. Smith); **235** National Gallery of Canada (P. Kane); **236** *top* RE (after F. Boas, 1888; T. Newman, 1974), *bottom* Denver Art Museum (F. Boas); **237** *top* RE (after R.L. Olson, University of Washington Publications in Anthropology, 1936), *middle* RE (after T. Newman, 1974), *bottom* LC; **238** *top* BCPM (W.A. Newcombe), *middle* Northwest Whitman College Archival Collections, *bottom* UW; **239** *top* UW (S.G. Morse), *middle* NWCAC (M. Eells); **240** *top* FMNH; **241** UW; **242** BCPM (C.F. Newcombe); **243** BCPM (C.F. Newcombe); **244** BCPM (C.F. Newcombe); **245** *top* BCPM (C.F. Newcombe), *bottom* USNM.P (F. Boas, 1889); **246** SBMNH (E.S. Curtis); **247** (L. and F. Shotridge, *Museum Journal. University of Pennsylvania,* 1913); **248** Vancouver Public Library; **249** AMNH (E. Dossetter); **250** *top* RE (after F. Boas, 1888), *bottom* BCPM (W. Duff); **251** USNM.P (F. Boas, 1889); **252** *top* BCPM (C.F. Newcombe), *bottom* BCPM (W. Duff); **253** *top* USNM.P (F. Boas, 1889), (F. Boas, 1927); **254** *top* BCPM (C.F. Newcombe), *bottom* BCPM (W. Halliday); **255** *top* SBMNH (E.S. Curtis), *middle* USNM.P (F. Boas, 1889), *bottom* BCPM; **256** AMNH; **257** AMNH; **258** *top* BCPM (E. Fleming), *middle* RE; **259** *top* RE (after F. Boas, Columbia *University Contributions to Anthropology,* 1930), *bottom* AMNH; **260** *top* AMNH (E. Dossetter), *middle* RE; **261** BCPM; **262** NMC; **263** SI; **264** NMC; **265** *top* FMNH, *bottom* UW; **266** AMNH; **267** UW; **268** *top* BCPM (C.F. Newcombe), *b left* RE (after D. Fraser, *Village Planning in the Primitive World,* 1968), *b right* RE (after J. and C. Smyly, 1973); **269** BCPM (C.F. Newcombe); **270** RE; **271** *top* BCPM (B. Atkins), *middle* AMNH (H.I. Smith), *bottom* BCPM (C.F. Newcombe); **272** FMNH; **273** *top* FMNH, *bottom* AMNH; **274** *top* RE, *bottom* RE; **275** RE; **276** SI (A.K. Fisher ?); **277** *top* (L. and F. Shotridge, *Museum Journal. University of Pennsylvania,* 1913), *bottom* SI; **278** LC; **279** SI; **280** NMC; **281** *top* BAE (F. Boas, 1916), *bottom* BCPM; **282** SI; **284** British Columbia Ministry of Tourism **285** RE.

Chapter 7 286 *top* RE, *bottom* BL.UCB (H.B. Brown); **287** LC; **288** YU; **289** San Diego Museum of Man; **290** *t left* Siskiyou County Museum, *t left* PN; **291** RE (after *Report on a Study of a Yurok Indian Village,* 1964); **293** California. State of, Department of Parks and Recreation; **294** *top* J. De Angulo, 1953), *bottom* RE (after W.R. Goldschmidt, *Nomlaki Ethnography,* 1951); **295** *t left* RE (after C.W. Meighan and F.A. Riddel, *The Maru Cult of the Pomo Indians,* 1972), *m left* RE (after J.W. Hudson, SI, 1890s), *b left* RE (after M.J. Moratto, *A Survey of the Archaeological Resources of the Buchanan Reservoir Region...,* 1968), *b right* LMA.UCB; **296** (W.C. McKern, 1923); **297** *top* LMA.UCB (H. Littlejohn), *bottom* D. Hill Coll.; **298** LMA.UCB (C.H. Merriam); **299** *middle* RE (after S.A. Barrett, 1916), *bottom* BL.UCB; **300** *top* (A.H. Gayton, *Yokuts and Western Mono Ethnography,* 1948), *bottom* BL.UCB; **301** (S. Powers, 1877); **302** *top* (C.H. Merriam, 1955), *bottom* BL.UCB; **303** SI (J.K. Hillers); **304** Oakland Museum (T. Hill); **305** *top* LMA.UCB (C.H. Merriam), *bottom* (C.H. Merriam and R.F. Heizer, 1966); **306** PM (H. Burger); **307** BL.UCB; **308** *top* LMA.UCB (P.E. Goddard), *bottom* PM (F.W. Putnam); **309** *top* SM, *bottom* LMA.UCB (C.H. Merriam); **310** Santa Barbara Mission (F. Deppe); **311** *top* SI, *bottom* SI (J.P. Harrington); **312** *top* LMA.UCB, *bottom* SM; **313** SBMNH (E.S. Curtis); **314** California Historical Society, Los Angeles;

315 SM; 316 SBMNH (E.S. Curtis); 317 *top* San Diego Museum of Man, *bottom* Los Angeles County Museum of Natural History; 318 *top* RE (after C.D. Forde, 1931; J.G. Bourke, 1889), *bottom* AMNH; 319 *top* SM, *bottom* MNM (B. Wittick); 320 MNM (B. Mollhausen); 321 PN.

Chapter 8   323 *top* RE, *bottom* ASM.UA (F. Hanna); 324 CHS (Pennington); 325 *top* RE, *middle* RE (after C. Mindeleff, 1898), *bottom* RE; 327 *top* RE (after Berard Haile, 1942; S. Kent, 1982; L. Lamphere, 1969; C. Mindeleff, 1898; L.C. Wyman, 1957), *bottom* National Archives; 328 *top* LC, *middle* LC, *bottom* LC; 329 *top* BAE (after C. Mindeleff, 1898), *middle* RE (after C. Mindeleff, 1898) *bottom* LC; 330 ASM.UA; 331 *top* RE (after S. Jett and V.E. Spencer, 1981), *bottom* (S. McAllester); 332 *top* MNM (C. Goodman), *b left* RE (after C. Mindeleff, 1898), *b right* NA; 333 RE (after S. Jett, 1987); 334 S.C. Jett); 335 *top* AHS, *bottom* CHS; 336 *t left* RE, *top right* RE; 337 Amon Carter Museum (L. Gilpin) 338 A. Hungry Wolf Coll.; 339 *top* MAI (E.H. Davis), *bottom* RE (after W.A. Longacre and J.E. Ayres, 1968); 340 AHS; 341 *top* ASM.UA (H. Teiwes), *bottom* AHS; 342 RE; 343 *top* SI, *bottom* University of Arizona. Special Collections; 344 *top* AHS (C. Abbott), *b left* AHS (C. Abbott), *b right* AHS (C. Abbott); 345 *top* SM, *bottom* AHS; 346 (J. Van Willigen, *The Kiva*, 1970); 347 ASM.UA (H. Teiwes).

Chapter 9   348 (P. Carr, 1979); 349 *top* RE, *bottom* SM; 350 FMNH; 352 *t left* RE, *t right* RE, *middle* RE (after S.P. Moorehead, R.S. Peabody Foundation); 353 RE (after E.W. Haury, 1936); 354 *top* RE (after J.W. Fewkes, *Journal of American Ethnology and Archaeology*, 1892), *b left* SI, *b right* ASM.UA (H. Teiwes); 357 *t left* RE (after F.H.H. Roberts, Jr., *Shabik'eshchee Village*, 1929), *t right* P.S. Martin et al., *Indians before Columbus*, 1947; 358 *t left* RE (after D. Fraser, *Village Planning in the Primitive World*, 1968), *t right* RE (after R.L. Knowles, *Energy and Form*, 1974), *bottom* FMNH (P.S. Martin); 359 *top* ASM.UA (H. Teiwes), *bottom* RE (after J.W. Fewkes, *American Anthropologist*, 1908); 360 *top, middle* Hayes, Alden C. et al., *Archeological Surveys of Chaco Canyon, New Mexico*, 1981, *bottom* SI; 361 (P. Logsdon); 362 National Park Service; 363 MNM; 364 *top* (P. Logsdon), *bottom* BAE (V. Mindeleff, 1891); 365 MNM (T.H. Parkhurst); 366 MNM; 367 SI; 368 (D. Kent); 369 *top* (D. Kent), *bottom* (D. Kent); 370 BAE (V. Mindeleff, 1891); 371 *top* BAE (V. Mindeleff, 1891), *bottom* RE; 372 *t left* MNM.SARC (B. Wittick), *t right, bottom* BAE (V. Mindeleff, 1891); 373 *t left* LC (HABS), *t right* BAE (V. Mindeleff, 1891), *bottom* Museum of Photography, University of California, Riverside; 374 *top* SI, *b left* National Archives, *b right* MNM (E.S. Curtis); 375 MNM (T.H. Parkhurst); 377 MNM (T.H. Parkhurst); 378 RE (after C. Mindeleff, 1891; M.W. Stirling, *Origin of Acoma and Other Records*, 1942); 379 FMNH; 380 (S. Stubbs, 1950); 381 MNM (J.K. Hillers); 382 PM; 383 RE (after W.E. Reynolds, 1981); 384 ASM.UA (F. Hanna); 385 MNM; 387 RE (after R. Swentzel, 1975); 388 SI; 389 SI; 390 (S. Stubbs, 1950); 391 *top* MNM, *bottom* MNM, 392 *top* CHS, *bottom* ASM.UA (F. Hanna); 393 LC (HABS); 394 LC (HABS); 395 MNM.SARC (B. Wittick); 396 National Archives; 397 (S. Stubbs, 1950); 398 *top* SI, *bottom* Los Angeles County Museum of Natural History; 399 SI; 401 *top, middle* RE (after K. Whitaker, *The Masterkey*, 1974), *bottom* MNM.SARC (B. Wittick); 402 Los Angeles County Museum of Natural History; 403 (S. Stubbs, 1950); 404 *top* Museum of Northern Arizona, *bottom* AHS; 405 FMNH; 406 MNM.SARC (B. Wittick); 409 SI.

GLOSSARY

Adobe wet clay mixture used for mortar or sun-dried bricks in the Southwest, sometimes reinforced with fiber.

Arbor a bent frame shade structure loosely covered with brush built in the southern Plains, or an open-sided post and beam shade in the Southeast.

Banco a bench-like shelf around the interior of a kiva or pit house.

Bent frame a frame of small saplings set into firm ground, then bent and tied together to form a domical structural frame.

Burial mound the elevated earthen grave of a Southeastern Indian dignitary, which often acquired an additional earthen layer with each subsequent ritual burial.

Cache a sealed subterranean cavity dug to store dried food or other possessions.

Cacique the traditional leader of a Pueblo, usually a position held for life.

Chinking sealing walls made of logs or wood by stuffing a filler material—grass, mud, etc.—into the cracks.

Clan group within a tribe whose members believe they share descent from a common ancestor (which may be human or mythical); individuals receive clan membership through their mother or father's line, and generally cannot marry within their own clan.

Compression shell usually domical roof structure which is self-supporting because individual elements distribute loads in all directions.

Conical cone shaped form.

Corbeled roof a compression roof frame of tiers of horizontal logs in which each upper tier decreases in size and is shifted in alignment for bearing. Used in some Navajo hogans and pre-Hispanic Pueblo kivas.

Cordage ties made of strips of hide or plant fiber which are used to join together structural parts of a building.

Cosmic tree the center pole in many Indian buildings which has religious symbolism. Also called the 'earth navel' or 'axis mundi.'

Cosmology a people's conception of how the universe is ordered.

Cribbed logs a method of walling with horizontal logs in which, as the walls rise, the tiers of notched logs overlap at the corners.

Curtain wall a house covering made of removable horizontal, overlapping wood planks lashed to upright poles; used on the Northwest Coast.

Dew cloth a liner hung inside Plains Indian tipis for insulation and to control drafts.

Domical round or dome shaped form.

Foot drums constructions of hollowed log or masonry which are often found in ceremonial buildings, and are struck with the feet.

Great Kivas large circular constructions built by pre-Hispanic Anasazi villagers for rituals and community use.

Horno the beehive-shaped outdoor baking oven found in most pueblos.

Italwa the Creek Indian term for "town."

Kachinas the supernatural beings which assist Pueblo Indians and which they impersonate in dances.

Kashim a large building used by Eskimos for social or ritual gatherings.

Kiva the special chambers, often semisubterranean, in which Pueblo Indians meet, conduct rituals, weave cloth, tell stories, and instruct children.

Latillas small round poles used to span between vigas in a pueblo roof structure.

Longhouse a general term for linear, multi-family dwellings, but particularly identified with Iroquoian buildings; recently applied to various traditional-style Indian meeting houses.

Moiety the name for each half of group which is divided into two social segments.

Palisade a row of upright logs, sometimes pointed and occasionally supporting an inner raised walkway to protect a village.

Phratry a term used to describe an associated group of clans when there are more than two such groups.

Pilaster a pier that projects out from a wall and usually supports a roof, as in some pre-Hispanic kivas in the Southwest.

Pit house a semisubterranean house, one-room with excavated floor, interior posts, and an earthen-covered roof generally rising from ground level.

Plaza a public central area in a community for festive, social, political or religious gatherings.

Post and beam a structure framed with vertical posts and horizontal beams, usually with sloping roof members (rafters).

Post molds the discolored ground remains in an archeological site which indicate where wooden supports for structures once stood.

Puddled adobe an earth mixture worked into a floor or wall while it is still wet as a finishing surface.

Puncheon slab-like planks which are split from a log.

Purlin the horizontal poles on a roof which are supported by the rafters.

Qarmaq inter-seasonal lodgings for Eskimos.

Ramada a sun shade built with logs.

Rectilinear a structure with 90° corners both in plan and section.

Smoke flaps the moveable extensions of a tipi cover which can be adjusted to deter wind and rain and control smoke release.

Stringers the members which are fastened on the exterior of a building frame upon which the roofing or walling material is attached.

Tipi ring a circle of stones left behind by Indians who used them to weight down the coverings of their dwellings.

Totem pole the popular name for cedar poles on the Northwest Coast carved with family crests, composed of stylized faces and bodies of supernatural beings and ancestors.

Travois the V-shaped frame of tipi poles which Plains Indians dragged behind dogs and horses to carry tipi covers and other possessions.

Truss a structural element made up of a number of members, usually to support a roof.

Tupik the traditional summer tent used by most Eskimo groups.

Umiak the summer boat of wood frame and walrus hide which Eskimo groups sometimes beached, turned on its side, and used for shelter.

Viga a round log beam used in the Southwest to frame a pueblo roof structure.

Wattle-and-daub a walling method employed predominately by Southeastern and Southwestern tribes which uses a frame of upright or interwoven slender saplings to hold mud fill.

Wigwam a general term for a domical dwelling framed with saplings and covered with mats or bark, built principally by woodland Indians of the Northeast and Great Lakes.

Wikiup a specific term for the domical winter dwelling of the Kickapoo Indians; also a name for the traditional-style Apache dwelling.

INDEX

3 EARTHLODGE, GRASS HOUSE, and TIPI

GREAT PLAINS

Mandan earthlodge

The earthlodge drawing *(above)* is taken from a pictographic chronicle by Mandan artist Foolish Woman.

Crow tipi camp

The photograph *(below)* of a camp on Little Bighorn River was taken about 1906 by Edward S. Curtis. Plains Indian architecture changed after horses were introduced by the Spanish, opening up wider hunting and feuding ranges for many tipi-building tribes.

In the spring of 1541, Francisco de Coronado led his horses, soldiers, and priests across the Mississippi River and into the southern Plains, where they soon noticed squiggly lines scratched into the ground alongside what appeared to be well-worn trails. Coronado's expedition followed the markings until they came upon a camp of conical tents wrapped in sewn buffalo hides near the present-day New Mexico-Texas border. The curving lines in the dirt were the traces of portable architecture—the drag marks of tent poles lashed to the backs of pack dogs. The camp probably belonged to eastern Apache hunters who lived on the Plains during most of the year. Coronado's scribe admired their dwellings as "tall and beautiful," and mentioned their inventive adaptation to a mobile life style: "Their pack dogs transport their houses for them. In addition to their other burdens they carry the poles for the tents ... the load maybe from 30 to 50 pounds, depending on the dog."

This was Europe's introduction to the Plains Indian house type that came to be known by the Siouan word *tipi*, meaning "used to dwell." The structure was framed with a cone of peeled poles and was covered with a semicircle of tanned and sewn buffalo hides. Its doorway usually faced east, and flaps at the tip of the cone could be adjusted to deflect wind and release smoke from the centrally placed fire. The oldest traces of Plains Indian architecture are "tipi rings," circles of rocks 5 feet or more in diameter that are believed to have held down the hems of small hide-covered tents. In one archeological survey of more than eight hundred tipi ring campsites on the northern Plains, most were found on ridges near watercourses, possibly to prevent snowdrifts from burying the small lodges.

Coronado arrived on the brink of a cultural renaissance inspired by the rapid spread of Spanish horses. Within the next century, tribes moving into the Plains would begin stealing horses from each other, raising them on their own, and streamlining old traditions, including architecture, to suit a new exuberant and mobile way of life. In 1541, however, there were few large tipi camps in the grasslands that extended from northern Alberta and Saskatchewan in Canada more than two thousand miles south to the Rio Grande. On the east the sprawling plains were bordered by the Missouri and Mississippi river systems. West of the river valleys, the tall grass prairies blended into short grass and desert scrub before reaching the Rocky Mountain foothills. Occasionally the flat terrain was interrupted by mountain outcrops, rolling hills, and wooded river valleys, but by and large it was a landscape of treeless horizon and immense sky.

Besides their small tipis, some early tribes who inhabited the high Plains between Wyoming and Alberta also used so-called timber lodges for hunting or rituals. These were large, stationary cones made of small trees stripped of their branches, which were leaned together and perhaps covered with brush. These early people also designed large circles of boulders known as "medicine wheels," which were commonly found on hills and often aligned to cairns many miles away. Recently, archeo-astronomers have debated whether they served a calendric function, because the main spokes of some point toward solsticial sunrises and the night's brightest stars. The sites remain sacred to contemporary Plains Indians, who claim an architectural motive behind the best-known medicine wheel in the Bighorn Mountains of northern Wyoming: "The sun made it to show us how to build a tipi."

In the Canadian and Dakota Plains, Indians also laid out rocks to resemble animal or human figures. These "petroforms" have been variously interpreted as commemorations of historical events or as evidence of effigy mound influence from southeastern Indian cultures. "Buffalo jumps," another early structural form, are twin lines of rockpiles that open wide at first, then narrow to a V-shape as they abruptly end at sheer cliffs. Herds of buffalo were lured into the V's wide neck, and the Indians would emerge from behind the rocks yelling and waving hides. Panicked, the animals stampeded over the cliff to their deaths and were butchered in a brush corral at the base.

Although the major population shift of peripheral tribes into the Plains did not occur until after Coronado's visit, agricultural towns whose signature house type was the earthlodge were well established along the Missouri and Republican river systems. They were built by tribes known as "village Indians," who tilled the floodplain terraces and occupied these stockaded communities from late February to late October, living in large wood-framed and sod-covered dwellings.

Grass houses, possibly an even older building type than the earthlodge, were constructed in the southeastern Plains by Caddoan-speaking tribes such as the Wichita, Hasinai, and Caddo. Their dwellings were squat, pointed domes enclosed with grass thatch. Seventy or eighty grass houses might constitute a typical village, which usually was surrounded by cultivated fields of corn, beans, pumpkins, and squash.

As the horse, or "sky dog," rapidly revolutionized Plains Indian life in the seventeenth century, the buffalo-hide tipi, whose poles and cover had once been transported by dogs, became larger and more elaborate. Prairie and woodland Indian hunters who before had only ventured into the grasslands for periodic hunts now moved into the Plains to stay. Tribes such as the Cheyenne, Arapaho, and the Crow from the east, the Comanche from the west, and the Blackfeet (known as the Blackfoot in Canada) from the north began jockeying for territory and prestige in an equestrian world. With horsepower to drag the long tent poles and weighty hide covers, it was possible to transport tipis twice the size of those used before. While the old-fashioned earthlodge remained the village farmers' house of choice, the sleek, tall tipi became the preeminent dwelling and symbol of the new Plains Indian.

Nearly all Plains tribes also used the dome-shaped sweat bath for personal cleansing and ritual purification. In summertime they erected arbors, usually roofing them with green willows. They constructed scaffolds to dry meat, vegetables, and firewood, and near their lodges they excavated deep pits, which they insulated with grass, to store the dried meat and vegetables in anticipation of hard times. There were also menstrual huts for women, special platforms for elevating the honored dead, and log shelters and open-air "beds" for sacred activities such as trapping eagles or vision-questing. Most Plains tribes also built a special structure for grand religious festivals: the Mandan constructed a permanent six-post earthlodge for their annual Okipa ceremony. Other Plains tribes built large Sun Dance lodges, circular frame structures with brush walls and rafters radiating from a sacred center pole.

The structural parts, spatial domain, and village patterns of earthlodges, tipis, and grass houses were often endowed with social and spiritual meanings. Rules and rituals governed their construction. Their use and arrange-

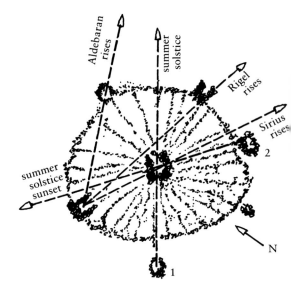

Bighorn Medicine Wheel

Found in the Bighorn Mountains of Wyoming at an altitude of 9,640 feet, these lines and stone cairns form a "wheel" with a diameter of about 70 feet. Possibly used by Indians as astronomical markers, the cairns seem to be aligned with key solar and stellar positions.

For example, from point (1) outside of the main structure of the circle, looking across the center of the circle, one sees the summer solstice sunrise. From point (2), looking across the center, one sees the summer solstice sunset. Other lines point to the rising positions of particularly bright stars.